Dancing With The Devil

The Battle for the Soul of God's Children

And the Life of a Christian Nation

❧

by

Kathleen Dryden

DANCING WITH THE DEVIL

Dancing With The Devil ©2016 Kathleen Dryden

All rights reserved. No portion of this book may be reproduced, stored in a retrieval system, or transmitted in any form or by any means—electronic, mechanical, photocopy, recording, or any other—except for brief quotations in printed reviews, and up to 300 words in papers and manuscripts without the prior written permission of the author/publisher.

Scripture quotations marked NLT are taken from the Holy Bible, New Living Translation, copyright ©1996, 2004. Used by permission of Tyndale House Publishers, Inc., Wheaton, Illinois 60189. All rights reserved

Scripture quotations marked NIV are taken from the Holy Bible, New International Version®, NIV®. Copyright ©1973, 1978, 1984, 2011 by Biblica, Inc. ™ Used by permission of Zondervan. All rights reserved worldwide. www.zondervan.com The "NIV" and "New International Version" are trademarks registered in the United States Patent and Trademark Office by Biblica, Inc. ™

Scripture quotations marked (AMP) are taken from the Amplified Bible, Copyright ©1954, 1958, 1962, 1964, 1965, 1987 by The Lockman Foundation. Used by permission.

Scripture quotations marked NASB are taken from the NEW AMERICAN STANDARD BIBLE ® Copyright ©1960, 1962, 1963, 1968, 1971, 1972, 1973, 1975, 1977, 1995. Used by permission of The Lockman Foundation.

Scripture quotations marked NKJV are taken from the New King James Version®. Copyright ©1982 by Thomas Nelson, Inc.; Used by permission. All rights reserved.

The King James Holy Bible (KJV) 1769 edition, public domain.

The opinions expressed by the author are not necessarily those of Revival Waves of Glory Books & Publishing.

Library of Congress Control Number: 2016914936

Revival Waves of Glory, Litchfield, IL

Published by Revival Waves of Glory Books & Publishing

PO Box 596| Litchfield, Illinois 62056 USA

www.revivalwavesofgloryministries.com

Revival Waves of Glory Books & Publishing is committed to excellence in the publishing industry.

Book design Copyright © 2016 by Revival Waves of Glory Books & Publishing. All rights reserved.

Published in the United States of America

Paperback: 978-1-68411-081-0

CONTENT

DEDICATION 4
INTRODUCTION 5
CHARACTERISTICS OF THE ANTICHRIST 9
BIBLE TRANSLATIONS 10
SCRIPTURES TO LIVE BY 10
PART ONE: A WORLD OBSESSED WITH EVIL THE BATTLE FOR THE LIFE OF A CHRISTIAN NATION 12
ONE: DANCING WITH THE DEVIL..13
TWO: WHO IS THIS DEVIL WITH WHOM WE DANCE? 41
THREE: A WORLD OBSESSED WITH EVIL 59
FOUR: A CHRISTIAN NATION MOCKS GOD 137
PART TWO: The Battle for the Soul of God's Children "Choosing the Broad Path" 186
FIVE: RELATIONSHIP ABUSE VIOLATING GOD'S PLAN FOR A HEALTHY SOCIETY 187
SIX: SCANDALOUS BEHAVIOR - PERVERSE SPEECH – ANGRY TONE: A RECIPE FOR DISASTER..249
SEVEN: MORAL IMPIETY "WHO TOLD YOU THAT YOU WERE NAKED?" "WHY DOES IT MATTER?" 285
PART THREE: The Battle for the Soul of God's Children Choosing the Narrow Path..318
EIGHT: KNOWING GOD/JESUS/HOLY SPIRIT 319
NINE: WHAT IT MEANS TO BE A CHRISTIAN - A SUMMARY -..........341
TEN: "BUT I HAVE THIS COMPLAINT AGAINST YOU".......................367
ELEVEN: "TURN TO ME NOW WHILE THERE IS TIME; GIVE ME YOUR HEARTS"..391
TWELVE: IN MY FATHER'S HOUSE 409
ABOUT THE AUTHOR 422
END NOTES 423
RCOMMENDED READING………………………………………..432

DEDICATION

"But to man He (God) said, behold the reverential and worshipful fear of the Lord—that is wisdom; and to depart from evil is
Understanding
(Job 28:28 AMP)

Dancing With the Devil
Is Dedicated
To Every Person Who Desires to
<u>Understand and Experience</u>
The Fullness of God's Redemption
And Eternal Life with Him by
Opening Their Eyes and Turning from Darkness to Light;
From the Power of Satan to the Power of God;
That They May Receive Forgiveness of Sins,
And an Inheritance among Those who are
Sanctified by Faith in Jesus!

Taken from *Acts 26:17-18*

INTRODUCTION

The Lord's description of the time of the Antichrist's rule, which He documented in the book of Matthew, is so alarming it should capture the heart of every person that reads it. However, in spite of those warnings and many others throughout the Bible, few Christians appear to take seriously the possibility that this horror could happen in our lifetime or in the lifetime of our children or grandchildren. In huge numbers Christians and non-Christians alike are violating God's commands, betraying Christ, and hating their brother—ignoring God's great mercy as though there is no accountability to His grace, the death of His Son. The battle armor God provided for those that believe in Jesus has been removed and cast aside for the pleasure of the light-weightiness of carefree irresponsibility.

Why is it so easy to ignore or reject this crucial protection, which God made available to us in His Word? Research shows that many Christians don't have a solid *understanding* of evil, which comes from the strategies of a dark spirit that wants to kill, steal, and destroy souls. To *understand* evil it's important to compare what the Bible says about it—where it comes from and how it affects lives—to the wicked actions and behavior clearly visible in both the Christian and non-Christian society today. Though many Christians believe it's important to know God's Word, few make studying the Scriptures a priority and too many think that their view about the Word is the correct and only view. Or, they say, "That part doesn't apply to me." Also, few take seriously the fact that an irate enemy of Jesus (radical Islam) is infiltrating western civilization—especially Christian nations—in an attempt to destroy all evidence of Him.

The target audience for *Dancing With The Devil* is Christians and the purpose for *Dancing With The Devil* is to minister to believers inclusively—regardless of denomination. There is no call to unbelievers (those who are slaves to sin) who have no obligation to obey the Word (Romans 6:20). Therefore, since it is not my purpose to offend non-believers, they should not read *Dancing With The Devil* for they *will* be offended; in fact, some Christians will be offended. However, I do welcome those unbelievers who choose to read with an open mind, and I challenge both believers and unbelievers to evaluate their heart by truthfully asking: "What kind of life am I living while awaiting the Master's return? Am I studying the Word daily and living accordingly—applying it to my life? Am I willingly obeying the Word of God, with a dedicated prayer life, or am I participating in the sins of the culture, which are orchestrated by the spirit of darkness?"

I am an advocate of the pre-tribulation rapture of the "true" Children of God—those that have accepted Christ and who have walked in repentance. The rapture or "catching away of the saints to meet the Lord in the air" is described in 1 Thessalonians 4:17. Some people aren't an advocate of the rapture and that's all right. But, I can't imagine why the Lord would call His children to continual repentance and faith in Jesus while they live life on earth in order to escape the things to come, and then sentence them to extreme persecution and death by beheading during the great tribulation. Each person must make their own decision about the rapture, but regardless of the decision there are two things that are important to know about the Great Tribulation: 1) if there is no rapture, each of us must be fully aware of the intense persecution that will affect all humanity during that time. 2) If there *is* a pre-tribulation rapture, as I believe the Word confirms, we should be prepared in advance to escape the persecution that will come to those unprepared. Being prepared means walking in repentance, serving and obeying the Lord with heart, mind, and soul. There is no other way of escape!

1 John 4:3 tells us that *"every spirit that does not confess that Jesus Christ has come in the flesh is not of God. And this is the spirit of the antichrist, which you have heard was coming, and is now already in the world" (1 John 4:3 NKJV).*

DANCING WITH THE DEVIL

Today's media confirms that the spirit of the antichrist is truly present in our world just as the Scriptures teach. According to the Pew Research Center's World Distribution of Christian Population 2010, 68% (4.72 billion) of humanity objects to Christianity. We would be foolish to suggest that the anti-Christ spirit that lives in 68% of our population has no negative impact on all it touches, including Christians. Clearly our world shows that it does. Daniel 7 indicates that the time of the Antichrist will be a Kingdom with a man at its head. The antichrist spirit that surrounds us is Satan's attempt to confuse us all, preparing us to willingly worship the Antichrist when he is revealed at his time.

Even though civilization still has a semblance of correctness through law enforcement, education, science and reason, and godliness, one need only observe our surroundings to *understand* that evil is gnawing at the very fiber of all that represents righteousness. Though we may be horrified by the increase of evil throughout the world, we have yet to see the real horror of complete lawlessness, which will happen when the One who is holding it back steps out of the way to let evil rule completely. The Prophet Jeremiah described it like this:

"I hear cries of fear; there is terror and no peace. Now, let me ask you a question: Do men give birth to babies? (If not) *then why do they stand there, ashen-faced,* (with their) *hands pressed against their sides like a woman in labor? In all history there has never been such a time of terror (Jeremiah 30:5-7 NLT).* Parenthesis added.

It is difficult to imagine what kind of evil could be worse than that already committed against mankind. But the Bible says that the evil that will come during the Great Tribulation *will* be worse. I believe it will because of the abundance of deadlier methods of warfare that were not available until recent times, and humanity's on-going and extreme rejection of Jesus combined with an acceptance of a wicked violation of His moral code, which orchestrates the most awful evil against humans.

DANCING WITH THE DEVIL

No doubt, there is a very real tug-of-war for Christian's souls, and the life of our Christian nation. *Dancing With The Devil* is about the evil strategies Satan uses to capture those souls and destroy America. But regardless of his strategies he cannot invade our lives unless we give him access through the choices we make that reject Christ's statutes. If we let this enemy inside any part of this temple of the Lord, or into our government entities we will begin to live a life of deep sorrow and regret.

Each chapter of *Dancing With The Devil* is my impassioned attempt to describe what I believe I *understand* about how God's children disobey Him, playing around where we shouldn't. It is written in such a way that it can be clearly understood by both the very young and the most mature adult, regardless of educational level. Through my own personal experiences, as well as those shared by close friends and family, I have come to realize how each of us contributes to our own demise, and to the brokenness in our families, which leads to a broken nation—physically and spiritually—through our sinful choices. We must stop and turn around; we must renew our mind, and change our behavior; only then will the Lord heal our land.

What you obtain and retain from this text depends on you, the reader, but my prayer is that as you read you will let the Lord open the eyes of your heart so you may *understand* how living in disobedience to His Word jeopardizes your soul and creates a world of evil—evil that begins with the smallest intent of the heart and mind, ends with the most wicked action, and sets up our nation for failure. When you *understand* His commands I pray that if you feel convicted of wrongdoing of any kind that you will make the choice to return to Jesus and give Him your heart before it's too late.

Kathleen Dryden

CHARACTERISTICS OF THE ANTICHRIST

Daniel 8:23 – He will know the unknowable by being deeply involved in the occult, which is supernatural, mystical, or magical beliefs, practices, or phenomena, and includes the paranormal, supernaturalism, magic, black magic, witchcraft, sorcery, necromancy, wizardry, the black arts, occultism, diabolism, devil worship, devilry, voodoo, hoodoo, white magic, witchery, and mysticism.

Daniel 8:25 – He is extremely arrogant and will magnify himself in his heart and make treaties he never intends to keep.

Daniel 7:8 – 9:26 – He will come from the reunited Roman Empire, which is primarily of Islam faith; he will most likely be Islam.

Daniel 9:27 – He will make a seven-year peace treaty with Israel but will break it in 3.5 years.

Revelation 6:2 – He will be a mighty military leader of an army he will create out of many nations. He will establish a one-world religion and will set up his image in the City of Jerusalem and those who don't worship him will be beheaded.

Revelation 13:1 – He is the beast from the sea; like a leopard, with feet of a bear, a mouth like a lion, and is given power, a throne, and great authority.

Revelation 13:3 – He will be shot in the head but will recover miraculously and the world will marvel.

Revelation 13:6 – He will blaspheme God's name, His tabernacle, and those who dwell in heaven.

Revelation 13:18 – The number of his name is 666. He will force everyone on earth to take his mark (Revelation 13:16-17) and those who refuse will be killed.

Revelation 17:11-13 – He will be a political genius, leading ten kingdoms, conquering three; the other seven will rule nations under his direction.

Paraphrased from Pastor John Hagee's Sermon of January 8, 2015

BIBLE TRANSLATIONS

Bible translations are based on two methods of interpretation—text for text and thought for thought. For the purpose of clarity and easy comprehension Scripture references used in *Dancing With The Devil* are taken from the New Living Translation Life Application Study Bible. Though several translations were used to compare the more difficult Scriptures, the NLT thought for thought method was chosen as the preferred Bible to best reach those who can *understand* only through the modern day language.

The Scriptures are our source for living and we must believe in them with all our heart. Included here are five Scriptures from the New Testament, which were selected as those we should live by. They are persuasive reasons all Christians should use the Holy Bible as their daily guide.

SCRIPTURES TO LIVE BY

"All Scripture is inspired by God and is useful to teach us what is true and to make us realize what is wrong in our lives. It corrects us when we are wrong and teaches us to do what is right. God uses it to prepare and equip his people to do every good work" *(2 Timothy 3:16, 17 NLT).*

"I solemnly urge you in the presence of God and Christ Jesus, who will someday judge the living and the dead when he appears to set up his Kingdom: Preach the Word of God. Be prepared whether the time is favorable or not. Patiently correct, rebuke, and encourage your people with good teaching. For a time is coming when people will no longer listen to sound and wholesome teaching. They will follow their own desires and will look for teachers who will tell them whatever their itching ears want to hear. They will reject the truth and chase after myths" *(2 Timothy 4:1-3 NLT).*

"So we tell others about Christ, warning everyone and teaching everyone with all the wisdom God has given us. We want to present them to God, perfect in their relationship to Christ *(See Chapter Five)*. That's why I work and struggle so hard, depending on Christ's mighty power that works within me" *(Colossians 1:28, 29 NLT)*. Parenthesis added.

"So get rid of all the filth and evil in your lives and humbly accept the Word God has planted in your hearts, for it has the power to save your souls. Don't just listen to God's Word. <u>You must do what it says. Otherwise you are only fooling yourselves</u>" *(James 1:21, 22 NLT)*. Emphasis added.

"For it is with your heart that you believe and are justified, and it is with your mouth that you profess your faith and are saved" *(Romans 10:10 NIV)*.

There is a way,
That seems right to a man,
But its end is the way of death!

Proverbs 14:12 NASB

PART ONE

A World Obsessed With Evil
The Battle For The Life Of A Christian Nation

ONE

~~~

DANCING WITH THE DEVIL

"The serpent was the shrewdest of all the wild animals the Lord God had made. One day, he asked the woman, "Did God really say you must not eat the fruit from any of the trees in the garden?" "Of course we may eat fruit from the trees in the garden," the woman replied. "It's only the fruit from the tree in the middle of the garden that we are not allowed to eat. God said, 'you must not eat it or even touch it; if you do you will die.'" "You won't die!" the serpent replied to the woman. "God knows that your eyes will be opened as soon as you eat it, and you will be like God, knowing both good and evil." The woman was convinced. She saw that the tree was beautiful and its fruit looked delicious, and she wanted the wisdom it would give her. So she took some of the fruit and ate it. Then she gave some to her husband who was with her, and he ate it, too. At that moment their eyes were opened, and they suddenly felt shame at their nakedness. So they sewed fig leaves together to cover themselves" (Genesis 3:1-7 NLT).

WHO WOULDN'T WANT TO BE LIKE GOD?

Satan told Eve it was safe to eat something God had prohibited. In essence, he convinced her that God had not been completely honest, that she and Adam would not die but instead would become like God. And, who wouldn't want to be like God, who is perfect in all His ways?

Eve believed what the devil said, and ate the fruit. When Adam was offered the fruit he too, was convinced that what God had said might not be right for them, so without question he also ate. This story is the very first recorded evidence of humanity's dance with the devil. Adam and Eve's choice has created havoc throughout the history of mankind and has resulted in relentless suffering that followed them throughout their life, and the life of their descendants. This book is not about why they made the choice to disobey. It is about the fact that they did, as have millions since that time, and the consequences that follow.

In Matthew 7, Jesus presented two distinct paths people could take in life. He said, *"You can enter God's Kingdom only through the narrow gate. The highway to hell is broad and its gate is wide for the many who choose that way. But the gateway to life is very narrow and the road is difficult, and only a few ever find it" (Matthew 7:13-14 NLT).*

Why is the narrow path so difficult to find and who are the few that find it? It's difficult because God has an enemy called Satan—the old devil—who uses His children for revenge. Satan makes the broad way look and feel good to most people. If we listen to his lies long enough he will convince us that the narrow road is too great a sacrifice. "Besides" he whispers, "God *really* doesn't care how you live!" That's his best tactic against Christians because we all like to have fun living a sassy lifestyle and still get to heaven. If we let Satan convince us that he can make us happier and provide better for us than God can (and we can still reach heaven in the end), most of us will gladly believe his lie. The heart that truly wins is the one that is sold-out to the Father and His Son.

When Jesus was led by the Spirit into the wilderness to be tempted, the devil promised Him the kingdoms of the world with all their glory. Clearly they were glorious if Satan thought that the Son of God might fall for his offer. He said to Jesus, *"I will give it all to you if you will kneel down and worship me."* But Jesus opposed him: *"You must worship the Lord your God and serve only him" (Matthew 4:8-10 NLT).*

Our life, both earthly and eternally, is about choices. God *really* does care how we live even though He gave us the freedom to choose. The path Jesus chose in obedience to the Father was His personal sacrifice for all mankind.

A QUESTION OF GOOD OR EVIL

In a 2009 Barna Group survey titled *Most American Christians Do Not Believe that Satan or the Holy Spirit Exist*, George Barna reported that of the 1871 randomly selected self-described Christians interviewed, only 26% (486) fully agreed they believed Satan was real. This means that 1385 (an astounding 74%) of those "Christians" did not agree with the Bible!

The Barna Group is an organization that polls individuals at random on various issues, primarily Christian, and then makes that information available to the general public. Their report is shocking and difficult to believe especially for those of us who genuinely *understand* that we have an enemy we must guard against at all times. Further, the Barna poll suggests to me that it is fair to say that true Christians should be gravely concerned about the salvation of those Christians who say they aren't sure about evil. Maybe it seems much easier to believe that a loving God would never allow anyone's soul to end up in an eternal torment. The Barna Group percentages support the Lord's warning that *the gateway to life is narrow and only a few ever find it!*

George Barna, the author of nearly four-dozen books analyzing research concerning America's faith suggests that Americans are constantly trying to figure out how to make sense of biblical teachings in light of their daily experiences.

Barna says, *"Most Americans, even those who say they are Christian, have doubts about the intrusion of the supernatural into the natural world. Hollywood has made evil accessible and tame, making Satan and demons less worrisome than the Bible suggests they really are. It's hard for achievement-driven, self-reliant, independent people to believe that their lives can be impacted by unseen forces."* At the same time though, he says, *"Through force of repetition many Americans intellectually accept some ideas that do not get translated into practice"*—such as the fact that, you either side with God or with Satan—there is no in-between. Barna also noted that Christians don't object to co-existing and maintaining relationships with people of other faiths, even Wiccans—those who practice witchcraft. However, he says *"open-mindedness is sometimes due to their limited knowledge about the principles of their own faith and ignorance about other faiths."* **Emphasis added.**

In his book, *Why We Fight*, Doubleday, April 2002, author William J. Bennett's comments reinforce the 2009 Barna poll. Bennett relates that in the wake of the bloodiest and most devastating attack on American citizens in our history, (9/11) some asked questions like, *"Did we bring this on ourselves by the way we have behaved in the world?"* Or, *"If we go to war against them, does that make us as bad as they are?"* Or, *"Shouldn't we work on getting rid of the poverty and oppression that are the root causes of terrorism, instead of just adding to the killing?"*

Bennett believes these questions showed our society's great need for clarity on the difference in good and evil. Asked by those we might define as sensible and patriotic Americans, these questions confirm that our nation has muddied the line of its moral code so radically that few are able to determine what is good and what is evil.

Why has this happened? When did "we the people" of a Christian nation, which was founded on the moral code of the Bible, cross over into such darkness that we need clarity about which action is good and which is evil? If we question the reality of evil and if we can't tell the difference in good and evil it is because we have allowed the very evil we question to confuse and deceive us about its existence and its power. If we don't know what a moral code is, then we have neglected our responsibility to generations of Americans, passing down to our children and grandchildren a dark and destructive confusion about godly morals. And we have allowed tolerance of a liberal mindset to weaken the power of the unquestionable rule that defines the correct moral code—the rule and code that come from the God of The Holy Bible. *"Fear God and keep*

DANCING WITH THE DEVIL

His commandments for this is the whole duty of man (or mankind). *For God will bring every deed into judgment, whether it is good or evil" (Ecclesiastes 12:13-14 NIV).* Parenthesis added

Is it any wonder many Americans are perplexed about moral clarity as proposed by William Bennett? Christians are supposed to be a light to the world. They should know, *understand*, and honor God's Word and His standards of behavior. Instead they willingly violate or condone the violation of His moral code—those harmful actions that cause pain, and offend or threaten others. If Christians don't honor His moral code then they cannot be a light to the world. If Christians show the world that they don't know the difference in good and evil how can they expect the world to know the difference in good and evil. If they fail to recognize or don't care that their actions are evil in God's sight then they won't care how the world sees any behavior they exhibit that is contrary to God's moral code.

Part one of *Dancing With The Devil* clarifies evil and demonstrates what it means for God's children to dance with the father of evil—the devil. It establishes biblical truth about who he is and gives evidence of how evil destroys. It also attempts to show how America is in danger of losing God's blessing not only because of our willingness to violate His moral code, but also our government's willingness to abandon Israel, God's chosen nation. Part two shows how we give the evil one access to our daily lives granting him the permission he needs to destroy our Christian walk and us as a society. Part three pleas with Christians to repent and turn their hearts back to Christ before it's too late.

Throughout this book you will see much emphasis on four very important words—*understanding* and *wisdom*, and *repentance* and *redemption*. Until we *understand* who the devil is and what it means to dance with him, and *understand* the real meaning of evil, we can't turn from it and fully to Jesus, letting Him redeem and renew us. *"Blessed be the name of God forever and ever, for wisdom and might are His. And He changes the times and the seasons; He removes kings and raises up kings; He gives wisdom to the wise and knowledge to those who have understanding'"* (*Daniel 2:20, 21 NKJ*). Emphasis added

To *understand* evil we must know *how* to *understand*. However, the importance and meaning of *understanding* is something even educators disagree about. But the Bible is relentless with Scriptures that admonish us to *understand* because *understanding* is the foundation for true wisdom, which helps us make the godly decisions that keep evil out of our lives. In like manner, repentance is Jesus' mandate for anyone needing redemption and salvation.

THE IMPACT OF UNDERSTANDING

"For the people's heart has become calloused; they hardly hear with their ears, and they have closed their eyes. Otherwise they might see with their eyes, hear with their ears, understand with their hearts and turn, and I would heal them" (*Matthew 13:15 NIV*).

"When anyone hears the message about the kingdom and does not understand it, the evil one comes and snatches away what was sown in their heart. This is the seed sown along the path" (*Matthew 13:19 NIV*). When the seed of the gospel is planted within our heart, we must pray and study to *get understanding* and protect that seed from the evil one. But educators believe it is difficult to define *understanding* because if the definition is based on a concept, which is a theory, notion or thought, then who is to say if the concept is right or wrong. In other words, who or what will set the standard for that concept. This brings us back to the need to know the difference in good and evil. Since good and evil are based on morality, where there are no good morals sin abounds and where sin abounds, the Word says that God shows His anger from heaven against the sinners (Romans 1:18).

Why does God get angry? Because wicked people *"know the truth about God because He has made it obvious to them. For, ever since the world was created people have seen the earth and sky. Through everything God made, they can clearly see His invisible qualities—His eternal power and divine nature. So they have no excuse for not knowing God."* Hidden means unseen, concealed, or disguised. If they are hidden then why does God get angry; after all, He has said that people can clearly see his invisible qualities? He gets angry because He put inside each of us an instinctive measure—a "sense"—by which we are able to evaluate good vs. evil yet we violate that sense often. To have a sense about something requires a certain amount of *understanding*. For the purpose here, the word "sense" will be defined as an *understanding* of a subject; where one is able to think about something and use reason to deal appropriately with that thought before it becomes an action that results in evil. But which standard of comparison shall we use—ours from our own *understanding*, or God's, from His Word?

The Bible cautions us not to lean on our own *understanding*. If we are commanded to *understand* but can't use our own way of thinking then we *must* follow a moral code designed by someone with perfect *understanding*; otherwise anyone's view can be accepted as the right one until someone else changes it based on their *new understanding*. This creates thinking void of accountability, and it creates chaos among humans and chaos brings war!

If minds can agree on a moral code from someone with *perfect understanding* (God), and that code provides fairness and justice, we will see greater opportunities for people to be more accountable to one another. But when minds are divided or confused (the devil confuses) about what represents a basic moral code by which we can judge evil, then we have leaned on our own *understanding* and the result is a free-fall in morality. No genuinely moral person can deny that our society is in free-fall mode and descending rapidly into complete moral decay. Also, from the information in chapter 3 of this book we get a clear picture of the results of those who lean on their own way of thinking.

One argument for accurately defining *understanding* suggests that to *understand* something one must be able to figure out a simple set of rules that explain it. This may be true in the broad sense, or when applied to inanimate objects (such as how machinery works) or thoughts or imaginations. But I argue that to *understand* evil we must be able to recognize its damaging effects on humans regardless of its origin. When we're able to see that bad things hurt and good things don't, then we begin to *understand* evil because we compared it to a given moral code—the one from God. *Understanding* is the key to wisdom. When used together, *understanding* and wisdom help us determine and implement an acceptable moral code to live by.

Another view for defining *understanding* suggests that knowledge is the simple awareness of bits of information; it is an awareness of the connection between the individual pieces of the information. This view also believes that *to understand* means to allow knowledge to be put to use, therefore, *to understand* represents a deeper level than simply knowing the facts—*understanding something* means knowing what to do with those facts and then doing it because we *understand* the consequences if we don't! To *understand* in the way that God requires defuses the confusion that comes from Satan.

Personally I support this point of view. We can have knowledge about something, but to *understand* it requires an open mind that is willing to investigate deeply all the relevant possibilities for *understanding* something based upon knowledge of the available facts. Once we are willing to thoroughly investigate a situation we can use *sensible reasoning* and a *compassionate heart* to find its proper and just moral code, and then act based upon that. The proper moral code does not cause harm, but instead it is just, and comes from God. If we rebel and refuse to judge issues based on the moral code of God, evil will rule and people will be hurt. Before we can recognize the effects of evil we must decide whether we believe evil really exists.

Impressed with the view that it is *understanding* which allows knowledge to be put to good use I chose the Holy Bible and other documented events to research evil and *understanding*. I discovered that the Bible is absolutely clear on the topics.

When Solomon, son of King David, was anointed king at a very young age he was concerned that he would not be wise enough to govern what the Bible calls a "great" people. Wanting to do the right thing, he prayed for an *understanding* heart and the wisdom to know the difference between right and wrong (From 1 Kings 3:9). He was old enough to know that he needed *understanding*, wisdom, and knowledge of right and wrong but he didn't have the wisdom to do as the Lord wanted unless the Lord gave it to him. The Lord answered Solomon's prayer and made him the wisest and most *understanding* man that ever lived.

The prophet Daniel was called by God and much of what we *understand* today about the end times is taken from Daniel's ministry. However, Daniel needed *understanding* so God sent a heavenly messenger to touch him. *"And he said to me, 'O Daniel, man greatly beloved, understand the words that I speak to you, and stand upright, for I have now been sent to you.' While he was speaking this word to me, I stood trembling. Then he said to me, 'Do not fear, Daniel, for from the first day that <u>you set your heart to understand</u>, and to humble yourself before your God, your words were heard; and I have come because of your words"* (Daniel 10:11, 12 NKJV). Had Daniel not set his heart to *understand* or prayed for *understanding*, God could not have used him to tell us what was to come in the final days. Daniel fully *understood* who the devil was and the demonic world he ruled with his evil.

Job 28:28 says, *"But to man He* (God) *said, Behold, the reverential and worshipful fear of the Lord—that is wisdom; and to depart from evil is understanding"* (AMP) Parenthesis added. This would imply that to avoid evil, one *must* have *understanding*. But exactly what are we to *understand*?

The footnote in *The New Living Translation Life Application Study Bible* for Job 28:28 says: *"The fear of the Lord means to have respect and reverence for God, and to be in awe of his majesty and power."* This is the beginning of finding real wisdom. We should ask: "Is wisdom useful to us if we have no *understanding*?" I suggest that God intended for us to connect wisdom with *understanding* so that we might do better at obeying Him.

IS WISDOM HANDICAPPED WITHOUT UNDERSTANDING?

"Wisdom is the principal thing; therefore get wisdom; and with all thy getting, get understanding" (Proverbs 4:7 KJV). This scripture is a commanding statement that shows the importance of attaining wisdom, calling it a principle part of mental, emotional, and physical wellness. However, the great emphasis here is that with all our ability to get, attain, and feel urgency about—with all the ability granted us by our Creator—we are to *understand*. To *understand* is to be able to comprehend, discern, and interpret. In other words, while wisdom is important, it is handicapped without *understanding,* and *understanding* is not possible without a humble and compassionate heart, which enables us to rightly evaluate a situation. *"Happy is the man who finds wisdom, and the man who gets understanding" (Prov. 3:13 NLV)*. Clearly the Lord is stressing the benefits of what it means to *"understand."* So just what is it that He wants us to *understand?* Indisputably He wants us to *understand* who He is, what His moral code looks like, who Satan is, and the difference between good and evil. Every aspect outlined in this book must be read using this paragraph as a reference and the key to *understanding,* wisdom, repentance, and redemption.

DEFINING EVIL

The Merriam-Webster on-line dictionary defines evil in the adjective form as follows: something that is morally bad—morally reprehensible—sinful and wicked; arising from actual or imputed bad character or conduct and which causes harm or injury to someone. There are other definitions for evil, but this one alone should cause every person to take notice of his own morals whether in thought or in action.

Evil is also defined as being disagreeable. Have you ever been bitterly disagreeable? Or maybe on occasion you were kindly disagreeable like the old devil was with Eve in the Garden. The Bible says he was seductive. Successful seduction requires persuasive charm, not bitterness. Immediately upon Satan's encounter with Eve in the Garden he disagreed with her when she told him that God said they would die if they ate the fruit from the tree of the knowledge of good and evil. Directly, the devil said, *"You won't die."* He disagreed with her, calling God a liar but he was not mean-spirited about it. He used such charm that she never questioned whether God would be displeased with her choice. From the Word we know that God is not the liar. John 17:15 tells us that Satan is the real father of lies, and is referred to as the "evil one." These biblical facts give us *understanding* about evil, that the works of Satan spawn it.

Evil is also known as "being marked by bad luck or bad events, destruction or misfortune; something causing discomfort or repulsion; something offensive or threatening; having the nature of vice." A vice stems from evil that births a thought or action.

Another definition of evil is "the *intention* of causing harm or destruction specifically from the perception of deliberately violating some moral code." Intention is when the mind plans something to achieve a certain goal. This definition confirms that even our thoughts can be evil.

As a noun, evil is defined as "the force of things that are morally bad; something that is harmful or bad—those powers of darkness; the 'fact of suffering,' of misfortune and of wrongdoing." Evil is also called "a cosmic force that brings sorrow, distress, or calamity."

From this we see that the primary definition of evil is something that is morally bad—the abuse of a moral code, which is a system of morality according to a particular philosophy, religion, or culture. A moral is any one practice or teaching within that code. For example, Christianity is based on a moral code as defined by God in the Bible.

"Morality" is from the Latin "moralitas," meaning manner, and manner is character, and proper behavior. Morality is a sense of behavioral conduct that differentiates intentions, decisions, and actions between those that are good (or right) and those that are bad (or wrong). Unless we have *understanding* we are unable to discern or establish moral clarity. But, as we have shown, most people cannot properly define *understanding*. Therefore they struggle to clarify morality.

To accept that morality means 'manner or character' is to *understand* the spiritual image of God, which He gave to us at creation. His attributes are moral and pure. When we violate the purity of the character of God, which is within us, we get a conscience conviction that helps us recognize when we are outside the boundaries of Godly behavior.

The following Bible stories are good examples of sin attitudes that ignored good moral character and indulged or tolerated evil that could have led or did lead to a "dance with the devil."

FIRST SIN ATTITUDE

Genesis 34 relates a disturbingly sad story that involves Isaac's son Jacob, Jacob's daughter Dinah, and Jacob's sons, Simeon and Levi.

While Dinah was visiting some young women in the town of Succoth, Shechem, the local prince and son of Hamor noticed her. Finding her irresistible he lusted for her, lost control, and raped her. However, the Bible says he fell in love with her and tried to make amends for his evil act by using tender words with her.

Tender words alone cannot repair a wrong. They must be reinforced with action, which is what Shechem did. He told his father Hamor that he wanted to marry Dinah. Hamor went to Jacob saying, "My son Shechem is truly in love with your daughter; please let him marry her." Then Shechem came and pled his case to Jacob, begging to marry Dinah and offering Jacob's family anything they wanted in return. Famous as angry and violent murderers, two of Jacob's sons—Simeon and Levi—devised an evil scheme that affected the entire town. Circumcision was a requirement by Jewish law so as part of the agreement to the union between Shechem and Dinah, Simeon and Levi demanded that all the men of Succoth be circumcised. Both families agreed so that the two groups could live peacefully together and intermarry.

Shechem wanted Dinah so he wasted no time taking action to get the approval of the town council. Because he was highly respected in his family his prevailing speech to the townsmen convinced everyone that circumcision was the right thing to do. Once the men of Succoth were circumcised Dinah went to live with Shechem and for a time there was peace between the two tribes. Dinah's shame of sexual impurity was corrected in marriage. However, filled with pride and anger and a need for revenge, Simeon and Levi wreaked havoc on Shechem and the entire town.

The Bible relates that before the wounds of circumcision had healed Simeon and Levi went into the town and murdered all the men—speculation is that their throats were slashed at night while they slept—and then they took Dinah back to their camp. Jacob's other sons came and plundered the town, seized the flocks and herds—both inside the town and in the fields—and they took the women and children captive; it was evil run amok.

When Jacob cried out to his sons that they had ruined him, they showed no remorse for their actions. The Scripture says they replied in anger, *"But why should we let him* (Shechem) *treat our sister like a prostitute?" (Genesis 34:31 NLT)* Parentheses added

Jacob did not punish his sons for their crime but he did wring his hands and complain that their behavior had brought him shame. Where did the thought come from that it was acceptable to destroy an entire tribe of people for the sin of one man? It came from the evil one! Numerous people were bitterly affected by the sin of one man.

The rapist conceived an evil thought orchestrated by Satan and then acted on it. Jacob's sons conceived the evil of murder, which comes from the one who steals, kills, and destroys, and then they acted on that thought. Simeon and Levi's reprimand didn't come until Jacob became an old man and had a family discussion about their future. He called them two of a kind—angry and violent murderers who killed men and crippled oxen for sport, and he vowed to scatter them throughout Israel among the descendants of Jacob (Genesis 49:5, 6).

One can easily see the good and evil in this story but it is clear that there was much more evil than good. Dinah was a guiltless victim of the evil behavior of those out of control. Jacob's sons were guilty of murdering innocent people as a result of uncontrolled wrath, pride, and vengeance, though God says vengeance belongs only to Him. When they killed Shechem they destroyed family security for Dinah. Together their behavior caused emotional stress, shame, and pain for their father. When pride and revenge are combined they create the perfect storm for dancing with the devil. When Jacob finished wringing his hands in despair, he simply packed up and fled.

Shechem started this massacre by letting his emotions rule. He danced with the devil when he raped Dinah, but he changed his mind, confessed his sin and repented, offering to right his wrong in several ways. He was told all was forgiven, then was met with deception and murder. Aren't we glad that when we dance with the devil and then go to Jesus and repent we can trust Him to redeem us? He doesn't fool us into thinking we are forgiven and then kill us with a sword.

SECOND SIN ATTITUDE

In 1 Samuel 25 we read about David—a great warrior before he became King of Judah—and how he was forced to reevaluate his view of right and wrong after an encounter with a very wise woman. Once again, this story about David and a sheep farmer named Nabal, and Nabal's beautiful wife Abigail, shows the evil in thoughts that are dead-set on destroying many for the sin of one. In the words of the characters themselves, it shows how God felt about such thinking.

DANCING WITH THE DEVIL

Abigail's little sermon to David was orchestrated by God, and was His way of telling David that if he carried out his thoughts of bloodshed and vengeance against Nabal and his men, his actions would create a staggering burden for him the remainder of his life.

Nabal was a very wealthy man who owned large herds of animals. Scripture defines him as a crook and a drunk—selfish and crude—mean in all his dealings. Abigail was his beautiful, sensible and wise wife. David and his warriors had often protected Nabal's workforce during sheep shearing time and much of Nabal's prosperity was due to David's vigilant protection. However, when David sent a message to Nabal, asking him to share his provisions with his hungry warriors, Nabal refused, hurling insults against David. When word of Nabal's remarks reached David, he strapped on his sword, and commanded four hundred of his men to do the same. Simply put, Nabal was rude and disrespectful toward David and the power of those unrestrained words set a field afire, and provoked David to kill.

Back at Nabal's ranch, one of the servants told the beautiful and wise Abigail that her husband had spoken unkind words about David to his servant. Realizing the potential for retaliation by David, Abigail took immediate action. She wasted no time gathering adequate amounts of food and wine, which she packed on donkeys, and along with her servants she set out to intercept David and his army. Her plan was to use eatable goods and diplomacy to make peace and protect those she cared about but she chose not to tell Nabal, a predictably cruel and unreasonable man. Regardless of any decision she might make, she had every reason to be afraid. In her husband, she would face cruelty. In David, she might face death. Obviously she knew what a warrior David was and how quickly he leapt to judgment. She and her entire entourage could have been raped and/or slaughtered when they encountered David and his warriors, and clearly David was very angry. I believe she went where she thought she could do the most good. Regardless of her reason, knowing David's reputation and what might lie ahead, she willingly put her own life in danger when she faced an army of 400 men to negotiate with a famous warrior on behalf of others.

By the time Abigail and her group approached a mountain ravine, an irate David and his troops were marching toward them. The Bible says he had just been grumbling to his men about how useless it was to help Nabal. *"We protected his flocks in the wilderness, and nothing he owned was lost or stolen. But he has repaid me evil for good. May God strike me and kill me if even one man of his household is still alive tomorrow morning!" (1 Samuel 25:21, 22 NLT)*

David wanted vengeance against all Nabal's men to punish one guilty man. From this story we see the trickle-down effect of vengeance and why it belongs to God. Had Abigail not intervened and left David to his own will, many innocent men, women, and children would have suffered because of the evil in one man—Nabal—and the unrestrained actions of another man—David.

A WISE WOMAN PLEADS HER CASE

Abigail was wisely defensive when she encountered David and his men in the ravine. She dismounted and bowed low to the ground before him. With an eloquent voice and diplomatic words she used truth to intercede for her husband and family and their entire workforce. Her speech is documented in 1 Samuel 25:24-31.

Abigail's strategy was remarkably wise! She called a spade a spade and described Nabal for what he was, a wicked and ill-tempered fool. And he was most likely a difficult taskmaster. She showed wisdom and *understanding* of a potentially dangerous situation when she took food and supplies to David and his men, and spoke words meant to deter evil.

Further, Abigail was obviously educated about the Lord because immediately following her comments about Nabal, she offered an epistle of praise for David's integrity, and admonished him to get control of his emotions before he sinned. Then she spliced it all together with a strong caution about him having to bear the staggering burden of needless bloodshed if he proceeded with his quest. Afterwards she prepared for her future asking David to remember her when the Lord showered him with blessing and power. This indicates that she knew David was destined to become a powerful man blessed by God.

Abigail's excellent presentation could do no less than cause David to come to his senses. The footnote in the NLT Life Application Study Bible says, *"David was in no mood to listen when he set out for Nabal's property."* It would be difficult to ignore a beautiful woman on a donkey surrounded by a group of servants carrying a passel of food and wine. Further, David's army was most likely hungry by the time they saw Abigail. Also, she was headed into a mountain ravine, which is usually narrow. With 400 men in armor on horses, David would have been somewhat hard-pressed to bypass her. Killing her would have been his only option for not stopping to listen, so he stopped. Then he praised her logic, which he confessed kept him from vengeance and murder. Otherwise not one of Nabal's men would be alive the next day. David accepted her gifts and said, *"Return home in peace. I have heard what you said. We will not kill your husband" (1 Samuel 25:35 NLT).*

When Nabal learned what Abigail had done he had a stroke and died ten days later. When David heard about Nabal's death he thanked God for avenging him against Nabal so he wouldn't have to do it himself. Then he sent for Abigail to be his wife.

Surely Abigail was concerned for her life and the life of those with her when she encountered David's 400-man army and all their war armor in that mountain ravine. David admitted that he might have killed her, yet she showed great bravery in spite of it. Further, Abigail still had to face Nabal when she returned home.

Based on the evidence here in the Word we can conclude several things: 1) God hates a bad attitude; Nabal had a bad attitude when he refused to assist David and his men. David had a bad attitude when he wanted to kill all the men in Nabal's household for the bad behavior of one man; 2) God can and will remove the enemy. Upon learning what had happened Nabal died within ten days; 3) God rewards a humble heart and obedience. Abigail exercised both in the action she took, and God provided for her.

In this story, we can see two separate but identical views of Nabal from two people who didn't know each other but each knew Nabal. Abigail said her husband was wicked and ill tempered. David said that Nabal answered good with evil. They both recognized evil and called it evil. If we don't recognize the works of the enemy and make choices that help us avoid his attacks, we structure ourselves to reap the long-term pain and consequences of our actions, which the Bible calls a staggering burden.

MORE EVIL ACTIONS BY DAVID

It didn't take long after David's resourceful encounter with Abigail for him to indulge other overzealous behavior that hurt his reputation and left him with staggering burdens throughout the remainder of his life. After David became King of Judah, he ordered servants to bring him a beautiful woman named Bathsheba so that he could have sex with her, which he knew was an evil act that violated God's moral code.

Bathsheba was married to Uriah, one of King David's top thirty warriors, who was still on the battlefield when his wife learned she was pregnant by the King. David then ordered Uriah home to spend time with Bathsheba so that she could say he was the baby's father. But out of respect for the soldiers that were still fighting, Uriah, exercising much more restraint than the King did at that time, refused to comfort himself with his wife. King David wrote a letter to Uriah's commander Joab, that Uriah was to die, and then he sent Uriah back to his unit unknowingly carrying his own death sentence. Wicked, indeed!

In those days a person was subject to severe punishment or death when a king's orders were neglected. Uriah died because he disobeyed the King's order to have sex with his own wife—a penalty the King orchestrated against Uriah to sustain his own lie. The Bible doesn't say whether Bathsheba objected to the King's demands but if she did object and if David gave her no choice, then he intended on forcing her against her will—the very definition of rape. Had she refused to go to the King she might also have died as Uriah died when he disobeyed David. This story is a biblical example of a great man of God who used his power and position to get what he wanted. We see this same kind of behavior among people with power and position in our world today.

The King's unrestrained sins needed unrestrained punishment so God punished him by taking David's newborn child, and cursing David and his family with uncompromising sorrows. David's dance with the devil brought him penetrating pain, catapulting him into bouts of depression, and ushering into his life a cycle of violence and death that would mock and criticize him throughout his reign as King.

UNRESTRAINED PUNISHMENT FOR UNRESTRAINED SIN

Kings and leaders are prone to rule as having "all knowledge" whether or not they are qualified as knowledgeable. And, it is usually the king who issues reprimands and punishments, not the ordinary person. But God loved King David, calling him a *"man after His own heart."* He wanted David to *understand* just how angry He was with him. He sent His prophet Nathan to confront David about his huge sin. Nathan's little speech to David was forceful and designed to pierce his heart, reminding him that he was just a king.

In 2 Samuel 12, God told David that it was He who anointed him king, and gave him his abundance and that it was He who loved David so much that He was willing to do abundantly more for him.

He set David straight about his behavior and showed him how broken-hearted and angry He was by calling out the details of every sin David had committed regarding Bathsheba and Uriah. Through Nathan God then told David exactly how He was planning to punish him. But with deep *repentance*, David confessed his sin to Nathan who then reassured him that he was forgiven and would not die because of it. However, Nathan said, *"nevertheless,"* which, by definition means, 'it ain't over yet!' *"Because you have shown utter contempt for the Lord by doing this, your child will die"* (2 Samuel 12:14 NLT). To have contempt for someone is to feel hatred, disapproval, and condescension toward him or her. To have *utter* contempt is to have absolute, complete or unreserved hatred. Nathan's words showed David how seriously God disapproved of his sin.

Soon after Nathan left, the Lord sent a deadly illness to afflict David's newborn child. For seven days David lay on the bare ground without food and begged God to spare his son, but on the seventh day the child died. David got up from the ground, bathed his body and put on lotions and fresh clothing. After that, he worshiped the Lord and dined.

It cannot be denied that God hates the sin of adultery. And He hates when His children dance with the devil regardless of the nature of the dance. Some readers may suggest that David's punishment was too extreme but God will not be mocked. Through Nathan, God wanted David to *understand* that He had blessed him far beyond the norm but David abused God's blessing and in God's words, David had shown contempt for Him. David knew beforehand that his behavior would displease God but he did it anyway, mocking God's statutes. God does punish sin.

Even though David was on his face before God repenting and asking Him to spare his son, he did not continue to dwell on his sin after the child died. He accepted the forgiveness God gave him through the Prophet Nathan and he moved on. We must do the same when we repent of our sins—accept forgiveness then get on with life so that God can use us. David repented, and God, in His mercy and love, forgave David's awful sin and contempt against Him. However, He did not give David a freeway to heaven with no challenges. He left him with a painful curse on his family. It would be David's own son, Absolom to whom God would give David's concubines in order to dishonor him.

2 Samuel 16 tells how Absolom conspired with Ahithophel to overthrow David's throne as Nathan predicted. They set up a tent on the roof of David's palace and Absolom had sex with his father's concubines in open sight. The sword against David's family didn't end there. Following the death of David's newborn son, another of his sons, Amnon, committed a crime that brought more killing and intense pain to the Royal family. It was sexual sin that David used to violate God's commands and it was sexual sin that affected David's children, bringing more disgrace to the family. Even though God forgave David and let him live, he allowed David to suffer intense shame brought on by the behavior of his children—a reminder to David of two things: 1) God was his boss, and 2) he should never forget the intensity of his sin. David's dance with the devil was due to evil thoughts that were not brought into captivity and replaced with good thoughts, but instead were left to rule the flesh.

AMNON, TAMAR, AND ABSALOM RAPE, REVENGE, AND MURDER

David's son Amnon was obsessed with the King's beautiful daughter, Tamar, who was Amnon's half-sister. Encouraged by Jonadab—a devilish cousin—Amnon pretended to be sick one day and pled with his father to let Tamar come and cook for him. The King agreed. When she arrived, Amnon sent away the servants, and raped Tamar despite her pleas for her purity.

Clearly he was in lust rather than in love as he had claimed, for afterwards he hated her even more than he had said he loved her before the rape. Amnon cast her away without mercy and Absolom took her in. However, she was consigned to a life of isolation and humiliation far worse than if Amnon had simply married her. Amnon's lust for Tamar was an unrestrained thought that led to evil both in rape and murder.

King David was known as one willing to kill men simply for speaking certain words or having a viewpoint he believed to be contrary to God's moral law, but the Bible doesn't say he did anything to bring justice to Tamar. The crime was simply swept under the rug until Absalom murdered Amnon to vindicate Tamar. However, regardless of the vindication he admonished her to keep the rape a secret within the family. This same kind of thinking strikes families of today—hide it under the rug and it will go away, but it never really goes away. Shouldn't someone be held accountable and punished for evil? Rape is an evil act!

King David and his family were royalty—the most exalted family in the land. He was famous as a great warrior and a God Chaser who always returned to God with a repentant heart, but he was pathetically weak when it came to his children. 1 Kings 1:6 tells how the King never disciplined his son Adonijah—not even to ask him "Why are you doing that?" Adonijah was handsome, arrogant, and appointed himself king, causing division in the family. King David had experienced God's severe punishment for his own sins, so he knew that his sons deserved to be punished for theirs, yet he did nothing. And, the Bible does not say whether he did anything to comfort Tamar in her circumstance—only that he was very angry about the incident. The Lord expects His children to help bring justice to the innocent and defend the defenseless.

LIES THAT LED TO INSTANT DEATH

Being the liar that he has always been, Satan loves to convince Christians that deception has no consequence. Even when we know better because it was taught to us, we will listen to his voice particularly when we think we will benefit if no one knows the truth.

DANCING WITH THE DEVIL

During the time of the New Testament Acts the disciples and the Apostle Paul were passionate about building the church and spreading the message of the Gospel throughout the Roman Empire. But conflict was widespread and the integrity, love, and moral code that Jesus wanted delivered to all people were challenged constantly. It was during this process of preaching the Gospel to both the Jews and the Gentiles that controversy arose and forced those who ministered the gospel to find resolve and punish sin.

Their effort to attain unity motivated the believers to share what they owned. This generosity was a good example of love and personal sacrifice, and it attracted many people. The Scriptures say that there were no needy people among them because those with many possessions would sell some or all and then bring the proceeds to the apostles to be given to those in need.

Ananias and Sapphira was one such couple. They sold their property and separately they brought the proceeds into the Church but each of them held back a portion for their own use. The Holy Spirit spoke to Peter about what Ananias had done so Peter confronted him. Ananias lied to Peter saying that he had brought all the profit he had received. Then Peter said, *"Ananias, why have you let Satan fill your heart? You lied to the Holy Spirit and kept some of the money for yourself. The property was yours to sell or not sell as you wish. And after selling it, the money was also yours to give away. How could you do a thing like this? You weren't lying to us, but to God!"* (Acts 5:3, 4 NLT). Immediately Ananias died and was carried away and buried.

Unaware of the incident, Ananias' wife, Sapphira came to the apostles a short time later to deliver the profits from her sale. When she was asked if her offering was the price she and her husband received for the land, she answered that it was. Peter admonished her, saying, *"How could the two of you even think of conspiring to test the Spirit of the Lord like this?"* (Acts 5:9 NLT). Immediately she died and was buried beside her husband. The Lord considers lying to be a serious offense. The New Testament teaches that no liars will enter heaven.

Ananias and Sapphira's punishment was an example of how much He detests evil and wants His children to do away with it. Today, we don't drop dead instantly when we lie. If we did, we *all* would be dead. But clearly in God's eyes lying is evil worthy of severe punishment.

CALLING GOOD EVIL AND EVIL GOOD

"Woe—grief, affliction, misery, despair—unto those who call evil good and good evil, who put darkness for light and light for darkness, who put bitter for sweet and sweet for bitter" (Isaiah 5:20 NIV).

Evil begins with the intent to do harm. The thought that is conceived and then fulfilled becomes the evil that destroys. Satan made it easy for Adam and Eve to ignore God by calling evil good and all humanity was affected by that action. This great master who orchestrates all evil convinced the Israelites to disrespect Moses and the Ten Commandments, though with their own eyes they saw God perform miracles. He was calling evil good.

Courts in America have used the biblical Commandments to take action against evil in our society and they still do to some degree. However, largely the Commandments have been cast aside in favor of a system that is itself corrupted by evil. Good is now called evil.

Irish Statesman, Author, and Philosopher, Edmund Burke (1729-1797) is credited with the following statement: *"All that is necessary for the triumph of evil is that good men do nothing."* It is a profound way of saying that when those who *understand* the difference in good and evil do nothing about evil they are calling it good and acceptable. God detests such behavior!

God was extremely gracious and merciful when He let David live after David hurt Uriah and Bathsheba. When Amnon raped Tamar, he listened to the evil one. When King David failed to take action against his son for the sin against his daughter, he was ignoring his responsibility as a father and his accountability to the God he served. Even though David was considered a good man, he danced with the devil when he tolerated the evil in his sons and committed adultery and murder. Absalom let anger and vengeance rule his heart and mind when he used evil to take action against evil and called it good. Had Peter not addressed Ananias and Sapphira's sin after the Holy Spirit revealed it to him he would have been calling evil good by tolerating their lies to prevent embarrassing them.

This is why we are taught to bring our thoughts into captivity to the character of Jesus Christ and submit to God so the devil will flee. Today we tend to wink at evil, afraid to speak up or take action against it. Rather than confront the issue and chance offending someone we often tolerate bad behavior for the sake of a temporary peace, supporting that person's slide toward hell.

Every Christian must choose to help reduce evil, bring justice to the innocent, and help turn people to Christ by using wisdom to make good choices. While we will never eradicate all the evil in the world, we must believe that it exists and accurately define it. Then we can judge and punish it, and take warlike action against it when necessary thus minimizing its effect on humanity. We are often called upon to fight against the wrong so that what is right can prevail. We can use Scripture to disarm the devil and his plans but if we don't recognize his tactics we will innocently buy into his deception. And, if we as the church and as society in general fail to teach about Satan and his plan to destroy Christians we will allow him access to our world through which he will lead us contrary to the Word of God. Our children and grandchildren who are watching our dance with the devil will become brainwashed against the Trinity in favor of the ways of Satan.

WHAT IS DANCING WITH THE DEVIL?

Only Christians dance with the devil; non-Christians already belong to the devil. Dancing with the devil is to ignore scriptural wisdom about how we should live, behave, and talk. Instead of obedience to the Word, we participate in evil, which destroys. We often allow ourselves to be manipulated and controlled until we are unable to escape the bondage to which we are held captive. We disregard, distort or minimize the Lord's instructions often refusing to *understand* or have compassion for a Christian brother or sister, including family members; in so doing we flirt with an evil attitude. We willingly trade biblical truth for personal lust while still claiming to be a Christian, attending church, and influencing those around us, especially tender hearts and innocent minds.

When Jesus addressed the churches in the Book of Revelation, He warned the Christians at Thyatira that if they didn't stop following the sexual sin encouraged by "that Jezebel" woman He would cause them to suffer greatly alongside her (Revelation 2).

The Jezebel woman was teaching a lie about God, and fooling the people causing them to believe and tolerate her views. Her false teaching gave power to Satan, diminishing the greatness of God. Not only does God punish Christians who tolerate sin in others, (Revelation 2) He also searches out the thoughts and intentions of every heart as to whether they are evil. So we too, must search our own heart and soul to see if we are like those in the church at Thyatira before we are required to face God's findings.

DANCING WITH THE DEVIL

CHAPTER ONE STUDY QUESTIONS

1. Do you question whether evil is real? If so, why?

2. What do you know about the rapture?

3. Do you struggle with moral clarity? If so, briefly describe your struggle.

4. Describe your own views about the connection between wisdom and understanding.

5. Define your own thoughts and opinions of the Antichrist.

6. What does it mean to call evil good and good evil?

7. What does dancing with the devil mean to you?

8. Search your heart to see if you can recall the last three lies or attitude of deception that you allowed to control you.

9. What is your opinion of Abigail's husband, Nabal?

10. Why do you think the narrow path is difficult?

If you believe that you are a "Christian" and you want to live eternity in heaven with Jesus when you die, yet you live your life contrary to the Word of God, then you are dancing with the devil and need to "stop" and "turn around" and "return" to Jesus with all your heart.

DANCING WITH THE DEVIL

TWO

❧

WHO IS THIS DEVIL WITH WHOM WE DANCE?

"Be strong in the Lord and in His mighty power. Put on all of God's armor so that you will be able to stand firm against all strategies of the devil. For we are not fighting against flesh and blood enemies, but against evil rulers and authorities of the unseen world (darkness), *against mighty powers in this dark world, and against evil spirits in the heavenly places. Therefore, put on every piece of God's armor so you will be able to resist the enemy in the time of evil" (Ephesians 6:10-12 NLT).* Parentheses added

Christians who read these Scriptures in Ephesians and then say they question the existence of a real devil or evil, or a place of punishment for those who reject the Lord's principals and commit evil are deliberately ignoring God's Word.

Yet, we see from the Barna Group poll mentioned in chapter 1 that a large percentage of American Christians question whether the devil, evil, and hell are real. The poll causes true believers grave concern for the salvation of these so-called Christians. Maybe it seems much easier to believe that a loving God would never allow anyone's soul to end up in a place of eternal torment.

For years I heard preachers and Sunday school teachers quote Ephesians 6, but never heard anyone use *understandable* clarity to explain how to stand firm against the strategies of the devil, or the evil rulers and authorities of the unseen world; I didn't *understand* mighty powers or the dark world or evil spirits in heavenly places. To me, and obviously to those preachers and teachers, these Scriptures were for another time, another place, and a different people—something far into the future, and they didn't apply to the present. But now, our world is faced with just such evil. So, exactly what does Ephesians 6:10-12 really mean?

Flesh and blood describes the physical bodies or humans we can see with our eyes. Principalities are defined as the powerful spirits—Satan and his angels—who fell in the revolt against God. They are the demon spirits in Satan's ruling council. Powers refers to authorities with executive influences such as thrones, dominions, or governments who oppose Jesus. Rulers of the darkness are those world rulers, who allow demons to use them to fight the true light of the world, (Jesus). They use seduction to blind people's eyes and lead them into darkness. Their power is used to darken people's minds as history has recorded about the world's most wicked leaders.

Spiritual wickedness in high places refers to an all-encompassing evil. The word spiritual comes from the root word "spirit," and "wickedness" means malicious—one who not only is wicked, but whose every deed and thought are wicked. All he does affects others in a negative way. Spiritual wickedness in high places may not specifically refer to people, but rather to the evil itself that inspires such principalities, powers and rulers of darkness. Just as peace, love, and goodness motivate God's angels, a terrible spiritual wickedness controls those of Satan's spirit world (See Col. 2:15-16 and 1 Cor. 2:8).

The Bible teaches repeatedly that the devil is the enemy of Christians, but as noted, many believe that God's love does not permit anyone to go to hell. That simply is not true. Because we were separated from God during the fall of mankind in the Garden, we live in a broken world filled with evil. Thorns choke out tender plants (Matt. 13:7); the enemy of humanity (the devil) plants weeds to contaminate what is good—the tender plants are God's children

(Matt. 13:28); both rain and sun affect the just—God's children—and the unjust—those who reject or disobey God (Matt. 5:45); all mankind is touched by evil.

God does love us and gives us free will! But He is also a God of justice. Truly there are angels, but our fairy-tale description of them bears no resemblance to how the Bible portrays them. When our loved ones die they do not go to heaven and then return to earth as angels to watch over us, nor do they float around heaven rearranging the furniture—a popular phrase by grief-stricken relatives of the deceased. Neither do our departed loved ones reincarnate in any manner. If we believe they do, we have been misled by false teachings that twisted the Scriptures.

The Bible says each of us is destined to die once and after that comes judgment (Heb. 9:27). All the angels that will ever exist are already created (Psalms 148:2-5). Angels that were cast out of heaven in the revolt will be condemned to an eternal hell at the judgment (2 Peter 2:4). Heavenly angels don't die (Luke 20:36). Only humans die a physical death just as God promised Adam in the Garden of Eden (Gen. 2:15-17). The death we see every day proves that what God spoke years ago is true.

If there were no judgment for evil would there be a need for heaven? And if there is no hell, is Christianity a farce? What good is living a godly life if even wicked humans, such as those you will read about in chapter 3, go to heaven because there is no place of punishment for them, as some Christians say they believe? Clearly there is no justice in such thinking. Without a doubt the Bible teaches that God is a "just" God who will not allow evil into heaven. While He will reward the righteous, He will condemn the unrighteous.

Jesus promised a place in heaven for the repentant sinner. He said, *"In my Father's house, there are many mansions. If it were not so, I would have told you. I go to prepare a place for you" (John 14:2-3 KJV)*. This promise was not given to the unbelievers or the wicked, but was given to God's children. When Jesus was crucified, two other men were crucified alongside Him. The Bible says both had committed evil. One of them said to Jesus; *"So, you're the Messiah, are you? Prove it by saving yourself—and us, too, while you're at it!"* But the other criminal challenged him saying, *"Don't you fear God even when you have been sentenced to die? We deserve to die for our crimes, but this man hasn't done anything wrong."* Then he said, *"Jesus, remember me when you come into your Kingdom."* And Jesus replied, *"I assure you today; you will be with me in paradise" (Luke 23:39-43 NLT).* Jesus never once acknowledged the cold-hearted criminal. By not saying a word to him, Jesus confirmed that He never knew him, and he was not welcome in the Father's house. If he was not welcome in the Father's house because he rejected Jesus and wouldn't repent, where did his soul go when his heart stopped that day on the cross?

If you are in the percentage of American Christians who have doubts about a real heaven and hell, or if you believe only in heaven but reject hell, it's time to wake up to the truth—that you have believed a lie that could cost you your very soul if you don't find the truth. Perhaps you've simply chosen to focus on positive Scriptures in the Bible, neglecting those that warn of the devil's plan to destroy you. The Lord says His people perish for lack of knowledge. (See Hosea 4:6). The person that refuses to believe in evil or a literal hell, or sees God as love only, without justice, giving prosperity without expecting obedience in return, does not *know* the God of the Bible.

THE RICH MAN AND LAZARUS

In Luke chapter 16 Jesus gave a chilling description of a rich man who died and went to hell and a poor beggar who died and went to heaven. The story is Biblical evidence of hell by the Savior Himself and shows how those who fail to listen to warnings while they are alive will find that after they die it's too late to warn others.

Jesus said, "There was a rich man who was splendidly clothed in purple and fine linen who lived each day in luxury. At his gate lay a poor man named

DANCING WITH THE DEVIL

Lazarus who was covered with sores. As Lazarus lay there longing for scraps from the rich man's table, the dogs would come and lick his open sores. Finally the poor man died and was carried by the angels to be with Abraham. The rich man also died and was buried, and his soul went to the place of the dead (the spiritually dead). *There, in torment, he saw Abraham in the far distance with Lazarus at his side. The rich man shouted, 'Father Abraham, have some pity! Send Lazarus over here to dip the tip of his finger in water and cool my tongue. I am in anguish in these flames.' But Abraham said to him, 'Son, remember that during your lifetime you had everything you wanted, and Lazarus had nothing? So now he is here being comforted, and you are in anguish. And besides, there is a great chasm separating us. No one can cross over to you from here, and no one can cross over to us from there.' Then the rich man said, 'Please, Father Abraham, at least send him to my father's home. For I have five brothers, and I want to warn them so they don't end up in this place of torment.' But Abraham said, 'Moses and the prophets have warned them. Your brothers can read what they wrote'* (the Scriptures). *The rich man replied, 'No, Father Abraham! But if someone is sent to them from the dead, then they will repent of their sins and turn to God.' But Abraham said, 'If they don't listen to Moses and the prophets, they won't listen even if someone rises from the dead'" (Luke 16:19-31 NLT).* Parenthesis added.

Some Christians do not believe this story reflects something that really happened but instead is an analogy of how the Lord wants us to be compassionate toward others. While it does seem to contradict the Scripture in Psalms 37:25 (NLT) that says, *"I have never seen the godly abandoned or their children begging for bread,"* (Lazarus was both righteous and begging for bread) I would never gamble my soul on the assumption that the story is an analogy. Rather, I am deeply moved because of the many ways God used to warn mankind about hell. But the main reason this Scripture touches me so is that many of us today are just like the rich man. We don't realize how deeply rooted we are to an attitude or behavior that is inspired by demon spirits and which can separate us from God if we don't repent.

DANCING WITH THE DEVIL

Scripture doesn't say much about the rich man; it doesn't describe him as a particularly wicked man, and I question whether he believed he was bad enough for hell. The only thing the Bible tells us about his character is that he was rich—needing nothing—yet he lacked compassion, something very important to the Lord. Evidently he was capable of caring because when he arrived in hell he had compassion for his family, wanting to keep them from the same fate. But in responding to the rich man, Abraham used reason and logic, compassionately calling him "son" to explain to him why he was now in hell. It's likely that the rich man passed Lazarus each time he left his home. Where did he get the notion that Lazarus was unimportant? I think he was able to ignore Lazarus without conviction due to an apathetic heart that was ignorant about the Scriptures. He did not know the Scriptures because he had not read and studied or prayed over them for *understanding*.

Delayed compassion has absolutely no spiritual benefit. When the rich man cried out, "No, Father Abraham," he was in anguish because he had not read the Scriptures and he knew his brothers would not read them. Was he too busy, or simply didn't see their importance? Had he read them, might he have *understood* why he needed a heart attitude that would keep him out of hell? Possibly! But now, experiencing the reality of hell, he *understood*, which is the very thing the Scriptures teach throughout the Bible. Suddenly the Scriptures became important to him and he realized that the only help for his brothers was for someone to return from hell to warn them. He was desperate for them to know truth. But once we die, it is too late for us to accept and obey the Scriptures.

What does the Lazarus in your life look like? In an article dated February 5, 2007, titled *American Lifestyles Mix Compassion and Self-Oriented Behavior*, the Barna Group reported that when compared to the national norms (for society in general) born-again Christians are more likely to volunteer for their church but are no more likely than the average person to help the poor and homeless. Unlike the

Lazarus of the Bible, maybe the Lazarus God wants you to help has no open sores for the dogs to lick, or other evidence of a great need. However, just out of sight underneath the skin there may be a festering wound of poverty or personal dysfunction that is threatening the life and soul of that individual. How often have you passed by, not taking the time to stop and inquire about his needs? Do you really know the needs of the people inside your loop of friends, family, co-workers or employees, or does your charity go far into the distance for its pleasure in helping others—maybe to a faraway country suffering from natural disasters or the devastation of war. Yes, these things are well deserving of your help but have you inquired of the person sitting next to you? A God-led connection might turn around their life, keeping them from sinking, or it might lead them to salvation through Jesus Christ. I have a personal testimony about being a "Lazarus" in the life of friends and family.

AN ANGEL TURNED BAD

Refusing to believe in a literal hell has monumental consequences for mankind. However, there is no difference in doing that and believing that God absolves us from the need to be holy. The Bible teaches that the devil, also known as Satan or Lucifer (along with many other names), was an angel created by God, who gave him great power and significance. God also gave Satan extensive access to His throne. But Satan developed a deep hatred for God because he wanted to be God and sit on His throne. However, God let Satan know that He was the only God and there wasn't room for two, so He cast Satan and his rebels out of heaven.

Angry over being deported, Satan waged war against God and all humanity with his attack of seduction against Adam and Eve in the Garden of Eden but even as it unfolded God had a plan for the redemption of mankind through Jesus Christ. Regardless, from the child in the womb, to the oldest person living Satan has used every method imaginable to hurt human beings. This is hauntingly sad, but even sadder is that we repeatedly give him plenty of opportunity to destroy us through the choices we make in life and our ignorance of the Word.

The devil's agenda includes sowing doubt, discouragement, diversion, defeat, deceit, and delay into the heart and life of mankind. Through doubt and deceit, he causes Christians to question God's Word and His goodness just as he did with Eve in the Garden. Through discouragement Satan causes us to focus on ourselves. We worry, rather than look to God for answers. The Bible cautions that we can't change a hair on our head, so why worry? Satan uses what may seem as logical truth but instead is partial truth to make wrong things attractive so we will desire those things more than the good things of God. Satan is thrilled when we take our eyes off of Jesus. He whispers to us that our failures defeat us so that we will become discouraged and won't press in and stay the course. But the Lord says that we can do all things through Christ Jesus who strengthens us. This is where we must choose to exercise our faith. Through delay, Satan causes us to put off doing something that needs doing so that it never gets done, derailing God's plan for good. When we put off God's work we accommodate Satan's goading towards laziness, slothfulness, wasting our energy and our time. The Lord cannot use us if we don't respond to His call.

Satan often uses our greatest unfulfilled God-given needs to deliberately foul the good race we are to run. When we fall for his deceptive tactics, either willingly or unwillingly, we are distracted from our destiny. But if we will evaluate our conscience, which can often take a long time, we will eventually discover we have been seduced.

A WICKED ADVERSARY

The devil is our adversary—an enemy, rival, opponent, antagonist, and challenger—who roams the earth looking for Christians to devour. To devour is "to overcome, overwhelm, consume, engulf, use up, demolish, and dispose of." The presidential campaign and debates of 2012 were excellent portrayals of adversaries. Instead of presenting a well-thought-out plan that would bring our nation back to the place of honor it once had a reputation for, each candidate endeavored to devour the other. The 2016 election debates showed no improvement over those of 2012. In fact there seemed to be more effort made to destroy adversaries.

As Christians, we should be constantly on guard against our enemy and his plan to do us harm. He doesn't walk around with a sign on his back that says, "Hey, I'm the devil. Watch out for me because I came to destroy you." No, you can't see him because he is in the spirit world, which is the reason he uses people for his dirty deeds. Therefore, we must be spiritually awake in order to see him working through people. When we see people behaving in ways that are contrary to God's Word we must conclude that they are listening to the whispers of the evil one and his demon spirits. Until they stop what they are doing and return to the Lord, we must be careful of our association with them, but we must pray for them. Unlike God, Satan isn't omniscient or omnipresent (all-knowing or everywhere at one time) but Job 1:7 tells us that Satan patrols the earth watching everything that is going on. Do you ever think about him watching all that is going on in your life, your family, and your job?

God gave Satan permission to test Job's faith. During that test Job lost all his abundance—children, animals, workhands, and property. Yet, God had defined him as blameless, perfect in everything, a man of complete integrity. It is difficult to *understand* why God would permit such a test of someone He esteemed so highly, but Job's suffering was an unparalleled test of his faithfulness to God in spite of his wealth. When the final curtain fell, Job had a much greater *understanding* of who God was. He said, *"I know that you can do anything, and no one can stop you. You ask, 'Who is this that questions my wisdom with such ignorance?' It is I, and I was talking about things I knew nothing about, things far too wonderful for me. You said, 'Listen and I will speak! I have some questions for you and you must answer them.' I had only heard about you before but now I have seen you with my own eyes* (he saw God in action). *I take back everything I said, and I sit in dust and ashes to show my repentance" (Job 42:1-6 NLT).* Parenthesis added.

Imagine it! Job was a Godly man so respected that even highly revered elderly men stood when he approached their turf. Even God said there was no man like him. He was a wealthy and highly moral man who made a covenant with his own eyes not to look at any woman besides his wife—a man who made burnt offerings every day for his children just in case they had sinned. Imagine that with all the knowledge, *understanding*, and wisdom accredited him by everyone who knew him including God, it took eight months—almost as long as it takes a child to enter the world after conception—before he had enough *understanding* about God that he could repent and confess that he knew nothing at all and God knew everything. When the great test was finished, and Job found his place with God, He restored to Job double what he had.

THE VISION

In 1974, the late Evangelist David Wilkerson wrote a book called *The Vision*, (out of print; revised as THE VISION AND BEYOND in 2003; see www.worldchallenge.org). He shared the insight that he had received from the Lord in 1973. He spoke of the *"tragedies that would befall all humanity in the latter days—economic confusion, drastic weather changes, a multitude of earthquakes, a flood of filth—all kinds of moral degradation—problems with our youth, and persecution madness."* He said, *"We had only a few good years to prepare for the calamities; that Satan would attempt to vex and deceive even God's chosen people."*

He spoke of how the world would be immersed in erotic filth, smut, and sensuality, even seducing ministers, and what he called very "religious" men and women. Wilkerson said that those who stand against this flood of filth will be few, and they would be looked upon as "out-of-step" with an "enlightened" society and a more relevant (or tolerant) church. He called it a full-scale war (page 52) against God's chosen, with more lovers of sensuality than lovers of God.

Wilkerson said that *"Christians who thought they were beyond temptation would be tempted the most and their number one temptation would be prosperity, having become so attached to their material possessions their loss of them would be an affliction far greater for them than afflictions due to poverty."* He wrote that some of the most respected and wealthiest churches in the country would *"replace prayer with séances, be intrigued by the supernatural claims of spiritualist and Satanist groups . . . phrenology, palmistry, fortune telling, and horoscopes."* He also spoke of the super church, which he said, *"would be spiritual in name only. Instead of worshiping Jesus it would speak freely of Him but would be anti-Christ—political, deeply involved in social activities, charity programs, and ministries of compassion."* They teach about the love of God but neglect to admonish the listener to live a life that crucifies the flesh and surrenders the heart and soul to Jesus.

Wilkerson also spoke about how people would *"turn to the prophecies and teachings of men rather than giving heed to the doctrines of truth* (from the Bible). *They would give heed to seducing spirits and doctrines of devils . . . and the new doctrines would be ornamented with trappings of asceticism"* (self-denial using personal willpower instead of trust in the Lord). It is the devil that causes all this madness for the Lord says that we can't do anything without Him *(John 15:5 NIV)*. Parenthesis added.

The super church Wilkerson referred to, can in part, be recognized today as "The New Age" or the "Emergent" or "Seeker-Friendly" church. These churches can also be known as mega churches. Not all mega churches teach heresy however, many do. Further, in an unbelievable move toward a refusal to listen to or to teach sound doctrine, mainstream denominational pastors and congregations are choosing to compromise the Word of God by endorsing certain authors who change the Word and still call it Christianity, supporting lifestyles that violate or abandon the true gospel, and which the Bible clearly calls sin. If you wonder whether your church teaches the true gospel, inquire with David and Deborah Dombrowski at www.lighthousetrails.com. If they can't answer your questions, they will help you find the answers you need.

THE SEDUCTION OF CHRISTIANITY

In 1985, only eleven years following the publication of Wilkerson's book, T.A. McMahon, and the late David Hunt—who went to be with the Lord while this chapter was in progress—published their masterpiece, *The Seduction of Christianity*. The authors offer information that reinforces much of Wilkerson's vision about the end times and the super church: *"We are in danger of making cults the measure of evil and being blind to anything else that doesn't fit a particular definition of cultism.* (He means that we won't recognize when cultism is being filtered through the church because Christians have neglected educating themselves on the cult and occult world.) *The church needs to recognize that cults are only part of a much larger and more seductive deception known as the New Age movement."*

In their book, McMahon and Hunt use the term "New Age" when referring to the "great delusion" or apostasy which the Bible warns will sweep the world in the last days, causing humanity to worship the Antichrist. *"It is a tragedy of our time that the average Christian is either too easily persuaded* (falling for every wind of doctrine), *or cannot be persuaded at all* (even in their agony they will curse God). *Too few seem willing to take the time to think the issues through and check the Scriptures for themselves. Those who would escape the growing seduction must get back to the Bible and know what they believe and why, rather than succumbing to the temptation of accepting facile* (superficial) *answers provided by* (so called) *experts."* Emphasis and parenthesis added

Many churches in America have allowed Satan's influence inside by welcoming a new arrival of demons that normally operate in other countries—those that worship gods that are not the one true God. For example, Yoga comes from the Hindu religion and is based on the union between two Hindu gods. From there it expands into any characteristic a teaching guru wants to sell. For years, Yoga gurus have competed with each other to get their individual brands of Yoga into the United States—a Christian nation that worshiped the one true God—yet the Kundalini spirit (meaning the serpent power) has taken America, her churches, and Christians by storm. Pastors: why aren't you teaching against this enemy of a Holy God and protecting the lives and hearts of those in your congregations? Instead, many of you are endorsing "Christian" yoga.

While the practice of yoga continues to rise in contemporary American culture, sufficient and adequate knowledge of the practice's origins does not. According to Andrea R. Jain, Assistant Professor of Religious Studies, Indiana University, with Academic interest that includes the history of modern yoga, *"Yoga is undoubtedly a Hindu movement* (anti-Christ) *for spiritual meditation."* Contemporaries of the Hindu faith argue that the more popular yoga gets, the less concerned people become about its origins in history.

These same contemporaries do state that while anyone can practice yoga, only those who give Hinduism due credit for the practice will achieve the full benefit of the custom. Yoga is marketed as a supplement to a cardio routine and is endorsed by Dr. Dean Ornish. But, marketing yoga in this manner *"dilutes its Hindu identity."* Christians must *understand* what this means; Yoga does one no good unless the participant gives Hinduism credit for the practice. To do so requires turning one's back on Christ because the god of Hinduism and the God of Christianity cannot and will not co-exist. Further, true Christians cannot serve and worship two different gods and attain heaven. Parenthesis added.

Yoga is now honored worldwide. On December 11, 2014, all 193 members of the United Nations General Assembly approved by consensus a resolution establishing June 21 as 'International Day of Yoga.' The declaration came at the request of Indian Prime Minister, Narendra Modi. The first International Day of Yoga was observed in

DANCING WITH THE DEVIL

2015. 35,985 people from 84 nationalities gathered in New Delhi, India for 35 minutes of yoga. The event ushered in two Guinness world records: the most people gathered for one event and the most people gathered from different nationalities.

If you are involved in Yoga of any kind, and call yourself a Christian, despite Dr. Dean Ornish's endorsement of Yoga, I encourage you to do a complete study of the history of Yoga, particularly Kundalini Yoga. Dr. Ornish is a follower of yoga guru Swami Satchidananda. Pray and ask God to show you *understanding* and wisdom about this enemy that is operating inside your church and probably within members of your own family. It is difficult today to find a family that does not have at least one member involved in Yoga.

The late Charles Colson wrote: *"The enemy is in our midst. He has so infiltrated our camp that many no longer can tell an enemy from a friend, truth from heresy."* (Note: Though originally a critic of postmodernism—later to become known as globalization—Colson eventually endorsed the ecumenical movement to unite all faiths throughout the world. Ecumenical is from the Greek word *oikoumene*, which means "the whole inhabited world." Christians are called to unify, but not create a "one-world religion" by compromising the truth of Scripture.)

Can you identity the enemy in your camp? Your camp is your church, your home, and your workplace. Jesus taught that in the end times the enemy would be in the pulpits of our churches and in our own homes. He cautioned us saying, *"And don't imagine that I came to bring peace to the earth! I came not to bring peace, but a sword. I have come to set a man against his father, a daughter against her mother, and a daughter-in-law against her mother-in-law. Your enemies will be right in your own household! If you love your father or mother more than you love me, you are not worthy of being mine; or if you love your son or daughter more than me, you are not worthy of being mine. If you refuse to take up your cross and follow me, you are not worthy of being mine. If you cling to your life, you will lose it; if you give up your life for me, you will find it" (Matthew 10:34-39 NLT).*

Whether we are boycotting sending troops into harm's way, or simply proclaiming well wishes to family and friends, we cry out for "Peace! Peace! Peace at all cost!" We celebrate the birth of our Savior by promoting "peace on earth and good will toward men." Yet in the words of the Savior Himself, He didn't come to earth to bring peace but instead a sword. Scripture does encourage us to live at peace with all people, but only as far as it is possible for us. However, living peaceably with others is not always possible because some people will have no part in peace. It is then that we must fight for what is morally right.

Is the enemy in your home? I have painful personal experience where the enemy was in my home until it exploded. Jesus said, *"Do you think I have come to bring peace to the earth? No, I have come to divide people against each other! From now on families will be split apart, three in favor of me, and two against—or two in favor and three against (Luke 12:51, 52 NLT).* The enemy works on those that are weak in spirit and who cave easily to his tactics.

Can you see the enemy in your workplace? Pay attention to the inappropriate words, behavior, views and beliefs of those around you. You may be shocked by what you learn.

Many in the pulpits, both in church and on television, are falsely teaching that humans are little gods. But there is only one God and He owns everything He created including us. We are simply beloved children He redeemed with the blood of His Son when we gave Him our heart. False teachers who claim to speak for God have an agenda and methodology that is contrary to the Word of God. Unfortunately they have captured the hearts and minds of multitudes of Christians that are being deceived and seduced in ways and thoughts that will enable them to easily follow the Antichrist. If you're wondering if the great deceiver is deceiving you, then go directly to God and ask Him to reveal His truth to you. He says His children will know His voice. He promises to let us find Him if we seek Him with all our hearts. He does not want anyone to perish. Your enemy could be using someone right in your own church to confuse the innocent.

How can you purge the sin in your camp? You must know and *understand* who the enemy is—the devil, Satan—and be able to identify his tactics—how he operates. The Bible calls him by many names and defines him so well that no one should question his existence, his power, or his intent. Because he hates God, he loves to hurt God's children, afflicting them with pain and troubles. His objective and quest are to take your soul. Don't let him have it! I encourage you to search the Scriptures with a hunger to *understand* who he is so that you will never have to say you were caught in his trap because you didn't recognize him. Purging is easy when you know what you are looking at and are willing to take action.

Every American should make a special effort to study the history of the Bible and the history of the world, and then take a good look at the evil that humanity has endorsed—the evil that came from the devil. Chapter 3 contains enough information about evil that no one should question whether there is a real devil that has no mercy on mankind.

CHAPTER TWO STUDY QUESTION

1. What is spiritual wickedness in high places?

2. What are the tender plants spoken of in Matthew 13:7?

3. What does the Bible say about how often a human can die?

4. For whom did Jesus promise a place in heaven?

5. Why do you think the rich man ended up in hell?

6. Why do you think the poor man (Lazarus) never attained prosperity and was never healed?

7. Provocative Question: Why do you think Satan turned against God?

8. Why do you think Satan (the devil) got so angry with God?

9. Are you aware of Satan's influence in your life?

10. What is the battle armor spoken about in Scripture?

DANCING WITH THE DEVIL

THREE

❦

A WORLD OBSESSED WITH EVIL

"And I the Lord, will punish the world for its evil and the wicked for their guilt and iniquity (sins); I will cause the arrogance of the proud to cease, and will lay low (humble) the haughtiness of the terrible, and the boasting of the violent and ruthless" (Isaiah 13:11 Amplified).

"Do you think I like to see wicked people die? Says the Sovereign Lord. Of Course not! I want them to turn from their wicked ways and live" (Ezekiel 18:23 NLT).

"Evil men do not understand justice, but those who seek the Lord, understand it fully" (Proverbs 28:5 NIV).

In the days of Noah, people had become so wicked that God said he was sorry he had ever made man. The following Scriptures from the New Testament Bible are a reminder to us that God created all things, and He has destroyed according to the wickedness that has prevailed, and He will destroy again. *"God made the heavens by the word of His command, and He brought the earth out from the water and surrounded it with water. Then He used the water to destroy the ancient world with a mighty flood. And by the same word, the same heaven and earth* (that was destroyed in the days of Noah) *have been stored up for fire. They are being kept for the Day of Judgment, when ungodly people will be destroyed" (2 Peter 3: 5-7 NLT).* Parentheses added

Space does not permit me to include all my research on the evil perpetrated against humans by other humans that has been documented since the beginning of time, both in the Holy Bible and in history since the Bible was closed. However, from the evil acts selected for the purpose of this book—to show the depth of darkness to which humans can fall when they serve Satan—it is easy to see the magnitude of evil throughout time and how it is still extremely active today. From the tiniest evil thought untaken, then brought into repentance and submitted to the Lord, to the darkest crime the human mind and heart can manufacture, even the strictest skeptic should be convinced that the devil is both very evil and very active. Those who still doubt his existence after reading this chapter should thoroughly investigate crimes against humanity during war as well as during peace. One of the saddest things about crimes against humanity is the fact that so few people are educated about the atrocities and so few care to be enlightened. Many people follow the views of a fifth grade student who said to me, "I don't know about it and I don't want to know about it. It is their problem; not mine!"

INSPIRED TO RESEARCH THE EVIL OF WAR

After hearing the testimony several years ago by a man who was the product of his mother's rape by five Nazi soldiers during World War II I became aware of the atrocities of war that had nothing to do with battle. They were simply evil run amok. My memory of what happened to the young man's mother is slightly fragmented due to the passing of several years since I heard him speak about it, but I am writing what I remember.

In that dark night of intense pain and torture, five Nazi soldiers entered her home, drank excessively, and exhausted all their violent hostilities against one defenseless woman until the late morning hours of darkness. (Isn't that something to be so proud of?) Though she was beaten and traumatized, the men went one step further. Before their departure they broke both of her legs and threw her from her home into the muddy yard to die in the cold rain. I often wondered why they didn't just shoot her like they did so many of the women but they clearly wanted her to suffer. Gloriously though, God had a plan of redemption for the victims that would eventually change thousands of lives.

After daylight, a neighbor passing by her home saw her lying in her yard. He came to her aid and tended her wounds. When she learned she was pregnant her courageous rescuer (truly one of the good guys) asked for her hand in marriage and she accepted. When her child—the man giving the testimony—was born, she was still too bitter to nurture him. She administered his basic needs but any affection he received came from his step-dad who accepted him unconditionally. The innocent victim of a barbaric crime, the child grew into an angry man, became a drug addict and finally ended up in prison. When Christians came to minister to him there, he met a young woman whom he later married. Eventually he, too, became a minister, teaching and sharing his story of redemption.

On the day I heard him speak, he said that after he accepted Jesus as Lord he pleaded with his mom to forgive her abusers so she could love and accept both him and Jesus but she steadfastly refused. Regardless, he was relentless in his quest for her to forgive and accept Christ for her healing and for salvation. Then after several years of preaching, he looked down from the pulpit one evening and saw her standing among those at the altar. Her heart had finally softened.

Though I had always been one who refused to read stories or watch movies that depicted the atrocities of war, this young man's testimony inspired me to a relentless search about war. I learned that the powers in Hollywood had not accurately portrayed the reality of war in movies about it. The romantic and heroic stories of military soldiers in combat did not reveal the inhumane crimes against all humanity, and especially the brutality against defenseless women and children.

Our government and media kept those horrors hidden from the majority of American civilians both during the war and in the years following the end of the war. The consensus was that our society should not be exposed to the atrocities of war. Most authorities agreed that Americans would not be able to deal with the trauma caused by what they would learn, that many would go mad with sadness, which is quite true! Even our military men and women today are plagued with Post Traumatic Stress Disorder (PTSD) because of what they saw and did during war.

Though the concerns about exposure to war horrors are justified, can we justify remaining ignorant about the reality of war? Presently terror is lurking at our door and human slavery at an all-time high. Can we use what we may call our *right* to a level of emotional and physical freedom that was bought and paid for by the blood of our forefathers and our present day soldiers as an excuse to stay ignorant about the intensity of evil? I think not! Women and children aren't safe anywhere in the world, including America, and this should not be in a country presently free of totalitarianism.

UNDEVIATING WORDS OF CAUTION

Though I offer no apology for the unusually graphic content of this chapter, I do give the reader caution as some may find the brutally painful acts against humans, emotionally disturbing. Beginning with my first research of these crimes, I became physically ill and for hours afterwards I surrendered to serious emotional trauma. Not wanting to invite those sad feelings back into my life, twelve months passed before I could continue my research. Most of the sites I visited and the books I read sternly cautioned the reader. Some apologized for what they felt they needed to write. Others explained that they were unable to make the atrocities known to the public because most people would probably panic. While I do give caution, I won't apologize for exposing evil for the sake of personal salvation and corporate growth through awareness.

DANCING WITH THE DEVIL

The first documented crime I discovered was the Horror at NeuStettin. It described the torture-until-death of young girls at Camp Vilmsee of the RAD—a camp housing 500 females of the Women's Reich Labour Service during WWII. The attackers were believed to be Polish men who agreed to entertain drunken Soviet soldiers (who occasionally moved from being entertained to being a participant) by torturing young German girls in a most horrifying manner. The amount of hate required to perpetrate and watch such unbelievable behavior is impossible to imagine. The military personnel who came to free the POWs following the incident said evidence was still very visible, and women that were left alive were walking around in a daze as if they had gone insane. The incident was so disturbing I will not relate the details here even though I believe that we all must be aware of the meanness humans are capable of. Those curious enough can find the reports online.

For as long as history has been recorded, leaders from around the world have participated in, encouraged and condoned inconceivably brutal pain and torture and degradation of human beings. While much evil has been addressed through wars and other kinds of invasions meant to destroy it, the aftermath remains and grows because it is allowed to do so. In this chapter I hope to show how humanity has embraced evil by rejecting the moral code of God—Christians and non-Christians alike—or we have remained uninformed about evil. It is not my desire to frighten or traumatize anyone; rather, I hope to enlighten so that people will know how to fight this great enemy called evil, *and* keep their faith. Some people may read the content presented here and then deny God, asking why a loving God would permit such things to happen to the innocent. Americans must be aware of evil as we could very well experience such behavior on our own soil unless something is done to stop any anti-God invaders who hate our citizens. Though difficult to read, the information I have chosen to use in this chapter confirms the depths of evil that humans will allow the devil to use them to destroy other humans.

Romans chapter 1 documents a letter from the Apostle Paul to both Jewish and Gentile Christians, the believers at the church in Rome. Paul gave a general description of and named the evil acts of wickedness men and women had committed throughout history, and told how God felt about them. As I searched through the Bible for the type of crimes Paul spoke of, I found a story in Judges 19, Chapter 1 that shook me to my core. Instantly I was angry, hurt, and questioned whether the God I thought I loved was really a loving God or a criminal. After all, the husband in this story was from the tribe of Levi, the lineage of Jesus, and the abusers were from the land and tribe of Benjamin—the twelfth and youngest son of Jacob from whom the twelve tribes of Israel descended.

The behavior of the farmer who gave shelter to the traveling man and his concubine and servant was intolerable. However, when I finished researching evil in the Bible, I discovered that the real criminal was the old devil called Satan, and that God was the loving God I had been taught He was. Though the crime in Judges 19, which I recommend as a study, was heinous, God's vengeance against the evil behavior in those of that time is spellbinding as it will be when He raises His sword against those who commit evil in our day and in the days to come. Israel had forgotten God. Laws were not enforced and crime was ignored. No one was willing to speak out against evil until atrocities had gone too far. Sexual perversion and lawlessness prevail easily when a nation disobeys or forgets God. Sounds very much like the United States of America today!

The content in this chapter about evil is difficult to read, but I hope it will not be discarded as too painful. Instead I pray it will be used to help awaken other sleepers who have been lenient with evil—those who ignore its power. To ignore the power of evil is to endorse evil, something a Christian should never do. Throughout the Scriptures, the Lord has clearly defined how destructive evil is.

UNRESTRAINED THOUGHTS BECOME UNRESTRAINED EVIL

As we saw in the stories in chapter 1 about Jacobs's sons, and King David and his family, unrestrained thoughts become unrestrained evil, which comes from the heart. God sees it as so important for us to avoid that he wants all people to be educated about it. Something that many consider insignificant such as disrespect—review the story of David and Nabal in chapter 1—is highly important to the Lord. A haughty look or insolence, which is rude behavior, is offensive to God because when it is not redirected to become good behavior, it will lead to evil behavior. This is why we are cautioned in Scripture to bring up children so that they will have a conscious conviction to help them avoid evil.

Malicious behavior usually begins with a small deception; a lie conceived from a simple thought grows into the most horrific evil the mind and heart will allow. There are two choices we can make when an evil thought comes to us: 1) we can allow it to take root in our heart and then act it out, or 2) we can refuse to submit or participate in evil, and take action against it. Taking action against evil in our own heart requires submitting our thoughts to Scripture and then asking the Holy Spirit to help us overcome those thoughts. In more severe cases where evil abounds and is perpetrated by others, you may be required to give your life for someone else—as a military soldier does for his countrymen, or a parent for a child, or in the manner of Dietrich Bonhoeffer during WWII. Bonhoeffer has said: *"There are things for which an uncompromising stand is worthwhile."* And, *"Silence in the face of evil is itself evil; God will not hold us guiltless. Not to speak is to speak. Not to act is to act."* Quote from Dietrich Bonhoeffer, Pastor, Martyr, and Spy (1906-1945). Read his story on page 108, 109.

The great Irish Orator, Philosopher, and Politician, Edmund Burke, who lived from 1729-1797 once said: *"All that is necessary for the triumph of evil is for good men to do nothing."*

DANCING WITH THE DEVIL

Writer and publisher John Stuart Mill—1806-1873 wrote: *"A person may cause evil to others not only by his action, but* (also) *by his inaction and in either case he is justly accountable to them for the injury."*

The Bible records vast accounts of evil, proving how long it has been with us, and it is ever with us today. We have a command from God to avoid evil where possible and fight against it, but in today's church teaching about evil is unpopular because of its unpleasantness. Regardless, there are times when we must face evil and deal with the fear it brings.

HEALTHY AND UNHEALTHY FEAR

Throughout the Bible the Lord admonishes us to not be afraid. In the New Testament we read that God didn't give us a spirit of fear, but of power, love and sound mind. Many Christians read this Scripture and then toss it aside as impossible to live by. To others it means that having any kind of fear is a great sin. But that simply isn't true. Those who easily toss these Scriptures around haven't lived with a violent dad or abusive mom; they have not experienced the pain and degradation of rape; they haven't faced the humiliation of bullying, or looked into the barrel of enemy guns; they haven't dealt with an intoxicated and angry husband or wife using words that terrify the spouse and children. Certainly we shouldn't *live* in fear, but having been in many situations where there was a need to be afraid, I found it difficult to draw from the Scripture about power, love and a sound mind. Fear is a natural instinct; our brain tells us when we are in danger. Even Jesus cautioned the disciples to avoid a certain road at certain times because those who wished to harm the disciples resided in a cemetery nearby. Jesus was telling them to use their common sense about evil.

The "spirit of fear" spoken of in the Bible is not the instinctive fear we feel when we are subjected to situations such as the ones I submit below. God's promise is that when we trust Him and don't panic in fear, no matter what happens to us we will live in eternity with Him. Being afraid of evil or a dangerous situation is normal and the one who says he isn't is fooling himself. There is an instinctive healthy fear that tells us not to do something ridiculous due to the danger involved—like avoiding the cemetery road because of those hiding there who wanted to kill them. There is fanatical or unhealthy fear that keeps us in bondage to an existence that prevents us living a resourceful life. God gave us common and spiritual sense to help us with both kinds of fear.

There were many times in my life when I was afraid. Once during a hike in Grand Teton National Park I experienced heart-thumping anxiety when I mistakenly took the wrong fork in a trail. My earlier visit with a park ranger about the trail assured me it was well traveled and I was not likely to encounter wild animals. What we didn't clarify was that I intended to hike full circle which included a part of the trail that was not often traveled. I didn't *understand* that most people only hike from the trailhead to the lake and then back the same way they came. The ranger didn't *understand* that I didn't *understand* routine hiking on this trail. I passed plenty of hikers on the first half that led to the lake but when I continued on past the lake I encountered only a couple of hikers along the way. With each step I took down that wooded and scary trail alone I became more and more hopeful to encounter other hikers, which would help to shoo away wild animals, but none came. I prayed the famous "God didn't give me a spirit of fear," prayer but all I could think of was that I didn't want to be eaten by a bear.

Fear is a natural reaction over concern for the safety of someone we love. When my son was a toddler he loved to play hide and seek when I took him shopping with me. He would hide in the clothing on the circular racks while I browsed. Then he would laugh and scream when I searched him out and yelled, "Boo!" One time, though, he sneaked through the clothing to hide under another rack. When I called out to him he did not answer. He played this game until he heard my voice change from laughter to concern and then to panic. It was when he heard the panic that he surfaced. I will never forget the rapid heartbeat and pressure I felt in my chest and thinking that my head would burst trying to make a common sense decision about what should be my next move.

Two more incidences of *game playing gone too far* in my life sent my heart pumping in fear. When my niece was a preteen I took her with me on a road trip to Colorado. While we were putzing around a small town awaiting the events of the day she decided on a secret solo stroll. After my search for her on foot and a couple of blocks in my car were unsuccessful, I returned to the cute little café where we had dined earlier. To my great joy I found her there sitting on the steps. When the human mind and body is consumed with fear of the unthinkable, desperation follows quickly.

One afternoon, my six-year-old granddaughter decided to play hide and seek with me at her school. When the end of day bell rang I greeted her through the glass of her classroom door and then waited for her to exit the room. At the appointed time she lined up with the other students and headed toward the exit doors of the building. I trailed along behind them for a brief time, but then got pushed aside by a crowd of a couple hundred students. When I finally reached the front exit doors, I couldn't see her anywhere. Recalling the former incidents and their positive outcomes, I didn't get too upset in the beginning but when my twenty-minute search and a fifteen-minute search with the school secretary turned up nothing, I became very concerned.

Exhausting what we believed to be all our options for search and rescue, mutually we agreed to notify authorities and my daughter that her daughter was missing. At the moment I gave the secretary instructions to call the police, my granddaughter walked into the office. She confessed that in the beginning of her game of hide and seek the fun and excitement of watching me search and worry kept her in hiding. Then as she listened to our worry turn into panic she became too afraid to surface. She had sandwiched her little body behind a large roof support column and the wall of the building just enough that she was fully hidden. It wasn't until she heard me instruct the secretary to call the police that she realized her game had gone too far.

In each one of these incidences, I thought I would lose my insides. They were three people I loved deeply and the thought that some evil had come to do unspeakable harm to them was crushingly sickening. In times like this fear will overcome us and there is nothing we can do. But it is important to work at being sensible, to know how to separate healthy instinctive fear from unhealthy fanatical fear in order to rightly apply the Scriptures about power, love and a sound mind.

Since the time of creation, war after war has plagued nations. From the closing of the Bible until present day, rulers, dictators and tyrants of nation after nation have terrorized innocent people beyond what one's imagination can conceive. Further, nations have produced serial killers, rapists and drug dealers that instilled immeasurable fear in their neighbors, their communities, and their state.

In chapter 1 you read Bible stories of danger or evil and saw their consequences. In chapter 2 we learned who the devil is, what his strategies are and how they affect all people of all time. In this first part of chapter 3 you have learned of my personal stories of fear when I was faced with what could have been. But what you will learn ahead in this chapter about men, women, and children who suffered horribly at the hands of those whose hearts were ruled by Satan both in times of war and in peace will probably bring fear to your heart as you read. The fear and heartache I experienced cannot be compared to what those people suffered. Nowhere is it written that we can rest assured there is nothing in the world to harm us. However, much is written that confirms there is plenty of evil in the world that all ages of people need to be aware of.

THE EVIL MEN DO! - "IT STILL MAKES ME SHUDDER"
France and Spain: Equal Brutality (War of 1810)

Witnesses of human massacre during the Revolutionary and Napoleonic Wars gave horrifying details of the brutality humans inflicted on other humans causing some to question which group was actually worse. In an article titled *It Still Makes Me Shudder*, Professor Philip G. Dwyer, Newcastle University, Australia, recounts the indiscriminate torture and killing of anyone who fell into the path of the Napoleon led French troops that gave themselves up to pillage, rape, and murder over a period of two to four days following the fall of the town of Jaffa, in what was then (1799) known as Syria.

During the Spanish war of 1810 French General Louis-Francois Lejeune, who was an eyewitness to the war, was captured by the guerilla(s) and saw the brutal killing of three French prisoners. Thirty-five years later he confessed to still being haunted by the noise of sabers hacking into their heads and shoulders. He reported, *"It has not ceased to reverberate in my ears and still makes me shudder with horror."*

Many years after the battle, Doctor Etienne-Louis Malus, who had accompanied the French army, recalled what he witnessed during those awful days of horror. *"The soldiers cut the throats of men and women, the old and the young, Christians and Turks . . . father and son on top of the other* (on the same pile of bodies)*, a daughter being raped on the cadaver of her mother, the smoke from the burnt clothes of the dead, the smell of blood, the groans of the wounded, the shouts of the victors who were quarreling about the loot taken from a dying victim."* Parentheses added

Following the initial massacre, more than 2500 prisoners were marched to a beach south of the city and slaughtered. To save bullets, troops were ordered to bayonet any prisoners not already shot. Doctor Malus reported that among the victims they found many children who in the act of death, had clung to their fathers—clear evidence of God's design for children to rely on their fathers for protection. (Note: Compare to the duty of fathers in chapter 5).

In his journal, a Captain Francois recalled the equally brutal ferocity of the Spanish: *"I have seen . . . officers, soldiers, and even women disemboweled from the womb to the stomach and their breasts cut off, men sawn in two, others with the noble parts of their bodies cut off and placed in their mouths; others again hung by their feet in a chimney and their head burnt."*

Professor Dwyer relates that reports given him illustrate three types of extreme violence one most commonly encounters in accounts of the Revolutionary and Napoleonic Wars—namely the slaughter associated with the sacking (plunder and destruction) of towns, the killing of prisoners, and the abuse of civilians, *particularly women*. He wrote that some testimonials showed that there were men who refused to participate in such cruelty against others. For those that did, such acts were done in an uncontrolled frenzy—the wildest of inhumane behavior, a giving of the mind, will, and emotions to the acts of the devil. Parenthesis and emphasis added

It is difficult for a compassionate person to believe that any human could gain personal pleasure from the suffering of another while he is the one causing the suffering. God is compassion and unless He has a strategic purpose (Job and Pharaoh come to mind) He does not inflict deliberate suffering on His creation. It is compassionless God haters that cause human suffering.

1812 FRENCH INVASION OF RUSSIA
THE COST TO SATISFY PERSONAL WILL

French Emperor Napoleon Bonaparte had a reputation for being self-willed, arrogant, brilliant, the greatest military strategist in history, and could have probably been diagnosed as narcissistic when compared to the official definition.

In 1812, Bonaparte organized 600,000 soldiers of his French "Grand Armeè," and on June 24 they crossed the Nieman River, and invaded Russia. The goal was to force Russian Emperor Alexander I to remain in the Continental Blockade of the United Kingdom, and to prevent a Russian invasion of Poland. Bonaparte had won numerous military battles since the beginning of his reign. His strategies are so famous they are still studied at military academies worldwide. But he greatly misjudged weather conditions when he set out to force Russia's Alexander to comply with the Blockade. This would cost him the lives of approximately 570,000 soldiers of his Grand Armeè, and probably an equal number of horses, and it would set the stage for his downfall as Emperor of France.

Though Russia lacked the military power necessary to battle the Grand Armeè, they had great respect for harsh winters. Russian military strategy was to retreat north, torching the land behind them and forcing the Grand Armeè deeper inland. Retreating may have been a wise military decision, but hundreds of thousands of Russian civilians died as the Grand Armeè sacked villages, towns, and cities on its historical march to capture Moscow. Russia's strategy of torching the land behind them left nothing for the French troops to forage. Threadbare, hungry and cold, they reached Moscow on September 14, 1812 with only about 100,000 of their original 600,000 soldiers. They found Moscow to be deserted. Anxious for a peace offering from the Russian Emperor Alexander, French Emperor Bonaparte and his army remained in Moscow until October 19.

Meanwhile, an unusually harsh winter came early, so when the offer Bonaparte expected from Alexander didn't come, he organized his demoralized, starved and frozen troops and marched out of Moscow along the same war-torn path he had used to enter it. Facing sub-zero temperatures and unusual snowfall, and no forage for the men and horses the Grand Armeè reached the Nieman River in late November, with only about 30,000 troops—a remnant of a half-million-man army.

Bonaparte's invasion of—and exodus from—Russia cost him much more than he anticipated. The harshness of a war inadequately thought-out provoked his men to a darkness of mind unfamiliar to militaries of today. Stories of men piling dead human bodies against walls of abandoned buildings to help insulate against sub-zero temps and cutting open dead horses and crawling inside to keep warm, and hunger and fatigue that caused them to surrender to cannibalism, all show the depth of man's will to survive. *"Without wise leadership a nation falls; there is safety in having many advisers" (Proverbs 11:14 NLT).*

POGROMS OF EXTINCTION
1821-1859-1871-1881-1886-1905 and Bolshevism, A Revolution

One term for violence—pogrom—is defined as the deliberately organized and particularly state-supported killing of a targeted group of people and the confiscation or destruction of their property. For thousands of years, the Jewish race has been targeted for extinction by those who deem them unfit to live, and the pogroms from the early 1800's forward proved successful at killing millions. The pogroms of Odessa, a port city on the Black Sea and present day Ukraine, are reported to be the beginnings of modern day ethnic cleansing. Particularly there were six different years (1821, 1859, 1871, 1881, 1886, and 1905) when the Jewish people experienced horrific abuse and destruction, but the most notable pogroms were administered under Emperor Nicholas Romanov II who reigned in Russia from 1894 to 1917.

Tsar (English slang "czar") Nicholas was first cousin to King George V of the United Kingdom and the British Dominions, and he was the Emperor of India. He was also the grandson of Queen Victoria and Prince Albert, and was first cousin to Kaiser Wilhelm II, the Emperor of Germany from 1888 to 1918.

In the same way the church in Germany trusted and supported Adolf Hitler, the Russian Orthodox Church, which affectionately named the Tsar "Saint Nicholas the Passion-Bearer," favored him and often called him Saint Nicholas the Martyr. But, critics nicknamed him 'Bloody Nicholas' because of The Khodynka Tragedy, Bloody Sunday, the anti-Semitic pogroms, his execution of political opponents, and his pursuit of military campaigns of unprecedented measures—excessively violent and aggressive decisions by a country's leader.

History confirms that from the beginning of his reign, Tsar Nicholas Romanov showed willingness to resort to violence at the slightest pretext. He used the Black Hundred gangs to carry out his atrocious commands, particularly against peasants. Also, the Tsar's anti-Semitism and genocide are well documented. In one month, up to 4,000 people were murdered and 10,000 more injured. Victims included Jews, socialists, and intellectuals as Tsar Nicholas vowed to never relent in his effort to destroy people he felt weren't fit to live.

The Black Hundred gangs were militant men who trekked the countryside urging peasants to rise up against anyone they knew hated Russia, and they staunchly supported Nicholas who had a direct connection to them. In effect, they demanded, *"Report the views and actions of your neighbor lest you suffer harm."* These gangs were racists who incited pogroms and were especially violent when they were loaded with vodka and prodded by the police. In obedience to leaflets that attempted to persuade the public to *"tear them to pieces and kill them all!"* 800 Jews were murdered, 5,000 wounded, and 100,000 rendered homeless in Odessa.

In *Bolshevism: The Road to Revolution by Alan Woods, Part Two: The First Russian Revolution,* Woods describes the Black Hundred gangs, as the "scum of society" protected by the forces of the state, and incited to commit the most unspeakable atrocities against defenseless people.

In referencing the Black Hundred gangs, Woods quoted Leon Trotsky, a leader of the 1917 Russian Revolution, and organizer of the Red Army--*"doss-house tramps turned king; an hour ago they were trembling slaves, hounded by police and starvation, he is now himself an unlimited despot* (dictator/tyrant). *Everything is permitted to him, he is capable of anything, and he is master of property and honor, of life and death. If he wants to, he can throw an old woman out of a third floor window along with a grand piano; he can smash a chair against a baby's head, rape a little girl while the entire crowd looks on, hammer a nail into a living human body . . . He exterminates whole families, he pours petrol over a house, transforms it into a mass of flames, and if anyone attempts to escape, he finishes him off with a cudgel* (a short heavy club). *A savage horde comes into an Armenian almshouse,* (poorhouse), *knifing old people, sick people, women and children . . . There exists no tortures, figments of a feverish brain maddened with alcohol and fury, at which he need ever stop. He is capable of everything."*

Numerous reports about the evil atrocities against humanity confirm how the amount of alcohol one consumes plays a huge role in provoking humans to commit awful crimes. Today's drug problem is no different. People are addicted to various types of prescription and street drugs, and they succumb to whatever the effect of the drug tells them to—usually the whispers of a demon spirit. Often what these people do is evil and is contrary to what the Scriptures tell us about how we are to live and treat others.

1914-1918 WWI: A NEW KIND OF WAR

The First World War began in 1914 and for the four years following, Europeans would see war as they had never before seen it—a "new" kind of war. During the forty years that preceded the war nations experienced growth and expansion, and conflicts and jealousies, which most likely led to greed. Monarchies and democracies were challenged to find ways to cope with the change while defending each country's authority. Though many European leaders felt peaceful about their future, others believed trouble was quickly approaching.

Throughout Europe the social, economic, and governmental aspects of authority clearly needed reform, but the real cause of what has been called the 'Great War' (WWI) is still questionable since none of these issues could be held directly responsible.

Other reasons for the war include: 1) Austro-Hungary's determination to impose its will upon the Balkans—a geographical designation for the Southeastern peninsula of the European

Continent which includes Greece, Bulgaria, Romania, Serbia, Croatia, Albania, Macedonia, Montenegro, and Bosnia; 2) many different nationalities combined in one country or another, which caused hostilities among the people; 3) Germany's quest for great power and world influence, which sparked a naval arms race with Britain—the greatest naval power in the world at the time and who responded by building new and greater warships; 4) The French desire for revenge after being defeated by Germany in 1871; 5) Russia's need for restoration and national prestige after a 1905 battering by the Japanese military. Reasons to declare war were numerous, and needed only a spark to ignite.

As previously mentioned, some of the leaders were related and unresolved family issues had plagued them over time. Offenses perpetrated by men in high places against other men in high places were raw and unpredictable. Some were prepared to fight at the first provocation. When a Serbian nationalist named Gavrilo Princip assassinated Franz-Ferdinand, the Archduke of Austria and his wife on June 28, 1914, the Treaty Alliance System—a formal agreement or treaty between two or more nations—was used to catapult nations into war to protect designated allies. Some historians believe that few leaders cared about Franz-Ferdinand and thought his death was a good thing, but his assassination was the spark used to ignite war.

Throughout time numerous documents confirm that hate for God and His son Jesus has been responsible for a huge amount of human persecution. Motivated by this hate and a blatant rejection of people who loved Christ, Austro-Hungarian soldiers began systematic attacks on the Serbian people, particularly Christians. Proudly, they photographed the Serbian Christian men and women they crucified.

Professor R.A. Reiss, a teacher of criminology at the University of Lausanne, Switzerland, wrote, *"The especially brutal atrocities against the unarmed, and defenseless Serbian population were committed by soldiers of Mohammedan religion,* (Bosnian Muslims)." Dr. Reiss also reported that these Bosnian Muslims were generally the leaders of the massacres. What justice could be found in fatally torturing Christians for the works of a "fanatic" named Princip? No wonder the Bible admonishes us not to hate because when left unchecked, it leads to appalling crime, and the evidence is visible in war after war.

Kaiser Wilhelm II of Germany came to Austria's defense, helping them punish the Serbs. Wilhelm's support of Austria served to push Russia's Tsar Nicholas into backing Serbia. Finally, Russia, France, and Britain allied for war against Germany and her allies. In spite of the assassination, which was committed by what some called a *fanatic*, not one country's leader used his position or any good judgment to avoid war. Instead, Germany, a fairly new country, wanted to be recognized as a major power among the older powers like France, Russia and Britain. With cousins fighting cousins, the aggressive rivalry between these countries brought death to a massive number of people—more than 17 million in what history has labeled *"a new kind of war."*

Weapons never before used (poison gas, and heavy artillery) ushered in a whole new way to fight a war of unprecedented levels of horror, suffering, and deaths stemming from hate and revenge. Military and diplomatic leaders of Austro-Hungary, Germany, and Russia saw war as the key to saving their honor and bringing resolve to the internal and international problems they believed they had. The surge to annihilate the Jewish people and other minorities was escalating. Every nation involved experienced extreme destruction. In Russia, masses of people were suffering from starvation and other issues. But the people believed they could find hope in a communist thinker named Vladimir Lenin.

On March 15 1917, Tsar Nicholas II was forced to abdicate, leaving his throne to a temporary Government, which supported the war effort but was unable to affect change for Russia. One month after the Tsar abdicated, Vladimir Lenin was transported on a sealed German railroad car from Switzerland to Sweden and then to Russia.

DANCING WITH THE DEVIL

In November 1917, he seized power of the provisional government that had been in place since the Tsar's collapse, and created a communist government. Lenin had become enthralled with the work of famed communist thinker, Karl Marx so on his first day in office, his regime abolished all private land ownership.

Lenin wanted Russia out of the war so he began truce talks with Germany immediately after taking the leadership role. In his impatient quest for peace he agreed to relinquish to Germany large territories in Finland, Ukraine, three Baltic States, as well as other minor locations. The agreement was documented in the Treaty of Brest-Litvosk, which is dated March 3, 1918. However, once Germany surrendered to the Allied powers in November 1918 the Bolsheviks (the Russian Social-Democratic Worker's Party) backslid on the deal. Eventually, most of that land became the newly formed Soviet Union, creating discord between the two powers. Lenin moved forward with drastic efforts to ban all political parties except his own; he strictly censored the press, and in his own words, he ruled the country by the Communist motto: *"based directly upon force, and unrestricted by any laws;"* unequivocally the thinking of a true dictator.

The two cousins—Russia's Nicholas II and Germany's Wilhelm II—especially hated the Jewish people, the 'tribe of Judah,' as Wilhelm so antagonistically called them. Some historians believe that Wilhelm II instigated the start of World War I. Along with various wicked plans to hurt many people he was particularly dedicated to his effort to extinguish the Jewish race. He believed that gassing these "parasites" as he called them was the best approach. The two men's hate didn't end with their reign or WWI, but it filtered down through time and continued under Germany's Adolf Hitler, and Russia's Joseph Stalin. Twenty years after Wilhelm's declaration to gas the Jewish people, Hitler managed a good start in gas chambers prior to and during World War II.

After much controversy, Wilhelm II of Germany abdicated the throne and self-exiled to the Netherlands. His cousin, Nicholas II, who was nicknamed 'Nicholas the Bloody,' his official title being Emperor and Autocrat of all the Russians, was forced to vacate his throne leaving it to a provisional government. He and his family had lived a royal life until he refused to stop the persecution of peasants and Jews, for which he would suffer severe consequences. On a dark night in July 1918, the Romanov family, along with their medical doctor, their footman, the maidservant, and the cook were murdered in the manner Nicholas had allowed so many other people to die. The assassins organized the royal family for photographs but instead of smiling before cameras, they faced the guns of their killers. Russian Bolsheviks regarded the local government officials in Yekaterinburg as the ones who made the decision to kill the Romanov's but historians strongly suspect that it was Vladimir Lenin who approved the order for the execution.

THE ARMENIAN MASSACRE – 1915 TO 1917
A GENERAL PERSECUTION OF CHRISTIANS

As Europe continued to battle over who was and was not worthy to live, America faced her own problems. The 1906 San Francisco earthquake, which brought about the financial panic of 1907 drained financial institutions across the nation as people rushed to pull their funds. The subsequent economic burden followed us into WWI while European battles raged on. From 1907 to 1915 Germany built warships, Serbia attacked Austria-Hungary; Italy declared war on Turkey, the Ottoman Empire and Libya. The Arabs attacked the Jewish Communities of Rechovat and Palestine; Chinese General and Emperor Yuan Shikai captured Nanjing; the German army shot Belgium priests, and finally, World War I began when Austria invaded Serbia following Franz-Ferdinand's assassination. Widespread suffering plagued the nations in Europe but the most shocking atrocities were committed against the Armenian Christians by the Ottoman Empire, which was inspired and sustained by Islam.

For 2500 years, Armenia has been a nation where 94% of the population call themselves Christian. It is a tiny country surrounded by Iran, which is Muslim, and Turkey, which is 90% Islam but has no official religion, with less than 1% of the population reported to be Christian and Jewish. Still, that low number is steadily diminishing. The other two countries that surround Armenia are Georgia and Azerbaijan. Georgia is about 90% Orthodox Christianity and 9.9% Muslim and it has a long history of religious harmony except under Soviet Rule, which ended in 1991. Soviet rule had brought severe purges of the Georgian church hierarchy and constant repression of Orthodox worship. Churches, priests, and religions diminished drastically during that time. However, since the collapse of the Soviet Union, Protestant denominations are stronger in Georgia. But despite Georgia's strength in Christianity, it places second to Armenia—the oldest Christian country of record.

Between 1892 and 1894, Muslim leader Abdul-Hamid II, the Sultan of the Ottoman Empire from 1876 to 1909, attacked Armenia. He hated Christians and intended to exterminate them all so he led the massacre of an estimated 100,000 Armenians. Over time, the total number of Armenians massacred in what is now known as the Armenian Genocide or Holocaust, is between 1 and 1.5 million Christians.

During the massacres committed by the Turks in 1915, approximately 18,000 Armenians were deported to Aleppo, Syria to die during a death march into the Syrian Desert. German Technical School Teachers reported on what they saw. From *Records of the Great War, Vol. III, ed. Charles F Horne, National Alumni 1923*, the following information is taken from *Memoirs & Diaries – The Armenian Massacres*.

Desperate to help, the teachers in the German Technical School at Aleppo pleaded with the German Government, which was fighting WWI, to stop the brutality against the wives and children of the slaughtered Armenian men. They reported how that after the men were killed, women and girls—except for the old, the ugly, and the tiny children—were abused by Turkish soldiers and officers, then taken away to Turkish and Kurdish villages where they were forced to accept Islam. Those not taken away were left to starve. Armenian children age five to seven were left to die of typhoid and dysentery. Starved for so long, they had forgotten how to eat when offered food.

The cry of the Christian German teachers was, *"amid such surroundings, how are we teachers to read German Fairy Stories with our children, or indeed, the story of the Good Samaritan in the Bible? How are we to make them decline and conjugate irrelevant words, while round them in the yards adjoining the German Technical School their starving fellow-countrymen are slowly succumbing? Under such circumstances our educational work flies in the face of all true morality and becomes a mockery of human sympathy."* (Note: A well-written description of the shame in tolerating evil. But still today, Muslim countries are killing Christians and forcing people to accept Islam or die and no one is doing anything about it. How often have you seen Christians kidnap non-Christians and torture or kill them because they would not convert to Christianity? Or violently force non-Christians to accept Christianity? Never!)

The report continues, *"Under the auspice of deportation to a new home, but* (instead) *moved from one place and then another, thousands are extinguished to remnants. Turks and Arabs alike* (those Moslems and Mohammedans who were compassionate and caring) *shook their heads in disapproval and spared no tears when they witnessed convoys of exiled Christian Armenians marching through their cities. Turkish soldiers bludgeoned women in advanced stages of pregnancy and also those dying and no longer able to drag themselves along."*

Germany was Turkey's ally and did nothing to stop the horrors. Teachers documenting what they saw wrote *"the atrocities in Aleppo were the last scenes in the great tragedy of the extermination of the*

Armenians." Christians in other provinces of Turkey had already undergone such slaughter.

German travelers and engineers of the Baghdad Railway who met convoys of exiles—women and children—were unable to eat for days because of what they had seen. At Tell-Abiad and Ras-el-Ain, Herr Greif, a German resident of Aleppo saw corpses of violated women, lying naked in piles on the railway embankment. Herr Spiecker of Aleppo saw Turks tie together the hands of Armenian men and roll them down steep cliffs where women standing below slashed them with knives until they were dead.

The German Consul from Mosul reported seeing the hacked off hands of children, enough to pave a road. All the girls found hidden in Christian homes were mentally deranged, having not spoken or smiled for months after seeing their parent's throats cut. One fourteen year-old girl had been raped so many times by Turkish soldiers in one night that her mind had completely lost any ability to reason, even to drink water.

Near Ourfa, hundreds of Christian peasant women were forced by Turkish soldiers to strip naked and drag themselves through the desert in 104 degrees temperatures until their skin was completely scorched. One eyewitness reported seeing a Turk tear a child from its Armenian mother's womb and hurl it against a wall.

The report by the German Teachers at the German Technical School in Aleppo believed *"it was a duty of conscience to bring these things into publicity, and, although the Turkish government, in destroying the Armenian nation, may only be pursuing objects of internal policy, the way this policy is being carried out has many of the characteristics of a general persecution of Christians. All the tens of thousands of girls and women who have been carried off into Turkish harems, and the masses of children who have been collected by the Government and distributed among the Turks and Kurds, are lost to Christendom, and have to accept Islam . . ."* Christian America: Please pay attention! The German teacher and author of this report, whose name was not shown, said, *"In this report I hope to reach the* (German)

DANCING WITH THE DEVIL

Government's ear through the accredited representatives of the German nation. Even apart from our common duty as Christians, we Germans are under a special obligation to stop the complete extermination of the half-million Armenian Christians who still survive. We are Turkey's allies and, after the elimination of the French, English and Russians, (whom it was hoped would be defeated in the war) *we are the only foreigners who have any say in Turkish affairs."* (Note: Why do you think the German government kept silent, refusing to help the Armenians? The present day threat against Christians by radical Islam or ISIS could mirror the Armenian massacre. But America and more than 59% of European residents hold to a hope that the election of Donald J. Trump as President of the United States will be an important step in destroying this great enemy of Christians and prevent a repeat of history.)

According to the Mazhar fact-finding commission, thousands of prisoners were released from Pimian prison from the end of 1914 to the beginning of 1915. Their purpose was to form the members of the fact-finding organization, but they were charged to escort convoys (mostly Christian women and children) of Armenian deportees. Vehib Pash, commander of the Ottoman Third Army, called those (prison) members of the special organization, the *"butchers of the human species."*

I can't imagine anything more horrifying than our justice system releasing thousands of America's hardened criminals from prison, and then commissioning them to march naked Christian females—wives, mothers, daughters, sisters and girlfriends—on a death march into the Mojave Desert where the temperature can exceed 120F. Due to overcrowding, and on the authority of Barack Hussein Obama, American prison systems are already releasing prisoners whose terms aren't finished. Though presently, the claim is that non-violent drug offenders are those being released, should we be concerned that the next group of released prisoners could be violent criminals? It is a very real possibility that should not be ignored.

DANCING WITH THE DEVIL

A question must be asked of the preachers and teachers of today who try to tell us that God's love for His Children brings healing, prosperity, and protection: "where was the God we sing about in our churches—the provider, the protector, the healer and comforter—when His children were tortured and killed simply because they were His children? Did He not love those Armenian Christians?" Of course He did! God doesn't always heal, protect, or give prosperity to His children. The Scriptures are clear that it is the condition of the leadership of a nation that helps determine what happens to its people—the wicked and the good.

The reason given for the Armenian genocide was that the Ottoman's began to suspect their loyalty to Russia and feared that they might actively support them if an invasion occurred. To prevent this, the Ottoman's devised this plan to eliminate the Armenians, leaving no sign of them in their territory. This resulted in a bloody and systematic massacre. Out of a combined 18,000 souls involved in the march, only 150 women and children reached their destination of exile—the Syrian Desert. *"The Massacre of the Armenians, 1915"* – *Eyewitness to History,* www.eyewitnesstohistory.com *(2008).*

The Muslims were wicked and completely barbaric in their torture. Anxieties over a fragmented Ottoman Empire were projected onto the dismembered, castrated, or beheaded bodies of the Armenians. Horseshoes nailed onto the soles of their feet became signs of subhuman status. Similarly, red-hot crowns applied to the heads of the "infidels," crosses branded into their flesh, stigmata (shames and disgraces) pierced into their hands and feet, and vital organs, and literal crucifixion all signified religious difference on the bodies of the Armenian Christians who refused Muslim Conversion. *The Edge of Modernism by American Poetry and the Traumatic Past by Walter Kalaidjian; c 2006, The Johns Hopkins University Press.*

Much is written that tells of the deep hatred Muslims have for Christians, and their crimes against the Armenian Christians would suggest that they were comparable to the present day ISIS. The persecution of the Armenians lasted three years and was an atrocity toward which many countries turned a blind eye, including America, which was not involved in WWI at the time of the genocide. And, it is true that our financial crisis and flu epidemic kept us focused on problems at home and motivated us to keep peace inside the U.S., avoiding all foreign wars. Nevertheless, we should have done something to help those tortured Armenians.

Today, many Americans complain that the U.S. tries to be the savior of the world. Though evidence of America's political and military involvement in the wickedness of a secret society called "the enlightened ones" or "The Illuminati," is gradually coming to public awareness, we have managed to maintain a certain amount of Godliness in spite of it and have done much to help other countries suffering under tyranny. No doubt, those tortured Armenian men, women and children would have been overjoyed to be rescued by soldiers from a Godly nation—soldiers they had no need to fear, who would offer them food, water, and medical treatment. Soldiers with integrity and love, able to exercise self-restraint and look with compassion at fragile humans rather than add to their agony. We should think twice before complaining when our nation obeys the Word, and helps the poor and defenseless. Unfortunately for the Armenians, their primary assistance from America came through volunteers and missionaries instead of an army of troops that could help stop the atrocities and establish peace.

An estimated 17 million people died during WWI. Imagine all that bloodshed within the last 115 years and the horrors of The Rape of Nanking, WWII, Viet Nam, and the mid-eastern wars hadn't yet happened. Believing that war ends anger or the hunger for control, and brings peace, is foolishness for when one war ends, hatred is still brewing behind the scenes and when it gets enough courage and power, once again, it attacks with restless aggression. As the Bible promises, there will be wars and rumors of wars before Jesus returns. If countries that value a moral code and equal justice for all humanity

DANCING WITH THE DEVIL

don't go into Godless nations to help bring order and peace to others some societies may never experience life without tyranny. The best deterrent to war is for people of all nations to submit to God but that will not happen until Jesus returns, when all people will recognize Him as Lord and bow to Him. Americans must ask if there is another country in the world that would willingly come to our aid if a tyrant dogged us into totalitarianism. Probably not!

No one can truthfully say that the United States jumped quickly into WWI. Not wanting to fight, the U.S. remained neutral even when on May 7, 1915, the German's sank two British passenger liners, the Lusitania, and the Arabic. All 123 Americans aboard the Lusitania and two Americans aboard the Arabic drown. At the time, U.S. Colonel Edward House, a close associate of U.S. President Woodrow Wilson, was in London for a diplomatic visit when he heard the news. In a telegram to the President, he wrote: *"America has come to a parting of the ways when she must determine whether she stands for civilized or uncivilized warfare. We can no longer remain neutral spectators."* Still, President Wilson refused to enter the war.

By the end of 1915, Austria-Hungary, Bulgaria, Germany and the Ottoman Empire were battling the Allied powers of Britain, France, Russia, Italy, Belgium, Serbia, Montenegro and Japan. Though Germany had agreed to suspend unrestricted submarine warfare in the North Atlantic and Mediterranean, they continued attacking unarmed merchant, passenger, and private ships. In March 1916, the German's sank The Sussex—an unarmed French boat in the English Channel. President Wilson threatened to sever diplomatic relations with them unless they refrained from attacking all passenger ships and allowed the crews of enemy merchant vessels to abandon their ships prior to an attack.

The German Government accepted these terms on May 4, 1916. However, following a wartime conference in January 1917, German Navy representatives convinced Wilhelm II and the military leadership that the United States had jeopardized the agreement when they supplied munitions and financial assistance to Allies, particularly a financially depleted Britain. Therefore, Germany justified violating the Sussex pledge. Throughout February and March 1917 German submarines sank several U.S. ships, resulting in the deaths of numerous seamen and citizens.

On January 19, 1917, British Naval Intelligence intercepted and decrypted a telegram sent by German Foreign Minister Arthur Zimmerman to the German Ambassador in Mexico City. The telegram promised the Mexican government that Germany would help Mexico recover the territory it had ceded to the United States following the Mexican-American War in return for an alliance with Germany in war against the U.S.

Regardless of the many unprovoked attacks by Germany against the U.S., President Wilson continually hesitated about joining the war. Finally U.S. public opinion supported the war effort and rested at President Wilson's side when Germany attempted to persuade Mexico to declare war on the U.S. An obvious implication of an approaching German attack on America, along with a dedication to our partnership with Britain, and a concern about massive amounts of propaganda eventually became the avenue that persuaded President Wilson to join the war in April 1917. This was three years after war had been declared. We did not *"jump quickly into war."* In light of the historical invasions by Germany imagine what would have happened to the U.S. citizens, first those in the U.S./Mexico Border States, had we not joined the war, and Mexico and Germany had allied together for an invasion against us.

On June 26, 1917, 14,000 U.S. troops landed in France to train for combat in WWI. From June 26, 1917 to November 11, 1918, more than two million American troops had fought on the battlefields of Western Europe, and 50,000 of them lost their lives. However, those well trained and equipped American troops proved to be a major turning point for the war, which had an anti-climatic ending. Though the war was one of massive human slaughter and property destruction, neither side accomplished a decisive victory. Germany boasted of victories in the east, and a conquest over vast lands, but still fell to defeat though they were never invaded. German behavior demonstrated no interest in seeking a peaceful end to the conflict but it was U.S. General John Pershing's plan to overwhelm Germany with foot soldiers in the coming months that forced Germany into a truce they didn't really want to make. Of German descent himself, Pershing, hailed as one of the most dashing men to don a military uniform, wanted the U.S. to occupy Germany and permanently destroy German militarism. Germany agreed to the truce in order to save the German people from an invasion that would have destroyed them. After Russia's Tsar Nicholas stepped down, Lenin, his replacement, pulled Russia out of the war nine months before it ended.

To *understand* what provoked the Second World War just 22 years after the First World War, it is imperative to *understand* what happened at the Versailles Conference following WWI and how the Treaty affected the war bullies. Due to no evidence of a win for either side after five years of death and destruction, both powers agreed to a truce or temporary halt to war. Leaders of Britain, Italy, France, and America met in Versailles to decide on a system of security for all nations.

Bear in mind that America had no desire to enter the war and did so only after three years of relentless attacks and threats by the German military. Russia did not want to be involved in WWI, as they were inadequately prepared for war. Further, they had no desire to join WWII until Hitler's quest for more Aryan "living space" motivated Operation Barbarossa against Russia—a military invasion of groundbreaking magnitude and what eventually became known as the largest military invasion in history. With more than 3 million troops and 3500 tanks, from the Axis powers of Germany, Italy, and Japan, Hitler set out to exterminate the Slav people, capture the Baltic States, Leningrad in the north, and Moscow in the center. This invasion forced Russia into WWII in June of 1941. Provoked into war once again (the first by Germany), America was forced into WWII when the Japanese bombed Pearl Harbor in December 1941. The combined efforts of Hitler, Hirohito, and Mussolini propelled the entire world into a war of extreme devastation.

Having served in WWI, Hitler was bitter about how the war ended—no decisive win. In 1914, Germany lost Eastern Territory to Russia in a fight over "living space." Hitler never forgot that loss. Wilhelm's Germany was relentless in provoking Allied countries into WWI and had been particularly destructive to France. Still today, very little love exists between the German and French people.

THE AIMS OF THE "BIG 3"

The Versailles Treaty was designed to place responsibility and guilt for the war on Germany—a punishment intended to stop future senseless wars of such magnitude. Though the war had devastated and bankrupted France and Britain, and caused a financial burden on America—who was forced to enter after having already loaned Britain and France huge sums of money to continue fighting—many believed Germany's punishment to be severe.

Allied leaders famous as the "Big 3" – U.S. President Woodrow Wilson, French Prime Minister, Georges Clemenceau, and British Prime Minister, David Lloyd George—wanted to put an end to wars of such bloody aggression. However, all three leaders had different ideas about how it should be done.

President Wilson was the mild-mannered son of a Christian minister. In addition to a degree from Princeton University (a private Ivy League research university in Princeton, New Jersey) he was also elected as Chair of Jurisprudence and Political Economy at Princeton. He attended The University of Virginia, and several other colleges and universities for minor studies, and he earned a PhD at Johns Hopkins University. Though Wilson held strong Christian beliefs he had no genuine understanding of human savagery and he was naïve about international affairs. In essence, he created and believed a fairy-tale image of what the world should look like. Despite both his secular and Christian education he proved to have no idea about evil—that it will not stop unless it is eradicated, which is what General Pershing wanted to do in Germany during WWI. But that didn't happen and just 22 years later, once again, Hitler was trying to rule the world and the majority of German people supported him. (Note: The only other way evil can stop is when it has a change of heart but an evil heart changes only when it respects biblical principles.)

Wilson believed that evil powers—not the people—should be punished for their wickedness. Personally, I agree, but history has shown that this is not the way punishment unfolds when wickedness prevails. It is usually always the people who are punished for the crimes of evil powers. Wilson's idea was to create world peace by establishing a League of Nations, an entity that would slap the hands of destructive aggressors. Though it was finally implemented Americans objected, so we didn't join.

French Prime Minister, Georges Clemenceau knew all too well the German threat to his country. No doubt he was educated about the history of French/German rivalry, so past resentments were not allowed to die. France possessed a large living space dotted with prime territories, two of which had already been lost to Germany in previous military engagements. A long border connected France and Germany, and French territory was ripe for the picking to a country hoping to create a master race that would eventually destroy all others. Germany initiated and declared war on Russia and France with a plan to fight both countries at the same time. Their eventual invasion of France brought massive destruction to the French people so when a treaty was on the table in Versailles, it was clear and understandable that Prime Minister Clemenceau wanted Germany to pay dearly for the destruction they caused not only to France but also to other allied countries.

DANCING WITH THE DEVIL

Clemenceau was frustrated with Wilson's naiveté about what could lie ahead for Europe if Germany's aggression wasn't stopped. He was also concerned by the British Prime Minister's middle-of-the-road view on harshness against Germany due to Europe's need for future trade with Germany. And, Clemenceau was quick to compare America and England's safety features to France's vulnerability to war when he said: *"America is far away, protected by the ocean. Not even Napoleon himself could touch England; you are both sheltered; we are not."*

British Prime Minister, David Lloyd George was famous as the middleman at the Versailles Conference. With a history in politics and a liberal view on social issues in his country he lead the public to believe that he agreed that Germany should suffer the full responsibility for the war because they had taken the first step to declare war. But he also was genuinely concerned about the communist Russian Revolution of 1917—that it would spread west and that Germany was the vast territory that separated the two countries. If Germany were brought to its knees by the demands of the Versailles Treaty it would be no help in stopping any future communist movement, which would devastate all of Europe and probably America. When asked by associates how he thought he had done at the Conference the British Prime Minister replied, *"Not badly, considering I was seated between Jesus Christ* (Wilson) *and Napoleon,"* (Clemenceau). Parenthesis added. In retrospect, the French Prime Minister's concerns proved to be accurate. Germany's attack on Dunkirk, France, during WWII supports Clemenceau's call to bring Germany to her knees after WWI.

The Versailles Treaty that brought an abrupt end to WWI became the catalyst for a second world war just 22 years later. World leaders were bitter and angry over the loss of 17 million people during WWI and no particular win for any country. The treaty's 15 parts and 440 articles reassigned German boundaries and assigned them liability for reparations. They were to pay Britain, France, and the U.S. the amount it had cost these countries to fight. This alone would cripple Germany's economy. The Treaty insisted that the Rhineland—the area of Germany adjacent to France—be demilitarized. Germany's army—the largest in Europe—beginning with 3.8 million soldiers was to be cut to 100,000 troops. The German army was to have no modern weapons, tanks, or aircraft like those used to revolutionize WWI. The German navy was to have no U-boats. The end of the Great War brought fear and un-neighborly mistrust by every country involved, so every line of the Treaty proposed German guilt and was designed to punish and weaken Germany.

In effect, it was a recipe for more disaster waiting patiently to engage war once again. Allied fear initiated the construction of several new battleships—a total of nine by the U.S., a series by Great Britain, and sixteen battleships and cruisers by Japan. Concerned that a competitive arms race was about to ensue, in 1921 U.S. President Warren G. Harding called a conference (which later became known as the Washington Naval Conference) hoping to set limits on the number of warships being built. This did not stop Hitler from rebuilding the German Navy a few years later, or constructing the *Bismarck*, a war machine battleship unrivaled in history.

For three months beginning November 12, 1921, attendees from nine countries convened in Washington DC to discuss naval disarmament and ways to relieve growing tensions in East Asia. Primary participants included The United States, Great Britain, Japan, France, and Italy—the largest naval powers in the world. Other leaders were concerned about an increase of Japanese forces in the Pacific. Subsequently, Secretary of State Charles Hughes wanted to limit that possibility. The British wanted to avoid an arms race with the U.S. as well as stabilize the Pacific, which would protect Hong Kong, Singapore, Australia, and New Zealand. Japan came to the table wanting their interest in raw materials, heavy industry, and the railroads of Manchuria and Mongolia to be recognized as valid. Britain and Japan wanted a naval treaty that would insure that the

U.S. would not be allowed to out-produce them should an arms race occur.

Following weeks of negotiations, a disarmament treaty was signed on February 6, 1922. Specific tonnage limits were set for each country but the Japanese representatives went away displeased with their allocation. The U.S. remained faithful to their agreement, and scrapped 60 percent of naval tonnage and reduced its military to 136,000 soldiers. Naïvely influenced by the opinion that national security could be attained and maintained through isolationism, America's leaders sought world peace without war unless attacked.

In 1929, just nine years after the Armenians fought their last war against the Turks, and only seven years after drastically reducing our military, the United States and the world fell into the worst depression in history. A war of massive casualties and destruction had bankrupted the major powers. Regardless of financial complications connected to the war and the depression, U.S. Government officials (along with other concerned governments that wanted to avoid future wars) found themselves continually trying to negotiate decorum between Japan and China. The potential for a full-scale war following several years of brief battles between the two countries was a grave concern. Japanese imperialists intended to dominate China both politically and militarily, and secure their vast raw materials as well as their food and labor. Despite the efforts to deter war, on-going military encounters between Chinese and Japanese troops intensified in July 1937.

A CALL TO RESTRAINT

Praising Japan as a first-class power, U.S. Secretary of State Cordell Hull encouraged the Japanese Government to endorse self-restraint regarding China, which he hoped would produce long-term benefits for Japan and the United States. If military restraint could be achieved, Hull proposed that Japan and the U.S. would have opportunity for world leadership, restoring and preserving stable conditions for business and peace. To discourage a full-scale war, Secretary Hull issued a Statement of Principles of international policy. The Statement proposed that any situation where armed hostilities were in progress or were threatened was a situation, wherein rights and interests of all nations either were or might be seriously affected. He felt it his duty to make a statement of the U.S. Government's position in regard to international problems and situations over which the U.S. felt deep concern.

The principles he advocated as appropriate and which the U.S. had endorsed were based primarily on the maintenance of peace, self-restraint and respect, and among other things, *abstinence from use of force in pursuit of policy*. Secretary Hull stated that the United States avoided entering into alliances or entangling commitments but believed in cooperative effort by peaceful and practical means in support of its stated principles.

The Statement of Principles was sent to the major governments of the world for comment. Regardless of Hull's appeal for restraint Emperor Hirohito ordered a military invasion of Nanking, China on December 13, 1937 after having captured Shanghai, China to the north. The city became a wild frenzy of terror as the soldiers committed shocking acts of torture and rape on unsuspecting citizens. This incident would become known as The Rape of Nanking or The Nanking Massacres.

AN ORGY OF BRUTALITY
Demons of Rape and Murder – Nanking, China 1937

The Rape of Nanking, which took place just four years before the bombing of Pearl Harbor on the U.S. Island of Hawaii, was a wild orgy of hatred, torture, and murder of unrestrained proportions performed by one culture against another.

Men were tortured and murdered. Pregnant women were sliced open and their babies cut from their wombs and hurled against concrete walls or other destructive objects, like bayonets. Women and children of all ages—from infant to the elderly—were brutally raped and then usually shot. Many had their tongues cut out, or were tortured until death. Females were vaginally brutalized with foreign objects. Bottles, swords, bayonets, pieces of steel, or bamboo sticks, were used to torture them in a most horrifying manner. Baby girl's genitalia were slit open with bayonets so they could be raped more quickly. According to one Japanese journalist embedded with Imperial forces at the time, *"The reason that the 10th Army* (responsible for the horrors) *is advancing to Nanking* (from Shanghai) *quite rapidly is due to the tacit* (understood) *consent among the officers and men that they could loot and rape as they wish."* (Second Sino-Japanese War – Wikipedia) Parenthesis added

Many living in Nanking at the time of the invasion refused to vacate preferring to stay and document what they saw. Eyewitness reports of the atrocities came from Chinese citizens that were present, Western foreigners wanting to help the civilians, and the diaries of John Rabee, a German businessman and member of the Nazi Party. Americans Minnie Vautrin, and Reverend James M. McCallum documented events of torture.

Reverend McCallum wrote in his diary: *"I know not where to end. Never I have heard or read such brutality. Rape! Rape! Rape! We estimate at least 1,000 cases a night, and many by day. In case of resistance or anything that seems like disapproval, there is a bayonet stab or a bullet . . . People are hysterical . . . Women are being carried off every morning, afternoon and evening. The whole Japanese army seems to be free to go and come as it pleases, and to do what it pleases."*

Un-relenting, aggressive, and brutal behavior by the Imperialists army, which was commanded by Hirohito—who referred to himself as a God, and who desired to rule the world—was the motivation for the use of the atomic bomb on Japan during WWII. Even John Rabee, who later renounced his membership in the Nazi party, defined the acts of the Japanese soldiers as *"brutal and bestial—inhuman; something humans would not do to each other."*

DANCING WITH THE DEVIL

Robert O. Wilson, a surgeon at the American-administered University Hospital in an established Safety Zone wrote in a letter to his family: *". . . the house of one of the Chinese staff members was broken into and two of the women, his relatives, were raped. Two girls about 16 were raped to death in one of the refugee camps."*

John Rabee wrote in his diary: *"You hear nothing but rape. If husbands or brothers intervene, they're shot. What you hear and see on all sides is the brutality and bestiality of the Japanese soldiers."*

Japanese soldiers gang-raped pregnant women, and forced families to commit acts of incest—sons against mothers and fathers against daughters. Monks dedicated to a life of celibacy were forced to rape women. Every brutal and humiliating act that a mind controlled by demon spirits could think of was inflicted on the Chinese people and was often condoned and justified by the Japanese military leaders. If the Chinese people had been armed and trained in defense, would the Japanese military have been so aggressive?

Peaceful civilized countries are presently seeing a spread of both deliberate and permissive evil. Just as the people in Europe so quickly accepted their dictators before and during WWII, I believe this is the devil's attempt to prepare people to willingly accept the Antichrist. They will accept him because of his promise to bring them peace but in reality he will bring disaster of unprecedented levels.

Many things motivate hate, particularly a superior attitude that says "I am better than you, therefore only I should exist. You must die!" Jealousy, a need to rule, (as in a dictatorship), and allowing the powers and principalities of darkness (the devil) to control the heart is clear evidence to me that a demon spirit of rape and murder ruled the Japanese soldiers.

We usually think of war as armed conflict between militaries of various countries. But war also comes out of a need for dedicated opposition to hostile acts against individuals, particularly injustice against the weak and defenseless, both provoked and unprovoked.

DANCING WITH THE DEVIL

War and its crime against civilians is also aggressive conflict usually stemming from one's personal anger or a dead conscience that is no longer able to generate compassion toward another human being.

For years, the majority of civilians not directly involved with war were kept in the dark about the behavior Hirohito approved and encouraged in his generals and soldiers. Our history books have not documented the intensity of the rape and torture of girls and women, which reaches into the millions including immediately before, during and after World War II. Nor were we made aware of the unbelievable number of abortions and suicides, or the shocking death of millions of defenseless children that was brought on by war. Yet, in more recent years, many people condemned America when they learned that Hiroshima and Nagasaki, Japan had exploded into a mushroom of atomic blast—an effort to stop the brutalities of a self-proclaimed "god" whose quest to win the war included a plan to use his own Japanese citizens as human shields to deter the invasion of enemy foot-soldiers along Japan's coastline during the war.

When faced with accountability, Hirohito attempted to protect his name by shifting the blame for the atrocities to his generals. When WWII was over, and on the advice of American General Douglas McArthur, Hirohito was given a full pardon for his crimes. Prior to his death to cancer in 1989 he was given all necessary medical aid inside the United States. As I studied the history of the Japanese invasion of Nanking and WWII I never found a documented reason for General McArthur's request to pardon Hirohito. Why was he given amnesty while so many other war criminals died? Why didn't he die in the manner he allowed his military to torture and kill hordes of people, particularly the Chinese? My research revealed that several tyrannical leaders from other countries who made life difficult for their countrymen and didn't provide good medical care for them came to the United States for their own medical care.

DANCING WITH THE DEVIL

For personal peace of mind, Americans must attempt to answer these questions: "Do you fully understand why our founding fathers abandoned their homeland to find a new land—that they were searching for a place to call home where people could live without tyranny? Do you understand why they established a Constitution that would give the people freedom to bear arms in order to prevent or strike down a tyrannical government? Do you understand what could happen to America if the citizens submit to disarmament, and why a superior military was established—that it was to build a national defense?" Since the end of the war, our preoccupation with "living" has brought about public ignorance or a lack of interest in the atrocities of war and because of that we have sanctioned many evil things. God says we are to defend the defenseless and we are to remove the evil from among us.

The stories in this chapter confirm our need to be educated about world history. In the history of the Bible, there has never been an unarmed godly nation. Even the children of Israel were armed during their Exodus from Egypt, for in one day friends and family members killed 23,000 of their own that had disobeyed God. Americans could very well be faced with the same kind of horrors that Europeans faced during the two world wars if we don't acknowledge that the devil wants to destroy the children of God and how he uses nations and governments—powers and principalities—to do his work. Every American (especially the Christian) is obligated to be aware of the evil that is treading our soil and our flag even as I write. Because America has earned the reputation as a Christian nation that trusts in God, and has defended the defenseless, certain regimes—and possibly even our present government—desire to destroy us as we have been known, and to execute a new system of government for our country. Each of us must make an effort to get educated about world history so that we will be able to compare what is happening to us today to what happened to those countries in whose footsteps we are following.

THREE, NO! FOUR DEMON POSSESSED TYRANTS
(One, an Ally)

Prior to WWII immigrants from war-torn countries marched across American shores looking for freedom from rulers that terrorized the citizens. Because they had already experienced mass tyranny they advocated neutrality at all costs.

However, Frank Capra's documentary film series *"Why We Fight"* addressed why America changed directions overnight and joined the war effort in Europe. They went from a mindset of *"peaceful existence"* to making more weapons of war, putting people in uniform ready to engage every enemy continent across the ocean. It was a fight between a free world that wanted to remain free and a world that could become one of slavery filled with horror.

Three demon-possessed tyrants deceived the majority of their countrymen with a promise that they could give them all they needed to survive. People were willing to believe anything they were told so they wasted no time in worshiping these earthly gods whose deadly poison affected all of Europe and Asia. Italy's Mussolini, Germany's Hitler, and Japan's Emperor Hirohito commanded the people to *"stop thinking, and follow me;"* Hitler: *"I will make you masters of the world;"* Mussolini *"Stop thinking and believe in me; I will restore the glory that was Rome."* Hirohito: *"Stop thinking and follow your god, Emperor, and Japan will rule the world."*

Mussolini planned to rule the world under Fascism, which is a radical authoritarian nationalism—combining elements of left-wing politics with right-wing positions. Historians, political scientists and other scholars cannot agree on the true nature of fascism, as each form is distinct. Though much has been debated about what fascism really is, most debaters agree that the leader has all power and dictates life, as he wants it to be for everyone else.

DANCING WITH THE DEVIL

Mussolini described fascism as a movement that would *"strike against the backwardness of the right, and the destructiveness of the left."* Unenlightened people find fascism easy to believe and follow.

Nazism, which is National Socialism, is defined in Britannica as a totalitarian movement (a system of government that is centralized and dictatorial, and requires complete subservience {by the people} to the state). In mass appeal and dictatorial rule it shares many elements of fascism except that Nazism is far more extreme in ideas and practice. It is anti-intellectual, (adverse to the views and methods of intellectuals or theoretical study), the dictator being the sole source of inspiration of a people and nation. In other words, "Your brain, if you have one, is no good, so let me tell you how you should think because I know everything!" Christians believe that it is the Word of God that should tell us how to think, not a Godless dictator. Parentheses added

Nazism proposes the annihilation of all enemies of the Aryan Volk, which Hitler believed to be a race of people superior to all others; therefore, all others must be destroyed. Had America refused to fight in WWII some of you might not be here today because your parents and grandparents might have been gassed along with the Jewish people and other societies Hitler tried to abolish.

Until World War II ended Japan basically had no religion, except for some Shinto beliefs—whoever held the position of emperor was God. As God, the emperor rules and dictates, and the people bow and capitulate. The *"God Emperor"* revoked their freedom, destroyed their human dignity and essentially created a herd of human savages.

As emperor, Hirohito's rule of Government was called the *"New Order of Enlightenment"* or *"New Order in Asia."* Since the Japanese people had never known the full benefits of freedom, it was easy for the God-emperor to take away what little freedom they had. Japanese men did not object to putting on uniforms and becoming the army of a sinister secret society under the symbol of the *"black dragon."* The Japanese people worshipped the black dragon because they believed it was responsible for those things that happened to Japan based upon how the dragon might have been offended.

Capra's documentary tells how Italy, Germany, and Japan had constitutional law-making bodies with elected representatives comparable to the U.S. Congress. But when the new dictators convinced the representatives that they could easily solve economic and political unrest and other pre-war issues, the representatives willingly gave their power to the new dictators. Soon the majority of citizens hoping for a "better life" joined the crusade after listening to propaganda about "heavenly bliss."

The stage was now set for three heartless despots to join together to take over the world. Hirohito dreamed of vindicating what he believed was the failure of his father's reign. And, he could not visualize Japan as anything other than "the leading part" of Asia. With the devoted support of his military, Hirohito single-handedly ordered the terrorization of China and other Asian territories in the years leading up to and during WWII.

Adolf Hitler, who had become Chancellor of Germany in 1933 after having been previously arrested and jailed for high treason, was now determined to vindicate Germany's loss during WWI. He also wanted to control the land mass and the people of Europe by establishing what he called a *"New Order."* His aim was to once again try to seize living space for the German people. Along with the help of Italy's Benito Mussolini, these three men were determined to rule the world.

Before WWII began, the citizens of Asia and Europe had witnessed mass murder and rape, the destruction of their properties, and numerous attempts to annihilate entire races of people. But nothing they had seen thus far would equal the destruction that was to come during WWII. In addition to the horrors committed by their own leaders, they also saw the destruction caused by the armies sent to stop the destruction, particularly Russia's Red Army that marched across Germany with an intensely angry aggression. While the three tyrants were yelling, "follow me" a fourth tyrant, Communist leader Joseph Stalin (not his real name, but a code name meaning *"Man of Steel"*) withheld no dreadful tactic to stop the Nazi movement despite former and strategic negotiations and various treaties between him and Adolf Hitler during the late 30's. The two tyrants were like 5th graders on a ball field; competition and the need to win motivated their every move. However, to win public approval they each used keen maneuvers and persuasive words to convince the people that they had their best interest at heart.

Fickle and propagandist in their feelings toward one another, Stalin and Hitler fought a personal vendetta before the real war began. Stalin needed materials and supplies of a military nature for Russia. Germany wanted food and oil from Russia and would be required by Stalin to pay for them in German goods that were needed by Moscow. On February 11, 1940 Russia and Germany reached a trade agreement for the eighteen months that would follow. In addition to their August 1939 trade agreement, the 1940 agreement required Germany to give Russia the German military cruiser *Luetzow*, the design plans for the Nazi battleship and war-machine *The Bismarck,* heavy naval guns and other gear, some thirty of Germany's latest warplanes, including the Messerschmitt fighters 109 and 110 and the Ju-88 dive bombers. Also from Germany, the Soviets were to receive machines for their oil and electric industries, locomotives, turbines, generators, diesel engines, ships, machine tools and samples of German artillery, tanks, explosives, chemical-warfare equipment and so on.

From the Soviets, the Germans received one million tons of cereal, half a million tons of wheat, 900,000 tons of oil, 100,000 tons of cotton, 500,000 tons of phosphates, considerable amounts of numerous other vital raw materials, and the transit of a million tons of soybeans from Manchuria—all within the first year of the agreement.

DANCING WITH THE DEVIL

Germany's Foreign Office's economic expert, Dr. Schnurre, who had masterminded the trade negotiations between Germany and Russia, wrote in the agreement that Stalin had promised to lend generous help in acting as a buyer of metals and raw materials from third world countries. This would give Germany an open door to the East, and effectively weaken the British blockade, the purpose of which was to restrict the transport of minerals, metals, food and textiles that Germany needed to sustain its war effort. At Stalin's promise of help, Hitler weakened and supported Russia's aggression against Finland, and accepted the threat of Soviet military occupation of troops and airmen, and bases in the Baltics, which would eventually be used against Germany. While German/Russian relations seemed solid to many onlookers, Hitler had no interest in keeping any agreement he had made with Russia. He had been planning his invasion and destruction of Russia since the days of *Mein Kampf* when he wrote: *"And so we National Socialists take up where we left off six hundred years ago. We stop the endless German movement toward the south and west of Europe and turn our gaze towards the lands of the East . . . When we speak of new territory in Europe today we must think principally of Russia and her border vassal states. Destiny itself seems to wish to point out the way to us here . . . This colossal empire in the East is ripe for dissolution, and the end of the Jewish domination in Russia will also be the end of Russia as a state."* (The Rise and Fall of the Third Reich" Page 796 - A History of Nazi Germany by William Shirer; 1959, 1960, 1987, 1988, 1990 Simon & Schuster, Inc.)

Number four of the seven things God hates as identified in Proverbs 6 is a heart that devises wicked schemes—such as those who speak friendly words to their neighbors while planning evil against them in their heart. Both Stalin and Hitler had hearts that devised wicked schemes but Hitler was particularly adept in this tactic. He was a heartless warmonger who would do anything to achieve his insatiable need to destroy those he believed weren't fit to live, and then create a master race whose lives he could dictate.

Russia was no stranger to mass destruction of colossal measure in the years preceding Hitler's 1041 attempt to destroy the Russian people and take over Russian land in what was called Operation Barbarossa. The largest military movement in history, the Nazi invasion spanned two thousand miles of Russian territory. Nazi combat effectiveness proved supreme and the best army to fight during the twentieth century. However, despite its size and ability, Operation Barbarossa was a failure due to human mistakes and misjudgments in the manner of Napoleon and his Grand Armeè's invasion of Russia in June of 1812.

Though Stalin was known as a tyrant who killed between 20 and 30 million of his own countrymen for one reason or another, and was a former supplies trader with Hitler, he was justifiably angry over the German invasion and fought back with his own form of wicked revenge. All four trailblazers combined built a powerhouse of savagery in those they ordered to fight, and as a result WWII would witness an angry communist aggression that would match the earlier concern of British Prime Minister, David Lloyd George at the Versailles Conference immediately following WWI. George believed that Germany would be the one country able to stop the advancement of communism but the world would soon see just how destructive an army of communists could become when provoked.

AN ORGY OF EXTERMINATION
Demons of Murder – Poland 1939

In the manner of Russia's Nicholas the Bloody, and Germany's Kaiser Wilhelm before him, Hitler's stated aim as Fuhrer of Germany was to exterminate the Jews living in all the countries he planned to conquer, including Russia, and to acquire more living space for Germany and a "puppet" breed of people that would do anything he demanded. In his book, *Mein Kampf*, Hitler continually referred to the Jewish people as parasites, germs, and vermin. Hitler and Stalin's invasion of Poland in September 1939 set in motion an orgy of extermination that reduced the Jewish population by record numbers in just a few years.

On September 1, 1939, Germany invaded Poland and on September 17, 1939, the Soviet Union attacked Poland as well. Within that month, the Germans and the Soviets had divided Poland, and aggressively weakened an already inadequate Polish military incapable of matching the Nazi strength in arms and troops, or the onslaught of the Russian Military. Germany's armored divisions, the dive bombings, and the aerial bombings on defenseless Polish cities served to terrorize, displace, and destabilize the nation. The invasion brought about a mass demoralization of the Polish citizens, particularly the Jewish people, who saw the construction of crematoriums designed to destroy them. But their persecution did not end with the war; it continued far beyond the war.

For hundreds of years before WWII, Poland was considered the refuge for displaced Jews ousted from other European countries, so the Jewish population there had grown to an estimated 3.25 million people by 1939. But, when the war ended in 1945 the population had been reduced to a number of less than 230,000 under German and Russian occupation. The Bible says that when Jesus was crucified the Jews willingly agreed to let His blood be on their hands and their children's hands (Matthew 27:22-26). Since that time when they rejected Jesus, God has allowed the Jewish people to be repeatedly targeted for destruction, however, at the appointed time, He will divinely intervene on their behalf. (Revelation 20)

A PLAN TO TAKE AMERICA BY SURPRISE - 1941
Demons of Deceit

During the twelve months preceding December 7, 1941, Japan's Emperor Hirohito secretly and strategically planned his attack on the United States while his army still occupied China following the 1938 invasion. Hirohito believed that the only way to conquer America was to take her by complete surprise. To avoid a leak of his plan, all Japanese officials including the Chiefs of Staff, remained uninformed of his attack strategy. Finally, during a speech to his cabinet ministers and Chiefs of Staff on September 6, 1941 he revealed his purposes for going to war against the United States, Great Britain, and the Netherlands. One of four reasons was his belief that if America did not support his proposed use of military force to put China under the complete control of his Empire, he would regard their decision as disclosing their true intention, which he believed was to *"bring Japan to her knees."* Hirohito believed that both the U.S. and Great Britain were a threat to Japan's survival so he defended his attack on Pearl Harbor in that if he missed that opportunity, Japan would have to submit to American dictation. Also, other countries, particularly Germany, wanted America involved in the war, hoping to destroy her.

When Hirohito was ready for his attack on Pearl Harbor, Sunday was chosen as the best day because spies had reported to Chief of Staff Nagano that U.S. personnel tended to drink in excess on Saturday nights and was lethargic by Sunday mornings, making them an easier target. At 6:00 A.M. on Sunday December 7, 1941, 182 Japanese planes including bombers, dive-bombers, torpedo planes, and zero fighters made their way to Pearl Harbor and within two hours they had destroyed so much of the U.S. Naval tonnage there was little left to hit when the second wave of 167 planes descended on the Harbor at 8:15. During the attack, 2,402 Americans died.

The attack rendered the U.S. naval fleet severely crippled or nearly depleted, having already been reduced by 60% to honor the arms agreement just a few years earlier. Now the U.S. was faced with an urgent need to rebuild the fleet. Remembering this, one might think that the United States would continually guard against being caught in a vulnerable position where any military or terrorists group could gain the upper hand militarily. But again in 2014 Americans watched as leaders reduced our military, neglected our borders, and lead by executive order instead of by Congress, the Constitution, or public approval.

Hirohito accomplished his surprise attack on America in 1941. President Roosevelt declared war on Japan and Germany, and Italy declared war on the United States. Thus began four years of great human tragedy, the majority of which American civilians knew and still know little about.

WWII - SIX YEARS OF HUMAN TRAGEDY
Demons of Destruction: 1939 - 1945

The combined declarations of war would eventually produce the great tragedies of our time, bringing about unbelievable torture and destruction, the results of which would linger for years beyond the end of the six-year war—four years of American participation.

The Japanese Imperialist army continued their inhumane attacks while Europe and the Soviet Union were unwavering in their effort to destroy at will. Their crimes against humanity—the majority being civilians—were excessive both by nature and in numbers. Crimes included death by beating, shooting, bayoneting, genocide and drowning as well as mass murder by machine gun, and beheadings. Torture by starvation, psychological and mental terror, and confinement in closed areas haunted daily the hearts and minds of the victims. People were doused with gasoline and burned to death or boiled alive in oil. Some were fully buried alive or buried only to the waist and left to the wild animals. Some were skinned alive, or injected with germ warfare (bacteria, viruses, and fungi) then dissected alive to observe the results of the injections. Other forms of torture included cold-blooded removal of body parts, (internal and external) including the heart.

There seemed no end to what their demon possessed minds could think of as they tortured human beings until they died, or until the persecutor decided to kill them. Other crimes included looting, arson, killing prisoners of war, and refusing to administer medical assistance. POW's under Japanese authority were forced to do push-ups in waste pits and eat feces. When they failed, soldiers shoved their heads into the pits until the victims nearly suffocated. But as cruel and predictable about brutality (including rape) as the Japanese soldiers proved to be, the troops of Russia and Germany followed close in their footsteps regarding the nature of torture. It would seem that the more known the Japanese techniques became other militaries endorsed their outrageous practices along with their own creations. (Note: Though Japanese cruelty is well documented, there are those that believe the Russians were the most cold-hearted of all militaries.)

Consumed with hate for certain ethnic groups, Adolph Hitler authorized his leaders to aggressively destroy millions of people. The 1939 Nazi occupation of Poland meant massive face-to-face shooting of the Jewish people by the Germans. As the genocide continued, reports surfaced that the moral of the Nazi troops was in deep trouble. Scientists began experimenting with other methods of extermination. Poison gas in chambers at concentration camps soon became the method of choice where millions died. Hitler organized generals that pledged him full allegiance in all military issues, and an extensive number of scientist, doctors, and other individuals to carry out his evil orders.

Targeted for disposal was Theologian and Lutheran pastor, spy and martyr Dietrich Bonhoeffer, who publicly opposed Hitler when the majority of pastors and churches in Germany supported Hitler or refused to speak out against him. In his opposition to Hitler's plan for Germany and in revolt of his treatment of the Jews, Bonhoeffer, along with other strategists, conspired to assassinate Hitler. When the attempt failed, Bonhoeffer was arrested and waited in prison for more than a year before his trial. When Hitler accepted his defeat, he ordered the execution of Bonhoeffer and his cohorts.

On April 8, 1945, Bonhoeffer was found guilty at a trumped-up trial and sentenced to death by hanging. On April 9 he was stripped naked and marched to the gallows. Bonhoeffer's death came just two weeks before U.S. soldiers liberated Flossenburg Concentration Camp where he had been held prisoner. It has been said that Bonheoffer was hanged more for trying to stop evil by opposing Hitler's system of government and for trying to persuade the Church to remain true to Jesus than for his attempt on Hitler's life. Hitler hated Bonhoeffer's pursuit of godliness for Europe both in its government and its citizens because *he* wanted to be worshipped as the god of the people. Consequently, he retaliated and God did not intervene for Bonhoeffer.

Richard Wurmbrand was another servant of Christ who experienced extreme torture by those who hate Christianity. Born a Jew in Romania, Wurmbrand converted to Christianity in 1938 and became a Lutheran minister operating in an underground church there. After his arrest for preaching the gospel and trying to convert communists, he endured 14 intermittent years of imprisonment where he was physically tortured, placed in solitary confinement for months at a time, suffered hunger and cold, and the anguish of brainwashing and mental cruelty. Finally in a deal to buy his freedom, he was released for the price of $10,000. In 1966, he moved his family to the United States where he founded his ministry, *Voice of The Martyrs*. Wurmbrand moved to the United States after his release because he could live free of religious persecution under the constitutional laws that were designed to protect his human rights.

Every form of torture I discovered was shocking to me. Countless men, regardless of their position in society, or their claim to religion or not, or their claim as good fathers and husbands or not, stooped to sadistic behavior during a time already overburdened with demoralizing trauma for every person directly involved in war and not just those carrying a rifle in hand-to-hand combat. Nevertheless, a greater shock to me was learning how terribly cruel female Nazi overseers were to female prisoners. As overseers, they were given very little power outside their ability to be brutal, yet prison survivors reported that the female guards were often more wicked in their torture than were the male guards.

Regardless of rank or purpose, as troops in battle moved across territories, they found new opportunities for sexual violence and torture enhanced by alcohol, which drastically elevated a soldier's willingness for brutality. To stop the atrocities committed by a heartless Nazi dictator and capture Berlin, Russia's Red Army—a U.S. and British ally—slashed its way across Germany on foot, by horseback, and in military tanks. They showed no mercy in their cruelty toward women and children, especially in Berlin. One Soviet soldier wrote: *"We were young, strong, and four years without women. So, we tried to catch German women . . . ten men raped one girl. There were not enough women; the entire population ran from the Soviet army. So we had to take young twelve or thirteen year-old. If she cried, we put something in her mouth. We thought it was fun. Now I cannot understand how I did it, a boy from a good family . . . but that was me."*

Military personnel reported seeing females of all ages forced to lay roadside awaiting incoming Russian troops, who lined up as many as 25 deep in front of each female waiting his turn with her. Some Russian troops were seen raping little girls then tossing them in front of oncoming tanks to be crushed. Others witnessed husbands and fathers killing their families and then themselves in order to escape the wicked cruelty of the Russian soldiers.

Girls that were fortunate enough to avoid a flying bullet while attempting escape chased after American troops in convoy hoping to be rescued. Some U.S. soldiers were brave enough to pull these girls aboard their moving Jeeps. Hopefully they were treated with compassion. But, not one country's soldiers, including our beloved America, fully abstained from some form of torture, especially rape, both individual and gang rape of defenseless victims. The end of World War II reported on America's Stain; more than 11,000 rapes committed by American soldiers on foreign soil. Statistics on the Viet Nam war do not give our military a clean record regarding rape.

Unlike the violations by our allies or even our enemies, many of the rape cases by U.S. soldiers were tried in court and convictions were handed down. Despite the Geneva Conventions and its continual updates to provide protection for victims of war, even today, brutality—especially rape—of the defenseless continues unrestrained.

Sadly it seems that there is no government or military force anywhere in the world that can generate effective outrage about senseless atrocities. Where is the human compassion needed to create a safe place for vulnerable citizens when the powers that govern decide to destroy each other? Where is the courage necessary to trust God for military replacements needed to fill the voids created by the punishment and removal of violators? People's minds are seemingly ruled by relentless hate and destruction. Continually I am perplexed by the stories about how people engage both natural and violent sex as their most important last rite before succumbing to death. Minutes before meeting their maker, they fear Him not! According to Adolf Hitler's secretary, Traudl Junge, who survived the war, some of the individuals isolated in his bunker succumbed to a shocking orgy of drunken sexual wickedness as Russian tanks rolled into Berlin at the end of the war.

In his book, *The Fall of Berlin 1945*, Antony Beevor writes that undisciplined soldiers without fear of retribution can rapidly revert to a primitive—a dark area—of male sexuality, especially in war, when there are no social and disciplinary restraints *(Beevor, Antony 2003-04-29 The Fall of Berlin 1945) (pp. 342-343) Penguin Books, Kindle Edition.*

Some of the kindest and most humane people that I have met did not accept the Christian moral code as the one by which they should live. Therefore, independent of Christianity or any belief in a "one and only true God," humanity has proven that it has the capacity to be decent to fellow humans. Some abide by that ability, but those with hate in their heart ignore it entirely. Particularly in war, men choose a path of destruction and meanness that is unnecessary to win a battle. They revert to a self-proclaimed freedom or right granted by war to inflict pain upon others. When a victor had control of his target and the target was fully submitted, the victor took great pleasure in continuing to exercise extreme torture over those they had defeated and captured.

The atrocities of WWII happened little more than seventy-five years ago. Many of us have living family members or friends or people we met at some point in life who were an eyewitness or remember what took place then. Austrian born Kitty Werthmann was 12 years old when Adolf Hitler was given control of her homeland. In a personal interview with her on April 3, 2012, Mrs. Werthmann shared with me about how the National Socialist Party and WWII changed not only her own life but also the life of her fellow countrymen, and Austria.

She said that in 1938 Austria was a depressed country with nearly one-third of the workforce unemployed, 25% inflation, and a 25% interest rate on bank loans. Bankruptcy cases were filed daily. People were without food and many were starving. Austrians were desperate for relief from their poverty and depressed environment. Germany appeared to be the best-qualified neighbor to render them aid. She said that Austrians had been told that Germany had low unemployment and low crime, and a high standard of living. The Austrian people had no knowledge of persecution of any kind perpetrated on any culture, Jewish or otherwise, by the German government. German propaganda reached the hearts of 98% of the population, so on April 10, 1938 they voted to let Germany annex Austria and they accepted Hitler as their leader.

Their hunger now arrested, and jubilant at the prospect of a prosperous life Austrians danced in the streets for three days and enjoyed extravagant foods in field kitchens put in place by the new NSP movement. The new government also established the Public Work Service, which created jobs for both men and women—an impressive act to hungry and destitute Austrians. But they would soon learn that instead of a compassionate leader, they now had a tyrannical dictator!

Because the population of Austria was primarily Catholic, the schools offered religion to students. However, after Hitler's election little time passed before he began to target education, and eliminate religious instruction for children. Mrs. Werthmann said that on the day Hitler was elected as Austria's leader she walked into her classroom and saw that a picture of Hitler and a Nazi flag had replaced the crucifix. Her teacher was a devout woman forced to stand before her class and tell those young students that they would no longer be praying or learning religion in the classroom. Instead they would be required to give praise to the Deutschland and participate in physical education.

She said that Sundays became National Youth Day and attendance was compulsory with first, second, and third degree penalties—the last being jail—for not attending. The first two hours of the day consisted of political indoctrination and the rest of the day involved unlimited sports promoted by free amenities including top-of-the-line sports equipment. This tactic was designed to indoctrinate the youth with political rhetoric and fun sports, and would help remove any conviction about accountability they might have felt towards the one true God.

Mrs. Werthmann said that her mom, a devout Christian, was very unhappy about the new school policy. She removed Kitty from public school and enrolled her in a convent where she would not be politically indoctrinated or brainwashed with sports, which were designed to make them stronger for the purpose of combat readiness. During holiday visits with her friends Kitty observed what living without religion had done to them. They had become extremely promiscuous. Unwed mothers were glorified for having babies for Hitler, so that he could build the Aryan race. Young girls were happy to accommodate the demands. Kitty soon realized what a great deed her mother had done when she removed her from a humanistic philosophy and enrolled her in a religious school.

Soon after Kitty's enrollment in the convent school, the military draft became law and Austrian boys and girls were required to give one year to the labor corps. By day, girls worked on farms, and by night they participated in military training alongside the boys. They were required to be skilled as anti-aircraft gunners and participate in the signal corps. After they finished labor corps they were sent to the front lines instead of being discharged. Mrs. Werthmann said that when she visited her homeland many years following the war, she discovered that most of the women survivors who were forced to participate in combat during the war had become emotional cripples due to the horrors they had seen.

After sending women into the workforce and battle, Hitler established childcare centers where children could be left around the clock under the total care of the government. The equal rights that had previously seemed so lucrative to most women had now offered a generation of brainwashed children raised entirely by the state with no spiritual or family teaching at all.

The medical industry, also affected by Hitler's reign, saw drastic changes when he established socialized health care, which was free to everyone. Consequently, people rushed to the doctor for every minor wound or illness. The overload forced those with major illnesses to wait as long as two years for treatment. Burdens from the overload as well as from low government salaries motivated doctors to leave Austria in search of a country where they would have more freedoms to practice medicine and earn better pay.

The production and service industries felt the impact of Hitler's leadership when the "business monitoring agency" and the "consumer protection agency" were implemented. Officials regulated such huge amounts of these industries that fledgling businesses could not survive. Consumer protection essentially abolished free enterprise as people were told how to shop and what they could buy. Agents would visit farms, count the livestock, and then tell farmers what to produce and how to produce it.

In 1944, Kitty, as I came to know her, was an 18-year-old student teacher at a small village in the Alps. One day she learned that 15 slightly mentally retarded adults who were good at manual labor (one was the janitor at her school) were taken away by the State Health Department under the pretext of helping them improve their work skills. Families of those adults were required to sign papers agreeing not to visit their relatives for six months. However, during those six months all 15 of the physically healthy adults had died. No one ever learned how or exactly when.

Following the attacks on Christianity, the implementation of socialized medicine, the forced work labor and military training for women, and business monitoring, the time had come to disarm the citizens. Disarmament meant that Hitler would now have complete control of the people. The first step was to enforce the registration of all firearms but soon after, the police required everyone to turn them over to the state. She said that because the police now had a record of gun owners, it would be futile not to comply voluntarily.

As totalitarianism slid rapidly into place Austrian citizens lost their free speech. Anyone caught saying something against the government was taken away. The National Socialist government fully controlled the press, so the citizens had no way of knowing what was really happening on a daily basis. Until the war ended in 1945 when Soviet troops entered and occupied Austria, which lasted until 1955, the people were fully controlled by the harsh demands of the German government. But it would be under Soviet occupation that Austrian citizens would experience the most brutal horrors. Soviet soldiers hated Austrians because they had allowed Hitler to lead their country. Forcing Austrian husbands and fathers to watch, they raped females from preteen to the elderly and massacred a large number. She told how that after being raped and brutalized by as many as 30 soldiers per woman many of the women were nailed alive to barn doors and left there to die.

In their effort to completely destroy Austrian land, the Soviets dismantled whole factories and sawed down entire orchards of fruit. What they couldn't destroy or take with them, they burned.

World War II ended in 1945. In 1950 Kitty Werthmann said goodbye to her homeland and boarded a ship bound for America. Though she was completely alone she was fully prepared—both mentally and emotionally—to begin life in a new and free county. Her happiest day came when the ship bringing her to American sailed past the Statue of Liberty standing in New York Harbor.

After the war, Kitty met and married Mr. Werthmann. She learned that he had been left for dead on the battlefield and when trucks came to collect bodies, two men picked him up and tossed him atop the mound of bodies already collected. Instead of getting back inside the cab, one of the men decided to climb on top of the dead bodies to smoke a cigarette. Suddenly he heard groans and saw movement in one of the bodies close by. They later discovered that his name was Werthmann. After a time of healing he came to America to begin a new life and eventually became a successful American radiologist, father and husband to Kitty.

During our two-hour interview, Mrs. Werthmann and I sat at the dining table in a beautiful historical Bed and Breakfast in the small town where we had agreed to meet. When our formal interview ended, she invited me to join her for an evening dinner at the local country club where I learned a great deal more about her and her life. At the time she was 86 years old and still very much an activist for the American Constitution. Though she was protected from much of the horrors of war, she is well aware of what took place and saw the consequences of war—the magnitudes of which the majority of Americans cannot even imagine. To hear her speak of it and to personally experience the variety of voice tones she used to express her concern for our country and its people was emotionally heartwarming. To witness her patriotism for a country that she chose over her homeland because she would live in freedom inspired me beyond what I am able to express. Sometimes accompanied by bodyguards when she travels, her courage and strength are unmatched by anyone I've met and she intends to fight for the American Constitution until she draws her last breath. I was honored just to sit in her presence.

Before voting Hitler into leadership and allowing Germany to annex their country the Austrian people were not bad people. They had no desire to see their citizens terrorized. They were simply destitute. They needed help and turned to their neighbor; one about which they knew little. In their desperation and their lack of knowledge, they believed a beautiful lie and because of it, they suffered horribly. In contrast, Switzerland had remained a neutral country since 1847. They understood Socialism, Nazism, and Communism and they knew the importance of being armed. When Adolf Hitler pranced his way through Europe building a plan to invade and destroy territories he deemed a threat to his quest for a master race, and the land to support that race, Switzerland was on his list to conquer. But when the war started in Europe in 1939, the entire population of Switzerland was armed and ready to wage a relentless guerrilla war against a threatening invader. The Swiss people strongly opposed Nazism and were prepared to fight to the death. Kitty said that every home had arms, and military arms were stored throughout the land. Though several of Hitler's military giants questioned his reasons, Hitler never gave the order to invade. Switzerland stayed neutral throughout the war and managed to offer itself as a place of refuge for displaced Jews.

For 700 years, Switzerland had stood firm for the ideals of democracy, federalism, and neutrality. (Note: However, staying neutral isn't a good thing if it threatens the safety of another). But, Switzerland's traditions were put to the supreme test during WWII and they were justified. After a good deal of research on Hitler, my opinion is that he had another reason for not invading Switzerland—a reason he never made known to anyone. Hitler had the means and the willingness to destroy or control any small country he chose.

Many good people have suffered under the leadership of their homeland. Aleksandr Solzhenitsyn was a Russian citizen who spent 11 years in labor camps and in exile because he made unfavorable remarks about Joseph Stalin, the Russian dictator. As hard as he worked in labor camps, he worked equally as hard on his book titled *The Gulag Archipelago*. His effort was to educate the West about the atrocities committed by the Russian government against its own citizens. In 1985, Mrs. Werthmann interviewed Mr. Solzhenitsyn by telephone while his wife translated. She said that his final comment to her was "America needs to wake up before it is too late." Solzhenitsyn's warning to America was 31 years ago.

POW Louis Zamperini, age 97 at this writing, was another who saw and suffered much during WWII. Laura Hillenbrand told the story of the Olympic runner and American hero's capture and quest to survive as a captive of the Japanese. In her book titled *Unbroken*, Zamperini relates that American pilots were well informed about the brutality by Japanese soldiers and the 1938 rape of Nanking, China. He said that the one thing they feared most was to be captured by the Japanese who hated Westerners and called them Anglo-Saxon devils. They tortured and humiliated Westerners with reckless aggression. Famous for this tactic with most people, they also used it on an affectionate little duck named Gaga.

Gaga was beloved by the prisoners which, Zamperini believed, provoked the guards to mercilessly torment her. Then one day in full view of the captives, the medical officer at the camp—a man they referred to as Shithead—decided to sexually violate Gaga. As if to prove that his power could not be thwarted, and motivated by his fascination with the suffering of others, an innocent little duck became another victim of evil as the officer dropped his pants and sexually abused Gaga until she died.

DANCING WITH THE DEVIL

Mr. Zamperini's story is one of sadness, sorrow, horror, and then eventually joy, courage, and encouragement. I recommend *Unbroken* as a "must read" for everyone. Also, a movie based on Hillenbrand's book, *Unbroken*, and personal interviews with Zamperini was released in December 2014. (Update: Mr. Zamperini passed away on July 2, 2014. I am thankful that he will never see how much brokenness the country who's integrity he fought for and suffered so much to protect has come to; he will never know the fullness of the shame our leaders inflict on our citizens and those Americans who have suffered in war; though he remained "unbroken" during and after WWII, I am thankful that he will never know how truly broken America is becoming.)

I was deeply saddened by the heinous crimes of war and for each of the victims no matter how they died. Whether healthy or sick, civilians—regardless of age or sex—and military personnel alike experienced the brute force of terror inflicted on them by soldiers who were just plain mean or were pumped up on alcohol. They believed that war gave them the right to torture and kill without consideration for the victims or any leaders who decried the horrors—though there were few.

Unfortunately, the original (1864) Geneva Convention agreement did not include war crimes against humanity and nations were not *required* to sign. The Convention was designed to make the neglect of those injured in battle a crime. After the atrocities against humans in WWI and WWII, the Convention was expanded in 1949 to cover armed forces on land and at sea, prisoners of war, and civilians. At a diplomatic convention in 1977, the Convention was expanded again. Now composed of four conventions and three protocols, basically, it is an agreement on do's and don'ts designed to protect vulnerable and defenseless individuals during military conflict. The underlying principle is that human dignity of all individuals must be respected at all times. Without any kind of discrimination everything possible must be done to reduce the suffering of people who have been put out of action by sickness, wounds, or captivity whether or not they have taken a direct part in the conflict.

The established rules and laws for good social and civil behavior, particularly the Ten Commandments were given by God for humanity to use as a guide for moral living and to corral our tendency toward evil and inappropriateness. Today, they are completely ignored, disregarded as if they are trash. Also, few people are interested in learning the beneficial aspects of the social graces. It's easier to do our own thing without regard for others. But the Lord says we are to consider others better than ourselves, be ye kind, one to another. That cannot always be implemented during war but where there is no threat, it certainly can be implemented, even during war. Nowhere in the Bible have I read that God said for people to abstain from abuse and torture, and sexual abuse and immorality unless of course you are in war; then it is permissible.

Books like Antony Beevor's, *The Fall of Berlin 1945* and *The Second World War*; Aleksandr Solzhenitsyn's *The Gulag Archipelago* and *52 Methods of Russian Torture;* Laura Hillenbrand's *Unbroken*, give us documented evidence of the evil in humans. Based on these books, I personally concluded that the Japanese may have been the most brutal and the most hate-filled of all military soldiers. However, I admit to being conflicted in my thinking because of the atrocities perpetrated by the Soviet soldiers against all people including their own, and Mrs. Werthmann's personal knowledge of their brutality, which places them first in her view. Christians who believe that there is no devil or evil haven't done enough research, studied enough history, or read enough police reports.

Pain caused by WWII isn't the only pain attributed to war. Today, war is still raging in the Middle East and other parts of the world. From the end of WWII through the writing of this book, heinous crimes in the name of war, religion, and everyday life rampage as the defenseless are held hostage by the brutally wicked and either beaten, drugged and raped, or viciously murdered. *"Men never do evil so completely and cheerfully as when they do it from a religious conviction."* Blaise Pascal 1623-1662.

THE ISLAMIC STATE OF IRAQ AND SYRIA (ISIS)

In his book, *Rise of ISIS, A Threat we Can't Ignore*, (Howard Books, 2014) Jay Sekulow, Chief Council of the American Center for Law and Justice, and his co-authors tell us how ISIS came to be. Sekulow says that they began as a group that broke away from the terrorists group, Al-Qaeda or AQI in Iraq. The new group rejected AQI because of their brutal tactics for killing. In AQI beheadings were not mercifully done with the quick slash of a sharp sword. Instead, the murderers reveled in torture, sawing away at a person's neck with dull knives. What the knives didn't sever, they finished the beheading by *pulling* off the head. Even Osama bin Laden objected to such brutality. Objectors broke away and organized the Islamic State of Iraq and Syria otherwise known as ISIS. But don't think for a moment that they aren't also brutal. Sekulow, whose stated goal for his book is to help people *"understand the horrific jihadist threat to Christians and Jews in the Middle East, a threat that will undoubtedly come to the United States if it is left unchecked abroad."* details their brutality.

Today, ISIS fighters have marked Christian's homes and businesses in much the same way the Nazi's marked the Jews of Germany. ISIS uses an Arabic symbol that has come to mean "Nazarene," a name for Jesus. They sell Christian women in the sex slave market of human trafficking, and behead children. Conquered Christians are forced to convert, or leave their homes, or die. Many are crucified in the manner of Jesus.

Hamas and ISIS jihadists (crusaders for a principle or belief) systematically violate the laws of war in an effort to create maximum human suffering. As I have done here in *Dancing With The Devil*, Sekulow and his cohorts have also done in their book, *Rise of ISIS, A Threat We Can't Ignore*: graphically described exactly how evil these enemies are. But he admits as I have, that the whole truth of their evil is simply too much for most people to bear. But I caution: "We must bear it. We must know all there is to know so that we can agree on how to fight this great enemy of the Christian should they bring their torturous cruelty to our people and our soil." Sekulow wants people everywhere to know that the evil acts witnessed by our own military, and the IDF (Israel Defense Forces) would re-create Auschwitz and Dachau during WWII. He says, *"Millions across the world support these enemies of Israel and the U.S., going to great lengths to strengthen terrorists and weaken the IDF and the U.S. military. This demonstrates that the spirit of murder and collaboration that haunted much of Europe under Nazi occupation has not disappeared."* He says, *"The U.N., Red Cross, and sadly our own President and State Department* (under the Obama Administration) *appease jihad, doing so with their eyes wide open, fully aware of the evil they empower. They should hang their heads in shame."* If you read only one book of those on my recommended reading list, please choose *Rise of Isis, A Threat We Can't Ignore* by Jay Sekulow. Parenthesis added

THE EVIL OF HUMAN TRAFFICKING
Demons of Rape and Torture and Murder

It is difficult to obtain an accurate number of women and children forced or sold into prostitution, (sexual slavery) but it is estimated at somewhere near or above 800,000 per year including the 17,500 transported into the United States alone. Some estimate the U.S. number to be as high as 60,000 annually but there is no way to know for sure. Estimates of trafficked victims worldwide are more than 20 million children and adults at any given time. Profits from the sex slavery market are estimated at between $7-12 billion U.S. dollars per year. Source: the *2014 Global report on Trafficking in Persons published by the United Nations Office on Drugs and Crime.*

Women and children are trafficked for sexual exploitation including prostitution, forced labor, and the removal and sale of their organs. Men are trafficked for forced labor and removal of organs, and children for all of the above. Victims of trafficking for the purpose of organ removal are often recruited from vulnerable groups such as those in extreme poverty. The traffickers are often part of transnational organized crime groups that include brokers, surgeons, hospital directors, health-care practitioners, ambulance drivers, and mortuary workers. *Source: UN.GIFT – The Vienna Forum to Fight Human Trafficking 13-15 February 2008, Austria Center Vienna – Background Paper Introduction page 2*

While this chapter was in progress the news reported that children were being transported into Cambodia from other countries for the purpose of sexual labor. Once they reached Cambodia their final destination was unknown, making their rescue basically impossible.

In early 2015, Malaysian authorities reported finding a series of graves in at least 17 abandoned human trafficking camps. The camps held Rohingya Muslims fleeing Myanmar. Prior to this discovery, police in Thailand unearthed dozens of bodies from shallow graves in abandoned camps on the Thai side of the border. Most of the victims were people fleeing their homelands to reach countries where they hoped to find work and live free from persecution.

This evil is not isolated to Cambodia or Malaysia or Thailand but is a constant fear for people everywhere. Even in the U.S. human trafficking is growing beyond our ability to imagine how it could be possible in a nation dedicated to destroying terror around the world, yet everyday our own women and children face the terror of being kidnapped and trafficked. Our states that border Mexico are suffering huge losses. Children of all ages are being snatched from their own streets, neighborhood playgrounds, and shopping malls. Our government's neglect of our borders and illegal immigration subjects our defenseless citizens to unimaginable terror. Once women and children are snatched they are transported to a "holding area" where they are initiated before being sold as sex slaves. Immediately upon arrival at the place where they are held before being sold, they are brutally raped and beaten then held hostage to repeated rape, beatings, and threats, and forced to perform unspeakable acts until they are completely broken and too afraid to fight back. Few escape to bring this atrocity to public awareness.

In contrast, girls from other countries are brought into the United States as mail-order brides, and as sex slaves in bars turned brothels—confined or imprisoned to prostitution in cities like San Francisco, CA. and Houston, TX. Many of these females are also taken through the "prep" centers before being sent to their final destination.

A shocking and despicable yet popular act against trafficked women is to rape her while she is pregnant—especially in her last trimester. For this reason, pregnant women bring a higher price in the slave market. Where birth control might have been previously encouraged it is now discouraged so that women will conceive. In these cases, the demon of rape and sexual perversion not only shows hatred for the female under his power, his hate is also directed at the child in her womb who is being terrorized by the act. What will happen to the child if it survives? A detective in a sex-trafficking documentary on the problems in his city spoke about the difficulties he faces trying to get help from law enforcement agencies, and in finding a place for rescued victims to reside until they are healed.

INHUMANE FEMALE GENITAL MUTILATION
Demons of Torture and Degradation

"One early morning in an African village not far from Nairobi, Kenya, young girls are roused from sleep and taken to a nearby river. The waters are cold, helping to arrest the bleeding from a first menstrual cycle, making their genitalia stand out and slightly numb. Soon an elder village midwife takes the children one by one and with a rusty razor, scissor or shard of glass cuts out the clitoris, slices off the labia and applies ashes, herbs or cow dung to staunch the flow of blood. As the girl writhes in pain, other women hold her arms down, her legs apart, her mouth shut tight so that she cannot run away or alarm the other unsuspecting

children waiting in their cool bath." (Reprinted from Women and Revolution No. 41, Summer/Autumn 1992)

According to the United Nations Children's Fund, 100 to 130 million females around the world have been genitally mutilated. This would translate to as many as 2 million or more being mutilated each year. This barbaric ritual, which is done without anesthesia, is to remove a female's sexual desire so that she will not chase after sex with unbridled passion, and to help ensure virginity before marriage and fidelity after marriage.

However, in almost all marriages where this custom exists, polygamy (having multiple wives) is practiced, therefore men argue for excision because it is difficult, they say, to satisfy all of their wives. So, they reason that it is just best that women don't desire sex. His many wives are simply slaves in his household; he can rape at will because the woman will dread each encounter. He doesn't have to please her, only himself. Genital mutilation, known as excision, is a modern day ritual exercised primarily in Muslim countries and is especially attractive to men with power and status who wish to dominate and control.

The savagery of the ritual, which is performed on girls from infants to the initiation into womanhood, subjects the females to revolting pain. In some parts of the Muslim world, genital excision includes infibulation where the two sides of the vulva are sewn together with catgut or held with thorns, and a matchstick shoved in place to ensure an opening the size of a pinhole. Part of the procedure in some cases includes binding the legs together from the hips to the ankles for as long as 40 days to encourage the formation of scar tissue.

Complications from this procedure include excruciating pain when trying to urinate, which can take as long as thirty minutes to empty the bladder due to the tiny opening, and menstruation is extremely painful for the same reason. Retention of urine and menstrual blood make the area overly susceptible to infection. Sexual intercourse becomes practically unbearable, especially on the wedding night. Consummation may take weeks, beginning with the husband having to open his wife's infibulation with fingers, or a knife, or a ceremonial sword, all of which are horribly painful. The woman must lie still with legs spread through repeated, bloody penetrations until a large enough opening becomes permanent.

Countries that practice some form of genital mutilation include the Muslim countries of Northern Sudan, Black Jews of Ethiopia, Catholic and Protestant converts in Nigeria, Burkina Faso, Mali, Somalia, Djibouti, parts of the Middle East and Pakistan, and among some Muslims in Malaysia, India and Sri Lanka.

Where is the civil law in defense of human rights? Where God is not honored, there is no moral code and no respect for humanity. People are ruled by their own way of thinking, which is motivated by the master of the world and not the God of heaven. Many man-made ideas surround the topic of female genital mutilation but we must conclude that it is simply another effort by humans to reject the perfect design of a perfect God, changing it into that which results in unimaginable pain, humiliation, and demoralization. The extent of the damage this procedure causes can't and won't be fully calculated and documented until more women decide to break free from these cult practices that do not follow the kind and merciful ways of a loving God. They must be discussed openly so that others will know what they have experienced.

Humanity must respect the fact that God designed every part of the human anatomy—both men and women—to function for a very specific purpose. In His brilliance He knew what would work best regarding a woman for a man and vice versa. Humans cannot and should not try to redesign what the living God has designed. They are not smart enough to make it work effectively!

Women in America live free of these atrocious rituals. They are free to see a doctor for medical treatment of sexual issues, and to preserve their genitalia, not have it mutilated. These freedoms were made possible by the blood of men who understood hate filled tyranny that haunted people under governments that hated God. These men put themselves and their families in harm's way to establish a way of life far better than what they had previously experienced, and they possessed a strong passion to provide the "good life" for those generations to follow. Their work and quest for human rights has had a positive and influential effect in America for more than 200 years.

Americans, who desire to keep our country free from those who wish to mutilate and torture women and girls, must carry on the freedom work of our forefathers. We must not forget that the Muslims desire to take over the world. They have made clear their hate for Americans, calling us "the infidels." Imagine what would happen to our infants, young girls, and women should America bow to the rule of worshippers of any god that is not the Holy God of the Bible who does not require that His children live under such cruelty. Though former President Barak Obama stated that genital mutilation is something we *"should not hold on to,"* he was not courageous enough to say that genital mutilation is repugnant and must be eradicated with fervent passion. Instead, he offered a suggestion only. (*From Obama's speech to the Washington Fellowship for Young African Leaders Educational Summit in Washington DC, July 28-30, 2014*)

Fortunately a few women in Africa abhor the horror of genital mutilation of females. These women are trying to teach those trapped as prisoners to this brutal ritual that there is a different life, which can be attained through laws of protection if they are only willing to fight for them. Like our forefathers did for America, these women have put themselves in harm's way and found the courage to speak out in order to make a difference in the lives of other female victims. They are being faced with a huge challenge because the men who fight for genital mutilation do not respect these women's efforts to eradicate it, so their work is beyond admirable as they themselves are often in danger.

WORLDWIDE RAPE, SEXUAL AND DOMESTIC VIOLENCE

Demons of Rape and Domestic Violence

Globally, women age fifteen to forty-four are more likely to be injured or die as a result of male violence than through cancer, traffic accidents, malaria and war combined. *(The Vienna Forum to Fight Human Trafficking 13-15 February 2008, Austria Center Vienna – Background Paper Introduction Page 1)*

The World Health Organization estimates that globally one woman in five will be the victim of rape or attempted rape in her lifetime. Other data suggests that in Canada, New Zealand, the United States, and the United Kingdom, the corresponding figure is one in six women. In South Africa, a frightening 40% of girls aged seventeen or under are reported to have been the victim of rape or attempted rape. In peaceful Geneva, a study of 1200 randomly selected ninth-grade students, a staggering 20% of girls revealed that they had experienced at least one incident of sexual abuse. Translated, globally the number of victims is estimated at more than 700 million girls and women. In the United States the estimations are at some 25 million and over 4 million in the United Kingdom. It is feared that these estimates are too conservative, for many sexual violations are never reported.

Sexual abuse of girls, often by family members, is widespread yet shrouded in taboo. In a treatment center in Nigeria, 15 per cent of female patients requiring treatment for sexually transmitted diseases were under the age of five, with a further six per cent between the ages of six and 15 years. In South Africa, one in four men report having had sex with a female against her consent by the time he was 18 years of age. Unfortunately, violence against women within the family is still largely treated as a private matter, rather than an urgent political and public problem, and a violation of human rights. These statistics do not include those females that have been trafficked into sexual slavery. Nevertheless, they are utterly unacceptable and must be given due consideration.

In the executive summary of the *Geneva Centre for the Democratic Control of Armed Forces, Women in an Insecure World, Violence against Women, Facts, Figures, and Analysis, in Slaughtering Eve, Page 1*, the United Nations estimates that up to 200 million women and girls are demographically 'missing.' The understatement hides one of the most shocking crimes against humanity. The author of the article chose the word "missing" as a milder form of the word that should have been used to define "how" they are missing—basically murdered because they were female and used up. The number of *missing* women, killed for gender-related reasons, is of the same magnitude as the estimated 191 million human beings who have lost their lives directly or indirectly as a result of the combined conflicts and wars of the 20th century, the most violent period so far in the history of humanity. Surprisingly, the average person rarely thinks of the female gender as paying such a high price for the rampant evil in our world.

Women constitute the largest group of the world's population exposed to universal and persistent violence. Victims are claimed in conflict, but they are also taken from the house next door. Causes are complex, but simply stated, the facts show that for all too many a female's life and dignity are worth far less than a man's. This situation is intolerable. If the stronger gender won't join forces and help, then the able women of the world must find an effective way to change the lives of the abused weaker gender.

Violence against women impedes the creation of a well-functioning security sector—those institutions capable of providing an adequate level of security for all citizens. Violence against women occurs at the domestic and community levels, and in situations of armed conflict, and under repressive governments. (Note: These are the reasons the U.S. has often aided the defenseless.)

In 2010, a young girl traveling on a bus with her boyfriend in India was attacked by a gang of six men who beat-up the boyfriend and then gang raped the young woman. Finally they disemboweled her vaginally with a tire iron—an act typical of the sexual violence during WWII. She died a few days later. Several other incidents of violence against women in India made headline news in 2013.

Also in India, the man who no longer wants the woman in his life simply throws acid in her face. It eats away so much of the flesh that she basically goes into hiding as no one wants to look at her; and she has no money for medical repairs. India, a country where Hindu gods are worshipped (the gods of inner healing and personal alignment, making one's life better, free of hate and struggles—the primary purpose of Yoga) carries an epidemic of sexual violence and Eve teasing, which is sexual harassment that often turns into rape and violence.

Russia has an on-going domestic violence problem, which is just recently being recognized. While the Russian government has no system in place to gather data on the issue, one private study of 2,200 people in fifty towns and cities across Russia showed that 70% of women suffered under at least one form of violence—physical, sexual, economical, or psychological—by their husbands. Further, annually in Russia, husbands are responsible for the murder of approximately 14,000 wives and approximately 36,000 cases of spousal abuse. (Note: Is it safe to say that the brutality the Russian soldiers inflicted on females during WWII was not left on the battlefield when the war ended, but instead went home with them and was passed down to their sons and grandsons?)

In a 2012 report by the Thompson Reuters Foundation on G20 nations, which is industrialized and developing economies dedicated to the key issues in the global economy, Russia was ranked the seventh worst country in which to be a woman—worse than Turkey (Armenian Genocide) and just above China, where for years, female babies were killed for being invaluable humans. Russia has no law defining or specifically criminalizing domestic violence. Therefore unlike America's laws against domestic violence, attaining a restraining or protective order in Russia is not an option.

DANCING WITH THE DEVIL

RAPE AND VIOLENCE ESCALATING IN AMERICA

Have Americans forgotten their Christian Heritage?

According to an article in *BBC News, U.S. and Canada*, dated December 15, 2011, rape affects almost 20 percent of U.S. women. A partner or husband, according to the Center for Disease Control, has attacked an estimated 25 percent. More than 24 people a minute reported rape, violence, or stalking. Experts at the *Centers for Disease Control and Prevention (CDC)* described the results of the first year of the *National Intimate Partner and Sexual Violence Survey* as "astounding."

It *is* astounding, and far removed from what we believe ourselves to be as cultured human beings. Based on our unwillingness to honor self-respect and the human rights of another, many people are returning to the ungodly pagan behavior of the gentile people before the Apostle Paul recruited them for salvation.

In 2012 and 2013 the American sports industry made front-page news validating the increase in sexual abuse against women at colleges and universities. We read stories about drunken football jocks gang raping young teenage girls who allowed themselves to slip into a drunken stupor, indolently succumbing, unable to escape the brute muscle hell-bent on getting their kicks at others' expense in what is known as the Steubenville rape case. (Ohio).

In his book titled *Missoula,* author Jon Krakauer shared the story of a fraternity brother he called Frank, who told how the fraternity brothers hunted and preyed upon girls to rape. He told how the frat brothers were on the "look-out" for good-looking girls, particularly freshmen girls—the really "young ones" because, according to Frank, they were the easiest to overpower. They were nervous at parties, so the men would start them drinking right away. Frank told how he was able to take sexual advantage of one of the young women after persuading her to drink alcohol-spiked punch. He then escorted her to a bedroom where he raped her by holding her down with one arm pressed against her chest while removing her clothes with the other hand. He said that she resisted him the entire time but that had no effect on him for when he was finished he adjusted his clothing and left the room. The young freshman went home devastated and too terrified to report the rape to authorities.

Most sexual abuse in civilized countries has been committed against women. But in the past fifty years sexual abuse of children—boys and girls—has escalated. There was a time when the higher percentage of sexual abuse among youth was against teenage girls but now there is a trend toward the abuse of girls younger than ten years. Also, sexual violence against children between the ages of newborn and twelve years has heightened to an unbelievable number of incidents.

Violators of newborns, infants, and toddlers under three years of age are not necessarily young boys or teens experimenting with sex. They are adult men. Even as I write, I examine reports about baby girls that are raped on the day of their birth. Their little bodies are mutilated. The pelvic bone is crushed and the child's reproductive organs are fully damaged. If they survive the abuse, several surgeries are necessary to remove or repair the damage. Think about it: a precious little child comes into the world then is taken home and forever damaged by rape. What a tragic way to begin life!

A man in northern Michigan was found guilty of killing his 15-week-old daughter during oral rape. In my list of research material on rape I have approximately 15 other cases of rape against newborns up to three days old, which I will not include here. But in one reported case of oral rape to an infant, a Texas man smothered his five-month-old baby daughter. At the time of the crime, the offender was a member of the U.S. military. It was learned that he had also violated other children.

The latest studies on military personnel show that men who serve or have served are more than twice as likely to have a troubled past than members of their non-military peers—differences that did not exist prior to 1973 when the draft was still in effect.

Information from a 2010 telephone survey conducted by the U.S. Centers for Disease Control and Prevention reveals that more than 60,000 adults questioned showed that 43% of men in the all-volunteer force reported emotional abuse in their past. 34% reported alcohol abuse in their home, 27% were exposed to domestic violence, 12% had a household member who was incarcerated and 11% had been touched sexually.

Of those that had served during the draft less than a third showed elevated troubles in only two areas—parental separation and alcohol abuse—instead of the five troubles listed for the all-volunteer force. The report showed that women who served were more likely than non-military peers to admit to a history of emotional abuse, household alcohol problems, and violence. Reports suggest that these women joined the military to escape their abusive situation but often encountered more abuse in their place of refuge. Branches of the U.S. military are seeing record numbers of accusations of sexual assault against women within their ranks. Reports show that the rate of assaults is increasing and top officers are under fire for condoning such acts. However, the fire isn't yet hot enough. If our military is not called to account what will keep it from becoming like the militaries that wrecked havoc on female civilians during WWII?

In a case of indecency with a child by a 69 year-old Texas man, a newspaper reported that his sentence was suspended because the crime was his first offense. The child victim was traumatized and will most likely be emotionally damaged for life, yet his offender goes free to face the temptation to violate again. Will the child fall into the military percentages as reported? No one knows for sure but according to the CDC Study the statistics indicate that the possibility can't be overlooked.

Violence of any kind and especially sexual violence has long-term and often fatal consequences for the victim. Physical pain notwithstanding, violent sex is the ultimate debasement of human character, integrity and the emotions of life that enable humans to love, cherish and care for others with balance and deep compassion. The anger we may carry due to our pain often interferes with our ability to forgive, or be compassionate. Primarily, the porn industry must be held responsible for present day sexual brutality.

Sexual violence must be punished, for no human is safe from another; particularly females and children are not safe from males, the very ones God designed to protect them. If civilized countries do not establish an unrestrained punishment for this unrestrained crime of brutality against the defenseless, it will prevail until the enormity of the act is in our face so often it will have no effect on our conscience. The seriousness of the crime will be uncompromisingly diluted.

Evil behavior comes from a spirit of darkness and we *must* define it as such. Christians *must* recognize, expose, and teach about these crimes of evil, particularly to our children for their safety, so that they will understand why they must be alert and careful. We must advocate a punishment that fits the crime because in many cases courts are too lenient in their punishment of the offender. The Lord says we are to defend the defenseless! Children are the most defenseless of humankind.

Every state in America has a registered sex offender website. My research shows that the majority of offenders used children as their victims. Why children? They are easily conquered. They trust quickly, are physically immature, and easy to terrorize with fear.

The violence against women and children as I have described in this chapter may seem exaggerated to us who have lived a life of comfort regardless of our personal tragedies. But humans have let Satan use them to treat other humans dreadfully and this should not be. To save our nation, Christians from every denomination must put aside their differences and their goals, do their own research and become prayer warriors who can move God deeply when they pray in the manner of Manasseh. (Read his story in chapter 8, pp. 322, 323 – Knowing God, Jesus, Holy Spirit.)

CHAPTER THREE STUDY QUESTIONS

1. Why did God say He was sorry He had created man?

2. Study Judges 19. What do you think was the cause of this heinous crime?

3. What is the difference in healthy and unhealthy fear?

4. Has there ever been a time in your life when you were desperately afraid? If so, how did you deal with your fear?

5. After reading about the horrors of war perpetrated against civilians were you shocked to discover how little you knew about these issues?

6. Describe briefly what you knew about female genital mutilation before reading about it in this chapter.

7. Have you or someone you know been touched by human trafficking? Explain

8. Why do you think that human trafficking has risen to such epidemic levels in America?

9. Why do you think rape in America has risen to such high levels and particularly on University and College campuses?

10. Write a 100-word article on what you knew about ISIS and other terrorists groups before you read about it here and before doing any other research on the subject.

DANCING WITH THE DEVIL

FOUR

❦

A CHRISTIAN NATION MOCKS GOD

But I assure you of this: If you ever forget the Lord your God, and follow other Gods, worshipping and bowing down to them, you will certainly be destroyed; Just as the Lord has destroyed other nations in your path, you will also be destroyed if you refuse to obey the Lord your God (Deuteronomy 8:19-20 NLT).

God detests the prayers of a person who ignores the (his) *law (Proverbs 28:9 NLT).* Parenthesis added

A wicked ruler is as dangerous to the poor as a roaring lion or an attacking bear (Proverbs 28:15 NLT).

"The Lord has made Himself known. He is fair in His Law. The sinful trap themselves by the work of their own hands. The sinful, all the nations that forgot God, will be turned back into the grave" (Psalms 9:19, 17 NLV).

King David knew that God had promised to destroy all who rejected Him so in his prayers he cried out to the Lord, asking Him to judge the nations that hated and rejected his God—the God of Heaven's armies. The men who ruled these nations wrecked havoc on God's children.

More than 2500 years passed from the time of King David's reign to the founding of the United States of America and the men who founded this great nation weren't like the leaders David mentioned in Psalms 9. Instead, our founders *understood* tyranny and religious persecution. In general, they loved God! Nations that reject God are those nations that serve the gods created by God's archenemy, Satan. We read about some of these nations in chapter 3.

Just as those today who seek freedom from persecution in their homeland find their way to American soil, so too were our founders looking for a place where they could worship God freely. Also they hoped to establish a new and better world with a system of government that allowed every citizen to live and worship without fear of persecution. Most importantly they used the Holy Bible as the foundation for making the laws that our nation would be required to live by, including our supreme law of the land—the Constitution, and the Constitutional Amendments that formed our Bill of Rights.

The Old Testament is a handbook that illustrates how God set up rational rules for leaders to follow. And, He gave specific instructions about how He expected them to rule. He wanted Israel's rulers to lead the nation with honesty, integrity, fairness, and purity. They were never to twist justice or show partiality or accept a bribe because to do so would blind the eyes of the wise and corrupt the decisions of the godly. He wanted true justice to prevail and insisted that court verdicts passed down by Levitical priests or judges be implemented without appeal. He required death for those that rejected a verdict and He required two or more witnesses against a person's crime before they could be sentenced or executed.

God promised His children prosperity to the degree that they would lend to others but they would never need to borrow. He promised to make His people the head and not the tail—meaning they would lead with anointing, power and authority. They would never be forced to 'follow' because no one would rule over them as long as they worshipped and obeyed Him. But Israel's kings refused to heed God's warning, so their bad behavior led to the downfall of one king and nation upon another. (From Deuteronomy 16:18-21)

History confirms that few leaders have led according to the will of God. Instead, more have leaned toward their own *understanding*, thus bringing about corruption based on their lusts for power, greed, violence, and fraud rather than trusting in God's commands. As a result, millions of innocent people have been massacred through the years and are still being massacred today because a dictator or a religion that objects to the God of the Bible wants to regulate all people.

However, the design for America was to be different; the government was to rule on the morals and principles outlined in the Bible and the justice system was to honor those principles. We were not to follow in the footsteps of the nations before us. The following excerpt from a speech given by Robert C. Winthrop in 1849 gives us clear evidence of our need for and the expected use of biblical content as the authority for ruling our nation.

On May 28, 1849, Robert C. Winthrop (1809–1894), descendant of Governor John Winthrop, first governor of Massachusetts Bay Colony, and Speaker of the House of Representatives addressed the annual meeting of the Massachusetts Bible Society in Boston, and said in part:

> *"All societies of men must be governed in some way or other. The less they may have of stringent State Government, the more they must have of individual self-government. The less they rely on public law or physical force, the more they must rely on private moral restraint. Men, in a word, must necessarily be controlled, either by a power within them, or by a power without them; either by the word of God, or by the strong-arm of man; either by the Bible, or by the bayonet. It may do for other countries and other governments to talk about the State supporting religion. Here, under our own free institutions, it is Religion, which must support the State. And never more loudly than at this moment have these institutions of ours called for such support. The immense increase of our territorial possessions, with the wild and reckless spirit of adventure, which they have brought with them; the recent discovery of the gold mines of California, with the mania for sudden acquisition for "making haste to be rich," which it has everywhere excited; the vast annual accession to our shores of nearly half a million*

of foreigners, so many of whom are without any other notion of liberty, at the outset than as the absence of all restraint upon their appetites and passions; who does not perceive in all these circumstances that our country is threatened, more seriously than it ever has been before, with that moral deterioration, which has been the unfailing precursor of political downfall? And who is so bold a believer in any system of human checks and balances as to imagine that dangers like these can be effectively counteracted or averted in any other way than by bringing the mighty moral and religious influences of the Bible to bear in our defense. As patriots then, no less than as Christians, Mr. President, I feel that we are called upon to unite in the good work of this Association. And let us rejoice that it is a work in which we can all join hands without hesitation or misgiving. There is no room here—I thank heaven—for differences of parties or of sects. There is no room here for controversies about systems or details . . ."

Ideas, opinions, and fantasies have occupied the mind of man since the beginning of time. History has recorded man's theories, proposals, and inventions, both successful and unsuccessful, as well as the possibility, probability and the belief by some that there is no evil—basically everything is good—God is all love, and the devil doesn't exist!

Mr. Winthrop's speech presents a clear picture of evil and our nation's need for a biblical moral code. Today, America bares little resemblance to the America that came out of our original design—an America united under God. Instead, we have become the "Untied" States of America. Once known as the greatest industrial power in the world, America has relinquished a huge amount of its industry to foreign countries, putting our own people out of work, and strangling the national cash flow. We have borrowed until our economic condition mirrors slavery, and we are floating on the tail of destruction like the nations before us that turned their backs on God and violated His commands. We have forgotten almost every aspect of Mr. Winthrop's speech of 1849, a mere 166 years ago.

To protect the people and help honesty prevail it truly is important that a nation has Godly governance. However, through several administrations America's leadership and also its citizens have endorsed secular humanism and so far have refused to return to biblical morals. America has been the most powerful leading authority in the world for many years but now through ignorance, selfishness, and rebellion against God, it is positioned for destruction by the hands of those who wish to see it decimated. What can we do to reverse this potential train wreck and salvage our country?

A DESPERATE CALL TO ACTION

"Godliness makes a nation great, but sin is a disgrace to any people" (Proverbs 14:34 NLT).

Regardless of where we stand in the process of our existence as a nation, Christians have a right to expect legal protection based upon a fair and just respect for their emotional and mental integrity, their wellbeing, and their religious beliefs. Further, they have a right to a government that takes seriously the laws of the nation as they were established at the start—the Constitution and its Amendments, the Bill of Rights. When governing authorities neglect their responsibility to the people of the nation under their care, they are deliberately challenging God's authority over them. When God gets angry enough at their behavior he will remove His hand of protection from that nation's offending authorities. Lifting that Godly protection allows an enemy to destroy according to the degree God lifted His hand. The entire population is affected by His wrath. However, there is hope for America if true patriots of the Lord—those who love His statutes, and believe in civil and human rights—will courageously object to totalitarianism—a system of government requiring the citizens to submit to state authorities. We must pray that God will help us restore His principles in our people so He can repair our nation.

DANCING WITH THE DEVIL

The rights to *"freedom for the people"* were never so eloquently defined as in the speech given by Patrick Henry to the First Continental Congress in Boston Massachusetts in 1775. Known for high character, Mr. Henry was said to represent that which defines a true man of God, *and* he was an advocate for the American Revolution. For more than ten years the American colonies had struggled under the unreasonable rule of Britain's King George III. Believing in civil rights for everyone Mr. Henry had great compassion for the people, and wanted to protect them from the burden of a high tax as well as other political and economic issues the British had forced upon them.

Mr. Henry's fight for freedom was an effort to convince the Continental Congress to contest the British control of the colonies, which eventually became a country united and free from foreign dictates. All previous diplomatic efforts with the British had failed and now in his famous speech, Mr. Henry was pleading with Congress to revolt.

To gain the support of his fellow countrymen, he orated the most compelling and compassionate argument for freedom ever presented to Congress. The strategy for the content of his speech was a heart's plea based upon reason and logic, and the rights given man by God. Within a month of his speech, which fell on the ears of 120 delegates including Thomas Jefferson and George Washington, the American Revolution began with the Battle of Lexington and Concord on April 19, 1775. It was a necessary driving force behind the freedoms all Americans enjoy today.

Mr. Henry was fighting not only for himself but also for those with whom he shared a country. While he had no desire to show disrespect for those that disagreed with him and insisted they exercise their freedom to debate, he desperately wanted them to *understand* the seriousness of the time. He felt so strongly about his need to express his views on where the country was headed if something wasn't done to deter it, that to keep them to himself would be tantamount to treason against the country, and disloyalty toward God.

Mr. Henry taught that experience is our great teacher and even though it is natural to hope, if we close our eyes to truth and ignore the past, we will most likely repeat it, once again becoming what we escaped. He admonished those listening that the past tells us what to avoid in the future, and he cautioned about the detriment in believing a lie as truth when the evidence by the aggressor clearly speaks of their intent to harm.

Evidence documented during the years immediately preceding WWII indicates that our leaders were focused more on reducing the size of our military and on speeches meant to negotiate world peace than realizing that in a year-long strategy the enemy was willfully and deliberately building weapons of war in their attempt to drag us into battle and eventually gain control of our country. When Mr. Henry made his famous speech to the Continental Congress, he was not ignorant of an enemy's calculating ways but since those first days in the 1700's America has repeatedly forgotten or ignored them.

Willing to have his beliefs subjected to criticism, Mr. Henry was adamant that every argument for peaceable negotiations had been scrutinized under the brightest lights possible and the only alternative for peace and freedom was to face head-on the undeniable storm that was coming their way—war! He called for a time to stop hoping for a solution through arguments, but instead, declared it was time to take action. Believing in a just God who presides over the destinies of nations, (clearly he had read Acts 17:26, 27) he pled for unity in a belief that they would not have to fight their battles alone, but instead they would be helped by the God of their faith. Pleading with those under the sound of his voice to *understand* that actually war had already begun, he insisted that his fellow countrymen were waiting in the fields for the sound of the "charge" trumpet. He classified retreat as submission and slavery, and suggested that the congress not sit idly by, but instead he called for war—the only solution that would bring the sweet fragrance of freedom from chains and slavery. Give me liberty or death!

Little more than a year following his un-paralleled presentation and after much bloodshed, the thirteen colonies that fought for our freedoms declared independence from the Kingdom of Great Britain on July 4, 1776. Through a process of events and legal documentation, this great country became the United States of America. Patrick Henry deserves the most credit and thanks for his righteous courage and persuasive passion that gave us our inalienable rights.

Through several administrations, the United States has not had a leader that thought like Patrick Henry thought. In fact, America has had no leaders—not in Congress, or the Supreme Court, or in the White House, or in the majority of justice systems across our land. There has been no one with Mr. Henry's *understanding* of leadership. Instead there has been a quest for political correctness, and capitulation to peers, as well as other individuals and entities demanding benefits in return for support. (Note: We hope to see the change promised under the Trump Administration.)

Mr. Henry's unrivaled speech should be required study for both natural born citizens and all those that were not born here. The true American that reads it will shed tears of pride for his patriotism and the patriotism of the countrymen of his time. Others will shed tears of regret at the loss of patriotism in many of our present countrymen.

John Stuart Mill (1806-1873) was a political philosopher and economist, with a logical *understanding* of war and why we fight: *"War is an ugly thing, but not the ugliest of things. The decayed and degraded state of moral and patriotic feeling, which thinks that nothing is worth war, is much worse. The person who has nothing for which he is willing to fight, nothing which is more important than his own personal safety, is a miserable creature and has no chance of being free unless made and kept so by the exertions of better men than himself."*

AMERICA AT THE CROSSROADS

"From one man, He created all the nations throughout the whole earth. He decided beforehand when they should rise and fall and He determined their boundaries. His purpose was for the nations to seek after God and perhaps feel their way toward Him and find Him" (Acts 17:26-27 NLT).

Every American should desire to take a close look at our country and determine whether they believe that God has decided the time is right for her to fall or if she can still be salvaged through repentance. America is standing at a crossroad where one sign says, *"Righteousness shall prevail"* and the other one says, *"Gimmie all you've got."* Where the Bible encourages truth and teaching others to fish to feed themselves, many prefer to receive subsidies paid for by the taxes of hard-working individuals with capitalistic integrity rather than making their own contribution to our national economy and workforce. Please *understand* that I am not referring to the disabled, the elderly, or those who have beaten down doors looking for work and yet can't get hired because they don't fit into a particular mold designed by an employer, or by a transformed society now unrecognizable to them—those that must get reeducated to learn today's new technology. I am speaking of an attitude of self-righteousness and entitlement that sets apart those who prefer to "take" from those who prefer to "earn." The Lord says everyone should do his fair share of work or he should not eat.

"One further order we must give you in the name of our Lord Jesus Christ: 'don't associate with the brother whose life is undisciplined, and who despises the teaching we gave him. You know well that we ourselves are your examples here, and that our lives among you were never undisciplined. We did not eat anyone's food without paying for it. In fact we toiled and labored night and day to avoid being the slightest expense to any of you. This was not because we had no right to ask our necessities of you, but because we wanted to set you an example. When we were actually with you we gave you this principle to work on: "If a man will not work, he shall not eat." Now we hear that you have some

among you living quite undisciplined lives, never doing a stroke of work, and busy only in other people's affairs. Our order to such men, indeed our appeal by the Lord Jesus Christ, is to settle down to work and eat the food they have earned themselves" (2 Thessalonians 3:6-12).

Such insight and straight from the Bible—if we want to eat, we must work! Where a person's character should prevail, their background and environment should be irrelevant, yet as a society we are sliding down a cliff of economic decline shaped in part by laziness and greed that will propel our nation into the worst depression in history if we don't change our thinking and conform totally to the biblical standards of good stewardship of God's blessings. That means everyone, not just a few.

The division in our country's moral character is unbelievably widespread, and drastically affects the church. As you will see in part two, our Christian society has mocked and rejected God's moral and ethical code, which He established as our guide to live by and He will not always remain silent. However, many from the pulpits and most elected officials do keep silent; that is, until they want to rule against God. Where moral law ends, tyranny begins. Moral law is an absolute principle defined by the criteria for correct action whether conceived as a divine (God inspired) ordinance, or is a truth based on unquestionable and responsible human reasoning. In 1980 the highest court in our land ruled that the Ten Commandments should be removed from public sites and from our classrooms *"lest the children should look at them and learn from them"* yet we have a Bible that tells us to never relent in teaching them to our children. Unfortunately we have a nation that forbids school children from even seeing or learning them. In June 2015, The U.S. Supreme court ruled in favor of same-sex marriage, destroying biblical marriage in America. It is now mandatory that school children tolerate all lifestyles—even those God opposes.

When the U.S. presidential election of 2012 ended,

commentators scrutinized the election results for more than twenty-four hours. Their responses ranged from speechlessness to disbelief to bewilderment. Though several possible reasons for the conservative loss were presented not one commentator could accurately evaluate why an unqualified and highly prejudiced non-Christian president was reelected to the highest office in a nation built exclusively on Christian principles and a strong work ethic. Americans from all categories of life as well as the leaders of our nation—regardless of spiritual beliefs, if any at all, and regardless of their ethics—showed that they had compromised the biblical requirements for living and for leading a nation. In a 2012 speech, Pastor Franklin Graham said it quite clearly; *"America has turned its back on God. We see people everywhere who claim to know God but do not live for Him. The only thing that will turn this nation around will be a spiritual awakening, sparked and fanned into flame by the Holy Spirit of God."* Today few Christians have eyes to see or ears to hear and are able to agree on what the Bible really says about how we are to live. How can God bless us with a "spiritual awaking" that will turn us around as a nation if we are unwilling to make a choice to correctly divide the Scriptures?

Our leaders have chosen to lead based upon their own thinking instead of seeking God for guidance. Our lawmakers, justices, and representatives have led our country without seeking God for so long they can no longer recognize a godly principle and in so doing they have danced deeply with a devil they may not even believe exists. It seems impossible to identify a principle of life within our society that offers recognizable values—those that are necessary to build a spiritually effective, cooperative and cohesive society of people.

When we must debate and get a court ruling on whether to fly the American flag anywhere in our country, when the majority must capitulate to a minority of people who hate God and want the rest of us to toss Him out, when our children are forced to remove jewelry or clothing that speaks of Christ or displays the American flag, and businesses are forced to perform a service for those they have chosen not to, we are truly a nation in trouble. When our Christian heritage and faith have been pushed aside and forced to take a back seat to any and all other religions because it has become offensive (though it was the governing foundation that gave the freedoms to those who wish to do away with it) then we are truly a nation in trouble.

When sexual promiscuity, sexual abuse, sexual slavery and human trafficking are at an all-time high for our country, and genuine Christianity at an all-time low, when the murder of babies both inside and outside the womb has become as simple and easy as flushing human waste down the sewer, we are truly a nation in trouble—in trouble with whom? God!

What can we look forward to when the majority of our elected officials don't seem to care what happens to America? How can we cling to hope, which expels despair? Residents of a nation should appreciate and praise the place that provides for them, and makes an effort to protect them, and offers opportunities that will fulfill their desires. Residents of a nation should be proud of their homeland and individually and corporately work to preserve it. Every resident, including representatives and governing authorities must purposefully ask not what their country can do for them, but what can they do to make their country better. We all must ask how we can help build a nation of united individuals with the same goal—to protect and preserve our infrastructure and the good that resulted because of it not only for the generations that occupy it now but also the generations of the future. That can only be done when there is agreement about the moral code to use as a guide. The only way an agreement will work is if the citizens and the governing authorities together respect that code.

THE DEATH OF CHRIST IN AMERICA

"When the godly are in authority, the people rejoice. But when the wicked are in power, they groan" (Proverbs 29:2 NLT).

The 2012 election results were not about who could repair and rebuild a divided nation with a broken economy and morals; they weren't about men verses women, political party gridlock or black verses white; they were about the death of Christ in America—a transparent disregard, and full rejection of the Lord we had agreed to honor more than 200 years ago. The evidence lies in the DNC's vote on whether or not to include the name of God in the party's political phrases.

The election campaigns did not offer a Patrick Henry style faith in a God that would never leave us but rather would help us; instead there was a vote as to whether God was worthy of being included in our nations politics, and certainly not worthy to call upon as our guide to wisdom. If American Christians don't fight for the right to Christian freedoms, we will find ourselves becoming numb to the power of the almighty God and then capitulating to a ruler that will take us places we don't want to go!

A Barna Group article dated October 31, 2006 and titled *A New Generation of Adults Bends Moral and Sexual Rules to Their Liking*, reveals that our nation's moral attitude is in a meltdown. People have difficulty agreeing on what a "moral" life should look like or how to make ethical decisions or define moral standards.

The Buster generation (born between 1965-1980) and the pre-buster or Baby-Boomer (born between 1945 and 1964) are divided in 16 different areas of moral and sexual behavior. The Buster group is less moral according to the traditional term. They are twice as likely to have viewed sexually explicit movies or videos, two and a half times more likely to report having had a sexual encounter outside of marriage, and three times more likely to have viewed sexually graphic content online.

Compared with half of older adults, more than two-thirds of

the Buster generation said that cohabitation (outside marriage) and sexual fantasies are morally acceptable behaviors and almost half of Busters believed that sexual relationships between people of the same sex are acceptable, compared with one quarter of older adults.

Busters are more likely to use illegal drugs, get drunk, be less civil or patient, use profanity in public, say mean things about others behind their back, tell a lie, get revenge for a transgression, steal, and physically fight or abuse someone. Busters are ten times more likely than older adults to download or trade music online illegally. The only areas where young and old were indistinguishable were that both age groups were equally likely to give someone "the finger" while driving, smoke cigarettes, buy a lottery ticket and place a bet or gamble. Busters and the older generation were equally compatible on three particular issues: accepting abortion, the "F" word on broadcast television, and divorce as no sin.

Two-thirds of those over age 40 said humans should examine God's principles to determine what is right and wrong morally, but less than half of Busters felt this way. Instead, nearly half of Busters said that ethics and morals are based on "what is right for the person." But the Bible says *"there is a way which seems right to a man, but its end is the way of death."* (Proverbs 14:12 – NASB) It also says that we are not to lean on our own *understanding*.

The percentages for born again Christians of all age groups interviewed by The Barna Group, did not fare much better in their moral and ethical behavior when compared to the Word of God. So, what does all this mean for America?

According to the Barna Group president, David Kinnaman, *"The morality of Busters comes from a very different background where Baby-Boomers took moral experimentation to new heights; a time when divorce, crime, single-parent households, and suicide were much more prevalent while Busters grew up. Busters now live in a world where such experimentation is the norm, not the exception. Busters are more disconnected, individualized, and have a less trusting spin on morality."*

DANCING WITH THE DEVIL

Kinnaman says, *"Young adults do not want to hear on-the-stage monologues about moral regulations* (such as this book). *To earn access to their hearts and minds, you have to understand each person's unique background, identity, and doubts, and must tangibly model a biblical lifestyle for them beyond the walls of the church."* How will Busters explain their anti-God demands to Him when they are called to account for their deeds as the Bible says we all will? Parenthesis added

Kinnaman also reported that *"it is striking to see sexual behaviors and attitudes that were* (once) *uncommon now becoming part of the accepted, mainstream experience of young people."* He added, *"We expect to see this mindset of sexual entitlement translate into increased appetites for pornography, unfiltered acceptance of sexual themes and content in media, and continued dissolution of marriages due to infidelity."* Kinnaman is concerned that *"a sexually unrestrained society will continue to lead to immoral scandals in government, sexual abuse by clergy, and sexually oriented school violence."* Thus far in America, he is right on all counts! In the ten years since Kinnaman's publication his predictions on sexual behaviors and attitudes are distinct. Many colleges and universities have serious rape issues and sexual indiscretion among clergy is at an all-time high. Parenthesis added.

He added that *"young adults are deaf to the same old complaints and cautions typically offered up by church leaders, whether those conditions are biblically accurate or not. Busters have created their own music, language, media, technology and relational networks.* (This explains why it is difficult for anyone over 45 to get a job today—the two ways of thinking and communicating are worlds apart separated only by a few years) *For Christians to connect with Busters requires fresh ideas and connecting points to help young adults deal with overwhelming amounts of sexually charged media. The strategies that affected Boomers are falling flat among Busters. We need thoughtful means of intervention and discussion, a new emphasis on biblical counseling, and meaningful forms of accountability."* Parenthesis added

Is it any wonder that many of today's churches whose secular themes of "anything goes" and "seeker friendly" messages advocating "tolerance" of all lifestyles—it doesn't matter what you believe, and "God just loves you so much He will tolerate anything your heart desires"—has become so popular? It is designed to reach the age group identified in The Barna Group Survey and anyone else hating accountability and personal sacrifice. It has no reverence for a Holy God and re-enforces the "freedom movement" of the Busters. These statistics are clear evidence of our society's growing disdain for God and His moral code for our country.

THE MILLENNIAL INVASION

Drastic social changes don't end with the Busters. Rising Millennia's—those born between approximately 1980 and 2000 aren't fond of tradition either. Having been indoctrinated by cable television, the internet, satellite radio, and movies that leave nothing to be imagined because everything is clearly visible, they are now positioned to take charge of their media given rights to the final level of their demands.

Recognized in the November 12, 2001 issue of *Newsweek*—as documented in the May 2013 issue of *Time Magazine*—in general, Millennia's are the children of Busters. Many are described as "wealth" minded, with little interest in politics or environmental issues, and are referred to as "Trophy Kids," a trend in competitive sports. They have great expectations of entitlement; participation instead of endurance is enough to gain rewards. The entitlement attitude gives way to concern for their future success as they may change jobs often due to disappointing expectations in the workplace. They are the most technologically savvy of all generations, and their sense of idealism gives them a false confidence that they can change the world. They are the ones most written about today and the ones getting the majority of jobs because they are young and technologically adept. They get jobs even when there is established concern about their ability to do the work and a faithfulness to job commitment.

They grew up witnessing and experiencing change: family break-ups, family moves, church change, technological changes, drastic moral changes, as well as racial and ethnic changes. They have been programed to accept everything and every change because they believe the world will be better for it. Though the majority claims to believe in the Bible, they are not likely to read it or be involved in organized religion, and they are skeptical of religious institutions, however they are quick to give Eastern religions a try because to them, their "Christian" family didn't represent true Christianity as defined in the Bible and they had become disenchanted with it. This is the generation that will be leading our country through a time when more than 50 percent of Americans want true Christianity eradicated. With the Millennia's views on the Bible, morality and self-satisfaction, what can we expect life in America to look like in 20 years?

We must realize that our Christian heritage and our rights are in a battle for survival in our own country and against our own people. Family members are divided drastically both spiritually and politically, and we must find a way to deal with that issue. It matters not if you are a pre-Buster, a Buster, or a Millennial, if you are playing church—attending for any reason other than seeking Jesus Christ and if you are looking for a pathway to heaven without Christ or one that does not include the moral code as defined in the Bible, I encourage you to rethink your purpose. Jesus said, *"I am the way, the truth, and the life; no man* (or woman) *cometh to the Father but by me" (John 14:6 KJV)*. But He also said, *"If ye love me, keep my commandments" (John 14:15 KJV)*.

The Scriptures tell us *"you can enter God's Kingdom only by the narrow gate. The highway to hell is broad and its gate is wide for the many that choose that way. But the gateway to life is very narrow and the road is difficult, and only a few ever find it" (Matthew 7:13, 14 NLT)*.

If we enter the Kingdom by way of Jesus Christ, we can only do so through a born again heartfelt obedience to Him and His statutes. So, what does the Scripture, "the road is difficult" really mean? We are all going to be judged according to our deeds, whether they are good or bad. When we stand before the Great Judge of all people, He will not judge us based on how bad our home life was or how pressured we were by our peers to individualize ourselves and do our own thing, refusing to acknowledge His moral code. When it comes to each person's accountability to his or her own actions, the Lord will not acquit anyone because they rejected Him due to their world being upside down or their need to do things their own way because of their spiritual indifference. He will look at the heart of each person, and see if there was genuine love for Him and a dedicated willingness to walk in repentance, and obedience in relationship with Him (See Chapter 11).

Difficult? Of course it is difficult! Especially when our nature is riddled with selfishness and sin, and the enemy who hates God's children is increasing his efforts to convince us we don't need Christ; and, we live in an ever-increasing variety of cultural beliefs that don't necessarily recognize God's principles. But regardless, each of us must make a choice about how we will live; we must test our ability to obey God by standing on our feet and running from temptation; we must endorse and live by the Scriptures—the instruction manual we must turn to when we are challenged in an area of secularism and conviction.

SPEAKING UP FOR THE DEFENSELESS

"Speak up for those who cannot speak for themselves; ensure justice for those being crushed. Yes, speak up for the poor and the helpless, and see that they get justice" (Proverbs 31:8-9 NLT).

Isn't something similar written on our Statue of Liberty? Christians are to speak up for the unborn, the poor, the crippled, the handicapped, the orphaned, and the ignorant susceptible to overbearing treatment by the powerful or highly educated that have not attained an ethical or moral integrity. In the 1968 movie *The Green Beret's*, John Wayne's Colonel character tried to comfort a young

DANCING WITH THE DEVIL

South Vietnamese orphan anxiously awaiting the return of the U.S. soldier that had befriended him. After learning that his comrade had died in battle the child asked what would happen to him now. He had no one to take care of him. The Colonel replied, *"You let me worry about that. You are what this* (war) *is all about."* Parentheses added.

America has often fulfilled those Scriptures that instruct us to ensure justice for those being crushed, to speak up for the poor and helpless and see that they get justice. Christians who believe in what the Bible tells us to be right or wrong are to fight for those being crushed by a system of law or government that has no respect for human life. We are not to remain silent. One day we may need a courageous person or country to fight for us.

Our Constitution and Bill of Rights were fought for, and blood was shed to protect them, and a majority voted them into existence. They were established to allow us full access to our inalienable rights. What does that mean? It means that our civil rights cannot be challenged, cannot be forfeited, cannot be denied, and cannot be disputed. They are to be set in stone and remain incontrovertible—in other words, they cannot be questioned! When they are, the offender—whether it is the justice system, the government, or a citizen—is dancing with the devil in the same way Christians dance with the devil when they misrepresent the Word of God. To change or question or declare impotent something that was established in the best interest of the people—whether it is God's Word for how we are to live as His children, or a system of governance that was based on His Word—is to put in place a "paradigm shift" on morals and ethics that will surely lead to a fully broken society and a fallen nation.

Just a few years before America became a nation in 1776, the colonies experienced a time of "great awakening." A remarkable theologian and philosopher named Jonathan Edwards preached sermons he believed would produce a new "sense of the heart" in the citizens. His desire was to promote godliness that would deter spiritual indifference, and help people repent of specific sins and embrace the gospel by faith. His great sermon, *Sinners in the Hands of an Angry God* caused many people to respond with true repentance. Profoundly moved, a large number cried out begging to *understand* how they could be saved.

At the time of Edwards' message, many nations were experiencing a crisis of some kind. England had industry related growing pains; Ireland and Germany were suffering under warfare and famine. European migration to British North America was overwhelming, creating an embattled frontier and changing the normal way of life for everyone—men, women and children. Vast differences in spiritual views, morals, and ethics played a huge role in the controversy. People were coming from countries where they had no religious freedoms and where life was dictated to them. In this new land we were fighting to establish a standard of life where all could be free, based upon a documented respect for one another. But the rule of human nature is that unless you walk a mile in someone else's shoes, you cannot *understand* what they have experienced. An influx of people, and harsh conditions destabilized our culture and brought about social chaos and confusion. Edwards cared deeply for the people and wanted to see spiritual order. He cautioned that the devil would use men's imaginations to produce irrational behavior. Today it is easy to see Edwards' caution being fulfilled!

The last two paragraphs of his speech, admonished men, women, and children of all ages who were hanging over the pit of hell to listen to the loud call of God's Word. He said that, *"when people neglect their souls they are in great danger of being given up to a hardness of heart and blindness of mind that if they don't repent, they will curse the day they were born when they do eventually see the wrath of God against those who do evil."* One Internet blogger wrote: *"This sermon is without a doubt . . . the greatest sermon ever preached in America. If Brother Jonathan preached this to the professing church today, he would be stoned to death because there is no 'best life now' stuff* (in it). *How desperately we need this kind of preaching in the apostate church today."* Parenthesis added. Edwards was a profound theologian, and a minister with great pastoral sensitivity. No matter the different opinions people may have of him, his passions and works reflect his dedication to loving people and God's Word. When I read Edwards' sermon, I feel motivated by the power in his words. The strength he uses to express himself, his passion for people's souls and for the Word of God is both frightening and invigorating. Primarily though, I am encouraged by his words because they help me remember that I have internal power that enables me to maintain my hope by seeking God in all things. *Sinners in the Hands of an Angry God, July 8, 1741 by Jonathan Edwards (1703-1758) Enfield, Connecticut* This great sermon is recommended reading.

As in the days of Jonathon Edwards, America is once again experiencing an influx of numerous nationalities whose environment and inherited beliefs and cultures are far removed from those our Founding Fathers used to build this nation. These immigrants have no idea what America has always stood for. They are clueless as to why they thought America *was* able to offer them the fullness of freedom they sought. With credit given to government greed, America is no longer in a position to fulfill the "freedom" dreams of illegal immigrants as thousands continue crossing our borders, infiltrating our system, and bringing with them all sorts of negative personal issues, not to mention the unexpected and unprepared for complications their presence here will inflict on our society. The invitation on our Statue of Liberty does not invite such an illegal influx of people. The invitation was meant to invite people to join us after being approved by a system that functions in the best interest of our nation and in the best interest of those wishing to enter.

But putting those things aside, what will any anti-American/anti-Christian views they may bring with them do to an already spiritually and politically damaged nation as the statistics show we are? Is our government building a powerhouse of individuals who will eventually become our military composed of people from many nations that will have no patriotism for America, or any compassion for the people who are already its citizens? We cannot discount this possibility. Our government's Selective Service System's mandate to register says that *"all male U.S. citizens and immigrants, documented and undocumented, residing in the U.S. and its territories must register if they are age 18 through 25."* The registration can be obtained at your local Post Office. Being a documented U.S. citizen is not a requirement for serving in our military; all that is required is to live in the United States. What can we expect from this influx of a new generation of people—primarily young men—from a culture most Americans know little about and whose language most of us can't translate? Revelation 6:2 says that the anti-Christ will be a mighty military leader of an army he will create out of many nations. It is estimated that between 11.5 and 20 million people live illegally in America. Presently, our government could build an army of people from different backgrounds and many nations, without ever drafting a natural born citizen. The U.S. government allows immigrants to attain U.S. citizenship by joining and serving in our military.

Is it safe to say that our lack of moral and political discretion is moving us forward into the kind of darkness that Dave Hunt and T.A. McMahan spoke about in their 1985 book, *The Seduction of Christianity*; or which David Wilkerson wrote about in his 1974 book *The Vision*; or which Paul Harvey spoke of in his 1965 speech, *"If I Were The Devil"*, or which Paul McGuire speaks about in his book, *Mass Awakening*?

The majority of U.S. citizens—including Christians who are supposed to be informed—are so far removed spiritually, emotionally, and educationally from what these inspired and prophetic men spoke of, they will be overwhelmed and completely surprised when complete lawlessness is allowed to prevail. Everywhere, people will be crying out, "Why didn't someone tell us what was coming?" Someone did, but few listened.

DANCING WITH THE DEVIL

HOW TO ENGULF THE EARTH IN DARKNESS

Paul Harvey was a great broadcaster gifted with wit, common sense and *understanding* about the condition of our country and the benefits of being a Godly citizen. Harvey wrote a speech about what he would do if he were the devil and wanted to engulf the entire earth in darkness. His gripping speech aired April 3, 1965.

IF I WERE THE DEVIL – by Paul Harvey

If I were the Devil . . . I mean, if I were the Prince of Darkness, I would of course, want to engulf the whole earth in darkness. I would have a third of its real estate and four-fifths of its population, but I would not be happy until I had seized the ripest apple on the tree, so I should set about however necessary to take over the United States. I would begin with a campaign of whispers. With the wisdom of a serpent, I would whisper to you as I whispered to Eve: "Do as you please." "Do as you please." To the young, I would whisper, "The Bible is a myth." I would convince them that man created God instead of the other way around. I would confide that what is bad is good, and what is good is "square." In the ears of the young marrieds, I would whisper that work is debasing, that cocktail parties are good for you. I would caution them not to be extreme in religion, in patriotism, in moral conduct. And the old, I would teach to pray. I would teach them to say after me: "Our Father, which art in Washington" . . . If I were the devil, I'd educate authors in how to make lurid literature exciting so that anything else would appear dull and uninteresting. I'd threaten TV with dirtier movies and vice versa. And then, if I were the devil, I'd get organized. I'd infiltrate unions and urge more loafing and less work, because idle hands usually work for me. I'd peddle narcotics to whom I could. I'd sell alcohol to ladies and gentlemen of distinction. And I'd tranquilize the rest with pills. If I were the devil, I would encourage schools to refine young intellects but neglect to discipline emotions . . . let those run wild. I would designate an atheist to front for me before the highest courts in the land and I would get preachers to say, "She's right." With flattery and promises of power, I could get the courts to rule what I construe as against God and in favor of pornography, and thus, I would evict God from the courthouse, and then from the school house, and then from the houses of Congress and then, in His own churches I would substitute psychology for religion, and I would deify science because that way men would become smart enough to create super weapons but not wise enough to control them. If I were Satan, I'd make the symbol of Easter an egg, and the symbol of Christmas, a bottle. If I were the devil, I would take from those who have and I would give to those who wanted, until I had killed the incentive of the ambitious. And then, my police state would force everybody back to work. Then, I could separate families, putting children in uniform, women in coalmines, and objectors in slave camps. In other words, if I were Satan, I'd just keep on doing what he's doing (American Broadcaster Paul Harvey, 1918 – 2009).

Harvey's idea about how the devil's evil tactics affect our nation as a whole is fully accurate and as we can see, much of it has come true.

WHY DO WE FIGHT?

Christians fight against evil to help salvage souls for heaven, and a Christian nation fights wars to remove evil that would harm its people and destroy their religious and civil liberties. But the question troubling many Americans today is "how do I know what is right and what is wrong?" As I mentioned in chapter 1, William J. Bennett offers convincing facts on how divided America is about what is and is not evil. Bennett says that U.S. citizens were intellectually and morally unprepared for 9/11. People he called "sensible and patriotic" spoke out against the U.S., and questioned whether

America had done something wrong to provoke the attacks on the World Trade Center.

Bennett gave no indication that American dissenters thought the 9/11 attacks might have been the actions of people who hate the God many Americans worship. However, he does believe these questions *"bespoke a deep ignorance not only about the rest of the world, but more urgently and much more disturbingly about America."* And, Bennett says, *"It bespoke an even deeper want for clarity about the difference between good and evil."* He is absolutely right. No one can deny that our country is divided about what constitutes a *moral code* that is best for everyone.

If people don't *understand* the moral code established by one who is fully moral, (God) how will they know they can fight for something better than what they have? If they don't know why they should stand, they won't stand. If they don't *understand* why they should fight for religious freedom, or against evil, they will have nothing that motivates them to fight, so they won't fight and people that won't fight are easily engineered.

As a nation, we must be able to recognize our enemy, and *understand* why he chooses to hurt our people, and what he hopes to accomplish by doing so. Does he hope to punish us for believing something that is contrary to his belief? Does he hope to punish us because he is jealous of our capitalistic opportunities? Or does he wish to control us for the sheer pleasure of conquest—to tell us how to live? The happenings in Europe, before and during WWI and WWII, offer proof that people do try to control and then destroy others for the power and prestige it gives them as well as for beneficial reasons, such as using them for work slaves. Kitty Werthmann, whom you read about in chapter 3, has traveled to many countries outside the United States. She says that people in other countries are deeply jealous of American prosperity and freedom.

Why *do* we fight? We fight to preserve our every essence of freedom from tyranny! And unless we *understand* what tyranny is— cruel and oppressive government—and what precedes it, (how we get to a tyrannical state) we won't know when to fight. Our churches are mandated to educate us about God and the nature of man, and our schools about history. We are to microscopically analyze the findings to see which parts of history we don't want to repeat, and which part of human nature we don't want to emulate or have power over us. Though parents are to have the primary role in educating their children on these most important issues, neither they, nor the church or the schools are doing a good job with their part. We must get educated, and *understand* what is happening to our country and our people. In the eyes of God there is no separation of religion and government, as both are ordained by Him and designed to protect the people. Nowhere in the Bible do we see a teaching on the importance of math or technology but we see many teachings that tell us to know history and God's moral code. Yet in our schools today, teaching His moral code is not allowed, and the teaching of biblical and world history is practically extinct. Our American freedoms are eroding at a rate that is incomprehensible. Change is happening so rapidly I struggle to close the pages of this manuscript due to continual updates.

    Christians who respect the Scriptures but who also operate businesses in the wedding and hospitality industry are now being forced by our government to violate their principles or be penalized or close their doors. Until recently, I was in business as a wedding consultant/caterer, and owned a vacation rental property but I no longer offer these services because my freedom to choose clients based on my religious values has been removed and the government dictates what I can and cannot do. Presently, I am a Christian substitute teacher but I am prohibited from speaking about God in the classroom. I have Christian friends who are photographers, florists, counselors, and teachers with great concerns about their future business. When I began advertising for wedding business, the very first call came from a gay couple. Immediately, I was faced with an important decision based on my spiritual beliefs. Fortunately, I was spared that conflict as they never called back but other businesses have been forced to decide and they have paid a high price for their decision.

In July 2014, the American Family Association distributed an email with a list of Christian businesses that were forced by the U.S. government to perform services for those they chose not to. Penalties for disobedience were inflicted and in some of the cases, the businesses had to close.

A Christian photographer in New Mexico was fined $6700 for politely declining to photograph a lesbian commitment ceremony. The Supreme Court upheld the fine.

A Christian baker in Oregon faced both civil and criminal penalties, including jail time, for politely declining to bake a cake for a gay wedding ceremony. Her business has closed.

The Washington state attorney general sued a Christian florist, Baronelle Stutzmanb, for politely declining to prepare an arrangement for a gay wedding ceremony.

Fox Sports Southwest fired Craig James after only one day on the job for expressing his support for natural marriage while he was a candidate for the United States Senate.

Jennifer Keeton was dismissed from the counseling program at Augusta State University for her religious reservations about the homosexual lifestyle. The same country that gave her freedom to speak also took away her freedom to speak.

The Wildflower Inn in Vermont was fined $30,000 and forced to close its wedding reception business after politely declining to host a lesbian ceremony.

Ms. Jillian John-Charles was dismissed from a doctoral program in education at Roosevelt University for expressing in class her belief that homosexuals aren't born gay.

In a 2014 report, Donald and Beverly Knapp, owners of The Hitching Post Wedding chapel in Idaho were being sued for refusing to perform a gay marriage ceremony. The Knapps confessed that they would close the doors to their 95-year business before violating their commitment to God's moral codes. (Update: On June 29, 2015, the United States Supreme Court ruled that all States in America must recognize and honor marriage between two people of the same gender. If you are an American Christian your freedom of choice, religion, and speech are gone!)

In 2013, The **National Health Interview Survey**, which is the government's premier tool for annually assessing Americans' health and behaviors, found that 1.6 percent of adults self-identify as gay or lesbian, and 0.7 percent consider themselves bisexual. That is less than 3 percent of our population. What's wrong with the rest of us—more than 97 percent of 316.1 million people, and our government, which is now clearly non-Christian—that less than 3 percent of our population is telling the rest us how we must believe and live.

I call upon sleeping Christians to awaken and pray! These rulings come from a government that built a supreme law of the land, which guarantees its citizens their religious freedom based on the moral code as outlined in the Holy Bible. Yet, it has turned its back on that code and now supports that which we Christians oppose, forcing us to do something that is highly contrary to our convictions. In this instance, our Bill of Rights no longer protects us. Our right to refuse service to anyone based on our moral principle is now removed to favor those whose beliefs don't conform to moral principles. We are being met with a challenge! What will we stand for or against? Will we speak out in favor of moral clarity and our right to honor morality? Our forefathers did! Read the documents they implemented and the speeches they gave. Americans who think as individualists—live and let live—without respecting a moral foundation for their individualism, can be easily changed into socialists. These are people who don't respect the Bible as their foundation for living. In the Scriptures, God continually challenges us to *"get wisdom and understanding"* of His moral character. And, He cautions us: "Woe unto you who call evil good and good evil." A day of His wrath is coming!

The American Family Association cautions that the professions being challenged are ones that American Christians will eventually have to give up, or submit to violating their beliefs by capitulating to a minority view. That which was once illegal in our country because it was evil is now legal and called good and acceptable, and when violated, the morally upright are persecuted. Without a distinct line between good and evil, those who have no reverence for the one true God will eventually rule the entire nation. Unless God intervenes, every Christian will become a slave to the ungodly just as the children of Israel were slaves to the unbelieving Egyptians.

In God's eyes, sin is an evil act against Him. Color, race, culture, gender, or the type of sin of an individual has no bearing on how God feels about what He defines as sin. Regardless, He gave every human free will to choose a lifestyle of sin or one free of sin. They can choose to stay in their evil behavior for as long as they like and God will be displeased but He won't force them out. But neither does He commune with them. When those who object to Christian principles lobby to have their anti-Christian behavior change the lives of those who abhor it and then mandate that the government and others uphold their desires against their fellow citizens, then they are creating a condition of tyranny for those individuals. To that, we must object. Every innocent child who has not yet heard of his or her option to choose the Christ that saves should be given that opportunity. That is why the purpose of the church was to be the safe place where children could go and hear biblical truth. If Christian pastors and teachers can't or won't speak out against sin, many children may never know that there is a Jesus whose moral code they are required to obey in order to enter heaven.

A NEED FOR NATIONAL REFORM AND RENEWED PATRIOTISM

Our nation is in position for reformation—to be returned to its original state and purpose minus the shameful part of our history—culture and race wars, and persecution. However, reform won't happen unless Christians are willing to speak out for freedom as Patrick Henry did in his famous speech before the Continental Congress in 1775. And, based on the rule of morality as outlined in The Barna Group survey, we will not get reform until there is a majority change in viewpoint about morals, regardless of race or culture.

Reform comes only when people of all ages, including those old enough to vote, attend college, and serve in the military, and those of very old age stop all they are doing that is self-indulged, and get educated about the topics—the most important one being our world history since the beginning of time and the history of America since its foundation. The findings must be compared to where we are today. Afterwards a stand must be taken to support the right thing, regardless of race or culture or offense.

Reform comes when we *understand* every aspect of the supreme law of the land, and why we fight to uphold that law; it comes when we recognize how far our government has deviated from those truths that we hold dear, and when we are willing to speak out for the purpose of liberty and justice. As American citizens we have a moral and civil obligation to *understand* and speak fluent English, whether natural born or not. We owe to our forefathers an attitude of respect and a willingness to learn American (and world) history with an unbiased mind, and dedicate our heart to respecting our history by the way we live. We must be willing to confront any government—including our own—that trespasses our rights to the freedoms our forefathers shed their blood to secure for us. Reform and renewed patriotism will not come until people *understand* what

America truly stands for and decide to make a difference by honoring their heritage.

There is plenty of evidence that millions of Americans still have faith in the patriotism that is owed our country and many still have faith in God. But does our willingness to help people whose culture is foreign to our supreme law and our biblical principles provide the opportunity those people need to adversely influence our original way of life? Probably! Countless people come to America introducing and sometimes demanding change that promotes tolerance, relativism, lawlessness, and godlessness, which may have been a standard of life for them in the country from which they wanted to be liberated. No doubt the patriotic among us are a compassionate people, wanting good for all mankind, much like former President Woodrow Wilson believed (see Chapter 3 page 90) but unless we are sensible and demand accountability, the side effect of "good for all mankind" can easily endorse that which numbs the mind about a proper moral code.

Our nation has an influx of nationalities that doesn't endorse the God Americans willingly honored when we established our country. Further, these people don't *understand* how much blood was shed so that every American could be free from a totalitarian regime. Consequently our country is divided on genuine patriotism. To add to this dilemma, our natural born citizens have deviated drastically from a godly moral code, and this too, divides us. Under such conditions a nation cannot stand united but instead it becomes "untied." People that we allow to cross our borders illegally everyday don't *understand* America's original system of government. They don't share in the traditional American loyalty. They have no experience or education on how we became a place where so many want to live and in many cases, want to change to something it isn't and has never been. If they can't *understand* why patriotism is important they won't support it. If our educational system loses respect for American patriotism and refuses to teach it, newcomers will never gain an appreciation for it.

Separating our nation's people into two territories and establishing two governments—one based on a strict moral code from the Bible and one based on humanism (which is human based morality that leads to lawlessness)—isn't a good option for a peaceful existence even though it may seem like it. Further, since we are unable to convince a majority to support moral standards, we are hanging in the balance whereby something simply has to tip the scale. The question is when and in which direction. Will it be civil war? We hope not! Maybe a divided nation would be a less tragic solution than war for solving our moral dilemma.

Still, never in our history have we faced so difficult a decision that could carry with it destructive and horrifying consequences for every man, woman and child presently in our country and for all those yet to come. Those who are coming to America to live a better life than they had in their home country, yet have no respect for America in their heart, should *understand* that when America falls, it will fall on us all. The Lord says that the rain falls on the just and the unjust. Therefore, regardless of race or culture or how people got to America it is in everyone's best interest to support her as she was founded, rather than oppose her because to change her will prove to be a colossal disaster for everyone. We all have the responsibility to take a close look at what lies ahead for our nation, because a nation divided against itself cannot stand strong. It will be defeated.

WHAT LIES AHEAD FOR AMERICA?

If America is invaded by foot soldiers, what will happen to our citizens? We suspect that China has military soldiers occupying territory in Mexico about 60 miles south of Laredo, Texas. Are they awaiting an opportunity to invade the U.S.? Is the present invasion of what our leadership calls "displaced children" from Central America an indication of what's coming? These are valid questions to which we must find answers.

DANCING WITH THE DEVIL

According to Judicial Watch, Inc. there are ISIS camps operating approximately eight miles south of the U.S. border in an area known as Anapra, which is situated just west of Ciudad Juárez, in the Mexican state of Chihuahua. Another ISIS cell to the west of Ciudad Juárez, in Puerto Palomas, targets the New Mexico towns of Columbus and Deming for easy access to the United States. In April of 2015, during the course of a joint operation, Mexican Army and federal law enforcement officials discovered documents in Arabic and Urdu, as well as "plans" of Fort Bliss—the sprawling U.S. military installation in El Paso, Texas that houses our army's 1st Armored Division. During the operation, Muslim prayer rugs were recovered along with the documents.

Official reports say that the area is dominated by cartels, which makes it an extremely dangerous and hostile environment for Mexican Army and Federal Police operations. Smuggling groups, such as those called "Coyotes" that are engaged in human trafficking and working for Juárez Cartels help move ISIS terrorists through the desert and across the border between Santa Teresa and Sunland Park, New Mexico. To the east of El Paso and Ciudad Juárez cartel-backed "coyotes" are also smuggling ISIS terrorists through the porous border between Acala and Fort Hancock, Texas. These areas are described as understaffed municipal and county police forces, making them relatively safe-havens for unchecked large-scale drug smuggling, which was ongoing before ISIS targeted the area for exploitation.

Mexico's intelligence sources report that present ISIS intent and activity includes exploiting railways and airport facilities in the vicinity of Santa Teresa, NM—a U.S. port of entry. "Spotters" have situated in the East Potrillo Mountains of New Mexico, an area largely managed by the U.S. Bureau of Land Management. They are there to assist with terrorists border crossing operations, and ISIS reconnaissance of regional universities, the White Sands Missile Range, government facilities in Alamogordo, NM, Fort Bliss, TX, and the electrical power facilities near Anapra and Chaparral, NM.

DANCING WITH THE DEVIL

To add to these grave concerns, several countries are experimenting with electromagnetic pulse weapons or EMP's. One weapon is capable of destroying the power grid in America, which would take about four years to rebuild. Though this weapon doesn't kill people instantly, any hope for survival is downhill due to contamination, disease, starvation, and violence. Many Christian Americans object to a discussion that these things could happen in our beloved America; many object to listening to commentaries on matters of nuclear possibilities aimed at the United States, but the Lord warned His people to be aware of the signs and times.

Paul McGuire is the "Christian's Watchman." Credited as a Syndicated Radio Talk Show Host, Professor of Bible Prophecy at The King's University and Seminary, Van Nuys, CA, Commentator for CNN and Fox News Network, Feature Film Producer, and author of 26 books, McGuire provides a world of important information for those listening.

My first knowledge of McGuire came in January 2011 while I was surfing the Christian Television Networks looking for a biblical teaching that went beyond milk or error. He was speaking on Bible prophecy. Intrigued by his comments, I turned off the TV and went directly to his website where I read several articles, and watched a few of his videos. I then searched the Internet for anything negative I could find about him, but found nothing I believed discredited him.

A year after researching and reading McGuire's newsletters, I purchased his 3-DVD production titled *"Are You Ready,"* and ordered his books *The Warning, The Day the Dollar Died, Are You Ready,* and *Mass Awakening*. For years I had been curious about the end times, Jews and Gentiles, and the war against Israel. McGuire's books cleared up some Bible prophecy I had been unsure about. *Are You Ready*, and *The Day the Dollar Died* contain a world of information that every U.S. citizen and Christian should have knowledge of. His latest book titled, *"Mass Awakening"* is a tough start but I found a true comrade by mid-page eleven. I encourage those truly interested in being better informed about what lies ahead for America to visit his website, paulmcguire.us and discover his work for yourself. I don't believe you will be disappointed but if you find his information a little unbelievable don't judge it negatively until you have done the kind of research and study he has done—thirty years worth. The information I am including here is taken from his book, *The Day the Dollar Died* and is used with permission.

McGuire says that the Bible talks about a coming one world economic system, a one-world government, and a global currency where each person must receive a mark on the right hand or the forehead in order to buy or sell anything. (Most mature Christians are aware of the Scripture in Revelation 13 that speaks of this but many Busters and Millennia's are not) McGuire cautions that this new world system is emerging right in front of our eyes; we are facing one of the world's greatest financial meltdowns while powerful nations are poised to strike at Israel, ushering in an Armageddon style conflict. He tells us that in an "unprecedented" manner, governments of the world, including the U.S., are buying industries in mass to avoid their collapse.

McGuire says that economists call this 'the nationalization of businesses and industries,' but he refers to it as economic socialism in the manner of Karl Marx—the father of Communism who believed that government should own the means of production. He cautions that our economy is being nationalized—a socialistic system that will move us into the one world economy and government that is prophesied about in the Bible. He questions whether the American people are prepared to face the truth about their world; he believes that most folks cannot process being told that they are the product of social engineering; instead they go into mental denial, separating themselves from the facts. McGuire says that a coming financial crisis will dwarf The Great Depression of '29, lead to radical changes in our standard of living—especially for the American middle class—and will raise the standard of living in other nations. Not only will this change affect Americans economically, it will have a devastating emotional affect, which could be overwhelming for many unless they are mentally prepared. As we learned in chapter 2, Evangelist David Wilkerson spoke of this same tragedy in his book, *The Vision*, which was written in 1974.

In McGuire's book, *The Day the Dollar Died*, readers will find facts from credible sources showing that much of what we see in the world is not the result of chance but instead, is part of a long-term plan to create the one-world system, as described above. McGuire believes that the ultimate conspiracy to a one-world system is a spiritual one consisting of people who don't believe in God, that individual lives are of little consequence, and that man must create a world system to solve our great problems.

Like McGuire, I believe there is plenty of evidence for a real God, and a very real devil. The reason for *Dancing with the Devil* is to help Christians *understand* how the devil wants to destroy them. McGuire is showing how the devil wants to use the governments of the world to accomplish his goal and he has not excluded the U.S. Chapter 2 of this book gives details about who the devil is and the rest of this book is to enlighten readers about how he operates in our lives. The struggles of power are between the forces of good and evil—God and Satan—and ultimately, each of us must make a decision about where we stand—whether for God or for Satan. We must awaken to what is and get educated so we don't despair when our luxury world falls apart. I recommend McGuire's books to all who recognize that something very serious is happening and who are weary with concern, wanting to help others. McGuire's research and interpretations offer plausible insight.

Pastor John Hagee, Cornerstone Church, San Antonio, Texas, tells us that three things must happen before the collapse of the dollar. We will see the destruction of our nationalism, patriotism, and the Christian faith. To some degree, we are experiencing these already. He says that afterwards will be the rapture of the saints and then a new one-world monetary system will be put into effect. However, some Christians believe the dollar will break before the rapture happens.

Corrupt leadership divides a government and its people and conditions a nation for a dictatorship like those mentioned in chapter 3. Under such an environment, many Americans will submit to hopeless despair; some will be poised for revolution, which is destructive beyond imagination. If American people and the government will repent of violating God's commands He promises to show mercy, but if there is no repentance, America will experience the wrath of God.

In Deuteronomy 28, the Lord told the Children of Israel that if they fully obeyed Him and kept His commands, He would set them high above all the nations of the world. Then He gave them a long list of blessings He would shower on them for their obedience. God gave His word to the Israelites that if they would avoid evil and not abandon Him, He would bless their towns, fields, crops, children, herds, flocks, fruit and bread, and everything they did wherever they went. He promised to conquer their enemies and fill their storehouses and give rain at the proper time. They would have such abundance the nations of the world would come to them to borrow.

However, God also promised that if they weren't obedient they would be overwhelmed by curses. If His people disobeyed his commands and abandoned Him, He would bring a distant nation against them. This nation whose language they would not *understand*, (because they couldn't translate it) would swoop down like a vulture and would be a fierce and heartless nation that showed no respect for the old and no pity for the young. It would be a nation whose armies would eat the crops they had worked so hard to grow, devour their livestock, and cause them to suffer under constant oppression and harsh treatment. They would go mad because of the tragedy around them. God promised that the foreigners living among them would become stronger and stronger while they became weaker and weaker.

The foreigners would lend money to God's children but His children would not be able to lend to the foreigners. Though God's children were as numerous as the stars in the sky, few would survive because they would not listen to the Lord their God.

After telling of the horror if they refused to obey, the Lord brought hope to His people. In Deuteronomy 30:10-20, He offered them a choice of life or death. But He gave another caution in Deuteronomy 32:39, *"Look now, I myself am He! There is no other God but me! I am the one who kills and gives life; I am the one who wounds and heals; no one can be rescued from my powerful hand!"* (NLT) If we think that God's love protects us from His wrath even when we live sinful lives and don't repent, we should think again. God loved those people yet He was willing to destroy them because of their sin. He will not allow us to sit high and mighty atop a fence and not choose sides. There is plenty of evidence that America is hated throughout the world. Hatred breeds contempt and then metastasizes into the vilest crimes.

A GOOD REPUBLIC FUNCTIONS IN THE LIGHT OF DAY, NOT IN THE BOWELS OF DARKNESS

"A ruler with no understanding will oppress his people, but one who hates corruption will have a long life" (Proverbs 28:16 NLT). The *understanding* spoken of here means to *understand* God's moral code and His statutes, and what He expects of the leaders of nations.

Chapter 13 of the book of Romans tells us to honor and respect the governing authorities over us because they are put there by God to help people know the right thing to do, and that we are to obey their authority. It also tells us that if we as a people are doing what is right, then we will not have to fear our authorities. The Word says we are to submit to these servants of the Lord, do what is right, pay our taxes, and keep a clear conscience.

But what are the people to do when the nation's authorities are not servants of the Lord and they no longer respect the God they are supposed to be serving as the Scripture says, and they begin to oppress the people? What should the righteous ones do when the majority of the nation's people are not doing what is right? For several years now most of our government leaders have fully endorsed America's broken moral code and don't care to correct it. Only a few have been decent role models for young people to emulate as someone to be proud of as the leader of a great Christian nation. Further, the people of America, including Christians have no reverence for God and His Son, Jesus.

No longer does the holder of the highest individual position our country provides—that of Chief Executive and Commander-in-Chief—respect that position or the people but instead declares us as no longer a Christian nation that honors Christ. Through several administrations the position of CE and CIC has become a sanctuary for the purposes and pleasures of those who desecrate the holiness of the Lord of our Bible, and the blood of our founding fathers by debasing their work in their battle to protect the governing rules of our country, which were based on God's Word. As Christians, we are partly at fault for the mentality of those who govern us today because we have sat silent and apathetic for too long, assuming that anyone willing to run for office is principled and smart enough to govern with ethics that benefit the people. Further, several reports say that more than 3 million self-proclaimed Christians didn't vote in the 2012 presidential election. Were they struggling with how to decide between a moderate Mormon candidate and a Muslim candidate? This wasn't a difficult decision for me. Also many people didn't vote because they were uninformed about the issues.

(Update: The elections of November 4, 2014 showed a great movement of the people toward a hope and a plan for a better government and country. However, on Wednesday following the election, commentators and politicians alike believed that conservative women were elected because they had compromised their stance on abortion, calling it an unimportant issue. In one report that I watched, a female Fox News commentator said that the issue of abortion was basically a minor issue that should be traded for much greater concerns like terrorism. Since the 2014 election most of those elected, including the Speaker of the House, proved their impotence in just one year.)

Sadly, we tend to neglect the abuse of moral issues we can't see, such as the beheading and mutilation of a child in its mother's womb, for those atrocities that we can see, such as adult beheadings in the news. Please understand: the all-seeing God sees all terrorism and will judge both the perpetrators and those who assist the perpetrators.

As the leader of our republic, a sitting president has the absolute responsibility to do everything necessary as well as all that is within the power of the office held, to protect and successfully lead with ultimate integrity the citizens of the nation. The leader of a nation has a legal and moral obligation to oppose political tyranny that may be dedicated to the destruction of the will and good of the people—not just those people of a favored culture or cause. This responsibility is founded on fairness and justice. It includes helping and protecting the innocent and defenseless citizens of our own nation as well as other nations who are being tortured and are dying at the hands of wicked dictators or regimes. North Korea's present day Camp 14 comes to mind.

A sitting president has a mandate to protect and honor the Constitution and Bill of Rights of the people he serves, and do what is best for the nation. When the person holding the office does not honor these prerequisites for leadership, and runs the nation by executive order that person is establishing him or herself as a God, and aligning their thoughts and deeds with the mind of the enemy of the God of the people who desire peace and harmony. When the power of the office is not honored, it can be used to bring into the leadership harem government representatives willing to sell their souls for personal recognition. It is also an opportunity for them to become powerful enough that they can easily forget the common sense integrity necessary to do the right thing. Power that is undergirded by control authorizes and supports a divided nation of people. *"Without wise leadership a nation falls; there is safety in having many advisers" (Proverbs 11:14 NLT).*

The Obama Administration was relentless in its attacks on our nation's Christian foundation and our freedom to teach and preach the gospel according to the Holy Bible. The Alliance Defending Freedom is a great resource for Christians needing information about government attacks against their religious freedoms. Wallbuilders.com has built a list of anti-God activities our leadership has committed against our constitution beginning in April 2008. Ann Corcoran's site, www.refugeeresettlementwatch.com offers daily updates on the condition of our country. Dinesh D'Souza has given us invaluable information in his book, *"The Roots of Obama's Rage,"* and we learned a great deal from his movie, *"2016 – Obama's America."* A more recent movie called *"America"* educates every American about their incredible country and was given an A+ grade at its opening in June 2014 and his most recent movie, *"Hillary's America"* released in July 2016 recounts the history of the Democratic Party. Finally, Obama himself educated us about his views for life in America in his books, *"The Audacity of Hope"* and *"Dreams from My Father."* However, in the manner of Hitler's *Mein Kampf*, few of us read them before going to the poles and voting him into office.

If we citizens are to obey the commands God laid out for us in Romans 13, then the authorities over us must also abide by the biblical requirements for ruling a nation—the rational rules God illustrated for leaders. Otherwise, they are inciting national anarchy.

A CALL TO HEAL A LAND OF BROKEN MORALS

"Where there is moral rot within a nation, its government topples easily. But wise and knowledgeable leaders bring stability" (Proverbs 28:2 NLT). The

DANCING WITH THE DEVIL

Lord says, *"If my people who are called by my name will humble themselves and pray and seek my face and turn from their wicked ways, then will I hear from heaven and will forgive their sin and will heal their land"* (2 Chronicles 7:14 NLT).

America is spilling over with moral decay; our government is setting itself up to be toppled. To be convinced is to watch the resettlement of illegal foreigners into our country.

Every person that recognizes God as the one true God is aware of 2 Chronicles 7:14 and knows it well because it has been quoted often from many pulpits and discussed among family and friends. But do we really believe it? Or do we simply listen to the words and then ignore them? Do we really know what it means to humble ourselves, to genuinely pray to God in the name of Jesus; do we deliberately turn away from our sins and truly repent—or do we even know what our sins are? So far, the evidence from the moral analysis of our country indicates that America isn't yet willing to repent, but eventually we must if we want God to hear our prayers and heal our land.

What lies ahead for America? Reflect on what you read in chapter 3 and think about the possibility of these things happening to us here in the United States. If our government continues to reduce our military, and we allow disarmament we will be unable to defend ourselves from invasion by ground troops or a police state. If the immigrants crossing our borders illegally are given citizenship or they become our military will they truly defend America or turn against her? If we continue to wink at the invasion of illegals from any country, we may very well find ourselves among foreigners who will become stronger and stronger while our nation becomes weaker and weaker.

The best way to take control of a land is to disarm its people, then take away their constitutional rights and their ability to support themselves. When people get hungry they become afraid, meek, and weak. Then panic follows. At that point, they are controllable because they are looking for a solution to their problems and are easily deceived. (Note: From chapter 3 remember how quickly the Austrians accepted Hitler, letting him take control of their country?) Hungry people will accept the first lie they hear that sounds good to them. When Adolf Hitler took control of both Austria and Germany their economical condition was in his favor.

Americans I talk with are quick to deny that ground troops could or would invade our country. However, America was eerily close to an invasion by Germany shortly after we entered WWII. Just 12 days after the Japanese bombed Pearl Harbor in 1941, the German Naval War Staff sent U-Boats to our Eastern seaboard. The objective was to cripple our merchant marine supply line whose corridor was the Eastern seacoast from Florida to north of the Carolinas. They were close enough to our shores to watch American automobiles drive the beach roads of North Carolina, and to listen to American music on their radios.

Their orders were to destroy our merchant shipping—the crucial supply lines that fed the war effort against Germany. Before we could react, the Germans sank 200 of our Merchant Marine ships and killed 2000 of our citizens. The assault was so deadly it was kept secret at the time and eventually called a cover-up. A second German advance against America was to send spies inland but only a few actually set feet on American soil. They were all found and executed. Looking back at the atrocities committed by the Nazi's against citizens during WWII, we must be eternally grateful that we weren't invaded by Germany's foot soldiers.

What will we do when faced with a need to defend the homeland? Will we imitate the people of Switzerland? Will we believe as our great statesman, Patrick Henry, in that we would call for liberty or death? Or will we hope to save our lives as the many Germans and German church did, and surrender to tyranny regardless of which government rises to rule us? Surrendering never works for good; instead it pushes people into slavery. Hasn't America seen enough slavery and bloodshed? It's time that we stop hating each other because of our past, and forgive former atrocities committed by those who came before us. We *can* unify for the sake of our country and stop being "The *Untied* States of America."

For years, the Lord has blessed America and in various ways He is still blessing her. But today, many American families are broken and this weakens the entire structure of our country. It creates a nation of emotionally fractured citizens addicted to self-indulgence designed to ease their pain. Addictions to technology, media, food, travel, fashion, drugs, and sexual immorality, will not help us survive an assortment of extreme disasters, or excessively cruel treatment by a foreign nation. America has been a country that God has set high above the nations of the world and blessed beyond expectations. But primarily we have dropped our Christian attributes and become a nation whose people and government have mocked God and laughed in the face of His principles. However, we can regain our high standing as a nation if our government will return to the God of our founding fathers and rule our country based on the Ten Commandments. Otherwise, God will eventually respond in a way we won't like. We have a choice between life and death, but which will we choose? Scripture says, *"Come, let us reason together."* Every patriotic American has a mandate from their forefathers and from all those that have shed their blood to keep the rest of us safe, to take a good look at the condition of our country, and then make a reasonable and sensible evaluation of what lies ahead for us. Those who fail to get their heads out of the sand and rightly evaluate our condition and where we are headed will be the first to clamor for help when the ax falls. Why not take action *before* it falls?

IT'S NOT TOO DIFFICULT TO UNDERSTAND

In the book of Deuteronomy, chapter 30, God gave a direct and specific declaration, which He said, "was not too difficult to *understand*" about what was required to occupy and build a great nation.

"This command I am giving you today is not too difficult for you to understand, and it is not beyond your reach. It is not kept in heaven, so distant that you must ask, 'Who will go up to heaven and bring it down so we can hear it and obey?' It is not kept beyond the sea, so far away that you must ask, 'Who will cross the sea to bring it to us so we can hear it and obey?' No, the message is very close at hand; it is on your lips and in your heart so that you can obey it. Now listen! Today I am giving you a choice between life and death, between prosperity and disaster. For I command you this day to love the Lord our God, and to keep His commands, decrees, and regulations by walking in His ways. If you do this, you will live and multiply, and the Lord your God will bless you and the land you are about to enter and occupy. Today I have given you the choice between life and death, between blessings and curses. Now I call on heaven and earth to witness the choice you make. Oh, that you would choose life, so that you and your descendants might live! You can make this choice by loving the Lord your God, obeying Him, and committing yourself firmly to Him. This is the key to your life. And if you love and obey the Lord, you will live long in the land the Lord swore to give your ancestors Abraham, Isaac, and Jacob" (Deuteronomy 30:11-20 NLT).

The Lord is practically *pleading* with His people saying, "IF you will, then I will." We must act first and then He will act on our behalf—not only for His people in Biblical times but also for their descendants. That includes those of us today who are grafted into the vine because we accepted Jesus. We replaced the unbelieving Jews who were cut off because they didn't believe in Jesus.

In the New Testament, Jesus pleaded with the people when He said, *"O Jerusalem, Jerusalem, the city that kills the prophets and stones God's messengers! How often I have wanted to gather your children together as a hen protects her chicks beneath her wings, but you wouldn't let me. And now, look; your house is abandoned and desolate. For I tell you this, you will never see me again until you say, 'Blessings on the one who comes in the name of the Lord!'"* (Luke 13:34, 35 NLT)

DANCING WITH THE DEVIL

The Lord tells us that even wicked people know the truth about God because He has made it obvious to them through all of His creation. And yes, God does say He will remember our sins no more when we repent, but we must abide in Him or He will remember our righteousness no more. Ezekiel, chapter 33 explains this well.

Is God saying to America, "O, *America, America, the country that endorses wickedness, abandons the homeless, refuses to protect the innocent and defenseless, hushes God's messengers, elects leaders that hate God, holds women and children in sexual sin and slavery, and kills babies while I'm knitting them together in their mother's womb; I would have gathered you underneath my wings of protection as a mother hen gathers her chicks in, but you would not come; no, you would not come! Because of your sin, I will bring a great nation against you and tear down your mighty fortresses!*" I believe that as the Lord watches us from heaven this may be the cry of His heart.

In some way, either through broken morals, a loss of integrity, or a quest for personal power and greed, nearly every American over the age of accountability has or does contribute to the fracture and eventual collapse in the structure of our nation. In part two of *Dancing With The Devil* readers will see how the documented results of our everyday choices (that neglect and rebel against God's statutes) create broken homes and families that contribute to the downfall of a nation, which He will not protect unless there is genuine repentance. We all, young and old, must keep our lamps burning. Our prayer must be that the Lord will bring us back to the days when His Word was the normal way of life for our country. If we don't unify on a genuine *understanding* of what evil is and establish a biblical moral code for separating good and evil, and if we don't fight to destroy evil whether in our own country or in others, we are doomed to collapse. If we love the Lord with all our heart and soul, we will also love our families and our country. We must support moral rectitude and argue against the abuse of it. We must choose "good" over evil even subduing the simplest thought that could lead us down the broad path. Maybe then we will be able to see God's protection over our country in that He would gather us beneath His wings as a mother hen gathers her chicks in.

The worst enemy to America is the American who has experienced the greatest of all this country has to give and then has turned against it. This is a TRUE traitor! Author Unknown - Emphasis added.

CHAPTER FOUR STUDY QUESTIONS

1. Were you surprised to learn that God laid out a plan for rulers to use to govern nations?

2. Were you surprised by the content of Robert C. Winthrop's speech to the Massachusetts Bible Society in Boston in 1849? If so, explain why.

3. Do you agree or disagree with Mr. Winthrop's proposal to use the Bible to govern humanity and nations? Explain your answer.

4. Do you think that America is at a crossroad and if so, do you have an idea for a solution?

5. Explain your feelings about 2 Thessalonians 3:6-12.

6. How do you feel about the removal of all references to God, Christ, and the Bible from educational institutions? Has this improved our country or harmed it?

7. What do "inalienable rights" mean?

8. Name three reasons for the American Revolution. Do you think Americans should submit to disarmament?

9. From your own opinion, why do we fight in wars?

10. Do you think our land needs healing and if so, how do you think this could be accomplished?

DANCING WITH THE DEVIL

PART TWO

The Battle for the Soul of God's Children
"Choosing the Broad Path"

FIVE

❧

RELATIONSHIP ABUSE
VIOLATING GOD'S PLAN FOR A HEALTHY SOCIETY

"Everyone who acknowledges me publicly here on earth, I will also acknowledge before my Father in heaven. But everyone who denies me here on earth, I will also deny before my Father in heaven. "Don't imagine that I came to bring peace to the earth! I came not to bring peace, but a sword. I have come to set a man against his father, a daughter against her mother, and a daughter-in-law against her mother-in-law. Your enemies will be right in your own household!" "If you love your father or mother more than you love me, you are not worthy of being mine; or if you love your son or daughter more than me, you are not worthy of being mine. If you refuse to take up your cross and follow me, you are not worthy of being mine. If you cling to your life, you will lose it; but if you give up your life for me, you will find it (Matthew 10:32-39 NLT).

We would be amiss to read these Scriptures and then question how serious the Lord is about our part in relationship with Him and with each other. He was and still is emphatic that we *understand* exactly what His coming meant; it wasn't peace as some may think but instead was division.

Not all members of the same household follow Jesus, and those that do won't agree on how it should be done. Disagreements create division and for the few that choose willingly to serve Him no matter what, life is a cross to bear. The Lord cautioned that if people hated Him and His righteousness, they would hate those who loved, honored, and spoke favorably of His sacrifice, which has the power to transform all humanity if they would only let it.

The presence of the Holy Spirit inside those living righteously convicts those living unrighteous, or those thinking about living un-righteously but haven't yet done so. Quarreling, and other forms of wickedness then permeate the home. Family members that stand firm against the one wishing to depart righteousness suffer agonizing oppression by the works of the enemy. The one that departs the good things of the Lord faces frustration as the Holy Spirit tries to woo them back. Discord increases as the tug-of-war escalates. Where this behavior is developed among family members inside the home it spreads to the outside like a poisonous gas that can't be identified until it has penetrated other's homes, the church, businesses, schools, and then on to governing entities.

Relationships are so important to the Lord that when they are violated He promises to punish the violator. Yet, in countless homes across America there is plenty of evidence of the division Jesus spoke about in Matthew 10 and a violation of every word He gave us in Ephesians 5. How is it that we can claim Christianity, and Christ as Lord of our life, yet completely ignore and live almost entirely opposite to these Scriptures? This chapter focuses primarily on what happens to families when the husbands and fathers—those creations God called to be the protectors, providers, and spiritual leaders in their homes—abandon their wives, and in many cases their wives *and* children, and move on.

In a personal poll of divorced "Christian" men, I questioned several about their views on love and commitment. Keeping in mind the Scriptures in Ephesians 5 about how a man must love his wife being willing to die for her, I was shocked to learn the number of "Christian" men that don't really believe that most men even fall in love, much less be willing to die for a woman; rather, I'm told they are more apt to believe that men fall into lust because so many can easily justify violating the Scriptures about fidelity and move on from woman to woman with no guilty conscience at all. Further, plenty of women accommodate their wanderings and in many of the cases, initiate infidelity. Yet this Scripture in Ephesians tells a man to love his wife as he loves his own body, even willing to die for her to salvage her for Christ. In contrast most women fall deeply in love but few genuinely respect their husbands, the very thing a husband wants from his wife and which the Scripture counsels women about.

Why can't women respect their husbands? How many husbands today are truly worthy of their wife's respect? How many wives are truly worthy of their husband's love? Only a few resemble what Ephesians 5 says God requires, and Satan is laughing himself silly!

When we sincerely look at the evil in the world, we must ask, "What has happened to the mind of mankind? Have we surrendered entirely to sinful thinking?" Most people and particularly Christians want the Lord to bless and protect them from harm, yet there is no doubt that since time began humans have neglected to guard their mind and heart against the tactics of the devil. Instead more have chosen to forget about the Lord's commands and listen and submit to Satan. The men in Malachi were one such group. They had violated their marriage vows and then complained because they couldn't get any blessings from the Lord. The Lord responded with a huge reprimand.

"Here is another thing you do; you cover the Lord's altar with tears, weeping and groaning because He pays no attention to your offerings and doesn't accept them with pleasure. You cry out, 'Why doesn't the Lord accept my worship?' I'll tell you why! Because the Lord witnessed the vows you and your wife made when you were young. But you have been unfaithful to her, though she remained your faithful partner, the wife of your marriage vows. Didn't the Lord

make you one with your wife? In body and spirit you are His. And what does He want? Godly children from your union. So guard your heart; remain loyal to the wife of your youth. "For I hate divorce," says the Lord, the God of Israel. "To divorce your wife is to overwhelm her with cruelty," says the Lord of Heaven's armies. "So guard your heart. Do not be unfaithful to your wife." You have wearied the Lord with your words. "How have we wearied Him," you ask. You have wearied Him by saying that all who do evil are good in the Lord's sight and He is pleased with them. You have wearied Him by asking, "Where is the God of justice?" (Malachi 2:13-17 NLT)

Most people demand justice against those who give them grief about something. But few people think the grief they cause others deserves equal justice. It's easy to reach this conclusion simply by listening to people discuss a situation whereby they feel they have suffered relationship injustice. Similarly many people want God to answer their prayers but they resent doing things the way God requires. It doesn't matter how close we walk with the Lord, He doesn't always answer our prayers in the way we ask Him to.

I have yet to find a stronger reprimand from God than the one in Malachi 2 that describes how much He hates it when people mistreat one another, especially men against women. God refuses to hear a man's prayers or accept his peace offerings, or have compassion for his tears when he has been cruel to his wife. God also lets us know how exhausted He gets listening to us call evil good and then say He approves. God never approves of evil and He hates a double standard. Just as it was in the days of Malachi, presently throughout our land people are calling evil good and good evil.

Relationships are highly important to the Lord and they begin with Him. He doesn't want half a relationship with His children. We are either fully dedicated to Him or we are not with Him at all. A lukewarm attitude is indifference and God assures us that it separates us from Him. So, how do we build a relationship with the Lord that He approves? It is through our faith in Him and choosing to obey

His Word; it is trusting that He watches over us, cares for us, and has our best interest at heart; it is making a purposeful choice to follow Him, both when things are going well for us, *and* when they aren't. It is committing to loving Him with all our heart, mind, soul, and strength.

When God told Abraham to take Isaac—his son of promise—to the mountain and sacrifice him to God He was testing Abraham, forcing him to *act* on his faith. If Abraham had taken Isaac and run, this would have proved he loved Isaac more than God. He would not have been qualified to carry out the Lord's plan for him to become the father of many nations. Abraham's obedience to God proved his love and trust for Him. Because of his faith God declared him righteous. In this instance, Abraham showed no signs of being a "lukewarm" servant of the Lord.

Through the Apostle John, the Lord told the Church of Laodicea how He felt about them: *"I know all the things you do, that you are neither hot nor cold. I wish that you were one or the other! But since you are like lukewarm water, neither hot nor cold, I will spit you out of my mouth"* (Rev 3:15, 16 NLT).

When my dad thought coffee wasn't hot enough for good taste, he spewed it from his mouth. These Scriptures in Revelation remind me of Dad's opinion of lukewarm coffee. Worthless! This address to Christians is a warning for us today. Jesus wants us to get spiritually serious about our relationships and especially the one with Him because it not only precedes all others; it enables them to function successfully.

Just as our passion for Christ must show in our behavior, attitude, compassion, service, and words, so also it should be with our spouse. Christian men won't have a successful relationship of any kind, especially marriage, until they have a "sold out" relationship with Christ. Christian women will not be able to *understand* a godly relationship with a godly man until they have a genuine relationship with Christ. Knowing Christ helps us renew our minds to become one with Him. When we are one with Christ, becoming one with a partner gets easier. Ephesians 5:21-33, and Malachi 2:13-17 indicate that God holds men responsible for initiating and leading a godly relationship in every part. He holds women responsible for finding a way to receive, complement, and respect man's attempt to do as the Lord admonishes him. However, history has recorded that humanity has continually violated and rejected the Lords commands. In this section about the breakdown in our society, which leads to evil behavior, I hope to show where our refusal to correct this behavior in everyday life contributes to broken relationships and broken families, which trickles down to a broken nation. The information offered is based on history, statistics, the experiences of people I know personally, and my own experiences. Building a relationship is a joint effort but if only one partner is trying, unity cannot be achieved. However, before we can build any kind of a relationship we must have a firm *understanding* of the different types of relationships, and the many different ways they impact our lives.

WHAT CONSTITUTES A RELATIONSHIP?

When I queried acquaintances from both genders about what a relationship meant to them, I was surprised to learn that most people believe that a relationship is sexual and/or romantic. Moreover, in that context, few could explain what a relationship would be like for them if after 25 years with a spouse sex and romance were not possible due to an unforeseeable change. They were unable to think of relationships beyond the surface of their emotional makeup.

Most agreed that a person had to *look good* for the sex to be good, and had to *do things* so the romance would linger. These desires are very important, but they are shallow when compared to the importance of substantial relationships—ones that endure through a lifetime of highs and lows. They must be shared with other important features that are necessary for growing a quality relationship with deep affection and compassion for another person. However, there are other types of relationships that have nothing to do with sex or romance and they too, don't function according to God's plan for a healthy society.

The word relationship has several meanings including having a connection to something for any reason—family ties, romance, business, and others. Each of these requires a particular type of behavior or action. Connecting to someone in relationship can mean an association through a business, or a series of events or actions that link us when we don't anticipate a link. For example, when we work for an organization we become linked to people we don't know simply because we do business with them. Often these relationships are short-lived, as people tend to move on from place to place and are replaced by others with whom we build new links. But sometimes there is a sense of loss when a person moves on in business even if we have never met them.

Correlated relationships are usually built on allied sentiment or assistance. We see these demonstrated between countries and in the judicial system. A government or military of one country may feel the need to ally with the powers of another country to prevent or stop the rule of an unreasonable and oppressive dictator. In a court of law, a defendant or a plaintiff usually finds it necessary to engage the help of someone who is detached from the disputes and who can testify on their behalf. Such correlated relationships exist only for the purpose they serve during the time they are required. Beyond that, there is no need for a connection; this makes them short-term.

Relationships of correspondence are simply ones where the only tie is communication by phone, or the written word. They can be either business-related or social interchanges between two people of any gender. Usually a relationship of correspondence is platonic—simply companionable, amicable, neighborly, or business—not sexually or romantically intimate.

Parallel relationships are those that refer to an expected correlation of behavioral outcomes, which may result from relationships between similar people. For instance, if we know someone who is unethical or is socially or morally improper, and then discover that person is abusive to others, we may correctly conclude that a second individual with similar behaviors may also be abusive to others. This can be a practical assessment to determine whether someone would make an acceptable lifetime partner.

Interrelated or interconnected relationships are well organized, serve a specific need, and are interdependent, as in retail merchandizing, corporate agreements, and in business. We also see them in marriage relationships where one relies on another for sustenance.

Business connections should represent every biblical aspect of Godly principles and code of conduct for proper ethics. The golden rule of civil respect, 'do unto others as you would have them do unto you,' should be the passion of all business dealings from the top executives to the least productive position in the organization. People have value, and they deserve respect at every level of employment, but from entry to ownership those people must also *give* respect. Regardless of the type of relationship, respect was never meant to be one-sided.

RELATIONSHIPS OF FAMILY TIES

Family ties are groups that are related by blood or marriage—people into whose life we were born—father, mother, and siblings. These are the most powerful of all relationships. Even when there is discord in a family, most family members—especially Christian ones—will defend and protect each other, particularly the older for the younger.

The bond in blood families is almost impossible to break and even when we try, the Lord will not let us stay broken forever, even amid conflict. He will not leave us alone for very long with our conscience without conviction. Even when the hurt among family members is so deep it seems to never go away, it must be dealt with before healing can be accomplished. When we disassociate ourselves from family due to hurts, or refuse to forgive, we exalt ourselves above Jesus who did no wrong. Though a whip with metal tips tore the flesh from His body and He died an agonizing death on a cross, He chose to forgive his persecutors. Dare we do any less than forgive those who have hurt us? When we refuse to forgive a blood relative because we think they don't deserve forgiveness, the Lord will not hear our prayers and will not forgive our sins when we ask Him to. If Jesus could forgive those who didn't deserve it then why can't we? Even when we know our prayers are on slippery ground, we still refuse to forgive. This is stubborn pride. The Bible says that stubbornness is like the sin of witchcraft and the Lord despises witchcraft.

Forgiving others is our direct connection to Jesus and determines our own forgiveness. And, it is the most difficult instruction from God for us to obey particularly when the offender has consciously planned to wound or destroy us. An unintentional offense is much easier to forgive. However, forgiveness is better achieved when we finally accept that it is required for our emotional healing, and for an obedient relationship with the Lord.

A minister once told me that the simplest way for a true Christian to forgive was to imagine the perpetrator burning in hell. He suggested that I study the Scriptures that described hell and then imagine myself there; afterwards, I would be able to imagine the person there I needed to forgive. I wanted to be able to forgive so I worked at his suggestions and found that he was right. Though memories of hurt lingered, the anger subsided and I was able to pray for those that hurt me deeply and move forward without a deeply rooted anger that could provoke me to revenge. The minister reminded me that people who truly love God, also truly love their enemies and when we can see our enemies as needing redemption as opposed to undeserving of God's love and mercy, then we will have compassion on them and forgiveness will come again and again. It is our compassion for a hurting or dying soul and our willingness to stop being angry with someone that enables us to forgive. However, forgiveness does not mean that when a human "snake" bites us repeatedly we must say, "Oh I forgive you; here I am; go ahead and strike again." Until the "snake" conforms to God's ways it is best to stay away from its poison. But even when we stay away, God won't let us keep our anger and un-forgiveness and He wants the so-called Christian "snake" to change his ways. We are to hate the sin and love the sinner.

Forgiveness means doing away with hatred and anger, which separates us from God. *"But I say to you that everyone who is angry with his brother will be liable to judgment; whoever insults his brother will be liable to the council; and whoever says, 'You fool!' will be liable to the hell of fire" (Matthew 5:22 ESV)*. Some versions say angry "without cause." The Greek uses "Raca," a term for abuse. The brother the Bible speaks of is any person who confesses Jesus as Savior and works at building a relationship with Him. It is not the person who clings to their so-called "rights" and is unable to say, "Maybe I was wrong," refusing to find a solution that respects the Lord's principles for Godly living. Our enemies are not the "brother" referred to here. Our enemies are unsaved people who don't care about us. While we are to love and pray for them we aren't being sensible when we let what an enemy does or wants keep us from a relationship with the Lord. After all, unrepentant offenders could care less whether we have a relationship with God because a relationship with God means nothing to them.

ROMANTIC RELATIONSHIPS

Romantic relationships occur when two people are connected by a sense of need or desire for each other. The attraction can be based on what the partners perceive to be love, a physical attraction, an emotion, a need, co-dependency, financial, or spiritual, but usually, and of course sadly it is physical attraction. Regardless of the reason for the relationship both parties are required to contribute a certain amount of effort or action to build and sustain balance and boundaries in romantic relationships.

Relationships are fragile. All wounds take a long time to heal unless they are nourished often with love and encouragement. This action diminishes fragility by gradually replacing it with stability and requires some form of respectful communication. If it is written it must appropriately fit its purpose. If verbal, it should represent truth in love and respect, and help build significance in the other person. Words and actions should bring resolve, and healing—not division or hurt.

Romantic relationships function much like a wood burning fire. When it is ignored it will smolder and eventually die, but if it is stoked, giving it air and more wood, it will burn hotter than before. When couples refuse to take action in their relationships, the passion and respect they once had will die and they will likely discard each other—usually through the judicial system.

Couples without compassion for the Lord will have none for each other. They will become fully ineffective not only in serving one another but also in service to Him. They may stay together for a time but the relationship will deteriorate unless they commit to change. Usually it is pride that prevents reconciliation once a relationship gets to a certain level of decline. People need people but if there is a refusal to work through the issues in marriage and a refusal to listen and have compassion for a spouse, he or she will either become a recluse in relationship or they will find someone who *will* listen to them. Today nearly 50% of all married couples divorce, with varying percentages applicable to first, second and third marriages. As in the words of a song called *"Husbands and Wives"* written and recorded by singer/songwriter/actor Roger Miller, *"It's my belief, pride is the chief cause, and the decline in the number of husbands and wives."* The Bible teaches that pride comes before a fall. Just as a house divided against itself cannot stand, a relationship cannot survive the arrogance of pride, as it is a stumbling block to good communication and compassion, the vital components of restoration.

We have no fundamental source of wisdom or *understanding* unless we are in right relationship with Christ and without that relationship it is impossible to build a quality relationship with those we live around. Further, a "right relationship" with Christ is not built on our terms; it is built on His terms and is typically the same as those for our earthly relationships, which also must be built on His terms. There is no room here for pride!

God designed human beings to need communication, physical presence and touch, sexual intimacy, security, laughter, comfort, protection, nurturing, reliability, trust, and reassurance, as well as the ability to forgive and be forgiven. We need mental and emotional assurance that there is someone close-by who is committed to caring for us and for whom we can care. We must be so transparent and "one" with our marriage partner that when they walk into our presence we can see whether they are in need, and then make every effort to help satisfy that need. Yet, that can only be accomplished when two people communicate well, forgive each other, and are careful not to take each other for granted. *"I told you I loved you when we married and that should be enough,"* doesn't work for very long. *"Yes, I promised to care for you in sickness and in health but I didn't realize you would get so sick."* Can you imagine Jesus turning us away because our sickness was too much of a burden for Him?

God created men and women with different physical attributes and for specific gender roles and I am convinced that equally men and women fail to make the effort that's necessary to understand how and why God made them different and to accept and respect those differences. Instead, they *compete for the power to persuade* the other to conform to their way of thinking and behaving. As a result, many men have become feminized and cannot lead their families as God intended them to. In contrast, many women have been coerced into giving up their God-given female characteristics and think and act as a man because their partner was unable to enjoy them as a perfect helpmate, with a woman's mind and courage that was designed by the Master himself. Instead some females must relinquish their initial design and become what their husband thinks they should be. That often means the woman must conform to the things he enjoys, which are usually masculine in nature.

Even among Christians, few commit to the study of God's Word deeply enough to learn His design for each gender and then build on that design. Instead, we turn our focus inward and refuse to completely surrender to Christ, letting Him lead us through the issues surrounding our differences. Surrendering to Christ requires a willingness to obey the Scriptures regardless of the situation at hand. But instead of finding wisdom and *understanding*, many couples find a way to tear each other apart. Current divorce rates confirm this and my marriage was no exception.

When a relationship is built with passion and compassion from both partners and then gets broken for any reason, pain and suffering can hang on for years to come. Loss is real and it reaches to the depth of our emotions when it is founded on compassion. The following stories show how humans react at the loss of a relationship, whether good, bad, animate or inanimate.

A MOTION SENSITIVE COMPANION

When I began writing this chapter on relationships only twelve days had passed since I had moved into my new home. One evening I was struggling with deep loneliness and my efforts to overcome seemed futile. Finally I decided to occupy mentally and physically by making granola by a recipe I had been tweaking for about a year. In the little village where I now lived snow or sleet had fallen for more than forty-eight hours, and a dear friend in Texas had texted that she was listening to a superb presentation on the Holy Spirit. Her message was encouraging so after exchanging a few comments, we wished each other a happy evening and I returned to my granola. I set the oven temperature and began collecting ingredients from the pantry and refrigerator.

Conveniently placed in my kitchen was a trashcan with a motion sensor lid. Each time I walked past the can the lid raised and lowered automatically. During the first week in my new residence I often spoke to it in a friendly manner. Occasionally I even got annoyed when it misfired and didn't react as I had commanded. Soon I began to recognize some companionship in the simple conversational habit I was building and realized that it might not be good for me if someone witnessed these conversations, so I decided to stop them.

The can's user-friendly placement in the arched doorway of my open-concept pantry quickly proved to be a nuisance, for when I passed it the lid opened and closed whether or not I needed to discard trash. To stop this unnecessary motion, I moved the can. This caused the lid to open but when it tried to close it got caught on the neck of a wine bottle in the wine rack close by, but I did not notice it at the time.

I walked passed the can several times gathering various recipe items before I realized there was no motion—no quiet little "swish" that I had heard so often before. Finally, I decided to investigate, and saw the problem. Immediately I felt a twinge of heart-felt compassion and apologized to my little chum for not paying closer attention to his dilemma. Quickly I moved the wine rack.

You are laughing? Yes, I know it was an inanimate object; it had no life, no breath, no blood, no heart, no oxygen, and no odor unless of course I neglected removing the trash in a reasonable amount of time. But that didn't matter. What mattered was the fact that our complementary motion created energy and a sense of life, which dispels loneliness. That loss of energy or movement was a distinct reminder of how alone I was.

DANCING WITH THE DEVIL

Before you judge me too harshly I want to share a story about a man's relationship with an inanimate object that became amazingly powerful in his quest to survive, and the story's sentimentality that earned millions for movie producers.

NO COMFORT HERE

In the year 2000, a movie called *"Cast Away"* hit the big screen generating over $200 million in revenue. Perhaps you've seen it. The story is about a man named Chuck whose Federal Express cargo plane crashed into the sea. As the only survivor he washed ashore on an island so isolated he found nothing even remotely useful. Without the means to cut open a simple coconut to drink the milk for food he struggled for weeks to endure the hardships of a rudimentary way of life and certainly no personal comfort. Then one day, cargo from the downed plane began to float ashore. Chuck opened package after package anticipating anything that would enhance the living conditions on the uninhabited island. There was nothing even slightly helpful until he found a Wilson brand volleyball. This piqued his interest! But it wasn't until he injured his hand trying to open a coconut that he discovered the ball's purpose in his isolated life. As blood gushed from the open wound, Chuck yelled at the ball, and then as if to place blame for his circumstances he picked it up and using all the strength he could muster he cast it far away from him. When his pain subsided he turned his attention to the ball once again and saw that his bloody handprint resembled a human face. In a quest to find comfort he immediately created a make-believe companion complete with hair atop its head, and named his new friend "Wilson."

During Chuck's four years alone on the island, Wilson became his playmate and valued companion, serving as a sounding board for all his frustrations as well as his attempts at reasoning. One day in a brave quest to get home, Chuck decided to leave the island on a makeshift raft. Enthusiastically he stabilized his good friend to a pole on the raft and headed out to sea. After a couple of days adrift on the water a storm arose and pounded away at the raft. Soon the bindings that held Wilson to the pole loosened and before long, he fell into the water where he was quickly swept away by the current.

When Chuck realized Wilson was overboard, he had drifted too far to be retrieved. In deep anguish, Chuck cried out at the loss of his make-believe friend—the companion that had sustained him emotionally during his isolation from humanity. As he gave up his effort to save Wilson, his human mind and emotions were certain that Wilson would feel abandoned, so he yelled out heart-breaking and sorrowful apologies that surfaced from deep within. One Internet blogger posted, *"Watching the scene where Chuck loses Wilson is the saddest scene in the history of movies."*

That a viewer could be so moved by an emotional scene about a tragic separation between a human and a volleyball is undisputed evidence of humanity's deep emotional needs and the damage caused by someone leaving. Chuck's emotional attachment to Wilson had become so intense that the human need to mend a relationship with apologies bursts forth from his gut without thought. Deeply troubled, Chuck suffered the same trauma, separation anxiety, and abandonment when he lost Wilson, as most folks do who find themselves divorced from a real person but didn't want to be.

Is God a motion sensitive God? Absolutely! And because he is a motion sensitive God, we are motion sensitive creatures. Life comes from the energy we create when we become active. With every promise God made to His people, there was an action on His part and an action on their part. Action is one of His primary requirements for us otherwise He would not have had such strong words for the Christians in the seven churches referenced in the Book of Revelation. I have written about the letters to the seven churches in chapter 10 of this book. He doesn't want us to be lukewarm or lifeless but to chase after Him with a craving desire to serve and worship Him. Clearly, inactivity brings death to relationships, even our relationship with the Lord.

ALONE IN THE WILD

In 2009 Ed Wardle, a freelance documentary filmmaker and adventurer set out to fulfill a boyhood dream of surviving completely alone, living off the land, and defending himself from the elements and the wild. Ed's test-quest required him to leave his girlfriend and family and head into the Yukon Wilderness of Northern Canada where he would attempt to survive for twelve weeks holed-up in a lean-to, which he built with poles he cut from trees.

A few weeks into his mission, he openly admitted to being ill prepared for the challenge. Food projections were inaccurate. The salmon didn't arrive in the rivers when predicted and the raw land offered little of the protein he needed to sustain muscle. Twice he moved to new locations to hunt for food. These unexpected challenges combined with his isolation from those he loved caused him to question his ability to continue. In daily video sessions he cried openly in a way that was shocking—certainly no Jeremiah Johnson mountain man or someone to count on for protection from unknown dangers.

Though he found huge patches of blueberries, he confessed that he lacked the skills to scavenge for food. When hunger took control and he began losing weight he still refused to defy Canadian hunting laws and kill a caribou. His search for food became an all-consuming quest and when his heart rate dropped to twenty-eight, in desperation he called for an airdrop of supplies. At that point he had a near-complete emotional breakdown that put him in danger of a heart attack. He cried and suddenly called out to God. No prayer—he simply spoke the word "GOD." Shortly afterwards he admitted to seeing himself as a failure and felt that the food drop was kindness. Surely he was able to appreciate those things, but maybe he felt unworthy accepting them.

Clearly Wardle lived in fear that he was about to die. Once he admitted to getting stronger, but then reverted to tears. Again and again he questioned whether he was going crazy. Finally he admitted that he was slightly ashamed that he had failed. Apparently he was plagued with guilt for not succeeding at his greatest challenge—to survive completely alone in the wild for a specified period of time. After day thirty his speech was continually negative: "I don't think I can do it." On day thirty-six he admitted to acting like a blubbering idiot. In his despair he confessed to feeling stupid and soon he couldn't videotape without crying. After fifty days he was airlifted out of the Yukon due to deteriorating health. He had encountered nothing that should make him sick except his emotions, which he allowed to take complete control of him.

Watching Wardle's behavior on the videos he made of himself moved me deeply. Much of his behavior was like an addict overcoming an addiction and was quite painful to see. He had embarked upon a difficult adventure that challenged every part of his capabilities, much the same way many of us begin a marriage—knowing very little about our mate and what it takes to build a life together. Although his attempt to be alone in the wild was admirable, once again we see how difficult it is for people to live completely alone. Like we who refuse to apply God's Word to our life, Wardle had not done enough homework in wilderness survival training before attempting such a journey. In like manner, we try to live a Christian life and build a marriage without referring to the handbook of instruction. Humans are not designed for being alone. We gain energy and sustenance from being connected to others and the only way we can be successful at it is when we obey God's Word.

Bible passages in Ecclesiastes say, *"Two people are better off than one, for they can help each other succeed. If one person falls, the other can reach out and help. But someone who falls alone is in real trouble. Likewise, two people lying close together can keep each other warm. But how can one be warm alone? A person standing alone can be attacked and defeated, but two can stand back-to-*

back and conquer. Three are even better, for a triple-braided cord is not easily broken" (Ecclesiastes 4:9-12 NLT).

ALONE WHILE TOGETHER

One evening in a restaurant, I conversed with a man who confessed to being angry because his wife had divorced him after a long marriage. He said that shortly after they married he fell in love with another woman, with whom he had an affair. He professed Christianity, so guilt and obligation to remain in his marriage motivated him to return to his wife, commit to her in relationship, and let go of the other woman even though—according to him—he loved her and she would leave with his heart. He said that several years after his incredible sacrifice to give up the other woman and return to his wife, she divorced him, leaving him struggling with anger and bitterness.

I suggested that perhaps the issue wasn't that his wife had left. Perhaps he had stayed with divided loyalties she could no longer tolerate and after finally losing hope that he would ever love her completely she released him. I suggested that she had made the far greater sacrifice, for the Scriptures had given her complete freedom to leave. Instead she was the faithful one that had not violated her marriage vows but forgave her unfaithful husband and accepted him back home.

As we talked, he referred to himself as a devout Christian because he had sacrificed much for the Lord and for his wife. Clearly he was proud of his "Christian walk" and his relationship with the Lord but I likened him to the men of Judah in Malachi 2—being unfaithful, weeping and groaning because of his unhappiness due to his own transgression.

He knew the Word of God and wanted the Lord to forgive his sin but he resented God's law. He didn't go back to his marriage with humble repentance or a broken and contrite heart. Instead, he let the other woman take his heart while he returned to his marriage with anger and bitterness buried in obligation. He didn't want to give of himself sacrificially but instead he wanted his wife to suffer as he was suffering for having given up the other woman. For years he sulked and was unforgiving, punishing his wife for a transgression that was his alone. When she decided enough was enough and gave him the freedom she knew he had wanted for years he felt rejected, lonely, and angry. He was indignant that she would leave him and resented her even more than during their years together. Because of his self-indulged attitude, he held God hostage to his commands instead of honoring God's commands.

By his own confession, he had sent his heart away with another woman. Now there was nothing in his marriage except perfunctory. The Lord says He will not tolerate a divided heart; we cannot worship other gods and love Him at the same time. He says, *"Turn to me now; give me your hearts before it is too late."* The man in my story worshipped another woman (or god, so to speak). His wife had given him every opportunity and he continually rejected her offer of forgiveness. Finally she gave him his freedom and got on with what was left of her life, leaving him in mourning for the woman whom he had let captivate his heart.

If we think that the temptation to violate our marriage vows will overcome us one day, it is of ultimate importance to be certain about whom we want to spend a lifetime with before we say. "I do" because the Lord hates divorce.

1 Peter 3:7 NLT . . . "you husbands must give honor to your wives. Treat your wife with understanding as you live together. She may be weaker than you are, but she is your equal partner in God's gift of new life. If you don't treat her, as you should, your prayers will not be heard." In the Old Testament book of Malachi the Lord gave a strong reprimand to the men who were being unfaithful and divorcing their wives. He said that if they didn't change their behavior He would not hear their prayers when they prayed. Again in the New Testament book of 1 Peter, He speaks to the men there, saying that if they mistreat their wives He will not hear their prayers. From the Old Testament to the New, and into today the Lord's statutes never change.

The Lord hears a husband's prayers when he is obedient to God's Word and when he is in right relationship with Him as well as in relationships with others. I am convinced that our answered prayers, our blessings, our peace, and our joy are dependent upon how we treat those with whom we are connected relationally.

ENDLESS LOVE - NEVER ALONE

My maternal grandparents were born and raised in the mid-South, and were married in the early 1900's. Though I have few memories of them from my early years, I do remember how much they adored and respected each other, and I have some vivid memories of certain events during my short time with them.

As married adults, they lived in what is called the "Big Thicket" of Southeast Texas where my grandfather, whom everyone addressed as "Pa," was a logger when logs were cut by hand with cross saws and pulled out of the forest with mule teams. A big man—six feet six inches tall and 300 pounds—he worked hard but moved very slowly.

My grandparents were poor, and because Pa's work required them to relocate often they knew very little about gardening, which could have helped feed their nine children especially during the Great Depression. However, during that time grandmother would bake bread, and make gravy from flour, lard, water, salt and pepper. Often that was all the family found on the table at dinner.

Transients often passed through their little community looking for work and begging for food. Grandmother always found a way to feed them a bite of something, and sometimes had to defend herself if Pa was away. Once when a man she fed showed he intended to harm her she reached for a butcher's knife and slashed at him. Right away, he moved on. It is sad that even while being fed to relieve his hunger, man can still desire to commit evil.

DANCING WITH THE DEVIL

At one point during their life, my grandparents lived next door to the community church and were always surrounded by people. Occasionally when our family went to visit, other relatives from nearby would drop in for the church service and an afternoon dinner and fellowship in my grandparent's home. Every unoccupied space in the tiny little five-room house was an open passageway for guests. No room was private or off-limits. My memory of the laughter in their home is reminiscent of a faint yet pleasurable scent of vanilla that drifts through a house where cookies are baking. I was always comfortable around them because they were as kind to me as they were to everyone else, something I have not always enjoyed from some who claim to love me.

My grandparents were dedicated to Jesus and lived His command to "love thy neighbor." Though both were highly esteemed in the community, Pa was the patriarch. True to their faith they were quick to assist where needed, making common-sense decisions on behalf of others. Neighbors often came to them seeking advice about their personal issues.

Ma and Pa were kind and tender toward each other. Not long ago Mom shared a heart-warming story I will never forget. Pa wore heavy denim overalls with shoulder straps fastened by metal hook-and-button closures. In those days laundered clothes were hung outdoors to dry. Sun-dried clothes were usually stiff, particularly denim. To make them softer, Ma dampened and then ironed them. With each stroke of the heavy cast iron she patted the legs of his pants and spoke a tender blessing: *"Bless his little pea-pick'n heart, Lord. Bless his little pea-pick'n heart!"* Though their poverty life never seemed to improve, my grandmother spoke a continual blessing over my grandfather each time she ironed his pants.

My grandparents owned few material possessions, but they had more love, honor, and respect for each other, their children, and the Lord than most people will ever be able to imagine in a lifetime. They knew well that it wasn't materialism that made a family, but rather how much they gave each other in love and compassion, and how they served the Lord and their community.

After my grandfather's death from a logging accident at the age of 63, everyone missed him terribly. Grandmother never adjusted to being alone. The joy I had seen in her through the years was now completely faded. In her attempt to move on through the loneliness she often visited her children, but at our home we noticed that she sat quietly, brushing her waist length hair. While still grieving the death of her beloved she died of congestive heart failure three years after my grandfather passed. Some say a broken heart took her life.

My grandparents had a healthy relationship filled with personal sacrifice. There was no selfish indulgence at the expense of family such as you will see in the story that follows.

COMBATIVE and UNCOMPROMISING RELATIONSHIPS

Regardless of denomination a true Christian *understands* that sin is disobedience to God's requirements for us about how we are to live life on earth. When we sin as Christians we suffer pain and loss whether it is our integrity—a mark of respect allotted us when we live by His truths—or the loss of our reputation or character. The pain we experience when we violate our own bodies, which are holy and consecrated, set apart for Jesus, also brings loss. Our transgression causes us to lose the respect of those closest to us as well as the respect of non-Christians who don't believe in God, but who once respected and admired us because of our commitment to Him. At this point we have lost our Christian witness and are no longer respected for the wisdom we once showed.

Occasionally I have considered myself wise, but I have not always made wise decisions. It's true that I wanted Jesus to rule my heart and mind. But because I desired real human relationships that I could see and touch—not just spiritual ones—I didn't always ask the Lord for help. As a result dreams and deception led to emotional bondage and heartbreak when I disobeyed the Lord.

Often young people make decisions based on feelings, which are deceptive, so at the age of twenty I entered my first marriage with big dreams, and little wisdom. Because of our age difference his life experience far exceeded mine, so we had nothing stable in common. Mom's advice against marrying him required me to think like her, so I ignored it. When we push forward indulging our own will, mistakes pile up until the closet of regret overflows with mountains of dirty laundry.

After three years of marriage, we divorced and two years later I made the greatest mistake of my life. I accepted a date with a married man whose impact on my life nearly destroyed me. He had all the right words to convince me that he couldn't live without me, so within six months he divorced his wife and we were married. I walked straight into a jail cell. He locked the door behind me and gave me freedom only when it was for his advantage. For thirty-two years, I struggled under his narcissistic personality traits while trying to right my transgression by making the marriage work, which would eventually prove to be impossible.

Our life together was a roller coaster ride of passion, deception, control, jealousy and infidelity that eventually destroyed our marriage. Although I was aware that we should have never married, I functioned under a lot of fear and was too young to be sensible about how incompatible we really were. After three years of his betrayals, foul language, and heavy drinking I requested a separation. But soon after, he came to me making promises—those I considered relevant for a successful marriage, so we reconciled six months later and agreed to accept Christianity as the foundation on which to build a new life. I rededicated my life to Jesus, and was baptized again. He accepted Jesus and was baptized for the first time. Now I believed our life together would be all right if I was a good wife, followed the Scriptures, and worked at creating a good marriage and home life. He knew nothing about the Bible so I poured my heart, soul, and mind into helping him know Jesus and building our marriage—a typical mistake of many wives. God holds each of us accountable for building a relationship with Jesus. No one can do it for us.

Years passed before I could *understand* that love is never jealous and that jealousy is a demonic spirit (James 3:14-16), which controls a person's emotional character, causing evil behavior. But in my faith and innocence I believed that anyone could change if conditions were right. However, after time and a great deal of research, I discovered that for those with Narcissistic Personality Disorder (NPD) conditions are never right for change because those with this disorder don't give up their self-appointed right to control. They change only long enough to manipulate and get what they want before reverting to narcissistic behavior. My husband was not diagnosed with NPD. However, after much research on the topic and its symptoms and comparing them to his behavior I realized that he was classic NPD.

During our marriage, I often felt that I was living two different lives. My inner self was consumed with shame and guilt; the life I let others see was prideful—pretending all was normal. I kept the really bad parts of our life together hidden from family for a long time. I refused to talk about them. The guilt side of me desperately wanted out of the marriage and free of the lifestyle I had agreed to live with him and though I craved a simpler and traditional life as a Christian I knew divorce had to stop. This thinking kept me bound to a struggle to make the marriage work but rarely was I able to verbalize my concerns, thoughts, or feelings to him without forceful controversy. Then after 32 years married and 29 years together in church, I learned of his true views about Godly morals and principles when he said, *"the Bible is a lie, there is no God, and Jesus isn't real!"* Heartache after heartache had been our history since our first date and finally after years of effort and personal sacrifice we had come to an end.

DANCING WITH THE DEVIL

My story is not so different from a large number of Christian marriages, so how do we reverse this breakdown that gets transferred to our children and grandchildren? By making an evaluation of our partner's personality before we enter into a marriage agreement with them, and refusing to participate in behavior that the Bible calls sin. In a potential partner we should look for characteristics that would violate how the Scriptures tell us to live. We must look at extended family members to see if there are characteristics that might bring future heartache to our own life or the life of our children. We must do our best to turn off our emotions if they are keeping us from being sensible and use our mind to get knowledge, our spirit to get wisdom from the Word of God, and then commit to being obedient to that. We must know beyond a doubt that there is a defined moral code we are to use to compare not only our own behavior, but also the behavior of others. If the person we think we love behaves, talks, and lives contrary to the Scriptures, we must not try to change them if they are adamant about their rebellion. This would create a power struggle, which could become violent. We must walk away from the relationship until the rebellious one shows positive signs of change for at least a year and in some cases, even more time is required. As it was in my situation, some never change.

I am fully aware that I should have never accepted the first date with this man who later became my husband. And definitely there should not have been a second date, but there was, and I cannot change that. Though the divorce was painful, and I eventually lost most of what I held dear, including people, I have discovered great joy in the freedom to serve the Jesus I love without having to deal with the objections of an anti-Christ spouse. After the divorce I made choices that proved to be mistakes but once I learned to let go of my fear of living alone, and repented of my sin, and asked the Lord to let me dance with Him, I discovered personal forgiveness, redemption and restoration. I became the apple of His eye and began to see myself through those loving eyes and heart. Though it does take a long time after a broken heart, I began to *understand* and experience genuine love, compassion, and peace by trusting in Him. Living a shame-free life brings comfort and joy that mere words cannot describe.

Often, I wondered how my life would have been different had I obeyed the Word of God. I wondered about the lifetime mate that was the Lord's choice for me. When I think about how my will diverted His plan, His assignment for me when He knit me together in my mother's womb and when I think of the heartache my choices caused others, there are times I shed tears of remorse, and lament the loss of that which never was—a life filled with the blessings of the Lord which would have come from a godly marriage and children purified through that union. I encourage anyone experiencing the difficulties of life, or personal lust and inappropriate behavior to turn from that broad path, which leads to hell, and get on the narrow path to eternity in heaven with the Lord.

It's been said that life's best lessons are learned in the school of hard knocks—I certainly learned my lessons there. But perhaps there are those who will learn from my painful experience and escape that fate. The worst thing about dreadful mistakes is that once they are done, they are done. The best thing is that we have an opportunity to pick up the pieces and move forward in the new life the Lord gives us when we let Him redeem us from our sinful one.

PARENT- CHILD RELATIONSHIPS

Including my own, the assortment of parent-child relationships is huge. Stories of tragedy and triumph between parents and their children could fill volumes in libraries around the world. Beginning with the heartache Adam and Eve surely suffered when their son Cain killed his brother Able, to Eli's troubles with his children, to King David's family cursed to live by the sword, there seems to be no end to parent child problems.

The modern day atrocities we hear on the news almost

daily—children killing parents and parents killing children—are so painful to hear we want to shut-out all knowledge of it just so we can move on in some kind of peace. News stories tell us how a child was forced by a stepparent to run in the heat until her heart gave out, and how other children have been kept as prisoners in boxes or small dungeon type rooms until they starved or were beaten to death. We learn about children and young teens that are held hostage for the purpose of sexual slavery—some by their own parents. These real life incidences have everything to do with relationships and the evil thinking behind their destruction. Who is the father of the evil that destroys? Satan!

There are all sorts of relationships, or lack thereof, between parents and children. In the same way that God our Father has called His children to an obedient relationship with Him, and declared that "if we would, then He would," God has called earthly fathers to be compassionate-yet-just spiritual leaders of their home in the same way He is a compassionate and just father to His children. He has also called earthly fathers not to provoke their children to wrath. However, family curses continue to move down through time and in nation after nation the children tend to repeat the sins of the fathers.

In contrast though, there are many stories where children have risen above family complications, chosen a better and more balanced lifestyle, and in many instances, they found the Lord and made a life-changing decision to serve Him and break the family curse by successfully raising their children to do the same. That is when God smiles!

There are many stories about parents who spend a lifetime treating their children as though they are still small children, using them for every advantage; there are numerous stories of children abusing parents, but the following story tells of children honoring their parents, and the beautiful relationship that results.

KEEPING THE COMMANDMENTS

Honoring fathers and mothers can be a difficult commandment to keep particularly when one or both are cruel, and not worthy of honor. But a Christian whose will is surrendered fully to Christ's will is more capable of being obedient to that Scripture, "doing it as unto the Lord." No parent is perfect and there are many that don't deserve honor but there are countless numbers that do, and for them "honoring" comes easy for their children.

When my 95 year-old-mom was 82, she became suddenly ill while sitting in church one Sunday. Realizing her sickness felt different to one she might take home and nurse by herself, she motioned for help from one of her daughters who was sitting close by. Instantly my sister and her husband came to Mom's aid. As they helped her out of the sanctuary Mom asked to stop by the ladies room where she vomited and then fainted.

After a few days in the local hospital another daughter, who is a registered nurse, took Mom to her home where she could use her medical knowledge to supervise Mom's care and observe her full time. Soon we learned that Mom was in kidney failure. The process to prepare her for dialysis treatments was a combination of tests by several doctors, and hospitalizations that required cooperative family assistance.

Caregiving a special needs person is difficult at best and Mom's RN daughter and her husband have been extraordinarily faithful to assist Mom in many different ways. When Mom is in their care, they make every effort to see that she continues to enjoy the average things of life—travel, food, special events, entertainment, and other forms of enjoyment. They have never once let Mom's special needs interfere with her joining in the fun. They make every effort to keep Mom's travel experiences as comfortable as possible. They often include Mom on their weekend trips willingly loading her power chair, wheelchair, walker, and toilet riser as well as all her personal needs such as luggage and meds. A special carrier is required for her power chair and a particular skill is needed to load and unload the carrier and the chair onto a vehicle. (Update: Mom now has a wheelchair accessible van, which is a huge help to everyone.)

My brother-in-law has always helped with a compassionate heart. He has pushed Mom in her wheelchair all over town for several hours while we women shopped from store to store just so Mom could enjoy the sights and be part of special events and the camaraderie we shared—an effort to help her feel wanted since she is too weak to walk more than a few feet before sitting down, and she can't stand for more than a couple of minutes. It is a personal sacrifice to inconvenience oneself for the pleasure of and service to a less fortunate person.

A few years following Mom's kidney failure, my sister and her husband who assisted Mom the day she became ill at church made an amazing personal sacrifice—one that would change their lives in ways they could never have imagined. My sister took early retirement from her job to engage full-time care of our mom, and her husband has been a faithful and dedicated partner and helper in this cause even though he helps with one of his own siblings. He is also chief of the local volunteer fire department and highly active in the local church, as well as assists as needed in the community. He is called on often for many things.

When they took on the responsibility of fulltime care of Mom, the all-encompassing impact of how it changed their lives cannot be defined or measured. Those of us looking on can only *imagine* to what degree it affected them. Care giving is a true labor of love that is often accompanied by frustration, concern, expectations, and needs and inconveniences no one can ascertain unless they have experienced them. Though my sister was active at church and with her own children and grandchildren, her responsibilities increased dramatically when she decided to care for Mom who needs assistance in many areas. Simple things like styling her hair, retrieving things she drops, helping her locate misplaced items, assisting her with her plate in a buffet line, shopping for her needs, making sure her meds are filled, and keeping track of her medical reports and appointments all take a chunk from the personal time, daily responsibilities, and the personal pleasures of another person. My sister and her husband have met those needs for our mom while another sister and her husband provide financial assistance. Prior to a severe leg injury in December 2015, Mom was able to get from the bedroom to the bathroom, bathe and dress herself, attempt to make her bed, and help somewhat in the kitchen. But since the injury she is no longer able to do those things. This condition has increased the amount of care she needs.

The dialysis clinic where Mom receives her treatments is 30 miles from her home—a sixty mile round trip three times a week. A sister-in-law has been extraordinarily faithful in assisting with Mom by committing to take her on one of the three days weekly. She has a great attitude, and proves her willingness to help out especially in last-minute needs. Her life has not been easy, either. My brother is diabetic and has a transplanted kidney. This is a situation that requires time given to close attention to special diet. Few daughters-in-law will give to a mother-in-law with such sacrificial love.

These examples of parent/child relationships according to the Scriptures are genuine and heartfelt but to our dismay, they are rare in today's society. More often, we see cases of parent neglect and abuse, such as parents being put away in a nursing home to die. The children or other family members go about life, never visiting the person who gave them life, but instead awaiting their death so they can inherit their "treasures." Humans are successful at relationships only to the degree they are willing to give of themselves.

However, accolades are due those children who have no choice except to provide care outside the home for their ailing parent. What one sees on the outside isn't necessarily what's happening on the inside of the story. Sometimes parents are too ill for the family to take care of; some parents must be "placed" so the family can work to provide not only for himself or herself but also for the ailing parent. There are numerous situations that determine how we care for our aging parents with needs, but the bottom line is that God requires children to honor their parents, and He requires parents to respect and love their children and not provoke them to anger. Mom was not perfect; none of us are. But when each of her eight children left home and married, she stopped seeing them as three or four years old; she never became a leech, refusing to let them go; she cut the apron strings and let each child find their own way in life and become adults in their own right; she also respected their place and role as adults. Though she might have disagreed at times, she never interfered and always listened when they needed to talk.

The book of Proverbs in the Bible is the Christian's handbook for living wisely every day. It begins like this:

"These are the Proverbs of Solomon, David's son, King of Israel. Their purpose is to teach people about wisdom and discipline; to help them understand the insights of the wise. Their purpose is to teach people to live disciplined and successful lives, to help them do what is right, just, and fair. These proverbs will give insight to the simple, knowledge and discernment to the young. Let the wise listen to these proverbs and become even wiser. Let those with understanding receive guidance by exploring the meaning in these proverbs and parables, the words of the wise, and their riddles. Fear of the Lord is the foundation of true knowledge, but fools despise wisdom and discipline. My child, listen when your father corrects you and don't neglect your mother's instruction. What you learn from them will crown you with grace and be a chain of honor around your neck" (Proverbs 1:1-9 NLT).

The Lord's plan for families was for the parents to teach the children but if they don't, how will the children gain the grace and honor the Lord promises them when parents teach and children listen? How many children today have parents they can listen to and who can give them wise Godly counsel? How many children today can follow their mother's instruction because it is based on the guidance of the Lord? How many children today can listen to and trust a father's correction because he is living righteously? Is the father still in the home or has he walked? According to the U.S. Census bureau for 2012, 24 million American children lived in homes where the biological father was absent.

The trickle-down effect of family dysfunction or neglect of the Holy Scriptures in the generations to follow can be difficult to reverse. Those raised in this environment often make mistakes with their own children before they realize what's happening. In these cases some damage will already be woven into the fabric of their lives and repairing that damage will take time and patience on everyone's part. However, with dedicated and sacrificial care, love, and prayer, children who were raised in a painful family atmosphere or abuse can make positive changes that will transform their own lives and the lives of future generations of children.

Though the book of Proverbs is filled with wise counsel for everyday living I can't recall when I last heard a sermon on its Scriptures. The story about my family's sacrifice to care for our mom represents a mentality of integrity we often find missing in many families. We hear more stories like the following report of what happens when daddies break relationship with their families, leaving them to struggle for survival on their own with no hope of help from him. The trickle-down effect from the perpetrator to other family members is astounding. (Note: While moms do leave their families the focus here is on dads because God called men to be the spiritual leader in their homes and the protector and covering for their families. See Ephesians 5:25-27; 1 Corinthians 11:3.)

WHAT HAPPENS TO CHILDREN WHEN DADDIES LEAVE HOME

During my research on divorce in America I read numerous stories and watched several videos that revealed the suffering caused by broken families. The heartbreak, loneliness, despair, anger, and personal need of those abandoned by someone who should have loved and cared for them were horribly painful. Those telling their story could barely speak as they sobbed terribly, with their head in their hands. Their broken heartedness had not waned after many years of abandonment and of those interviewed no one was remotely close to being healed.

Though some of the following statistics are not as current as I would like (1991) they still show us the damage caused to children when daddies leave home, and the numbers are even greater today. Individuals included in these percentages come from fatherless homes.

80% of rapists who are motivated by displaced anger.[1]
71% of all high school dropouts.[2]
70% of juveniles in state institutions.[3]
85% of all youths sitting in prisons.[4]
63% of youth suicides are from fatherless homes.[5]
85% of children with behavioral disorders.[6]

Fatherless children are at a dramatically greater risk of drug and alcohol abuse, mental illness, suicide, poor educational performance, teen pregnancy, and criminality.[7]

The absence of the father in the home affects significantly the behavior of adolescents and results in the greater use of alcohol and marijuana.[8]

Boys who grow up in father-absent homes are more likely than those in father-present homes to have trouble establishing appropriate sex roles and gender identity.[9]

Even governing the variations across groups in parent education, race and other child and family factors, 18 to 22-year-olds from disrupted families were twice as likely to have poor relationships with their mothers and fathers, to show high levels of emotional distress or problem behavior, [and] to have received psychological help.[10]

Children whose parents separate are significantly more likely to engage in early sexual activity, abuse drugs, and experience conduct and mood disorders. This effect is especially strong in children who were under the age of five when their parents separated.[11]

Compared to peers living with both biological parents, sons and daughters of divorced or separated parents showed significantly more conduct problems. Daughters of a divorced or separated mother evidenced much higher rates of internalizing problems—such as anxiety or depression.[12]

Father hunger often afflicts boys age one and two whose fathers are suddenly and permanently absent. Sleep disturbances, such as trouble falling asleep, nightmares, and night terrors frequently begin within one to three months after the father leaves home.[13] (Note: When my first grandson was three years old he began to cry to me that he had monsters in his stomach. His father had abandoned his mother while she was pregnant with him.)

Children of never-married mothers are more than twice as likely to have been treated for an emotional or behavioral problem.[14]

Children from mother-only families have less of an ability to delay gratification and they have poorer impulse control (that is, control over anger and sexual gratification). These children also have a weaker sense of conscience or sense of right and wrong.[15]

80% of adolescents in psychiatric hospitals come from broken homes.[16]

Ronald E. Johnson, C.Ph.D and author of *Teaching Eagles to Soar*, Tate Publishing, 2009 says that when dads fail to mentor or bond with their sons, the boys will show symptoms of being angry, volatile, argumentative, easily discouraged, and untrusting of adults. He says that they are less likely to be committed, they want immediate gratification, they focus on subculture habits such as attire, music, speech, and mood swings (conscience), and a short attention span. Dr. Johnson goes on to say that boys who aren't mentored by or bonded to their dads have a victim mentality, and short-term negative practices, and they are void of radiance.

With forty-five years as a youth educator and conference speaker to his credit, Johnson believes that the increasing condition of father-challenged homes has resulted in millions of youth damaged so severely that failure in school, in home relationships, and in careers demands that mentors (parents, teachers, coaches, correctional personnel, pastors, and probation officers) provide the instruction he calls *Laws of Eagles* or philosophy of life that youth should receive from their biological fathers. Otherwise, Johnson says, American teenagers likely will not be trained in basic skills needed for successful employment and marriage. (Also, how will they become quality leaders?)

A recent report from The Bureau of Census, Survey of Income and Program Participation collected and published in *Living Arrangements of Children, 2009,* reveals that in that year, 7.8 million American children lived with at least one grandparent, a 64 percent increase since 1991 when only 4.7 million children lived with a grandparent. (Note: There are many reasons grandchildren live with their grandparents and it isn't always because they have been abandoned by their parents, however, many have.) Among children living with a grandparent, 76 percent also were living with at least one parent in 2009, not significantly different from the 77 percent who lived with at least one parent in 1991.

In 1991, 5 percent of white, 15 percent of black and 12 percent of Hispanic children lived with at least one grandparent. By 2009, 9 percent of white, 17 percent of black and 14 percent of Hispanic children lived with at least one grandparent, a significant change for white children but not so much for black or Hispanic children. (Note: This statistic shows us the measure of advancement of moral and economical decay in our country—just one of the reasons more and more grandparents are assuming the responsibility for the care of their grandchildren.)

More than half of the children living with no parents were living with grandparents. Percentages for black children (64%) and non-Hispanic white children (55%) did not differ from Hispanic children (61%), but the percentage of Asian children living with no parents but living with grandparents was lower, at 35%.

In 2009, 69 percent of the 74.1 million children under 18 lived with two parents and 4 percent (2.9 million) of all children lived with both a mother and father who were not married to each other. (Note: 2.9 million children are being trained to accept social and sexual immorality. This does not include the influence of divorced grandparents who care for their grandchildren yet are cohabitating outside marriage.)

Between 1991 and 2009, children living with only their mother increased from 21 percent to 24 percent. What must we do to reverse this trend so that the leaders of tomorrow will know how to genuinely love and care for their own families? We must stay connected and teach.

The percentage of children living with their mother without a father present varied widely among race and origin groups in 2009, from 8 percent for Asian children to 50 percent for black children. Seventeen percent of non-Hispanic white children and 26 percent of Hispanic children also lived with their mother only. Seven percent of all children lived with one unmarried parent who was cohabiting. The percentage of all children who lived with a cohabiting parent ranged from 2 percent for Asian children to 9 percent for Hispanic children. Falling between these were non-Hispanic white children (6%) and black children (7%), not different from each other or the percentage for all children. Overall, 16 percent of children lived with a stepparent, stepsibling or half sibling. Thirteen percent of children living with one parent and 18 percent of children living with two parents lived in these blended families. Most children (78%) lived with at least one sibling. Among those, most (83%) lived with only full siblings from the same biological mother and father. Fourteen percent of children who lived with siblings lived with at least one half sibling, sharing only one biological parent.

Will we continue to forget the children, neglecting our responsibility to them, or will we make a choice to reign in our selfishness, stop this destructive trend, and build a more compassionate and loving society? If you have not considered how destructive this pattern is, the following information might help you understand the need for change.

Videos of interviews with men in prison showed that those prisoner's dads had abandoned all of them either before they were born, or at some point shortly after their birth. In some of the cases, both the mom and the dad abandoned. Moms that were interviewed confessed that they simply couldn't deal without help so they walked away. Many of those mothers that did stay after the fathers walked away were forced to be the strength for the family—the provider, director, adviser, homemaker, maintenance and repair person, and spiritual leader (if they believed in God)—and often on a lower income than what the income would be if a man lived in the home.

When daddies leave home, their daughters walk down the aisle alone on their wedding day or they walk with someone less attached emotionally unless they were fortunate enough to have an amazing step-dad. Still, as a former wedding consultant, I witnessed the sadness a bride feels when her "real" dad is willingly absent on her wedding day.

Although reports vary, some show that about 95 percent of men in prison come from fatherless homes. In his book *Fatherless America*, David Blankenhorn says that *"fatherlessness" is the most harmful demographic trend of this generation and is the leading cause of declining child wellbeing in our society.* He said, *"It is the engine driving our most urgent social problems, from crime to adolescent pregnancy, to child sexual abuse, to domestic violence against women."* Men are supposed to protect their families and clearly they abandon this role in huge numbers.

Based on these statistics can we doubt that God created family relationships for the purpose of mental, emotional, and physical stability, which He wanted to be carried on generation after generation? We forget that we have an enemy whose goal is to destroy our family unit. I believe that the trauma we see in our society today is due to years of adult self-indulgence that considered accountability to relationships invaluable. My plea is to Christians who are allowing the enemy inside their home. Throw him out and break the cycle! That means being willing to take a close look inside you before challenging a partner's issues.

A Christian man, who spoke at my church one Sunday morning, shared in his testimony that when he was just a toddler his daddy left him and his mom and moved down the street to live with another woman and start another family. He said that every day he waited for his dad to come by for a visit, or say hello, but he never came. His mother obviously did a great job raising him because he grew up to become a godly man, determined to never abandon his own children, his wife, his mom or the Lord. He made a decision not to pass down to his son the pain his father had passed on to him but instead to stop what could have become a generational curse—the demon spirit of abandonment.

There are heartaches of many kinds; there are tragic and inhumane treatments of men, women, and children, but the heartache of growing up just down the street from your dad and seeing him there playing ball in the yard with his new family, his new son, and knowing he doesn't love you is awfully painful to a child.

When a man leaves a woman and the child he bore with her, then goes on to establish a new family, forgetting the old one entirely, he has hardened his heart and filled it with deep resentment for both the mother of his child, and his child. When a man has this attitude toward his first family no amount of goodness he bestows on his new family will justify him before God regarding the poor treatment he gave his first family. Until he repents of his behavior and attitude toward them, God will not hear his prayers. See Malachi 2:13-16 – 1st Peter 3:7.

The very first step a man must take to become a good father is to make a commitment to love and follow the Lord and then commit to love and respect his wife—the mother of his children. Until he is able to think with his heart, putting God first in his life, he will not be able to carry through with any commitments to family because worldly seduction is so powerful. Abandonment hinders a child's ability to become a confident and productive adult. I believe that the breakdown of the American family due to uncultured paternity can become the primary reason for the fragmentation of our nation as a whole. Whether you are the mother or father or both trying to build a quality family unit, it will take sacrifice, putting others first, and thinking with integrity about what is in the best interest of the entire family.

Another reason for the breakdown of the family unit in our nation is ill-tempered and unpredictable parents left unchallenged. Unreasonable demands on children and spouses, and a violation of the scriptural admonition, "Fathers, (or mothers or stepparents) provoke not your children to anger," serves only to ill-prepare God's precious gifts for a healthy future as mature adults. Unrestrained anger instills fear in others, obstructs compassion and love, and hinders forgiveness. I am convinced that forgiveness can be achieved only when we stop being angry.

When children live life under unreasonable demands made by parents, they are more likely to make foolish decisions when the time comes to choose a life partner. Further, they may struggle to invest prudently, or acquire the skills needed for a productive career. Neither can they mature into quality leaders. Sadly, after such a childhood much of our adult life is spent learning what wise and loving parents should have taught. Parental behavior that forces children to survive by their wits teaches them unhealthy habits and fails to equip them to trust as God intended. These children are more inclined than others to become victims and are easily confused about what is acceptable behavior according to God's plan. They willingly dance through life with the devil until one day they realize the negative impact it has on their earthly relationships as well as on their relationship with the Lord. The same integrity and behavior required of the average citizen applies to the leaders of a nation. Where family commitment is achieved through the renewing of the mind and heart, reliable leadership will follow. Integrity and respect for a moral code builds a nation of leaders who will lead with compassion and concern for the country because they will lead with a caring heart, which they learned in a committed family environment. But as long as the statistics on fatherlessness continue to rise we will have a nation of completely desensitized men fathering children whether or not there is a family present, abandoning homes, and running our nation. When that happens, (if it hasn't already) we will be past the point of return to human decency, and indeed will be in trouble.

    Maybe we think these stories and statistics on relationships affect only the families that don't know the Lord. But that isn't true. This pain has touched millions of Christian families. Documented facts throughout history and into today reveal how men who hate God and behave accordingly, and men who say they love God but behave as though they don't, have adversely affected God's original plan for humanity and wreaked havoc on our society. Because of this, women and children have especially been treated disparagingly. As fathers, husbands and curators of man-made laws for society, and willing abusers of biblical Scriptures, men have and still do rule the world. The evidence in part one of this book shows that the results haven't always been good for humanity, particularly the defenseless. Leaders of churches have abused through legalism, intimidation, and manipulation. Author Ronald M. Enroth's book *Churches that Abuse* offers undeniable evidence of just such behavior. When those we need to trust prove to be untrustworthy, the damage can affect the victim for a lifetime.

Abandonment is devastating to anyone touched by its pain. My personal experiences and the numerous true stories I have heard on the heartache of abandonment help to motivate my plea for men to reconsider before leaving one family to create another. We must make a choice to reverse our unhealthy society and build a healthier one if we expect to live at peace with one another. Yes, women have walked away from responsibility, and deserted their husbands and children; they have committed violent crimes and treated men badly; they have lost their feminine charm and gracious manner and committed adultery, but the percentages are *far lower* than those for men.

This is especially troubling when the human design for a female is to rely upon the strength, provision, and character of a loving husband and father—the called leaders and defenders of home and country. Yet we see men behaving badly in almost every aspect of family, church, and business culture where they should be standing for integrity, good character, and a decent moral code their children can emulate and their wives can be proud of. As they walk their path of rebellion they are taking with them, wives, girlfriends, children, grandchildren, siblings, and acquaintances, and God *will* hold them accountable.

INCARCERATION MAYHEM

As documented in the statistics for *What Happens to the Children When Daddies Leave Home* the evidence confirms that it is the male gender that has consistently perpetrated pain and hardships on humanity. From *'Trends in U.S. Corrections—State and Federal Prison Population 1925-2011'*–there were fewer than 200,000 U.S. citizens (men and women) imprisoned in 1925. *Bureau of Justice Statistics Series*

Just eighty-six years later in 2011, the number had increased to an astounding 1,600,000 with significant increases beginning in 1976 and escalating at a phenomenal rate from then through 2011. Clearly the aftermath of World War II, the rebellious freedom movement of the sixties, drug abuse, illegal immigration, and the abolition of the military draft—which required men to be responsible and accountable—have had an impact on the number of people incarcerated. Rebellion against God and traditional morals, as well as disrespect for the law that judges good and evil has exposed itself in prison numbers. Freedom isn't freedom when it hurts others, and when people are hurt they retaliate, sometimes to the ruin of their social and respectable character—and often for a lifetime.

The U.S. Department of Justice, reported 1,499,573 men under the jurisdiction of state and federal correctional authorities at the end of December 2010. The number of women incarcerated at that time was 112,822. At the time of the 2010 prison report there were 5,182,890 more females than males in the United States, and 378,356 men had been killed in war since 1925. As of 2010, approximately 1.7 percent of Americans identified themselves as gay or lesbian; reportedly there are more gay men than lesbian women. It is estimated that more than four million men in America are out of circulation for a traditional family. These statistics show that our society is in serious trouble unless we get a healthier attitude about the importance of family relationships as designed by our Creator.

In an article titled *The Spirituality of Moms Outpaces that of Dads* dated May 7, 2007, the Barna Group poll on spirituality in the family, shows that while *"men may enjoy advantages in physical strength, they are much less likely than women to exercise their spiritual muscles."* The study reports that men are much less likely than women to attribute importance to faith; moms are more likely than fathers to attend church, pray, read the Bible, participate in small groups at church, (fellowshipping and getting acquainted with others) attend Sunday School, or volunteer to help a non-profit organization. The only faith-related activity in which fathers are just as likely as mothers to engage is volunteering to help at a church.

David Kinnaman, President of The Barna Group and the director of the study clarified the role of gender in shaping a person's spiritual profile. *"Whether they are a parent or not, women in America have high levels of spiritual sensitivity and engagement. Men generally lag behind the spirituality of women—particularly so if they are not a father. In other words, having children intensifies the spiritual commitment of men, but even so most fathers still do not measure up to the spiritual footprint of their parenting counterparts."* Kinnaman says, *"Imagine the impact on our society if fathers were to simply match the intensity of their parenting peers."* (*The Spirirualty of Moms Outpaces that of Dads May 7, 2007, The Barna Group*)

Men and women are taught by the Christian world and much of the secular world that the most important thing a woman needs from a man is security, which translates into money, a home, clothes, and food. We are taught that men are to be the primary wage earners for the family. This is why courts have enforced the "provide for your family" law for men wanting to leave their families and move on to something different in life, often a new woman and a new family or simply to go "find" him self.

No one should deny the importance of life sustaining material provisions for women and children. But hasn't humanity—the couples in court, the lawyers, the judges, the jury, and maybe even friends who testify—forgotten something equally important? I believe we have. We have forgotten God's design for our spirit and emotions, as well as our need to love and be loved—to be wanted by those who brought us into the world, and by those we chose as mates, as well as by our children, whether natural born or adopted. All these needs are connected to relationships and are called a family unit. But an unbelievable number are broken for a variety of ridiculous reasons, usually greed or a refusal to work at *understanding*. The broken families end up in the hands of the court whose system is too over-loaded to take the time needed to help restore them. Instead it gives an order, pounds a gavel and broken people walk out of the courtroom with no one to help them assemble the pieces of what's left of their lives. And few churches are willing to help without imposing denominational legalism.

DANCING WITH THE DEVIL

Would most Christian women give up material securities for a man who can live up to David Kinnaman's challenge to imagine the impact on our society if fathers were simply to match the intensity of their parenting peers regarding spirituality? Having already experienced more material possessions than I actually needed, and the pain of two bad marriages, I can truthfully say that I would have traded many "things" for a man of honor, respect and integrity, who refused to indulge immoral passions! And, I believe there are many other Christian women who would as well. If men would engage these attributes it would change every aspect of our culture and help women exchange an immoral attitude for a moral one. From the accolades given Actor Ralph Waite at his death, we see evidence of what the majority of people, particularly females, want and need a man to be for them.

As I tweaked this chapter Ralph Waite, who played John Walton on the long running television series *The Waltons*, passed away. Being a huge fan of the show and the awesome character Mr. Waite played, I was deeply saddened by his death as if it were a personal loss. But I struggled with feelings of foolishness about my sadness over the death of a man who may or may not live a life exemplary of the one he portrayed on television. I decided to see what other people might be saying about him at his death and what I discovered was even more shocking to me than my feelings of foolishness.

Numerous people from around the world had gone online to visit Mr. Waite's memorial sites and post their thoughts about him. Though they had never met him they referred to him as "daddy" and fantasized about him being *their* daddy. Women confessed of dreaming about him as their husband, for in their own life they had not enjoyed the kind of husband Mr. Waite portrayed on his show. Both men and women wrote about how he had made a positive impact in their life and how much he would be missed even though they knew him only through his role as John Walton. Letters about the integrity and patience of the character he played were impressive and those posting comments hoped the show would always air because it gave them genuine feelings of a balanced life. Does this not speak volumes about what people really want their relationships to be like?

Per his own admission, Ralph Waite was not always a good man. He confessed to alcoholism but made a choice to exchange that behavior for one exemplary of the man of integrity he played so well on *The Waltons*. Eventually he went into the ministry of the Presbyterian denomination, and accolades given him by countless people confirm his good heart. Michael Learned, Mr. Waite's TV wife confessed that when she was waiting in her dressing room for her time on the set she would listen to the dialogue and wish that her own life exemplified the one she played on *The Waltons*.

Mr. Waite's life became a powerful testimony as one the majority of us would like to have but have somehow failed to attain.

MEN WHO CHASE AFTER GOD'S HEART AND THE HEART OF THEIR FAMILY

If you are a man who doesn't fall under the description of those written about primarily in this chapter, but instead you are of the character of Mr. Waite, please do not be offended by these negative statistics about the male gender, but lift your head and *understand* how the masses love and appreciate you and how much God loves you, because you are rare in your gender. Also, please look at the reality of the negative statistics—a broken humanity that needs repair. Be willing to do what you can to help snatch from the fire the many men that have drifted so far from a holy God who deeply loves them.

Countless men have forsaken their professions and dedicated their lives to helping other men in mental, emotional, sexual, and spiritual battles. There are numerous other types of *really* good men in the world. Some are working quietly behind the scenes and have no need to have their egos boosted through front and center exposure. Others may be outspoken movers and shakers with no agenda to abuse or use another human being. Men of integrity are not consumed with greed, power, or status, and when tempted to compromise ethics and morals they are willing to put aside ego, which often drives men, and do the right thing based upon their love for God's Word and the people in their life.

 These outstanding men have no desire to stop by a bar on the way home from work but instead they willingly go home to mow the lawn (though they may not enjoy it) or grill for dinner, play with the children, and spend time with their wife. They are family men based on God's plan and purpose for humanity. They don't lean on their own *understanding* but if you look closely you can find them studying the Word looking for the wisdom they need from God to help them *understand* how to fix any problems in their home life, which they certainly have, as we all do.

 These confident men have no need to sneak around looking for a private place to watch porn, or call "the other woman" and plan a liaison because they work at being content with the woman they chose. Good husbands *understand* that their wives are due equal human rights, and that it is right to respect her and her role in their life. Equally, betrothed men who are just and fair *understand* what is required of them to become responsible husbands. They desire the very best for their wives and fiancée's and they deliberately search out the best.

 These "good" men care when their family members are ill, hurt, or upset about something. They have compassion and willingly show it to others. Instead of destroying relationships they are fully committed to restoring and building relationships. These good men fight wars yet have compassion for the defenseless; they teach in our schools and churches. They minister to prisoners, travel to mission fields, become "Big Brothers" and open orphanages where they mentor young boys who don't have fathers. Strong and confident males have certainly touched our world through the business industry, which they established based on a moral code they honored, and through dedicated community service.

Unlike the perpetrators of human trafficking, men of integrity do what they can to help stop this horror because they are brokenhearted for the victims and for the abusers lost in the clutch of Satan's hand. Many "good" men pray quietly and seriously with their families—some talk a lot, and some say very little. I am aware these men exist because I know some of them personally, but I also know they are not the majority; sadly for us all they are the minority—just a "few" good men as compared to the populace. Once while visiting in a small town I saw a genuine country boy get out of his pick-up truck with two toddler girls in tow and one in a carrier. He had his hands full yet he gently corralled the girls, insisting they hold hands and then latch on to him so he could be in control and know they were safe. I was loading groceries into my vehicle and stopped to commend him on fatherhood, his precious family and the love he showed them.

In this publication, I have particularly addressed the issues of men flirting with or deeply involved with sexual sin of some kind, or abandoning their wives and children. Statistics show that many men who say they are Christian are violating the Scriptures and the Lord is displeased with them—simply put, their hearts and behaviors are contrary to God's commands yet they confess their love for Him. But the number of women willing to step outside their Christian roles as respectable wives and mothers is rising dramatically. As they allow their disrespectful behavior to grow it hardens a heart that was once tender and committed to the Scriptures. Once a person violates the Word of God it becomes easier to repeat and accept attitudes and behaviors the Lord objects to, hoping He will overlook them at judgment if they have remained active in church.

Most Christian women prefer a mate who loves and defends them, and helps provide as best he can for the family, and who loves the Lord. But clearly many females have moved from looking for mates that have integrity—honesty, reliability, and trustworthiness—to seeking a man based on her willingness to conform to his sensualities, or an interest in the amount in his bank account. To find and keep a man many females have chosen to remove all restraints that would protect their respectability. Erroneously many believe that they must become what men want instead of what God wants. Or presumably what the entertainment industry tells men they want—wild and unrestrained women willing to do anything—a woman that will give him a challenge and keep his life interesting, so to speak. Often females are prone to neglecting their precious moral code hoping to win a man's heart by doing as they think he likes, hoping he will stay with them for a lifetime instead of wandering away after only a few years together.

Men who need a continual challenge aren't satisfied with one partner for long so they move on to another challenge. But once a woman steps outside the boundaries of a spiritually healthy relationship because she thinks a different behavior will keep him satisfied she is continually under pressure to find a way to keep him from wandering. However, some men eventually discover that what they thought they wanted—a wild and unrestrained woman—completely violates their natural born instinct about what a woman should represent both to them and to a civilized society. While they may be quick to use her unrestrained behavior as their excuse to indulge promiscuity, it doesn't take long for them to become hardened by her freedom of expression, which they admired so much in the beginning, but which now makes it easier for them to leave the relationship. These behaviors are a constant challenge for men and women looking for a lasting healthy relationship. Perceived greener grass always comes with its own set of issues.

FEMALES IN RELATIONSHIP

Young Christian men dedicated to achieving a life free of immorality are confessing how difficult it is to find a true Christian female who refuses to violate God's moral code before marriage. Instead, they say these females are more apt to initiate sexual promiscuity even on the first date. But, I am convinced that in many of these cases females willing to violate the rules of moral decency would gladly reign in their disgracefulness in favor of genuine commitment from a godly man who praised their good behavior and expressed displeasure at the bad—whether the one praising is a father, a boyfriend, or a husband. Surely under these more desirable circumstances only a rare few would continue their waywardness. These character weaknesses, which are so evident in many Christian women today, confirm our gender's bent toward flawed morals—those flaws that are contrary to Biblical mandates and which do not coincide with the definition of "lady," the true meaning being "one who is courteous, decorous, or genteel." To be courteous is to be polite, respectful, or considerate in manner. Decorous means keeping with good taste and propriety, being polite and restrained. To be genteel is to be polite, refined, or respectable. Few women who claim to be Christians can be called lady based on the accurate definition. Instead of calling on the Holy Spirit for help they yield to their senses and surroundings, lean on their own *understanding,* and give power to poor behavior.

MANIPULATION: Many people in both genders—including children—are pros at manipulation but women more than men are accused of being manipulators. Men complain that women set their mind on something and determine to get it at all costs. When the one manipulated gives in to the manipulator without a reasonable protest that is founded on Scripture, the manipulator is then able to build a system of manipulation that controls all those they touch. Equal rights and manipulation are not, and cannot ever be bedfellows.

SEDUCTION: When I was a young woman an older woman admonished me to "take care of my husband" because there were plenty of women waiting to seduce him and take him away. She said that men are weak and they will go. She was right. Women are a woman's worst enemy. Women will dress, talk, and behave seductively in order to get the attention of a man knowing full well it is wrong, and they will do this directly in front of the man's wife or his girlfriend. Adultery was in my past and it came full circle back to me. However, men must remember that God called men and women to the same moral purity and He won't excuse their behavior because of any weakness they claim. Jesus punishes and corrects those He loves—men and women. I know that He loves me because I have felt his severe punishment. And amazingly, it seems His punishment always suits the crime. However, I would rather experience His punishment here on earth than to live it eternally in hell.

SELFISHNESS: A poison that destroys a person's ability to think intelligently, behave compassionately, and live life appreciating others. It can be either passive or aggressive in nature.

A passively selfish female whines and pouts in an attempt to get what she wants, claiming to have a greater need than others, whether or not it's true. This is a form of manipulation. She makes all the decisions. She insists on driving her car when traveling with friends, and chooses the music on the radio. She decides where to dine, where people will sit at the table and makes suggestions about what others should order from the menu. She decides the topics of conversation, hers taking priority. She may be likable and fun but basically she is selfish, needing things her way. Should those with her object they are seen as difficult! In a conversation with family and friends, her topic and her view about her topic is the only one with credence. To disagree with her is to be labeled a dissenter.

The aggressively selfish woman screams and yells, and is sometimes violent—hitting, and throwing objects. She blames others even if they aren't guilty and she makes demands based on what she believes to be in her best interest while conveniently ignoring those around her.

CONTROLLING: This female is always in charge and her behavior includes all the characteristics previously listed. Many of today's young women wear the pants in the family, have little respect for their husbands and even belittle them in the presence of others including their own children. Plenty of TV sitcoms teach them how. The father of her children is stupid and can't do anything right. She is the only one qualified to make decisions regarding the children and will continually override her husband's input. She complains because he never offers to help but finds fault with his performance when he does. We must ask, "Who agreed to this marriage?" How can we wonder why some men leave home? Women that are out of control in the "control department" (the micromanagers), yet question why they can't have peace in their homes must make every effort to self-analyze based on the Scriptures.

DEMANDING: The demanding female has to be right whether or not she is. There is a saying, which I find highly objectionable because it is a direct condemnation of the female gender inclusively. "If momma ain't happy, there ain't nobody happy." When such a comment is made as a blanket statement it incorporates all females in all situations where all truth is unknown. It offers no mercy to those females that are abused, or that genuinely follow the Scriptures in their behavior or that carry the load for the family. How sad that the attitude and behavior of some is applied to all. This is equivalent to categorizing all men as bad. We women should strive to reverse this complaint men have against us and rebuild our reputation as gracious ladies.

OVERBEARING: Females that talk incessantly refuse to let others join in the conversation. Women who violate these sensitive areas in relationships believe their knowledge supersedes all others and that what they have to say is more important than what others might have to say. One of the most widespread faults of females is talking over another person's conversation and feeling perfectly validated in doing so. They refuse to learn when it is proper to be quiet and just listen—something they should have learned how to do in grade school—actually before kindergarten.

INSENSITIVE: As strange as it seems, insensitive women often give sacrificially, but they do it without considering how the recipient might feel. And, while they may never admit it, deep inside they think they have bought a portion of the person's life because they have been so generous toward them. Because of their generosity they want to be consulted about every decision made by the recipient of their gift. They suggest what should and should not be done with the gift they gave, and they pass judgment when they disagree with the recipient's decision. When a gift is given, it is no longer to be controlled by the giver. The gift now belongs to the receiver who decides what to do with it, so let it go. One who holds the strings to a gift is being insensitive toward the recipient. Regardless of the kind of gift I give I try to tell the receiver to use it as they please.

CRAZY: (According to Men) The definition of crazy is 'mentally deranged as manifested in a wild or aggressive manner; to be extremely annoyed or angry; to be foolish; to be overly enthusiastic.' Some young men say they find females their age unpredictable or "crazy" and that older women are more stable and tend less to embarrass them in public. If you are a young Christian woman who men call crazy because you embarrass them in public due to your overzealous behavior I encourage you to take a class in the social graces.

COUGARS: These are females that have gained a reputation as sexual predators because they prey on younger men who advertise themselves as sexual studs. I pray there are no Christian women involved in this custom but one never knows for sure. There may be those caught in such behavior, as there are Christian men and women addicted to porn. In wealthier Cougar circles many men get paid for their services. This behavior is saddening. Equally, men are notorious for "keeping" the much younger woman whether or not he is married. In my opinion, there can be no legitimate criticism of older women with younger men or older men with younger women as long as it is reasonable, and reasonable to me is no more than ten years. And, as the years pass ten might be too many. My views are based on personal experience and other's stories. Beyond ten years on either gender, one should seriously evaluate the reasons for the relationship. If after the evaluation no ulterior motive was found then age doesn't matter because the relationship was based on true love.

GOSSIPS: James 1:25-27 says *"Those who consider themselves religious and yet do not keep a tight rein on their tongues deceive themselves, and their religion is worthless."* Females will gossip about others both willingly to do harm, and also in the name of Christianity— *"I'm just telling you this, not to gossip, you see, but so that we can pray."* High on the list of social faux pas, as well as being an offense to the Lord, gossip appears to have a carpenter's clamp on the minds of women who it seems have nothing better to do. It is always best to govern our tongues and avoid offering too much information in any situation. I have learned this lesson the hard way—trusting while not realizing those I trusted would prove to be untrustworthy.

WILLING TO SAY ANYTHING: The social media has weighed in heavily as an avenue for causing astronomical hurts to others, and Christians conform to this trend in mass. I watched my daughter cry a cup of tears and then slide into the pit of angry wrath about words written to or about her on the pages of these information highways, which are often used to sow discord and create jealousy. Even law enforcement agencies are trying to teach people what is and is not appropriate communication in social media but is anyone *really* listening? It seems there is a race to see who can spend the most time socializing online, dispatching their most private information, gossiping, and using the vilest language to hurt others. Further, cell phone and social media mania now rules at just about every event, including those with family. Because of this, people no longer share relationships of any depth because they love their social media more; but media relationships are superficial.

VOID OF MORAL OR COMMON SENSE BEHAVIOR: Traditionally, men have made it known to society that pride is something they need desperately in order for them to feel good about themselves or to see themselves as successful. Pride strolls hand-in-hand with haughtiness, which God hates, but unfortunately many men function according to how proud they are of themselves and their possessions, regardless of what the Lord thinks.

Though God tells us it is a humble and apologetic heart that pleases Him most, society in general—especially women—knows that most men cherish pride over an humble and apologetic heart. Therefore they will appeal to a man's pride to get what they want. An appeal to pride does not respect a moral code and does not accept common sense behavior but instead is foolish and overly aggressive. We are never immune to falling for the kind of pride that builds ourselves instead of God. Women particularly behave in ways that appeal to and build a man's pride—usually always to gain something.

There is no question that we females are broken today, but the question to ask is how have we managed to fall so far without finding a way to pick ourselves up before hitting bottom? How did we lose our title as "the gentle sex" exemplified by dignity, grace, self-respect, social graces, good manners, moral correctness and other godly characteristics that were evident in the majority of us beyond a half-century ago? How did we become the seductive, promiscuous, foul-mouthed, manipulating, demanding and selfish, argumentative individuals we are today? How did we lose our moral standing so much that we will watch, and participate in sexual behavior, that even when we repent, the hurt and devastation follows us throughout life?

Some readers may wish to question me about these issues that plague Christian women of today, but I challenge you to a test. If you are a person with Biblical *understanding*, listen quietly to female acquaintances, friends, and family members, and then make your own evaluation. Listen to young women who dominate a meeting, or a classroom discussion, or the conversation at a wedding or baby shower. If you are a "biblical" Christian what you hear will probably shock you. When I overhear the "not so discreet" conversations of women sitting at a table or booth next to me in a restaurant I have often wondered why they share their personal lives within earshot of strangers. Why not choose more lighthearted topics for dining out, or at least speak more quietly. Further, in your evaluation of females take time to listen to their verbiage, observe their appearance, and their unmovable stance on a topic. Compare it to Scripture, and then decide if what you have just seen and heard tells you something about their character. Does it respect the Lord's principles?

Many females who read this will object, saying "I did what was necessary to survive in my relationship;" or "my boyfriend or husband demanded it;" or "your thinking is old fashioned—we live in a modern world where anything goes!" Yes, we do live in a modern world, but it is a broken world and we must refuse to contribute to more brokenness. Females are now being incarcerated annually at an astounding rate, and this is scary for our children and grandchildren. Injustice is mean and destructive. An "anything goes" mindset does not respect the Higher Authority who sets the bar for our moral value system.

Christian husbands and fathers: please listen! Are you respectfully taking your position as the spiritual leader in your home? Are you committed to being the protective covering your wife needs, and as the Scripture says, washing her clean to present her as the bride of Christ. Are you able to be a covering without dominating? Are you concerned that God will hold you accountable for your behavior and neglect, or do you think you are exempt from the rules? Absolutely not! Men and women alike will answer for the irresponsibility they endorse.

THE BEST RELATIONSHIPS
MOVE FULL SPEED AHEAD

In a simple analogy, I think of a good relationship as functioning much like the steam trains of the past. Like these trains of old, a relationship must have fire in its belly so that all parts can go full speed ahead to their destination. For their best use, trains were composed of a steam engine and a caboose with cargo cars in between the two. I relate the engine to the husband or father, the caboose to the wife or mother, and the cars to the children and the issues of life. Much like the way God created man, the engine was designed first and was built for fire, strength, and power—the energy that was needed to move the train forward. I like to call this energy or stimulation, the force that goes before the rest of the train and faces any obstacles with great authority, courage, and power.

However, the engine (father and husband) must make important decisions along the way and the rest of the train (cars and caboose) relies fully on those decisions to be in the train's best interest. The engine must stay fired up or motivated, and behave appropriately. If it doesn't, it will jump the track taking the rest of the train with it and crashing to its destruction.

The freight cars carry the cargo. In a family this means the children, the issues in life and the commonalties of life—finances, household, work, church, school and so on. If these things aren't balanced, one car will carry more baggage than others and become heavily burdened. All the cars might suffer in some way but the one that is overburdened will suffer the most. Therefore it is imperative to keep track of what is going on between the engine and the caboose just as it is imperative to know what is going on between the father and the mother in a real life relationship. Both parents must be aware of and in one accord about what is happening with the cargo—particularly the children.

Just as Eve was created after Adam because God saw that he was better with his much-needed helpmate, the caboose was crafted post engine because of the special needs of the rest of the train that weren't realized until after the engine had been in use for a time. The caboose was an important part of the entire system and oversaw the efficiency of the train. It was designed with a lookout tower called a cupola, so that an overseer could maintain a watch of the track and the rest of the train. The caboose also served as a storage room for tools or other extra needs of the conductors. It housed an office, held cooking supplies and other essentials for long trips on the rails and served as a resting place to reenergize those workers needing a break from their responsibilities.

The caboose pushed right along behind the train and served as an observation deck so that the condition of the entire train could be monitored. The caboose was the train's helpmate much like a wife and mother is to her husband and children. Her purpose is to observe the needs of the family, to use love, wisdom, and *understanding*, common sense, integrity, and good values to make the entire unit function to the best advantage of all concerned. She is where the family goes for rest and reassurance, to be nurtured and energized. She defines the Biblical moral code for the family and her husband is in agreement. The Bible says, *"A wise woman builds her home but a foolish woman tears it down with her own hands (Proverbs 14:1 NLT).*

In the same way that all three parts of a train rely on each other for support, the partners in a relationship must carry their designated role to the best of their ability and sometimes they must function in not only their own role but also the role of the partner who, for whatever reason occasionally can't function. We call this "carrying the load for the family," which we may be required to do at some point. It isn't always easy but if there is love and support, encouragement and *understanding*, and if our hearts are turned to Jesus, the Word says we can do all things through Him who strengthens us. People of integrity and commitment don't run away. The members in a healthy family love and cherish each other. Family members that can't perform their relationship duties for a period of time must not remain in that condition. Instead, with the help of others they must work at becoming stable once again—unless a medical condition permanently prohibits it.

Relationship building begins at birth but as our world becomes more progressive and traditional family values continue to erode role models and genuine godly teachers become fewer and fewer. Therefore, building a strong family relationship becomes more and more difficult. It is imperative that as Christian parents we take a microscopic look into our relationship behavior. Is it consistent or do we have several different ones we use when it's convenient? If we could see the Lord in the room with us, would we behave the same as when we could not see Him? And when our children are around do we behave in a Godly manner or do we really care what kind of behavior they see in us? As a substitute teacher I can listen to my students talk and determine how their parents teach or train or not. Can we define our behavior as being full of integrity or is it mixed with various characteristics—some respectful, some disrespectful, which surface depending on our situation?

God saved us because He loved us and wanted to be gracious and merciful toward us despite our sin. We believe in Him through our faith that He is real even though we can't see Him. Obeying Him through good behavior is an act of our faith and is accounted to us as righteousness. Our faith in God and our desire to glorify Him over man is the greatest possession we have, which we must cling to with all our might. God is motion sensitive, and expects us to get moving in our relationship with Him and in relationships with others.

John 10:27-30 shows us the three types of action involved for a good relationship with the Lord. God speaks to His children through His Word and the power of the Holy Spirit! We listen and we follow. He then gives us eternal life with a promise that we are secure in Him. The part, which I believe so many of us miss, is this: *listening* to His voice and *following* and *obeying* Him! Only then are we secure in Him. We cannot do our own thing, violating His Word and still remain secure in Him. The Lord wants His children to allow His character to become fully developed in their lives; again we *listen*. (Galatians 4:19) for we are shown to be right with God by what we do (an obedient action) not by faith alone (inaction) (James 2:24). God desires that we stay connected to Him through praise and worship, and obedience to His commands.

Whether we are a biological, blended, or broken family, we will get through difficulties more easily when we make a choice to relate to each other as the Lord desires us to relate to Him. We will be more successful at closing the gaps of dysfunction when we make a better effort to listen to each other, follow the spiritual leader in the family (hopefully there is one), and obey the biblical requirements laid out by the head and the helpmate—the mom and dad.

Where families are already divided and the children are blended into new families the adults from both sides have a mandate from God to put aside their anger and their differences in order to find solutions for their problems. When one family is Christian and the other is not, the Christian family must follow the Scriptures as best they can and make family decisions based on the best interest of the children. This may involve legal issues that hurt the non-Christian side if they refuse to cooperate on behalf of the children.

Christian families must realize that when children are trying to survive in a combined Christian and non-Christian environment their mental and emotional state of mind is overwhelmed and confused by issues they can't *understand*. Under these circumstances, it is the health and the salvation of the children that are most important. As parents, our *understanding* of Scripture and our prayer life together as a family will take a lot of our time. We may not see the results we would like right away, but any verbal and visual seeds planted in the minds and hearts of the children will someday prevail.

Are you involved in a relationship that is emotionally, physically or spiritually destructive? Are you grieving over any poor choices you made in life, yet you cling to an unhealthy relationship and environment because you think you will never be happy without someone to live with? Regardless of the legitimacy of your relationship, I encourage you to "let go" and "let Jesus" love you and be your companion. Getting out of any relationship is painfully difficult and it affects every aspect of your life but I am convinced that a relationship that hinders your walk with the Lord and puts you at risk both physically and spiritually is far more costly to your wellbeing than divorce, and I am one who strongly objects to divorce because of its destructiveness to everyone it touches. God forgives and redeems because more than anything He wants a relationship with His children.

CHAPTER FIVE STUDY QUESTIONS

1. Why do you think it seems easy for Christians to claim that they have a life dedicated to Jesus but they live entirely opposite to His commandments?
2. If you have experienced failed relationships, why do you think they failed?
3. Search your heart with honesty. Based on Scripture, how did your actions contribute to a failed relationship?
4. From this chapter, have you learned anything about relationships that will help you have a successful one or improve the one you are in presently?
5. If you have been affected by a shattered relationship as a child or as an adult, what steps have you taken to attain healing in your heart and emotions?
6. What are the three actions required for a good relationship with the Lord?
7. Whether you are the father, the mother, or the child in a blended family, how would you describe your family environment compared to what you know to be God's expectations for family relationships?
8. Honestly search you heart. If your blended family is struggling to survive how have you contributed to the chaos?
9. Do you use a biblical example when relating to other family members in your home or do you use your own way of thinking?
10. What action do you take to help build a Christian atmosphere in your home, setting a Christian example for your children?

SIX

❦

SCANDALOUS BEHAVIOR - PERVERSE SPEECH – ANGRY TONE: A RECIPE FOR DISASTER

"Those who are dominated by the sinful nature think about sinful things, but those who are controlled by the Holy Spirit think about things that please the spirit. So letting your sinful nature control your mind leads to death. But letting the Spirit control your mind leads to life and peace. For the sinful nature is always hostile to God. It never did obey God's laws, and it never will. That's why those who are still under the control of their sinful nature can never please God" (Romans 8:5-8 NLT).

"To fear the Lord is to hate evil; I hate pride and arrogance, evil behavior and perverse speech" (Proverbs 8:13 NIV).

The heart of the Godly thinks carefully before speaking; the mouth of the wicked overflows with evil words (Proverbs 15:28 NLT).

A hot-tempered person starts fights; a cool-tempered person stops them (Proverbs 15:18 NLT).

Most likely each of us knows someone who is in a position requiring wisdom, and is believed to be wise based on responsibility alone but in reality operates in foolishness, behaving inappropriately. President Clinton's time in the Oval office comes to mind and certainly fits that description. Our nation's support and love for immorality surged Clinton's approval rating to a high of 73% during the Lewinsky scandal. But Clinton isn't the only offender. Many of us behave in ways inappropriate for our place in life. When Jesus was teaching about fruit in people's lives He said this: *"Just as you can identify a tree by its fruit, so you can identify people by their actions"* (Matthew 7:20 NLT).

If we truly know the Scriptures we can look at how a person acts and determine if he or she is serving Jesus. As Christians we are to imitate Christ in all things and live our life following His example, (Ephesians 5:1-2) being careful not to bring sorrow to God's Holy Spirit by the way we live (Ephesians 4:30). We must build our faith on a solid foundation—the Word of God—and we must act out our faith accordingly so that others can see Jesus and His holiness in us. Though Jesus's death brought grace to sinners He taught that to be His true children there is accountability to that grace, and there are consequences for ignoring that accountability (Romans 6:15-16).

Jude, brother of James, taught that ungodly people had wormed their way into churches saying that God's marvelous grace allowed Christians to live immoral lives. Jude said that God had condemned those people long ago because of their denial of Christ and he wanted to remind the Jewish Christians that people who did whatever their instincts told them brought about their own destruction (Jude 1).

Much of today's church looks like the church in Jude's time. Even for redeemed Christians, following the Lord's instructions and commands is not easy. It requires "thinking" about them and "actively working" at trying to apply them. We will occasionally fall short, but it is when we deliberately fall short that we set up ourselves to reap the consequences Jude spoke of.

In Roman's 8, the apostle Paul taught that if we were dominated by our nature to sin we would think about sinful things all the time and if we let it control us, it would lead to spiritual death because we would never please God. In those Scriptures there are key words that tell us how we can separate ourselves from God—dominated; think; control; death; never.

DANCING WITH THE DEVIL

In order to please God we must choose Him as the Power over our life, and *understand* that He owns all souls—both those that choose heaven and those that choose hell. Once we recognize Him as the ultimate power over our soul we must choose to change our thinking so the Holy Spirit can control our behavior. If we don't let the Holy Spirit control our behavior then we do not belong to Him but instead are slaves to sin and in that case, we have no obligation to do right (Romans 6:20). We can choose to do right when the Holy Spirit lives inside us, for all who are led by the Spirit of God are children of God. We will make mistakes but we will immediately realize that they are just that—things that need to be confessed and repented of.

Because God created us humans with such great minds it is often difficult to turn them over to something we can't see . . . something in a spirit world. Often I find it difficult to let the Lord rule my thinking in even the simplest things such as when I am fully aware that eating something I don't need will add to my weight problem and infringe my good health. I moan and complain about being overweight but when I get the opportunity to violate the diet that is right for me, I go ahead and indulge while telling myself I shouldn't. I fail at this more than I succeed.

Paul expressed his grief over a concern he had for the Corinthians. False teachers had impressed and deceived them into believing they could still sin and gain favor with God. In a letter, Paul wrote, *"I am afraid that when I come, I won't like what I find and you won't like my response.* (In effect Paul was saying that he wouldn't like their behavior and they certainly wouldn't like what he would say to them—probably, that if they continued in their sin, they would eventually be separated from God.) *I am afraid that I will find quarreling, jealousy, anger, selfishness, slander, gossip, arrogance, and disorderly behavior. Yes, I am afraid that when I come again, God will humble me in your presence. And I will be grieved because <u>many of you have not given up your old sins. You have not repented of your impurity, sexual immorality, and eagerness for lustful</u>*

pleasure" (2 Corinthians 12:20-21 NLT). Paul was talking to "Christians," not unbelievers!

When these Scriptures in Corinthians penetrated my heart, I felt convicted to scrutinize my life. I found that there were things I had not given up, as the Scriptures require. I challenge readers to be willing to take a look into your own life. How many of these things will you truthfully admit might apply to you? I read these Scriptures and mentally acknowledge my inability to refuse the foods I love as being a lustful pleasure for me, which it is! But, what shall I do with my knowledge? I work at finding balance; otherwise, I will go out of control, which does not please the Lord. Jesus taught, *"Not everyone who calls out to me, 'Lord! Lord!' will enter the Kingdom of Heaven. <u>Only those who actually do the will of my Father in heaven will enter"</u>* (Matthew 7:21 NLT).

The letters to the seven churches in Revelation show us how important obedient behavior is to God. A passage in 1st Peter is another admonition for the children of God to behave honorably. *"Dear Friends, I warn you as temporary residents and foreigners to keep away from worldly desires* (lusts of the flesh) *that wage war against your very souls. Be careful to live properly among your unbelieving neighbors. Then even if they accuse you of doing wrong, they will see your honorable behavior, and they will give honor to God when he judges the world (1 Peter 2:11-12 NLT).* Parentheses added. Eating the wrong foods doesn't wage war against my soul. The Word says that it is not what enters my mouth that defiles me but rather what comes out of my mouth. (Mark 7:15) Nevertheless, what enters my mouth can wage war with my body. When I compare my inability to control the food I choose to my inability to control issues that wage war against my soul I am able to see not only the power that causes me to do what I want, but also I get a mirror reflection of my disobedience. One kills my soul and the other my body. In either situation I must choose. For some, the choice is easy; for others of us it is a battle, so we find ways to change the Scriptures into what we need them to say for our situation.

Just like unbelievers, Christians make poor choices that bring them great shame. They cannot undo the thing they did, but they can make a choice to repent of it and rebuild their tainted reputation. God forgives even though others may not. It is often the Christian rather than the non-Christian who struggles to forgive. Broken relationships of any kind can easily move us into a great need to find personal significance and fulfillment, and if we aren't careful, that search can be destructive.

SEARCHING FOR SIGNIFICANCE

People that are completely honest will admit that they have a need to feel significant in a special way. Most of us will search until we find some kind of significance whether we find it in evil or in good. It took many years for me to learn to stop searching for personal significance in a way that sometimes violated God's moral code, and to trust Him entirely for my worth—to see that it must be based upon my identity in Christ, and not upon my own efforts or the opinions of others, particularly men.

Eventually, I realized that in my search I let what I had been taught during those young years in Sunday school get lost in the persuasive tactics of others. I knew that I absolutely wanted Jesus in my heart and mind, but I also wanted something I wasn't convinced that I should rely on Him for—something I needed to find for myself.

Like most young women, I imagined a dream life of comfort—beautiful home, nice things, a husband who would long to be near me, and a family that would love and respect me. I was one who used a lot of energy and romance to build relationships and because I was of this nature I visualized a passionately romantic husband. With those things in mind I searched for the ideal mate based on my thinking, not God's. I was willing to sacrifice for this perfect relationship but if all things weren't perfect I would simply work harder to make them perfect. But there was one thing I hadn't realized—it takes two lovers of God's Word to work through the issues that surround behavior that violates His commands. I had not behaved well nor had I been sensible about a mate so I did not have that asset on my side. And, my husband had certainly not behaved well. Also, he disagreed with the major biblical points for a godly marriage so I was trying to build a relationship that was one-sided. Years passed before I could *understand* that words of praise, and promises made without acts of kindness and respect for a godly love are deception. This leads to regret. In the end, what I finally attained was far from the dreams of my youth—those dreams based on fairy tales alone.

Having grown up unaccustomed to words of praise, it's not surprising that those who used this technique on me met my deep need for validation and easily won my heart. When I listened to enticing words and indulged behavior I knew violated Scripture, I was truly dancing with the devil but at the time I did not recognize it as such. Too young to realize how serious a mistake I was making, I exchanged one bad relationship for another, not thinking of the consequences and certainly not the loss of my relationship with the Lord. Even after my divorce, it would be another man's words of praise, approval, romantic jargon, and promise of a lifetime together that would catapult me into a relationship that eventually left me completely shattered. Following the breakup, four years would pass before I could stop the hurt caused by grieving. I had never before loved so deeply or given away my heart so completely to anyone and even today, I must actively work at overcoming my love for him and the beautiful memories of what I call a "near perfect" relationship. Though complete healing does take time the process is easier when we stay in relationship with the Lord. But, the choices we make that violate His principles bring us heartache because we *failed to understand* the importance of distinguishing between good and evil behavior based on God's Word.

Life is full of regret and few people are exempt. If we could question Eve about her choice to listen to Satan instead of God on that fateful day that changed the course of life for every human born after her, surely she would speak of deep remorse and sorrow. But the devil is indiscriminate about who he chooses to confuse—even the elect, if possible, and there has never been anyone more "elect" than Adam and Eve, God's first creations.

Hoping to separate us from God, the great deceiver tries to convince us that God doesn't care how we live and that many of His biblical admonitions don't apply to us today. As we can see from Adam and Eve's experience, this is not a new tactic. Satan uses people to tell us that as long as we believe in Jesus we are secure in Him because His blood has covered our sin. But it is when we repent and stop willfully disobeying Him that we are kept safe in Him. There is no covering when we choose to remain in sin. Many things in life determine how quickly or not we come to realize that we must look to Jesus and His principles for our significance. From these principles, we learn to respect ourselves. When we respect ourselves, we make fewer immoral choices. If we don't respect ourselves as God's child we make a mess of our lives.

MAKING A "MESS" OF OUR LIVES

Within the last ten years, I have personally met numerous young men and women living in familial relationships that include children but who are not married to each other. From chapter five we learned that 2.9 million American children live in such an environment.

These arrangements are popular in the entertainment industry. Celebrities looking to establish individualism and gain publicity often choose non-traditional behavior to express their distinctiveness. Young people looking for ways to rebel against their parents or shock their peers will sometimes emulate a celebrity that is loved by the masses but is living immorally. Choosing a lifestyle that involves other humans but which is not balanced in the best interest of all concerned, especially children, is selfish, and lacks wisdom.

When a man or woman is willing to live with a partner outside the bonds of marriage and have children together there is no spiritual or legal requirement that allows anyone—woman, child, or man—any kind of security for traditional family benefits or commitment to Christ that leads the family to salvation. Further, domestic laws were designed and implemented to protect an individual's rights for the purpose of insuring the pursuit of happiness including financial sustenance. Happiness includes a promise that we can expect to receive everything a partner can offer that is in line with a traditional family and which embraces the following features, positions, and appearances of life as God established. The Bible teaches that the person who has God for his Lord is a happy person. Living in sin inhibits our happiness, takes away those provisions designed by God, positions children for failure, and jeopardizes souls.

FEATURES: Provision for Home, Finances, and Aging.

When two people cohabitate there is no marriage law of financial protection if or when the relationship ends. The partner with no ability to sustain a quality life outside the relationship may find it difficult to win financial provision. The financially stable partner wanting to dissolve the relationship may strongly object to dividing assets with the person they live with. This may also apply to a long-term marriage where divorce becomes necessary.

The following story is about a woman whose husband wanted to leave their marriage after more than thirty years together. It is typical of what often happens when couples try to divide what they both spent a lifetime trying to establish a financially stable life together. She was 58 years old when the marriage ended. She had been a homemaker and family business partner during their marriage and was not yet old enough for social security. Further, her husband was trying to keep her from her rightful settlement. His solution to her needs was for her to live with and care for her elderly mom. What the wife didn't know was that her husband already had another woman in the holding pen and wanted to keep more of his wife's settlement for his new woman.

The wife's mom needed fulltime care indeed, but her home was several years old and in need of repair. Further, her mom had already moved in with another daughter. Her husband was suggesting that in addition to her no longer being worthy of deserving the legal and biblical rights given to her through the marriage commitment of 'til death do us part,' or a unified family that she had spent years building, she should also be sentenced to a lonely life in a dilapidated home caretaking someone else. He was making it clear that he didn't want to keep or care for his wife in marriage, or after the divorce.

While they were negotiating a separate maintenance agreement prior to the divorce he insisted that she not get a penny from him until the divorce was final. She had no income, no way to care for herself and was living with a sister and brother-in-law. When she asked for living expenses before the court ruled on separate maintenance, her husband suggested that her brother-in-law could take care of her financial needs. When the lawyers met to discuss the separate maintenance amount, her husband argued that she would get no more than the monthly amount he had allowed her when they were living together, which was $300. Fortunately her lawyer and the judge refused to even consider such a figure and awarded her a more reasonable allotment.

Her husband's annual earnings exceeded $100,000 plus quarterly capital distributions. He had built his own significance justifying his right to personal toys and other indulgences, though she had helped build their business twice during their marriage, and managed their home entirely alone. His heart had completely hardened toward her and she was terrified by the battle for her survival. She could find no compassion in him at all; none for the years they had shared together, and none for her as a human being.

He showed no compassion or mercy for her old age but he had taken every part of her youth, using it to his benefit and declaring his right to do so before discarding her for another woman.

Even in marriage it can be difficult for a rejected spouse to get what is rightfully theirs because the one who earns the larger income feels entitled to take more both during the marriage and in a divorce. In some cases this may be justified but the rejected partner should never be left without the means to survive. Couples that cohabitate outside marriage, should reconsider this arrangement. When one partner decides to leave, the other is usually always left short of necessary support and since there is no certificate of marriage, there is also no protective law.

POSITION: The Right to the Intimate Endowments of Marriage

In marriage, each partner holds a God-ordained position to the rights of the intimate endowments of marriage. The Bible confirms that they each have full rights to the body of the other for personal pleasure—your body is mine and mine alone, and my body is yours and yours alone. (1 Corinthians 7:3, 4) But Scripture does not permit taking by force. Even in marriage this is rape and it destroys any opportunity for a tender and compassionate love between two people. Also, this Scripture does not permit any sexual behavior that does not conform to God's design for respectable sex between a man and a woman.

Marriage gives each partner the right to pursue the other for sexual pleasure. It establishes the right to expect fidelity and to know each other well. Sheltering secrets is unacceptable and particularly in marriages where partners are cooperating with each other. However, if the marriage looks like the marriage between the biblical Nabal and Abigail, (refer to their story in chapter 1) secrets may be necessary to protect others until a change can be made.

APPEARANCES: Rights to Respect in Private, as well as Public.

The marriage position also gives each person the right to expect and receive from the other a verbal approval of his or her existence. In a good marriage relationship where both approvals are given each partner knows instinctively how the other feels because they both make an effort to help each other feel comfortable and secure about life with them. Each partner has a right to expect total devotion from the other, which should be exercised in private as well as in public. Partners must understand that setting a good example of the Christian life requires behavior that is typical of devotion. I have witnessed partners treat each other affectionately in a semi-private setting, and then have seen one or the other, and sometimes both, rip each other apart in public. Constant criticism from one or both partners simply destroys the marriage. Whether it is the man or the woman acting out this poor behavior—power struggles, pride, arrogance, a need for the world to think you are the one in control of your marriage—they make a mess of their lives and destroy everything of value.

When a couple links together in marriage or in a non-binding agreement, an emotional bond is created that isn't easily broken. This emotional bond, which brings two people together in the features, positions, and appearances of life, is symbolic of twisting and pressing together two different colored pieces of clay. As time passes, the two pieces develop into one color, having been melded together in the traditional occasions of life. Whether the occasions were happy ones (children, grandchildren, special events, business, school, family, friends, sports, etc.) or sad ones (illness, tragedy or death) they twist and bind together the two pieces of clay until they are visually inseparable. Such an entanglement should produce love, *understanding*, compassion, respect, concern and happiness; not divorce!

DIVORCE: THE ULTIMATE REJECTION

Years ago a young Christian friend whose Christian husband left her and their infant child for another woman who carried his child from their affair said this: *"divorce is the ultimate rejection of another person."* But I say it is more than rejection; it is exemplary of abortion. Someone will die in several ways.

To physically separate a married couple by divorce is like trying to separate those two pieces of different colored clay that were pressed together until the colors were indistinguishable. Basically it requires breaking off tiny pieces searching for the original colors so that they can be separated. Divorce requires the same procedure. The result is complete brokenness because the person that left took with them a piece of the other person's heart and it can't be returned. Bones that were joined together through the events of life were broken. Emotions, which are required for love, were shredded because someone decided to stop loving or stop working at love. When we try to convince ourselves that emotions aren't important and divorce won't hurt, we are fooling ourselves and creating even more emotional trauma. It doesn't matter how good or bad a relationship is, divorce hurts. Though the rejected partner can still breathe, they leave the marriage with some form of brain injury, a sliced-up heart, emotionally broken, and physically burned out. When we forget or reject God, it's easy to forget and reject people.

My friend's husband's behavior almost destroyed her. They were Christians, but in today's world, Christianity doesn't seem to matter much when one person decides to leave the other. In the manner of her story many more tell of husbands that leave their wife and small child at home for the other woman who is now pregnant with his child outside of marriage. How does one justify such a change and believe that any good can come from leaving one family group to make things better for the other family? Until we women get gumption and refuse to join in an adulterous liaison with a married man and married men take a stand to honor their marriage vows, families will continue to be shattered. We make a mess of our lives when we decide to marry before we *understand* the responsibilities and commitments of marriage. And, we make a bigger mess of our lives when we decide we can't or won't use the

Scriptures and accountability to God to work through the difficulties of being partnered in marriage with someone.

How do we find it so easy to un-love another person? Is it because we never really loved them? Were we angry about something we refused to address? Was there too much pride to forgive even if we addressed it? Maybe one partner was adamant about not finding resolve. In these instances, time and the unsolved issues combined with a mound of hurt deaden the love we once had or thought we had. Two hearts—not just one—must be willing to find resolve. I suggest that the real reason we "unloved" someone is because most of us don't really know what true love is. Divorce among Christians is equal to or higher than divorce in the secular world. Adultery in the church is higher than it has been since the time of the Great Awakening when promiscuity in America was rampant. Even among people today who claim to love Jesus, it is a challenge to see in them a biblical worldview. Though many may say "yes," to Jesus, and attend church on Sunday, they continue living life as they want. This thinking and behavior has increased divorce numbers.

SEVEN THINGS GOD HATES

Proverbs 6 speaks of seven things the Lord hates and which are detestable to Him. When they are implemented they lead to scandalous behavior and are often contributing factors in divorce.

1) A proud or haughty look: This translates into arrogance, self-importance, conceitedness, snootiness, and superiority—characteristics of body language that are demeaning to another person and devastating in a marriage relationship.

2) A lying tongue: Satan is the father of lies. John 8:44 tells us that lies are his native tongue and there is no truth in him. We are most like Satan when we lie. Though we *understand* how much God hates lying it seems to be the one offense that is easiest to commit, the easiest to hide for the longest period of time, and the one offense against God that all mankind can easily justify. Spouses lie to each

other; children and parents lie to each other; employers lie to employees and employees to employers; politicians lie to each other and to the public even when they know there is evidence to the contrary—*"I did not have sexual relations with that woman!"* - Former President Bill Clinton on the Lewinsky scandal.

Ministers lie and deceive in their ministries. For some dark reason, we think we can hide this great sin from God. But as the words in a song written by my good friend Matt Nolen say, *"why do we think"* we can hide? (Emphasis added) We may be successful at hiding our lies from humans for a while, but from the moment the lie was conceived in the mind or heart we have not begun to hide it from the Lord. There isn't anything that we can hide from Him for He is the one who searches even our thoughts and our hearts, so He knows our lie before it ever leaves our mouth and hits the ears of the one for whom it was intended. No liars will enter heaven (Malachi 3:12 – Revelation 21:8). Please take a moment to review the story of Ananias and Sapphira in Acts 5. From it you will get a clear *understanding* of what God thinks about lying. Lying is the most destructive offense in marriage because it destroys trust. Remember the lie Satan used to convince Eve not to trust God's word? That one lie changed the course of humanity, and created chaos for the entire world for as long as the world exists.

3) Number three on the list of things God hates is "hands that shed innocent blood:" One doesn't need to think for long in this day in time to *understand* what 'hands that shed innocent blood' means. Killing rampages around the world reach headline news before we have time to heal from the last one. Daily, the blood of unborn children never ceases to flow. According to the World Health Organization 125,000 babies are dismembered in their mother's womb throughout the world each day. Their report on world statistics also shows that between 40 and 50 million babies are aborted annually.

DANCING WITH THE DEVIL

The womb is the place God designed to be the safest and most perfect to knit together a little human and keep it protected until it is capable of living on its own life support system. By bringing together a man and a woman, God made a plan whereby the child would have parents (a family) to nurture and teach him or her about Him. But humanity has listened to the father of evil and sanctioned greed and selfishness to find ways to use the great things God created—humans—to destroy His great creation—humans.

On February 18, 2010, the FBI and state police raided the Women's Medical Society, in Philadelphia, PA. The so-called "clinic" was owned and operated by Kermit Barron Gosnell. Because of the atrocities found by the investigators, Gosnell was convicted on three counts of first-degree murder, one count of involuntary manslaughter, and hundreds of other similar charges.

The investigation brought to light further information about unsanitary operations, use of untrained staff and powerful drugs without proper medical supervision and control. The investigating team told of a "filthy, deplorable, disgusting, unsanitary, outdated, horrendous, and by far, the worst conditions for a medical clinic" that these experienced investigators had ever encountered. The facility reeked of urine. Cats and their feces were found throughout, and filthy surgical rooms with blood stained floors resembled bad gas station restrooms. Investigators found fetal remains stored haphazardly throughout the clinic in various human food containers and even in cat-food containers. A surgical incision at the base of the fetal skulls (partial birth abortion, which has become illegal in America) was the cause of death for many of those defenseless babies. In the basement, investigators discovered medical waste piled high, and in one area of the building they discovered several jars filled with the severed feet of babies.

When convicted, Gosnell agreed not to appeal if the court would not seek the death penalty for him. He was sentenced to life in prison without possibility of parole. I find it interesting that the evidence suggests that Gosnell appears to have never thought twice about ending the life of those defenseless babies but used blackmail against our judicial system to salvage his own life, placing the responsibility of his care on American taxpayers.

Most people treasure their own lives so much they run to a doctor with every minor cut, wound, or illness. Who would have imagined that living, thinking humans could believe that it was morally acceptable to shed "innocent" blood—kill babies in their mother's womb? Maybe abortionists can't remember that they too, grew inside of a woman's womb before they came into the world. But they and those choosing abortion see no harm in killing other humans growing in the womb. The acceptance by so many people, even Christians that the child inside the womb is not a real human is a shocking paradigm shift from the moral code that defines Christianity. Even if people agree that the child in the womb is a human being they see it as not worth keeping. This thinking is directly opposed to the scientific evidence directly related to conception, fetal development, and finally, birth. It should not be difficult to *understand* that in order for anything—plants, animals, or people—to grow it must be connected to a life support system. Ask the mom still hurting because the child living inside her womb died and exited her body in what is called a *miscarriage*.

In order to stop the growth of anything living, it must die. To kill plants they must be sprayed with a chemical that kills the root system; or they must be pulled from the soil to which they are attached for nourishment, and then starved until they are completely dead. As a former gardener I found that there were two things that grew beautifully there—vegetables and weeds; but the weeds stole nutrition from the vegetables, which I needed to feed my body so I could stay healthy. The weeds weren't eatable, so I pulled them from their source of life. Watching them wilt and die, subjected to the elements without the protection they would get attached to the soil and drinking in the rain and sun, was easy. They were a nuisance in my garden and meant nothing to me. However, being a nuisance does not mean they were not alive or were not a *real* weed when I pulled them from the soil. *Real* children are plucked from their mother's womb because they are considered a nuisance—trouble of some kind. It doesn't mean they weren't a living person for if they weren't, there would be no problem.

A flower forms into a bud or bloom and then grows into a fully developed work of art because it is attached to a secure and rooted vegetal that nurtures it. Whether it begins dying while still attached, or at the point it is harvested and made into an arrangement for one's personal enjoyment, its ultimate demise is death.

To stop the birth of an animal it must be detached from the source of its nutrition found inside the mother's womb. When it is detached before its full term, it will die because in order to live until it can survive on its own life support system it must get life-giving sustenance from its mother. A child is no different. In order to grow it must be alive. In order to die it must have its life stopped by some method. Humans are the only creatures God made with a soul accountable to Him, and that soul can materialize only when a sperm and egg are joined to become a unified living organism and then is allowed to grow attached to its mother's uterine wall. For the sake of those who might not have a clear *understanding* of conception and fetal development let's review what happens from the moment a woman's body releases an unfertilized egg from her ovaries into her fallopian tube.

FROM OVARIES TO TUBES AND BEYOND

About two weeks following a female's last menstrual cycle, the ovary releases an egg, which carries two X chromosomes and which travels into the fallopian tube where it remains until it is either fertilized by a sperm or is discarded vaginally during her next menstrual cycle. Male sperm carries one X or one Y-chromosome but never both in the same sperm. If an X chromosome sperm fertilizes the X chromosome egg, the child will be a female; if the sperm carries a Y chromosome, the child will be a male. The genetic makeup of a child is carried in the chromosomes of the sperm and the egg. Fertilization takes up to 24 hours so at the moment fertilization is complete, the child's genetics and sex are determined. Most Christians believe that it is at this moment the fertilized egg becomes a child with a soul. Within three days of fertilization, the egg moves through the fallopian tube and attaches to the mother's uterine wall where it is fed for nine months while being knit together well enough to live separated from its mother's life-support system—the umbilical cord.

Once the fertilized egg is attached to the uterine wall, it begins to grow very fast and the cells begin to divide. Some of the divided cells become the placenta, which provides oxygen and nutrients for the baby and removes waste products from the baby's blood. Also, the umbilical cord arises from the placenta. Other divided cells become the embryo, which is the first stage of development from the moment of fertilization. At five weeks from conception a heartbeat can be heard on an ultrasound, and the child's brain, spinal cord, hands, and legs have begun to form and develop. At eight weeks, the child is no longer called an embryo but is given a new name—fetus. At this point, the child's liver, brain, and kidneys begin "functioning" inside the tiny body, which is between a half and an inch long. Through these two stages, the embryo and the fetus get nourishment from the mother's uterine tissue or the amnion. Meanwhile the placenta is developing, becoming the life-source (umbilical cord) for the baby—providing oxygen and nourishment from the mother's body.

The heart pumps blood throughout the tiny body, enabling all bodily functions. The Word says that life is in the blood, but it is the heart that moves the blood through the body. Since we know from Scripture that the heart is the wellspring of life, and that the Lord pleads with us to give Him our hearts, we know how important our heart is to Him. To stop a beating heart is to shed innocent blood and end the life that is in that blood. It is a lie from Satan—the father of evil—that helps us justify the death of the unborn by saying that the child inside the womb has no significance until it fully exits its mother's body through the birth canal. In the depths of our hearts we have to know that this is a lie.

On May 24, 2015 the USabortionclock website showed the following statistics on abortion. Since 1980, more than 1.3 billion babies worldwide have had their life support system disconnected. Their heart had to be stopped so that it could no longer send life-giving blood throughout the tiny infant's body.

The pro-abortion 'Alan Guttmacher Institute' reports that nearly 50 million babies were aborted in America since 1973. 93 percent of all abortions are performed for social reasons; the child is unwanted or inconvenient, (a nuisance like the weeds in my garden?) and most often the result of someone's unrestrained lust. America has great sin and blood in her soul and in her soil. The hearts of the people and the government are calloused. God is patient and merciful but He will not continue to look at our sin without bringing justice.

Usually when God punishes for the pain we cause others, it is a punishment of equal or greater pain than the pain we caused. The Bible teaches that during the battle of Armageddon in the valley of Megiddo, blood will flow as high as the horse's bridles. (Revelation 14:20) No one knows exactly when this battle will take place but considering the number of abortions per minute as documented, might we speculate that the blood of the innocent children murdered in their mothers wombs will be enough to reach the bridles of the horses in the Valley of Megiddo?

Romans 1:19-22 tells us that, *because that which may be known of God is manifest in them; for God hath shewed it unto them. For the invisible things of him from the creation of the world are clearly seen, being understood by the things that are made, even his eternal power and Godhead; so that they are without excuse: Because that, when they knew God, they glorified him not as*

God, neither were thankful; but became vain in their imaginations, and their foolish heart was darkened. Professing themselves to be wise, they became fools (KJV). Every mother has a mandate from God to do all she can to protect the unborn child growing inside her womb. Every man that causes the conception of a child, and knows it has been conceived has a mandate from God to protect and provide for both the mother and the child. As we have shown, neither the mother of the child nor the father respects God's mandate.

Physiciansforlife.com posted a report on their website of quite a long list of young women who were murdered by their boyfriends and in a few of the cases, their husbands. These women were pregnant by men whose dark side they knew nothing about or refused to acknowledge. They were murdered because the men didn't want the babies and when they demanded that the women get abortions, the women refused. Both mother and child lost their lives because of hands that shed innocent blood.

The men were willing to use the women for sexual gratification (and the women allowed them to), but under oath at trial they admitted to wanting their freedom. Not wanting to be tied down by a wife and child, or be forced to pay support for the child, they snuffed out two lives to salvage one—their own. But what foolish thinking; the murderers who killed to gain their freedom from responsibility went to prison where they lost all their freedoms and became criminals supported by the taxes paid by law-abiding citizens.

While many men have turned their backs on the children they fathered, we must not forget those men who fathered a child and wanted their wife or girlfriend to keep the baby. But, their voices were silenced by their partner's pro-choice view and the legally given decision-making power over her own body. In these cases, the Lord who hates the shedding of innocent blood will also hold the law-making authorities responsible for the baby's death.

I know several women who have had abortions and their life has been a roller coaster of emotional highs and lows. A few have gone to the Lord for forgiveness and the healing it brings, and they have attained that forgiveness. Others are still in need of healing and are struggling through that process. Still, some females can't see how the Lord feels about hands that shed innocent blood so they don't believe they need healing or forgiveness. When we truly seek God, and get to know Him through the Word, we will begin to see a perfect view of His heart regarding the death of these tiny babies.

If you are the father or mother of an aborted child, or the person who paid for an abortion for someone else, please know that the Lord is not pleased with your decision, but He loves you deeply and wants you to *understand* that you need to repent if you haven't already done so. The Word tells us that *"God so loved the world that He gave his only begotten Son, that whosoever believeth in Him should not perish but have everlasting life" (John 3:16 KJV)*. Jesus died to redeem us from our bad choices—the sinful things we do that separate us from God. He is our great healer and He loves when people turn to Him and let Him heal them and be their Father. He is the God of a divine comfort that only He can give (1st Corinthians).

Females that are dating a man who shows a side of himself that is contrary to what the Word teaches about godly living should pay close attention. He has a dark side. Refuse to give your body to men for sexual pleasure outside of marriage. Love the Lord first, then your body, your brain, and your emotions; respect yourself enough to know a great deal about a man's character before dating him. Abstain from sexual misconduct and reserve this great pleasure for marriage. Further, pull from your common sense instead of your emotions and don't marry a man until you know how he feels about the Lord *and* children.

Though it is not popular and is often ridiculed even among Christian men—"men will be men," so to speak—I am not ashamed to plead with fathers, asking them to teach their sons that sexual sin violates Gods commands, violates their own bodies, and violates the body of the female they joined themselves to. Please teach them to be humble and respectful toward females beginning with their moms. Regardless of how promiscuous the world becomes, the Lord will not permit or ignore sexual sin, whether committed by women or men. Nowhere within the Scriptures can we find that the Lord gives men permission to have sex outside of marriage but women must remain pure. Instead the Word tells us that both must remain pure for the marriage; in fact, the Word teaches that if men even look lustfully at a woman they commit adultery with her in their heart (Matthew 5:28).

Christian men should respectfully reprimand wives, daughters, and girlfriends who promote sensuality by the way they dress, speak and behave. They must be willing to walk away when a female behaves in a way that says she is willing to be sexually intimate. Just because she is willing doesn't mean you must oblige her. The Lord holds you accountable if you do submit, and he will bless you if you don't. If more men will speak out against the behavior of females who are violating the Lord's moral principles, more females will surely rethink their behavior and change their minds. We must stop respecting what Hollywood says is the acceptable moral code for mankind but look instead at the Word of God, for the Lord is the one who will ultimately decide our eternal fate based on how our heart served Him. We don't want to give Hollywood the honor of deciding what happens to our soul. Do we?

Fathers, please teach your daughters how to be unpretentious, and morally pure ladies and see that your children and teens learn proper social graces. Their physical, mental, emotional, relational, and financial wellness throughout life depends on what they think of themselves—their self-respect—and how they present themselves before others. In addition, please love your children because next to the Lord, their father's love and acceptance gives them the confidence they need to become strong and productive God-fearing adults who are able to pass that same wellness on to future generations. Don't do this, though, if you are deceiving your family, secretly involved in extramarital affairs or pornography and attending church pretending to be godly while railing moral sanctity at your children. To do so makes you a hypocrite setting them up for failure. One day they will learn of your traitor's heart and will compare your actions to what you taught them. At this point they could easily turn their hearts against Christianity. Without a father's teachings on moral and personal character, a child will have no idea what accountability is. If dads aren't accountable, the children won't be accountable. The only way to know if a man or a woman truly loves the Lord is when his or her actions line up with their words, which should be rooted in God's Word.

4) The fourth thing on God's list of things He hates is a heart that devises wicked schemes. The Lord looks at the heart to see the true attitude of a person. He knows if it is humble and contrite and practices the love recommended in 1 Corinthians 13:4-13. He knows if it is wicked, looking for ways to hurt and deceive others like those who speak friendly words to their neighbors while planning evil in their hearts (Psalms 28:3). Wicked schemes can be in business deals, the abuse in a marriage, murder, politics, government and trade agreements. These are just a few examples; there are many others. From the details in chapter 11 about how God sees our heart it will be easy to understand why God hates a heart that devises wicked schemes.

5) Number five on God's list of things He hates is "feet quick to rush into evil:" these are the feet of those that hate God, or they believe in Him but refuse to honor Him, preferring instead to chase after evil and sinful pleasures for themselves. Take a look at the history of the world, and chapter 3 of this book to see the results of millions of humans with feet quick to rush into doing evil.

6) God says He hates "a false witness who pours out lies." Have you been asked to testify about a court case but were instructed to avoid certain aspects of the truth, or to bend the truth? Were you asked to say things a certain way to show favor to one side over the other? Have you witnessed a friend do something wrong and when

they were brought to account you testified falsely on their behalf? Have you seen a friend in an adulterous relationship and then lied to their spouse to help cover their sin? God hates a false witness who pours out lies, and He expects His children not to participate. When they do, He expects them to repent.

7) The Lord also hates "one who stirs up dissension." Gossip has become one of the most destructive offensives in our society today, and it is present at every kind of gathering of people. The one who gossips stirs up dissension among brothers and destroys the peace in the life of another. God hates that. The Scripture tells us that *"if possible, as far as it depends on you, live at peace with everyone"* (Romans 12:18 AMP).

Throughout history, both godly and ungodly nations have risen and fallen. In those that fell, cultures came against each other in battle for one reason or another. Usually the reason was greed and hate—one group of people believing another group to be inferior and therefore unfit to live. Further, "we want the land you live on, so you need to vacate." Someone or group "stirred up dissension." Regardless of race, color, or creed, each of us has a command from the Father to do all we can to live at peace with everyone else. If we refuse to find a way to exist peaceably we will destroy ourselves with hate and bloodshed.

According to the Scriptures there is one more thing God hates: divorce! (Malachi 2:13-16 Amplified). All the other behaviors that God says He hates can easily lead to divorce. The Word is our guide to complete service to God. It is like a mirror to us and when we compare it to our life, we are able to see ourselves as we really are, whether our behavior represents the Lords commands or serves His enemy, the devil. *"Don't let evil conquer you but conquer evil by doing good"* *(Romans 12:21).*

WORDS THAT HEAL – WORDS THAT KILL

"The good man brings good things out of the good stored up in his heart, and the evil man brings evil things out of the evil stored up in his heart. For out of the overflow of his heart his mouth speaks" (Luke 6:45 NIV).

Jesus' half-brother, James instructs Christians about daily living—those behaviors that represent the Christian life. James cautions that the tongue is a flame of fire, a whole world of wickedness that corrupts the entire body; it is restless and evil, full of deadly poison and often used to praise our Lord and Father, and sometimes to curse those who have been made in His image. Blessing and cursing come pouring out of the same mouth and this is not right. But where does the tongue get its fiery motivation—from the heart.

Passages from the Bible tell us people break vows and use sacred language casually and carelessly. Routinely we hear people using God's name in the middle of a normal sentence or in anxiety. But Jesus said, *"let your yes be yes and your no be no, and anything beyond this comes from the evil one." (Matthew 5:37 NIV)*

"Let no foul or polluting language, nor evil word, nor unwholesome or worthless talk [ever] come out of your mouth; but only such [speech] as is good and beneficial to the spiritual progress of others, as is fitting to the need and the occasion, that it may be a blessing and give grace (God's favor) to those who hear it" (Ephesians 4:29 Amplified).

Appalling language is so prevalent today it's impossible to go anywhere without hearing it. Once while sitting in the steam room at the fitness center I heard such ridiculous language from a female I decided to leave because I was embarrassed in front of the men who were also present. In some churches we may hear language from the pulpit that would have never been tolerated as recent as twenty years ago. Christians speaking about a personal experience or giving a report in church think nothing of using slang words such as "jeez," (a saying derived from the phrase "Jesus Christ!" displaying anger, disappointment, or "wow" towards a person, object, or event);

"gosh-darn," (a play on the words, God-Damn—gosh is a gentler way of saying God and darn is the nicer way of saying damn. They are used separately or together to express anger, surprise, hurt or fear. They mean the same thing as God-Damn); "what-the-hell," (a reaction to anger or frustration); "dammit," (damming something with a curse); "frigging" (a backdoor entrance to the "F" word—the short term, "frig" is used as a euphemism (meaning substituted for) the "F" word. Also, it means, "masturbate" and it means to exclaim, such as expressing extreme anger, annoyance, or contempt). When we extend the word "frig" into "frigging" we are actually saying the "F" word. Routinely, these words come from the mouth of Christians. I implore you to please rethink any habit you may have using any of these words, for it displeases the Lord.

It seems few people care where they spew their angry attitudes. One day as I walked toward my vehicle after leaving the fitness center I heard a man yelling. I couldn't see him but his voice was loud, so I knew he was close by. Finally I spotted him across the street in a vacant lot. No people were around him except for those in passing vehicles but he was so angry that I could see the veins in his neck as he yelled and thrust his body forward, flailing his arms and tossing his head. His body language and his verbal language were terrifying and I became anxious and very frightened. I maneuvered my way to my vehicle hoping to stay out of his sight. I tossed in my things, and then quickly jumped inside and locked the doors. *"He who restrains his words has knowledge, and he who has a cool spirit is a man of understanding" (Proverbs 17:27 NAS)*. This man made no attempt at restraint.

A footnote in the NLT Life Application Study Bible tells us that, *"Our contradictory speech often puzzles us. At times our words are right, pleasing to God but at other times they are violent and destructive. Which of these speech patterns reflects our true identity? We were made in God's image, but the tongue gives us a picture of our basic sinful nature. God works to change us from the inside out. When the Holy Spirit purifies a heart, He gives self-control so that the person will speak words that please God."*

I don't know if the man I heard near the fitness center was a Christian or an atheist, or if he simply had not been taught about Christ, but even Christians think nothing of using the "F" word and "Jesus Christ" in the same sentence. If the Lord gives the Holy Spirit to us Christians for guidance, and surely He does, where do we hide Him so well that we can't draw from His source when we need to? I suggest that we hide Him behind our emotions, which we allow to control us instead of allowing the Holy Spirit to control us.

James tells us that our speech should be full of peace, and wise. *"But the wisdom that comes from heaven is first of all pure; then peace-loving, considerate, submissive, full of mercy and good fruit, impartial and sincere. Peacemakers who sow in peace raise a harvest of righteousness"* (James 3:17 NIV). *"What causes fights and quarrels among you? Don't they come from your desires that battle within you . . . ?"* (James 4:1 NIV)

Words! How they can kill and how they can heal! I have been in supermarkets and on playgrounds or sports complexes where I heard parents speak horribly to their children. I had to restrain myself to avoid confronting them about the abusive language they were using. Just like when we listen to spouses complain about each other and we can't determine what the exact truth is, neither can we know for sure what the issues are between a parent and a child. But I have witnessed all kinds. I have seen when a child was difficult in public and should have been taken home and dealt with, and I have seen when a child did nothing but ask a simple question and received a verbal thrashing no human should have to endure. It not only destroyed the child's confidence it also embarrassed bystanders. This should not be. Whether we are in public or in private, our need to flare-up should be restrained.

It is rare today to encounter people who genuinely know how to speak—how to form a correct sentence and say what they mean. More often we hear, "well, that's not what you said!" and then the response: "But, that's not what I meant." Why don't we know how to say what we mean? Is it because we didn't apply ourselves in school? Or was it because the school system passed us just to get us through the grades? Or maybe it was a little of both. In many cases fear and anxiety interfere with our speaking abilities. Parental abuse or criticism also determines how we talk. Maybe anger affects our ability to *understand* what someone is saying because we have a pre-determined mindset of that person, which solidifies our opinion of him or her. One reason we can't express ourselves well is because our limited vocabulary won't let us form an explanatory sentence. If we could reverse the damage that has been caused by being under-educated linguistically, we would have a greater chance at building and maintaining good relationships.

Kindness in today's world is almost a lost art. Criticism is more the model even in businesses where one would think most entities would value and encourage friendliness toward those laying their money down for a product or service. When I overhear employees in the service industry gossiping about other employees' work, or complaining about their boss, or an earlier customer, immediately I know that I am not immune to their wrath even if I have done nothing to provoke them. The reason is that this personality trait has no respect for anyone because it has no self-respect. Where respect is lost, self-discipline is also lost. Friendliness and kindness are not the standard in our modern day business world, so when I encounter someone who exemplifies the love characteristics the Lord laid out for us in 1 Corinthians 13 I compliment them for being friendly, which is simply the art of communicating kind words in a kind tone of voice and a non-threatening body language.

In 1 Corinthians 13, the Lord defines love as patient and kind, not jealous, nor boastful, nor proud, nor rude, or demanding, or irritable. It keeps no record of being wronged and does not rejoice about injustice but rejoices whenever the truth wins out. Love never gives up, never loses faith, is always hopeful, and endures through every circumstance. True love speaks kind words that calm fearfulness because they are spoken with genuine compassion and respect, which comes from the heart. When we implement these things, we are honoring God's command to love one another.

BODY LANGUAGE: MUCH MORE THAN WORDS

Life experiences have taught me that tone of voice and body language are lovers—one is never without the other and together they speak much more clearly than words and can be a powerhouse of either comfort or distress. In a loving attitude the tone and body language are comforting and reassuring. They don't threaten, or impart rejection toward others. But when the tone is angry, those close by may feel threatened in some way.

The principal of my elementary school was a kind man with a sweet and gentle spirit. He never quarreled or raised his voice though he was a firm disciplinarian. He had laughing eyes and a full-time facial smile though he might not have been deliberately smiling. He always joked with the students on the playground and never once did I hear him chide kids to make them feel bad. He encouraged students and we all loved him and felt completely safe in his presence. I personally felt that he respected and appreciated us—definitely one of the "good" guys. (Imagine if we feared God as our teacher!) It takes a special personality to teach because educating students involves much more than teaching the basics of reading, writing and arithmetic.

While we may not be able to reach all students at every level of their need, educating includes helping them *understand* that they are good enough to achieve what they set their minds to, and they have no need to fear their teachers or instructors. It is a *sweet-spirited* tone of voice and a friendly and appropriate body language that helps people learn. This tone dispels student's fear, expands their self-confidence, teaches them how to love and be kind, and enables them to transfer that same ability to others.

When we are contentious our tone of voice and body language expose our true feelings either about someone or something. The two together can be volatile enough to cause those around us to believe they are being threatened in some way. Those within earshot may feel they are hated, or unworthy, and stupid or wrong about something even though they are not. Maybe the bystander feels threatened physically. Others may become overly uncomfortable and either back off or retaliate.

Words have great power, and when they are spoken in anger accompanied by a frightening tone of voice and aggressive body language they separate people and hinder reconciliation and healing. *"The words of the Godly are a life-giving fountain; the words of the wicked conceal violent intentions" (Proverbs 10:11 NLT).*

HOW DO OTHERS SEE US?

For three summers, I worked retail in an up-scale contemporary western boutique in a ski resort town. The boutique accommodated folks from all walks of life locally, as well as from around the world. In an economically sound summer we would see as many as 30 customers in that small store at the same time, so it was impossible to avoid hearing their conversations. Usually I could tell right away which couples were married to each other and which were not. I could tell newly-weds from those aggressively climbing the ladder to corporate success as well as those couples that were downright tired of each other. They were the most obvious and the most routine. I could tell which wives were married to dictators and those married to a disinterested husband. The hen-pecked and abused husband was rare but occasionally I did see them. There were three telltale signs that helped me determine who fit where: words used, tone of voice used, and body language.

Rarely did women come into the store alone because most were vacationing with someone. The fairly balanced couple walked through the store together. Men companions were often quiet—clearly uncomfortable in a lady's boutique, but occasionally willing to comment on an item they thought she might like. The woman gave a low umm and moved on. Usually male partners made one round trip through the store with their female companion. When their conversation got stagnant at his question, "how do you like this?" and she ignored it with her reply, "umm, this little item is cute" and no serious interest was shown for his suggestion, yet she refused to leave the store, most men would then go and sit on the bench just outside the door, and wait for her to join him.

This behavior revealed a great deal about both personalities in that particular relationship. The husband's comments showed his approval for his wife to buy. Her lack of response but refusal to leave the store told him he should give her some space and let her think it through. When she had finished shopping she would meet him outside the door, open her bag and show him her purchase, and then he would approve. Some readers may say, "What a boring relationship." But those relationships are strong because they are built on trusting one person's ability to make a decision without fearing the other person's response to that decision—something I was never able to enjoy in my marriage.

Occasionally, I saw the couple where the man was 20-30 years older than the woman. Clearly, spending was not a problem for him since his ego was fully charged by her youth and sensuality. He was in complete control of the relationship and she was willing to submit to that control. He made selections for her and she usually agreed whether or not she approved. She would then ask for several items he hadn't mentioned but which she knew she would get. It was clear that she was either the new wife after the divorce or death of the former one, or she was the mistress. She presented herself as beautiful, sexy, classy, and obedient. She was allowed to talk but never dared to cross him. She had sold her soul for beautiful things and an opportunity to see the world; he had sold his soul for what he considered the luxury of authority and sex.

The overly dominant husband was rare but I did occasionally see one. He had no respect for his wife. Clearly she was the abused partner regardless to whether it was physical or verbal. She knew that any decision she made would be wrong, so she had to ask permission for everything. Her shoulders were bent as if she carried fifty extra pounds there, and a crease rested between her eyebrows. I knew these women like the back of my hand because I had been one. Once inside the store the husband would show his discontent at having agreed to even enter there by letting her know he had no time to spare because he was anxious to move on to something he wanted to do; and besides that, to his thinking "there wasn't anything there she really needed!" His body language, tone of voice and lack of willingness to encourage and inspire her usually meant there would be no sale. Unless she followed him out the door immediately, he would leave the store grumbling that he would wait on the bench a bit. Actually he was saying, "Don't take too long." In these cases, I would make a point to smile and say complimentary things to the woman, trying to take her mind off of her problems. Women with these issues rarely purchased anything, but they lusted and usually always returned in the afternoon while their husbands were napping. However, I never tried to sell to them because I could tell by their manner that they would be in trouble if they bought and I did not want that for them. I left them to make their decisions without any coercion from me.

Occasionally, I encountered the couple where clearly the man was abused. The abusive woman was sharp-tongued, demeaning, demanding, rolling her eyes, and giving him death-threatening looks. He showed signs of weakness and when he expressed an opinion she criticized him for his views, not caring if she embarrassed him in front of others.

DANCING WITH THE DEVIL

On occasion, I saw the husband who was so foolish it was easy to understand why the wife was frustrated; at times even I wanted to boot those guys right through the door. Regardless, from these couples I learned what I wanted and didn't want in a relationship at home or in public and I knew how I wanted others to see my partner and me.

The most impressive couples were those that came through the door smiling, and slightly touching or holding hands. Together they conversed kindly and onlookers knew instinctively they approved of each other. They were not exaggerated in any direction—neither overly sexual nor distant with each other. The man was affirming in his actions, his words and his tone of voice, and the woman responded in kind. He was gracious and generous toward her and she was respectful, and loving toward him. They made those around them feel comfortable and I knew by their behavior that I could be at ease and try to sell to them. They were strong enough in their individual roles to make sensible decisions and they never flamboyantly threw money around although clearly they might have had plenty. Often I would learn that these couples were not only in love with each other, they both were in love with Jesus. At their departure I always felt a little cheated that I was missing out on something of splendid value if I didn't immediately lock the doors to the store and meander around town together or join them for a glass of wine while getting acquainted over dinner. Combined, their actions drew me to them.

God set a standard that people should use for becoming good Christians. When put to use, this standard builds Christian relationships and homes that He approves. What standard would your spouse find if he or she were to truthfully evaluate your character based on your actions, your words, your tone of voice, and your body language? Would the evaluation meet God's standards, making you worthy of your spouse? *A gentle answer turns away wrath, but a harsh word stirs up anger (Proverbs 15:1 NIV)*. Anger always provokes retaliation whether verbal or physical and it is a recipe for disaster in relationships.

DANCING WITH THE DEVIL

CHAPTER SIX STUDY QUESTIONS

1. In your own words, describe what Mathew 7:20 means to you.
2. Have you found or do you presently find it difficult to turn your mind over to something in the spiritual world, which you can't see? (The Lord) If you overcame this problem, explain how.
3. Examine yourself. Do you feel insignificant in any way? If so, did you search for significance and how did you go about it?
4. Are you living in a relationship environment that violates the Scriptures according to what you have read here in chapter 6? If so, what will you do to change that environment and create one that aligns with the Lord's standards?
5. From the section, "Making a *Mess* of Our Lives" beginning on page 255 can you identify with any of those relationship characteristics? In what way can you identify?
6. From your own opinion, why do you think people find it so easy to un-love someone?
7. Do you think the unusually high divorce rate among Christians can be reduced? If not, why? If so, state your ideas about how it can be done.
8. Search your heart deeply and state your position regarding the seven things God hates. Don't leave any stone unturned because how you think about these seven things determines where you are in relationship with Christ.
9. Carefully review the Scriptures included in this chapter. Do you see yourself conforming to or violating these teachings?
10. God set a standard for becoming a good Christian. If you were to be evaluated by the person closest to you in relationship would they find in you a standard that meets God's standards?

DANCING WITH THE DEVIL

SEVEN

⊛

MORAL IMPIETY
"WHO TOLD YOU THAT YOU WERE NAKED?"
"WHY DOES IT MATTER?"

Don't you realize that those who do wrong will not inherit the Kingdom of God? Don't fool yourselves. Those who indulge in **sexual** *sin, or who worship idols, or commit adultery, or are male prostitutes, or practice homosexuality, or are thieves, or greedy people, or drunkards, or are abusive, or cheat people—none of these will inherit the Kingdom of God (1 Corinthians 6:9,10 NLT).*

Because we belong to the day, we must live decent lives for all to see. Don't participate in the darkness of wild parties and drunkenness, or in **sexual** *promiscuity and immoral living, or in quarreling and jealousy (Romans 13:13 NLT).*

You say, "Food was made for the stomach, and the stomach for food." (This is true, though someday God will do away with both of them.) But you can't say that our bodies were made for **sexual** *immorality. They were made for the Lord, and the Lord cares about our bodies (1 Corinthians 6:13 NLT).*

Run from **sexual** *sin! No other sin so clearly affects the body as this one does. For* **sexual** *immorality is a sin against your own body (1 Corinthians 6:18 NLT).*

And don't forget Sodom and Gomorrah and their neighboring towns, which were filled with immorality and every kind of **sexual** *perversion. Those cities were destroyed by fire and serve as a warning of the eternal fire of God's judgment (Jude 1:7 NLT).*

*And we must not engage in **sexual** immorality as some of them did, causing 23,000 of them to die in one day (1 Corinthians 10:8* NLT*) (During the Exodus out of Egypt).*

When tempted, no one should say, "God is tempting me." For God cannot be tempted by evil, nor does he tempt anyone; but each person is tempted when they are dragged away by their own evil desire and enticed. Then, after desire has conceived, it gives birth to sin; and sin, when it is full-grown, gives birth to death (James 1:13-15 NIV*).*

WHO TOLD YOU THAT YOU WERE NAKED? WHY DOES IT MATTER?

Generally I associate evil with a form of torture, or the killing of humans, so I was shocked that my research revealed how much evil is directly related to our sexuality. From nudity to extreme sexual violence, humanity has practiced sexual evil—particularly nudity—since time began. However, humanity doesn't always call evil what God calls evil.

I pondered my new discovery and then searched the Bible beginning with the fall in the Garden through The Book of Revelation until I grasped the intensity of God's warnings to His children about avoiding this great sin. Even so I was still haunted by, what seemed to me, duplicity of some kind. If it was acceptable for Adam and Eve to be naked before the fall, why was their nakedness not acceptable immediately after the fall? Why did they now feel guilty when they hadn't before? Why does nakedness matter, and why does it lead to evil behavior? Why do people want to expose their bodies and view exposed bodies—and who cares if they do?

Very little feels better than stripping down to the bare skin, free of anything that binds, and relishing the comfort of the birthday suit. For years I dreamt of frolicking naked in the snow atop a mountain—with a loving husband, of course. I struggled with my thoughts for some time, wondering if there was something dark and vastly inappropriate about me, something abnormal that I needed to fix before I could enter heaven.

One day my concern was liberated in the words of a five-year-old child. As we were traveling together to the supermarket he sat quietly, fastened securely in his car seat. I noticed that he was pensive as he gazed through the window at the snow outside. I watched him in my rear-view mirror and wondered if he was troubled about something when suddenly he spoke without hesitation or changing his gaze. In his child's vocabulary he said, "Kafaleen, someday I want to take off all my clothes and go play in the snow." Taking a few seconds to swallow my shock over his words, I giggled softly and replied, "So do I, sweetheart! So do I!"

My little friend's comment debunked the silly disquiets I had about romping in the snow in my birthday suit with a husband that loved me, but I still needed to find biblical answers about why being naked was a hesitation in the first place—after all, we were meant to be naked. So I returned to the Genesis account of the fall. *"Now the man and his wife were both naked, but they felt no shame"* (Genesis 2:25 NLT). Then the serpent arose and persuaded them that it was okay to disobey God. So they ate and instantly their life changed for the Scripture says, *"At that moment their eyes were opened, and they suddenly felt shame at their nakedness. So they sewed fig leaves together to cover themselves"* (Genesis 3:7 NLT).

Why did eating the fruit suddenly cause them to feel shame about their bodies? After all, it was not sexual sin that caused them to fall as it has so many since them. It was ignoring God's instructions that caused the fall. When they heard God walking in the garden they were afraid. Before they ate the fruit they were not afraid or ashamed for God to see them naked. Suddenly it was disgraceful to show uncovered skin, particularly before a Holy God.

In the beginning, God had put Adam in charge of the garden and instructed him not to eat from the tree of the knowledge of good and evil; therefore Adam was the one He questioned. *"Then the Lord*

DANCING WITH THE DEVIL

God called to the man, 'where are you?'" He replied, "I heard you walking in the garden, so I hid. I was afraid because I was naked" "Who told you that you were naked?" the Lord God asked. "Have you eaten from the tree whose fruit I commanded you not to eat?" (Genesis 3:9-11 NLT) Right away, Adam faulted Eve, telling God that it was the woman He had given him. From that moment forward the battle between the sexes has raged.

Instantly human nakedness became an urgent shame, a disgrace that needed to be corrected immediately after the fall. God didn't take the time to weave an overlay from vines or spin grasses into fabric that could be used for clothing. Instead, he used animal skins to cover their nakedness. *"And the Lord God made clothing from animal skins for Adam and his wife" (Gen 3:21 NLT).* When He did this He made an indisputable statement that fig leaves were not good enough to cover the human body. Throughout Scripture God refers to nakedness as a shame or disgrace. For years humans have used that aspect of Scripture to humiliate people. When Jesus was crucified, he was stripped naked and the soldiers gambled for his clothing. Before being marched to the gallows to hang for treason in 1945 Germany, Pastor Dietrich Bonhoeffer was stripped naked. To humiliate the Jews during the war their enemies forced them to walk around naked in public. During the Armenian massacre Christian women were forced to strip naked during their march to Aleppo, Syria. To expose their nakedness in such a manner was to shame and humiliate them since human eyes are not to look upon human nakedness. For Christians and Jews to do so violates God's moral statutes and leads to sin.

The key words in Genesis 3:7 are *"their eyes were opened."* When they ate the fruit, they saw the evil side of lust—sexual perversion and a desire to see with their eyes what fed their flesh. Satan, the father of evil, knew this and would use their nakedness to pervert their thinking about this great pleasure that God had made beautiful. Because the eyes would now lust (have strong and sometimes uncontrolled desires) for this pleasure God used clothing to place a veil between the flesh and the eyes, otherwise people would lust often for just about anyone. Pornography has validated this concept. It is visual material—both alive and printed—containing the explicit description or display of sexual organs and the activity of those organs.

This display is intended to stimulate erotic (*which is relating to, or tending to arouse sexual desire or excitement*) rather than aesthetic (*something that is appealing or beautiful*), or emotional feelings (*which is open affection*). God made the appealing, the beautiful and the emotional aspects of the human body. But Satan has deceived people, convincing them that God didn't know what He was doing when He clothed humans after the fall. Satan has caused people to believe the veil is obsolete and inappropriate. He has sought to entice us to remove that veil (our clothing) and use our eyes to indulge the lust that we let our mind think that our body needs. The beautiful pleasure of the human body that was made by God has been perverted into a multi-million dollar annual porn business in the United States alone. This industry has led to the ultimate violation of our bodies and of God's command. Also, it has destroyed many human lives.

For believers, Satan has teased and aroused their intimate nature and caused them to put aside God's ways in order to justify exposing their sexuality by choosing revealing clothing. This has convinced many of God's children that He doesn't mind if they are sexually promiscuous, and it makes abstinence a greater challenge. For unbelieves, Satan has convinced them that they are free to take what they want from other human beings—such as all types of sexual violence.

My young friend's and my desire to frolic in the snow naked was not evil. However, because of the fall, had someone seen us it could have provoked evil, if only in a thought. The clothing God made from animal skins was meant to fully cover the human body.

Fig leaves tear, rot and fall apart. Animal skins are strong, last longer, cover a larger area and are not transparent.

That God has already destroyed the earth once because of the perversion of man's heart, and history has recorded that covered human flesh has not abolished the evil of sexual immorality, there is still much evidence that covering our bodies does help put moral restraints on our mind and emotions. Covering our flesh is part of God's caution for the believer to run from the temptation to indulge this great sin against the entire body, which belongs to the Lord. Had God not made clothing a requirement, possibly sexual evil would have been much worse than it has been and is today. Clothing has helped many Christians prone to sexual misconduct bring their thoughts and behavior into accountability to God's word.

THE SINS OF THE CULTURE BECOME THE SINS OF THE CHURCH

The sins of our culture can be defined as those behaviors that reject God's moral and civil code, which Christians are required to honor. Our government once prohibited viewing immorality over the airwaves. Today it is allowed, and is accessible to us around the clock. Through this medium humanity has given Satan the freedom to use evil to continually tempt people to commit lustful misconduct. In today's culture, no one is likely to turn on a television and watch a program or movie that isn't soaked in sexual innuendos or immoral behavior of some kind. We have seen it so much until its inappropriateness no longer convicts us. The statistics on pornography substantiate that few, including Christians, rush to close a computer website, or a magazine, or change a TV channel showing indecent exposure of flesh or indecent behavior of some kind. Rather, it has been accepted as normal.

When one of my brothers underwent a time of physical healing following surgery, he spent a couple of years without access to television—the avenue through which moral decay is permitted to enter our homes. When he finally reconnected to TV he was shocked to see how rapidly immorality had advanced. Immediately he was forced to make a personal decision to deliberately think about what his eyes were watching and make the spiritual choice to change the channel. We discussed how this new morality would affect the tender and impressionable minds that were still searching for the right moral code and how difficult it would be for them to choose God's morality when so much personal freedom without accountability was available for viewing.

Regardless of where we are we cannot avoid the sins of the culture. To do so we would have to leave this world. Though horrifying that they exist at all, it is baffling that this anti-Christ behavior has been accepted by Christians and considered by many as "the Church keeping up with the times." The Church is not obligated to keep up with the "times" because times change according to what people can manufacture in their own minds. But the Lord's character—His ways and His purity or holiness—is the same yesterday, today, and forever. His children are called to follow Him in His ways, not the ways of the world that come from mere human thinking provoked by a deceiver hoping to capture our soul.

Following an intense study of the Scriptures, I realized how, at times, I had violated God's moral code. What I learned showed me that I needed to forsake forever any behavior that resembled the sins of the culture, which had become the sins of the church, and which I had allowed to capture me in certain ways. After all, I was secure in my salvation because my confused understanding of grace covered me! In my mind I was a good person who loved the Lord and believed that He loved me enough that I could do life my way and still reach heaven as long as I believed in Him. I was saying with my mouth that I loved Jesus and I was attending church but I wasn't doing what He said to do.

My quest has been to gain a clear *understanding* of why humanity was and still is so different from the godly plan laid out for us in Scripture and why humanity continues down a path of moral decay when we have the means not to right at our fingertips. Further, I have needed an acceptable answer to when and why immorality began to control our lives. Why did we become so perverted that God used water to destroy the entire earth because of it? Why do we continue down the same path today, awaiting His promised wrath if we don't turn around? Presently statistics on immorality in America give Christians every reason to be concerned about where our children and grandchildren are headed based on their morals, and we are past the time to take notice and reverse the deadly advancement.

AND GOD MADE MAN, SPLENDID INDEED!

When God made Adam from the dirt, which He had just created, Adam was nothing more than a lifeless hunk of mineral matter. Though God created him splendid indeed, it would take something more to make Adam useful to God and to himself.

Maybe before forming Adam God knew exactly each step He would take in the process of creation, but then again, maybe He thought it up as He went along. We don't know the answer because the Bible doesn't specifically tell us what God was thinking beyond the creation account as Genesis confirms. Once the Lord blew His spirit and breath into Adam's nostrils Adam could then feel emotion, love, hunger, compassion, appreciation, patience, kindness and other characteristics that came from God's spirit to man's spirit.

This is also why God cautioned His children to *"Guard your heart above all else for it determines the course of your life" (Proverbs 4:23 NLT)*. Some translations say it is the wellspring of life. Wellspring means the source of everything, yet the Word tells us that the Lord is our source. From this we can safely conclude that God is the source starting from the moment He used His breath to give us His spirit. We are to guard our heart because through it, God enabled us to live both physically and spiritually. When the heart stops, the body dies and returns to the dirt from which God made it. When a person gives their heart to Jesus, and then dies, the Lord removes the soul (spirit) from the body and takes it to heaven where it gets a new body and dwells with Him eternally.

If a person chooses Satan as their master, and then dies, God removes their soul (spirit) and it goes to hell where it will live eternally with Satan, but the heart returns to dust. Satan does not have the power to remove our soul from our body; only God has that power. *"Don't be afraid of those who want to kill your body* (including the heart); *they cannot touch your soul. Fear only God, who can destroy both soul and body in hell" (Matthew 10:28 NLT)*. Parenthesis added

God owns our soul whether it serves Him or Satan and He will do with it according to our deeds when we were alive on earth. From personal testimonies of those who have died and then regained life, we have evidence that when we die, our spirit does leave our body. This means that from conception to death, the only significant part of the human body is the spirit (the soul), and not the sexual organs, which have become more important to humanity than the spirit.

WHY WAS DEATH THE PUNISHMENT FOR EATING THE FRUIT?

We know that the spirit or soul of man is important to God because it is where He placed His holiness—where the Holy Spirit comes to live when we accept Jesus as our personal savior. When man defiles his character and his body, he is defiling God. Death was the punishment for eating the fruit because for God to maintain control of everything He created, including humanity, he had to reclaim the part of our body that cannot decay—the spirit of man, which God gave to us all at creation. Our body, including the heart is corruptible and cannot enter heaven. To enter heaven, we must have a new body (spiritual) washed clean by the blood of the lamb. When God said don't eat the fruit and if you do you will die, death would not have been a punishment for the crime if the body had no spirit. It would simply go back to mineral matter. But when the body dies, the brain, which enables man to achieve in life, and the heart, which enables him to love and be loved and where the good characteristics of the Lord are stored, (guard your heart for it it's the well-spring of life) deteriorates with the body. Only the spirit, which God owns—whether good or bad—survives. *"If we live, we live to the Lord; and if we die, we die to the Lord. So whether we live or die, we belong to the Lord"* (Romans 14:8 NIV).

A BAD WRAP FOR EVE SINCE THOSE DAYS IN THE GARDEN

Jesus called a little child to Him and put the child among them and then He said to the adults around Him, *"I tell you the truth, unless you turn from your sins and become like little children, you will never get into the Kingdom of Heaven. So anyone who becomes as humble as this little child is the greatest in the Kingdom of Heaven. And anyone who welcomes a little child like this on my behalf is welcoming me. But if you cause one of these little ones who trust in me to fall into sin, it would be better for you to have a large millstone tied around your neck and be drowned in the depths of the sea. What sorrow awaits the world, because it tempts people to sin! Temptations are inevitable, but what sorrow awaits the person who does the tempting"* (Matthew 18:2-7 NLT).

Instead of turning from our sin and becoming like little children as the Scripture says we should, more often we find it easier to revert to heinous behavior despite what we were taught. To *understand* why we are so susceptible to temptation it's important to return to the beginning of creation and take a moderate walk through history, starting with the Garden of Eden. The Word tells us very little about Adam and Eve except for how they were created and what God required of them. But when I think of them, I see them as little children even though they were created with adult bodies. Almost by the snap of a finger, they "became," having no history before "becoming." Birth and the various stages of growth that humanity has experienced since Adam and Eve doesn't necessarily let our imagination see them as created adults. Rather we tend to see them as having gone through the same growth process that we have because that is what is familiar to us.

We have little *understanding* of them because we, who were born after them and lived, grew from infancy to old age experiencing the different stages of life, the trials and tribulations, and the results of the fall and being born into sin. Hopefully we matured and gained some wisdom along the way. From the Word we see that Adam and Eve did not do that; they were created perfect (without sin—not born into it as we were) and they were placed in a perfect world where they knew only beauty, love from God, and tranquility. They knew no evil until Satan came along, entered the serpent, and beguiled them. They were much like children, wide-eyed, full of the pleasures of life, and very trusting of everything around them.

To my knowledge, the Bible doesn't say how long Adam and Eve were in the garden before Satan came along to tempt them. Scripture doesn't give us a history of their life adventures prior to the fall. We know only that they were in a covenant relationship with God and obeyed Him, and they had no reason to question the snake before that fateful day. After all, he was their friend like all the other animals in the garden of perfection where they were living. Further, I have found no indication from the Word that anything unusual or questionable happened between the snake and Adam and Eve prior to Satan's arrival. When the old devil came along with his beautiful seduction, Adam and Eve simply trusted their old friend, the snake. Afterwards, God cursed the snake and condemned it to crawl on its belly in the dust and dirt as punishment for its part as the host body for Satan to deceive His children. Even today thousands of years later, most of us want to kill every snake we see because we see them as evil and full of poison. Further, there is no question why Satan, the great deceiver and tempter of God's "little ones," will be condemned to hell! *"Oh what sorrow awaits the one who does the tempting!"*

For years, I was peeved at Eve for what I thought was her

desire to sell out all humanity for her personal pleasure and particularly that her selfish action made me invaluable as a woman, qualified for only certain things. I have heard sermons that accused her of being evil, intent on becoming like God. One day while reading the account of the fall in Genesis, I could find no evidence that what many pastors taught about her being full of evil and selfish ambition could possibly be accurate. She has been given a bad wrap about her intent, for the Bible says that neither Eve nor Adam knew evil until they ate the fruit.

If we accept this as truth, which we must do if we believe the Holy Spirit inspired the Scriptures, it is inconceivable that they could have had evil intent of any kind in their heart. They were babes, still on milk and still learning. They didn't have a Book of Instruction to read every day to help them make the right choices like we do today. They didn't have preachers and teachers and television or seminars, revivals, and books upon books to show them there is evil in the world they should watch for. But they did have God who walked with them often in the Garden (Genesis 3:8) and told them how He wanted them to live. Adam and Eve's mistake was that they did not recognize deception because they didn't know what it looked like, and they trusted the word of something they had no previous reason to doubt and they had no fear of the God who was their friend. Their sin was in listening to and trusting something that was contrary to God and believing that God would be cool with it because up until then, they had witnessed nothing but love from a loving father. They simply didn't follow His instructions. Clearly they believed like many of today's Christians—that God would never permit such a horrible punishment as allowing people to be tormented for all eternity.

Today, God doesn't walk with Christians in the same way He walked with Adam and Eve. He wasn't separated from them until after they fell into Satan's hands. Today, we are separated from God due to the fall until we accept Jesus as our Savior. Afterwards, we have the Holy Spirit to live inside us and we have the Holy Bible as our Book of Instruction. It is our acceptance of Jesus and our obedience to the Word that builds the bridge that reconnects us to God. Regardless, many Christians today don't take seriously God's Word about sin, believing He is okay with it. For example: If you identify yourself as a Christian but are living with a partner outside of marriage, or are having sex outside of marriage, you are willfully and deliberately violating God's commands from the Book of Instruction and saying it is okay with Him. When we refuse to forgive someone knowing that God says we must if we want to be forgiven by Him, we are deliberately choosing to believe that we are an exception to His rules. If we compare Adam and Eve's sin to what we know to be our sin today, and which we willingly participate in despite many warnings and instructions, books and teachings, their sin dulls dramatically when compared to ours. This is one reason I believe the Lord has cautioned us repeatedly throughout scripture to *"get understanding."* He wants us to *understand* from Adam and Eve's mistake that He is trustworthy, and Satan isn't, and that those things that are contrary to His Word also are not trustworthy. We are quick to blame Adam and Eve for being weak or for our sinful nature, which came to us because they fell. But we are no better than they were because we have no more of an ability to recognize deception and resist temptation than they had even though God's Spirit walked and talked with them and we have our handbook, the Bible.

In the light of complete honesty we all could tell stories about how we have seen a mature, experienced individual trick, deceive, or manipulate through a lie, a joke, or the seduction of an innocent child or even an innocent adult. Maybe we have even done this ourselves. For example, when a man and woman fall in love and get married, they trust each other completely if the relationship was balanced in the beginning. That trust remains intact until one of them does something to break it. Once trust is broken it is difficult to repair.

Children are no different. They trust innocently until they are misled or humiliated by belittling jokes, harsh teasing, harassment, or unjust criticism. These things cause damage to their self-image and when it continues throughout life they hold on to the damage caused by such actions and begin to put up walls to avoid the pain. As time passes and they mature, they create a defense mechanism that includes a "fight back" mentality loaded with sarcasm.

When God talks to His children He doesn't joke around about things, or tease, or harass with unjust criticism. Instead, He speaks sensibly and with loving concern for them. Satan was able to trick Adam and Eve easily because they were like innocent children, having no former knowledge of evil or deception.

I have witnessed men and women from all stations in life and all ages seduce, manipulate and beguile an innocent person for personal pleasure even if it was just for the sake of a laugh. Ahead in this chapter, I offer many examples of seduction like what happened to Eve in the garden. Evil came to destroy good and to hurt God. If we don't *understand* that humanity is in a battle of good versus evil, and if we don't know the Word of God, we can't recognize or *understand* how evil works, and we will become its victim. We Christians tend to find a few positive Scriptures in the New Testament, and repeat them to ourselves until we have them memorized, and then we live according to those few. In so doing, we set ourselves up to live a fairy tale life that doesn't see reality or the evil around us and we are then unprepared to fight attacks by the enemy because we don't have the battle armor of God. We only have the "feel good" Scriptures. Focusing on these Scriptures and ignoring those that warn us about evil is the same as eulogizing a person for their good characteristics and never addressing any of their behaviors that caused others pain.

We can ask repeatedly why Satan chose to tempt Eve instead of Adam but no one knows the true answer. Many speculate that she was weaker emotionally making her an easier persuasion. But if she was, then what happened to Adam that he so completely succumbed to Eve when she offered him a bite of something he knew to be against God's commands? Was he operating on weak emotions? If he was designed to be the stronger, wiser, more emotionally stable protective creation, which we have been taught for years that men are—compared to women—what happened to him at that moment? My understanding from the Word is that Adam and Eve were created equal, which includes mentally and emotionally. No one can accurately define what took place that day; we just believe that it did because we believe the Bible. Part of the problems between men and women today, so many years later, are that each blames the other for the fall and the curse that God placed on the earth and everything in the earth. Regardless, when each gender is able to *understand* and accept that we all live under the same curse due to the incident in the Garden we will do a better job of living at peace with one another.

I'm confident that Adam was often frustrated with Eve over the suffering they experienced due to the curse. As life became more and more difficult for them surely he questioned her repeatedly about why she disobeyed God and ate the fruit. I often wonder if he ever questioned himself about why he obeyed Eve instead of God and why he didn't send Satan packing. The fact remains they both disobeyed God. Both are equally responsible. And, in every relationship since Adam and Eve, both partners are responsible for obeying God and making it work.

WHAT DO YOU WANT FOR YOUR LIFE?

Sooner or later we all ask the big question, "What do I really want out of life as I live it on earth?" Most of us will say that we want to be happy and loved. But do we ever really achieve what could be called *true* happiness or *true* love and if not, do we know why?

Scripture tells us that happy is the man (person) who's God is the Lord. But evidently that isn't true for many because there is immense unhappiness in people's lives today, whether Christian or not. Is it safe to say that the reason we are so unhappy is because we have let our mind be seduced away from the Lord's characteristics and into humanism—a belief in human based morality?

Possibly morality and modesty have become one of society's greatest downfalls because so many do not *understand* what they mean. From chapter 1 we learned that people have trouble *understanding*, particularly the difference in good and evil. But the Lord Himself said that His Word is not difficult to *understand*. Therefore since morals and modesty are a huge part of His Word, it's important to *understand* the vocabulary that characterizes them—the words, terms and expressions we use to communicate about them.

Modest means to be self-effacing and efface means to do away with or remove without a trace. Therefore to be modest we must make a personal effort to remove from ourselves every hint of inappropriateness according to the Word of God. It also means to be unassuming. One of the adjectives for unassuming is to be inconspicuous, and to be inconspicuous is to be unnoticeable, unremarkable, subtle or ordinary, or not immediately obvious. For something to be unremarkable, it must not show any characteristic that would cause another to remark about or notice. Therefore, if humans wear clothing that reveals parts of their body that would cause others to look at them with lust, they are positioning themselves to be "looked at" in an inappropriate manner.

Isaiah 53:2 tells us that He (Jesus) had no beauty or majesty to attract us to him, nothing in his appearance that we should desire him. Considering the amount of sexual promiscuity in the world since the "fall," imagine what it would have been like for Jesus had He been splendidly handsome. Both men and women would have chased after Him with unbridled passion and not for salvation! Also, there is no evidence from the Word that Jesus walked around naked.

To be modest is to be unpretentious. Pretentious means to be exaggerated, showy, self-important, haughty, flaunting, spectacular, arrogant, ostentatious, etc. The antonym for these words is modest. Therefore, to be immodest is to capture all the adjectives for "pretentious" and act accordingly. There are several aspects of modesty as it is applicable to our character. To be modest is to dress in a way that doesn't draw attention to our self but which is nice, decent, and complementary.

Because God immediately dressed Adam and Eve in animal skins following the fall, Christians must believe that covering human skin was of ultimate importance to Him; otherwise He would have simply left them naked. Even though the fall was not due to sexual sin, it brought about sexual sin—the human body suddenly became significant to mankind, particularly the female body to the male body.

The Bible says women are to dress modestly, doing nothing to cause another person to fall. To fall means to decrease one's own core value due to the influence of someone else's behavior. The Proverbs 7 woman was dressed like a prostitute and was intentionally crafty. A prostitute earns money by selling her body to a man for the purpose of his sexual pleasure. One of the ways she attracts a buyer is by intentionally exposing and presenting her body in a language that will cause him to desire her more than he does already.

Since one of the definitions of evil is 'the *intent* to cause harm,' the prostitute's behavior—intentional craftiness—is clearly intent to cause another to fall. God calls this sin. If a Christian woman dresses in a manner that exposes her flesh, which clearly God wants covered, then she is disobeying God's plan for her modesty and purity. Her disobedience is no different to the prostitute who is intentionally crafty or Eve's disobedience when she listened to Satan and ate the fruit. The Lord is displeased with the behavior in all three cases.

In contrast, the Proverbs 31 woman is "clothed" with strength and dignity. Her dignity is exposed in her appearance and her general attitude; therefore her dignity includes the way she dresses. To be dignified is to be gracious and honorable. Under these characteristics the Lord is pleased.

Frankly, I am offended when I see women dressed promiscuously. Wherever I go they are there, flaunting their exposed bodies in my face—something I don't care to see. Some of the worst offenders are Christians, and age does not matter. Immodest dress is not only an offense by the very young, it also has captured women well into their sixties, an age when, as Christians, we are supposed to have gained enough wisdom from the Word to know what modest dress means and how immodesty affects others, particularly men who have allowed themselves to be hugely affected by the fall.

One year on Father's day, I was listening to a Christian radio talk show. Modesty was the topic and since it was their day men had been invited to call in and share their thoughts on immorality. In large numbers, Christian men responded with an urgent and desperate cry for women everywhere to reconsider the immodest way they dress publicly and especially at church. One caller, who was trying hard to choose words that would not offend the opposite sex, literally pleaded with women to consider a more spiritually acceptable dress code, which would help men deal with the sexual issues in their lives. Again we ask, "Why does it matter that we are naked?" This young man's plea is a good answer!

Sadly women rebel at the request for a more modest dress code! They like their bodies and want to show them off especially if they have a good-looking body. Beginning at the age of 12, girls, especially those well endowed, wear apparel that reveals much more of their bodies than is acceptable—that which, according to the Scriptures, would be displeasing to God. But even at this young age, their hearts and minds are already calloused or indifferent to the biblical teaching, and parents remain silent.

Who is teaching females how males think sexually? If they are being taught, is it an accurate teaching done with love or is it a corrupted one done with slang? Remember Job in the Old Testament? The Bible says there was no man like him but even he recognized that looking at women—the lust of the eyes for the flesh—could become a problem for him so he made a covenant with his eyes not to submit to this very real temptation.

DANCING WITH THE DEVIL

Shortly after I launched my business as a social graces instructor I was given an opportunity to write a weekly newspaper column titled *"A Matter of Manners."* One of my articles on modesty was an appeal to women asking them to reconsider their inappropriate dress code in light of the flood of pornography, divorce due to infidelity, and the affect immodesty has on children. The articles were written from a Christian perspective based on Scripture but the public response was that I was reversing the advancement of women in society, taking them back more than 100 years. I found it interesting that the complaint wasn't that I had used a biblical mandate to urge women to rethink their behavior; their complaint was that through my plea, I was attempting to put a roadblock in the advancement of women in business and in society in general. But in reality, the complaint showed me that my request had convicted my opposition to resist immorality and stand for morality, and they weren't ready to do that. Choosing to take a stand comes from conviction and conviction is uncomfortable. Taking a stand often makes us unpopular with the masses, which is also uncomfortable.

Under conviction females would need to rethink their clothing purchases. They would need to decide whether or not to buy styles from a famous designer who was getting wealthy by helping degrade women and girls by selling sex. But what surprised me most was learning that many women really do believe they advance in business and social arenas more quickly when they are sexual—whether in dress or in body language—so instead of fighting for their own good and the good of their gender they submit to the ways of the culture and to the men who yearn to see their flesh.

Where did women get the belief that they advance more quickly in business if they are sexual? Did their parents teach it to them, or did the church? Did they learn it in college or through the media and film industries? Did they get a hint of it during a job interview with a male? Or was it when they took a position under male superiors whose words carried undertones of sexual blackmail? Has the male gender convinced females that they can advance much further in life with them or in the business arena if they will feed his visual or maybe even his physical lust by the way they dress? Or did these females simply listen to the sensuality of their own bodies? Where does the real issue lie with women who believe this way—in their ego or in their belief that they will gain financial security through quicker advancement? I leave it to you, the reader, to do the research and decide, but I will add this from my personal experience. Over the years, I have worked subordinate to several male supervisors. Only three didn't try to convince me that I would advance further in my position if I would show them sexual favors. These employers were in church with their families on Sundays. Fathers are you teaching your young daughters how most males think? Are you preparing them to safely leave the nest? Are you aware that rape on many college campuses is at epidemic levels? I assure you that teaching godly morality to your daughters is important and it will have a greater impact if it comes from fathers!

Some women have told me that they dress immodestly because their husbands demand it. This may be true in many cases. Men endowed with an over-active ego have a reputation for being prideful. They have a need for their buddies to see them as powerfully virile, and able to get any woman they want because of it. The woman he chooses to escort on his arm helps promote that image. Therefore, if she isn't already a willing participant of immodesty, he will encourage her, and to please him, she will usually use his request as an excuse to cover any guilt she may carry due to any Biblical awareness she has about immodesty.

Though people have tried to invalidate God's requirement for clothing, to my knowledge, He has never changed his mind about where He stands on the subject. Christ says, *"Remain in me and I will remain in you."* When we make the choice to "remain in Him" with our purity, those who don't treasure what we treasure will call us

Christian fanatics, old-fashioned, frigid, puritan, holy roller, something from the Victorian era, and anything else those who disregard Christ's commands can think of to say. Some of us are simply discarded for a younger female who is more willing to violate her virtue. If men could realize that many of the women they have culled as a potential partner due to her moral values are, in reality, motivated sexual partners in a good marriage relationship, they might regret their decision. Instead, some men have discovered that the woman they chose due to her willingness to expose her body wasn't necessarily a quality long-term partner.

The comment I heard most often when I refused to indulge an improper sexual encounter was "aren't you a consenting adult?" Christian females: please don't be intimidated by this question; decide in advance how you will answer when it is asked of you. Please don't capitulate to the one trying to coerce you into taking off your clothes or exposing more of your body than is morally correct. And if you are prone to sexual promiscuity with a man through your own aggression, please dress yourself with moral restraint and turn from that habit or need. Instead, separate yourself from the world. Your body is valuable. It belongs to the Lord, and is reserved for your husband after marriage and as a nurturing component for your children. Look at yourself in the mirror; love and appreciate your body as sacred; keep it clean and pure for the Lord, something you will never be sorry for. Once you truly fall in love with Jesus you will discover that indulging promiscuity will eventually lead to deep regret for violating His statutes and hurting His heart. Please don't dress in a way that tells a man you are willing to experiment with sex when in reality you are not. And please don't talk in a way that gives a man permission to disrespect you. The Lord wants you to be decently clothed and is calling you to holiness and any promiscuity you indulge will return to haunt you when your daughter matures into womanhood. Do you not realize that your body belongs to the Lord? It is not yours to do with as you please. He has the final say.

DANCING WITH THE DEVIL

Scripture says, *"You say, 'I am allowed to do anything'—but not everything is good for you." "You say, 'I am allowed to do anything'—but not everything is beneficial. Don't be concerned for your own good but for the good of others" (1 Corn 10:23, 24 NLT)*. These Scriptures are New Testament teachings about the discretion we are to use not only about those things God prohibits but also about those things that He allows that may be beneficial to us as individuals, but which may not be good for others. Immodest attire violates the scriptural call to purity, and it benefits no one—male or female.

Most pastors are reluctant to address the issues of personal appearance and behavior in church. They are concerned about offending and/or losing a portion of their congregation. And, some pastors believe the issue simply isn't important enough to address, but I assure you that it is. God is very serious about how important our morality is.

Different versions of the Bible use a variety of words to describe "modest" apparel. The NIV says decency and propriety; NLT says decent and appropriate clothing; ESV uses respectable, with modesty and self-control; NASB uses proper clothing, modestly and discretely. Young's Literal Translation says: "In becoming apparel, with modesty and sobriety." The Darby Bible says, "Dress themselves with modesty and discretion." My personal favorite is The Holman Christian Standard Bible translation: *"Women are to dress themselves in modest clothing, with decency and good sense."* (1st Timothy 2:9) This is clear enough for any Christian—male or female—to *understand*. With such clarity from the Bible itself, Christian females of all ages have no excuse for violating God's requirement for modest apparel. If Christian men want to truly please God and follow Him obediently, they must be willing to ignore the secular world's view on morals, putting aside their own appetite for immorality that feeds the eyes, and help the females in their life honor God's commands. Both genders must work together, helping to abolish the moral decay that is destroying people of all ages and our nation as a whole.

PORN: TAKING AMERICANS BY STORM

In a survey of Christian men who agreed to talk, the results showed that 63 percent of those interviewed and who regularly attend church visit online pornography sites routinely. Some admitted to addiction, which is idolizing sex. Thirteen percent of those interviewed were pastors or someone in church leadership. Why must they visit porn sites when sexual freedom in America is at an all-time high and there are several million more women than men? Because there is an addiction that takes place once raw and erotic sexual behavior has been seen with the eyes. Usually when this happens, decent and respectable sex as God designed for a man and woman no longer satisfies so the only way to gratify an insatiable lust is to unclothe the body and view it in its most provocative light. Once a person removes their clothing so their bodies can be viewed for sexual pleasure, it becomes easy to indulge unlimited sexual violations of the body.

At a meeting I attended on human trafficking, I learned that videos of children being raped were being sold as online porn. Law enforcement officers confessed that it is one of the most difficult crimes against children to stop because of the difficulty finding the videographers. Also, websites are easily shut down and new ones opened before law enforcement agencies can locate the builders. By then damage is done. Heinous crimes against children satisfy those in the porn industry in many ways. The rapist and the videographer enjoy the crime. Those watching the videos satisfy their own sexual perversion. But, these pleasures are temporary for in reality those promoting and watching child rape have sold their soul to the devil. They can still find Jesus if they will stop, repent and turn around. The child being raped is most likely ruined for life. This new child rape porn is big money in the United States and law enforcement agencies are scratching their heads about how to stop it.

Porn has created such a high volume of revenue that it is now being allowed into mainstream entertainment with no restrictions at all from the movie industries rating board. As the movie, *Fifty Shades of Grey* testifies, glorifying porn has taken on a new role. It is no longer satisfied to reach its audiences through a more secluded venue where people have to make a concerted effort to view it—behind the shelves or curtains of adult bookstores. In the past, porn had an undisturbed home in dark places where there was little if any interference by the majority of people who respect decency and who regurgitate at the horror of the behavior of humans who think we all should get on board with this kind of treatment of young girls and women—and in many cases boys. Instead of it remaining among the genres of entertainment designed to feed the appetites of those with a sadistic bent it is now easily available to those of us who choose to live a life of respectability and holiness.

The power of suggestion is commanding! To deliberately suggest that females should enjoy such treatment as BDSM is to submit entirely to a deceptive seduction that if not restrained, will destroy the physical, emotional, sexual, and spiritual value and soul of millions of people. BDSM stands for bondage, discipline, sadism and masochism. "Bondage" is to restrain someone by tying up that person in a way that full control is given to the one doing the tying. "Discipline" is enforcement that is regulated by the threat of punishment to help insure that given instructions are carried out. "Sadism" is engaging in aspects of pain or humiliation for the sexual pleasure of the one inflicting the pain. "Masochism" is the tendency to derive pleasure, especially sexual gratification from one's on pain or humiliation. Certain disorders accompany BDSM. "SPD", Sadistic Personality Disorder, also known as Antisocial Personality Disorder, is a term proposed for individuals who derive pleasure from the suffering of others. "SSD", Sexual Sadism Disorder, is a medical/psychological condition for sexual arousal from inflicting pain/humiliation on unwilling, non-consenting victims.

For years females have fought for the right to say "no" without consequences, and be protected by the legal system against aggressive physical and sexual violence, such as date rape, harassment at work, domestic abuse and any other act that destroys her wellbeing. Now that the mainstream movie industry has given a green light to this entertainment, there will be too many shades of gray to easily convict a man when a woman files a complaint against those who insist on this kind of sexual violence. The movie's "power of suggestion" says that women want this kind of treatment and should submit to it if they want a stable future with a man.

A YouTube review by Grace Randolph portrays the movie as clearly the porno version of Cinderella; she says that the targeted demographic is largely women and the focus is on wealth. Anastasia's character was designed to be an innocent and inexperienced not so physically desirable female who is challenged to BDSM behavior by a wealthy and supposedly handsome suitor who wants nothing more than to usurp power and control over women in order to feed his insatiable appetite to rule. The purpose of this movie is to seduce women into behavior that violates every aspect of human decency and self-respect.

A quote by Sophie Morgan from her review of the book, *Fifty Shades of Grey* by E. L. James, for the Observer, August 2012: *"For me, the book is as much a fetishisation of capitalism as it is a discourse on BDSM. Christian Grey may be a stalkerish sort with epic amounts of emotional baggage, but the accouterments of wealth he offers – designer labels, helicopters and expensive gifts – are deemed enough that our virginal heroine should stick with him, endure his peccadilloes* (wrongdoings) *and keep trying to change him. It's very much focused on ending up married and settled and financially secure . . ."* How sad! Parenthesis added

Author E. L. James has created a character comparable to Satan—one full of power, seduction, and a promise of the enjoyment of great treasures if he could be worshipped as king—in this instance, sexual king. The movie suggests that he is right. This movie has been given permission as mainstream entertainment at a time when efforts are being made to expose and eradicate human trafficking and sexual slavery. It does great damage to our efforts by portraying such behavior as romance and security.

Dancing With the Devil was written for Christians—those of us that love the Lord and want to obey Him, and live with Him eternally. Sadly, many Christians will read *Fifty Shades of Grey* and watch the movie. I plead with every Christian—male and female—that might be tempted: "please don't read the book or watch the movie and if you have already please don't fall for the seductive suggestions this book and movie portray. To do so will lead to a sexual addiction and emotional and physical pain and bondage that you may never overcome."

In his book, *At the Altar of Sexual Idolatry,* author, and former police officer, Steve Gallagher shares his story about the pain of sexual addiction. Steve testifies to the torment for the person caught in the claws of sexual addiction and how easy it is to fall prey to it even when you thought you had been set free.

Steve reveals his deep entanglement with sexual sin, and how he believed that becoming a Christian would put all those issues behind him. But just several weeks after a dramatic conversion to the Lord, he found himself in bewildered shock that he had entered an adult bookstore and acted out the same compulsive behavior that had kept him bound for fifteen years. He says that the message of his book is one of hope for anybody willing to apply biblical principles to his life. Out of his love for God and those in sexual sin, he founded Pure Life Ministries in Dry Ridge, Kentucky where he has committed to helping others break free of this obsessive trap.

Steve says that sexual addicts have built their "need system" upon a false foundation of sexual activity, that they reward themselves by bolstering their fragile egos, and escaping the pain of reality. But, what was it that actually caused the original addiction? In chapter 1 of his book, Steve shares several cases about how men become addicted to sex.

He tells us how a little boy named Jimmy was introduced to

pornography when he was seven years old. His older brother took him to the house of a friend whose father sold pornographic movies.

Richard was introduced to sex for the first time when friends invited him to their house for a giant orgy. He was seventeen.

Bob became addicted after he discovered porn under his father's bed. (Hello! Dads? Know your children's friends and their parents!)

John became addicted as a teen when he found a large box of pornographic magazines that had been tossed on the side of the road.

Steve says that in all these cases, these young men spent years in compulsive sexual behavior. When people over-emphasize the importance of sex in their lives, it begins to dictate life-style. Their minds become obsessed with thoughts of sex and they lose control of how often, with whom, and under what circumstances they indulge. Christians are not exempt from this powerful temptation.

What initially begins as fun and satisfying urges gradually becomes a mire of bondage and if one continues therein without repentance God will give them over to a reprobate mind. As the person addicted to porn creates a ritual of browsing magazine racks he finds his lust heightening, and then he moves on to the movie arcade where he fulfills his lust. (Note: the person addicted begins his journey by feasting on uncovered flesh that God insisted we cover.)

Steve tells us that a child molester will establish a different routine. He may or may not begin by looking at porn, but regardless, at some point he sneaks into the child's bedroom where he will act out his lust. CM's that molest at home convince the victim that they want to show them "special love" and that it must be kept their secret.

An exhibitionist usually acts out his routine in the confines of a car. He may be driving to the supermarket when the fantasy of exposing himself to a female enters his mind. Preoccupied with his thoughts, he soon acts out his fantasy in the presence of the unsuspecting victim.

DANCING WITH THE DEVIL

The indecent caller is aroused as he rings the number where he hopes to find the naive woman who will answer and innocently listen to what he says; he has fulfilled his lust.

The "peeping tom" cruises streets looking for an open window to steal a glimpse of uncovered flesh. The addicted "peeper" may be sitting at home watching television when the thought to "peep" enters his mind. When the family goes to bed, he takes a ride. (The Lord tells us to bring our thoughts into captivity—to think on pure and wholesome things . . .)

In slight contrast, the "john" cruises a town's "red-light" district fantasizing until his lust is so high he finds the prostitute that will end his drive. (When a force inside us pushes too hard we must make a choice to stop and turn around!) Parenthesis added.

The nymphomaniac might act out her routine in bars going from man to man until she finds the one she wants to take home. Her greatest satisfaction comes when she is able to seduce the least attentive man, who may be reluctant because he is married. She is satisfied when he gives in. (Used by permission)

Hollywood producers, porn filmmakers, magazine publishers, and those who participate in supporting movies like *Fifty Shades of Grey*—moviegoers, publishers, the actors, and all who pour money into this travesty—contribute to the moral breakdown of the innocent and those caught in the clutches of this painful destruction of human decency and the basic laws of our country—laws originally designed to protect humanity.

"So I want to remind you, though you already know these things, that Jesus (Lord or God or Christ) *first rescued* (saved) *the nation of Israel from Egypt, but later he destroyed those who did not remain faithful.* (God destroyed 23,000 in one day because of sexual impurity and perversion) *And I remind you of the angels who did not stay within the limits of authority God gave them but left the place where they belonged. God has kept them securely chained in prisons of darkness, waiting for the great Day of Judgment.* (The angels were having sex with human women and the

results were the giants spoken of in the Bible. In fact, David killed one of those giants with a slingshot when he was a young man before he became king and while he was still a warrior.) *And don't forget Sodom and Gomorrah and their neighboring towns, which were filled with immorality and every kind of sexual perversion. Those cities were destroyed by fire and serve as a warning of the eternal fire of God's judgment"* (Jude 1:5-7 NLT). Parenthesis added

MINISTERS OF GOD: CAN WE TRUST THEIR MORALS?
CAN WE TRUST THEM WITH OUR CHILDREN?

Immorality in ministry has been around for years, but in the last fifty years America has seen a significant increase in the number of pastors that have fallen because of it. Both openly and secretly, ministers of the gospel have flirted with and seduced church members or they have become addicted to pornography—many having fallen completely while others repented. But in spite of their sin, some are able to maintain their leadership positions due to the amount of power given them by an apathetic congregation, and the approval of their accountability staff, composed primarily of men since many denominations still don't allow women to function in church leadership positions.

A former member of a large church in California shared with me that the pastor and his wife were both involved in extramarital affairs. The wife confessed her sin before the congregation, repented and asked to be forgiven, but instead of receiving forgiveness she was asked to leave the church. However, her pastor husband was not brought before the church but instead was given a year's salary, a new church, and was allowed to cohabitate with the woman of his sin. This is just one of many stories about abuse in the church that you will find if you inquire.

Child molestation in ministry is far greater than you would think and is a dark side of Christianity that should be dealt with and abandoned. And, it is not necessarily confined to one denomination or non-denomination. Though the Catholic Church has been the most publicized offender, the protestant church now has numerous stories that are nothing less than shocking. Often the incident is kept quiet, or the perpetrator is fired but the crime remains unexposed as he or she moves on to the next church employment opportunity. They get hired again only to abuse again.

In 2014 a Christian radio talk show host in Houston, Texas, revealed that a pastor there was caught entering a sex slave brothel. In another incident news reports revealed that a pastor at a church in Huntsville, Alabama confessed to being sexually active with members of his congregation, while knowing he had AIDS. He had been a minister there for 23 years. When we make the choice to submit to sexual sin we allow our sin to affect every one we know and love. God requires the same moral accountability for those He calls to preach and teach, that He requires of the average Christian sitting in the congregation listening.

Our nation has willingly done away with the Ten Commandments as our moral guide. We have basically removed ratings on what we are allowed to view from the film industry; we have accepted profanity on radio and television; we have permitted pornography on television and computers; and we have granted a no-fault divorce law that allows people to easily walk away from family responsibilities. These acts have contributed to the complete disregard for moral purity such as we are seeing in our world today, even among Christians. The result is a desensitized society willing to indulge any behavior God's archenemy, Satan, orchestrates for it.

Many Christians who read this section (part two) of *Dancing With The Devil* will be able to identify with it in some way. They can make one of two choices about their discovery: 1) use it to beat another person over the head, charging them with some of these crimes, which will accomplish nothing toward a new relationship together or life in Christ; or 2) be willing to use this information to look inside themselves for those characteristics that cause them to stay bound to ungodly behavior and then choose to change. Once a person completely lets go of pride, which is the real killer of relationships, and decides to make a change in their life, and then humble himself or herself before God they will *understand* when He is speaking and when the enemy is speaking. God will never tell His children it's ok to do something that is contrary to His Word. Just trust and obey Him! Each of us must willingly do our part to expand God's desire for a healthy society.

If you are living a promiscuous life, I encourage you to stop dancing with the devil and start dancing with Jesus. It truly is rewarding, but because of the free will choice He gives, you must make the first step. Ask Him into your heart, and obey Him. Life won't be perfect according to human standards but Jesus won't step on your toes. If you remain in Him, He will stabilize you when you miss a step and He will never abandon you. Unlike we who use words to crush those we love, Jesus won't use His words to crush you when you talk to Him. He will comfort you through the Scriptures and the Holy Spirit, bringing you peace.

It is difficult to imagine how much the Lord loves His children. His mercy is amazing. He is slow to anger, and full of compassion wanting all to be saved, but we must remember that He is a God of justice. In part three of *Dancing With The Devil* you will discover who the Lord is and why it is so important to serve Him. You will discover how to get on off of the broad path as has been described here in part two of *Dancing With The Devil* and then get on and stay on the narrow path that leads to eternity with Christ. You will *understand* how Jesus sees your heart, how to live a Christian life, and what your home in heaven will be like.

CHAPTER SEVEN STUDY QUESTIONS

1. Have you bought into the humanistic view about morality? If so, have you changed your mind after reading chapter 7?
2. Are you able to recognize the sins of the culture that have captured the church or do you sense that there is a fog in your mind about some of these issues?
3. Are you now involved or previously been involved with or tolerated others involved in sexual behavior that violated the Scriptures referenced in this chapter?
4. How will you change any improper conduct or opinions to conform to the Lord's commands for proper morals?
5. What steps are you willing to take to break free of bondage to sexual sin and find healing?
6. Why do you think God clothed Adam and Eve after the fall? Why did He use animal skins?
7. What does the Scripture "Remain in me and I will remain in you" mean to you?
8. If you know someone who has been abused by a minister, have you taken the proper steps to help those affected by this sin?
9. Do you know what pride is and whether it is an issue in your own heart?
10. How will you use the information in this chapter to help bring healing to spiritually dysfunctional issues in your home life?

DANCING WITH THE DEVIL

PART THREE

The Battle for the Soul of God's Children
Choosing the Narrow Path

EIGHT

❧

KNOWING GOD/JESUS/HOLY SPIRIT

"There is no other God but me! I am the one who kills and gives life; I am the One who wounds and heals; no one can be rescued from my powerful hand! Now I raise my hand to Heaven and declare, "As surely as I live, when I sharpen my flashing sword and begin to carry out justice, I will take revenge on my enemies and repay those who reject me (Deuteronomy 32:39-41 NLT).

"God is Spirit, so those who worship Him must worship Him in spirit and in truth" (John 1:24 NLT).

"This then is the message, which we have heard of Him, and declare unto you, that God is light and in Him is no darkness at all" (1 John 1:5 KJV).

"The Lord is Righteous in all His ways and holy in all His works" (Psalms 145:17 KJV).

"And we have known and believed the love that God hath to us. God is love, and he that dwelleth in love dwelleth in God, and God in him" (1 John 4:16 KJV).

Thou art worthy, O Lord, to receive glory and honor and power; for thou hast created all things, and for thy pleasure they are and were created (Rev 4:11 KJV).

The Bible portrays God as Creator, Sustainer, Judge and Redeemer, and the Only God. There are other attributes applicable to

Him but in this section of *Dancing With The Devil* we will focus on these five. The Book of Genesis is designed to help humanity *understand* how life came to be and the one who was responsible for it—God. From that beginning and throughout the Scriptures we are instructed to *"get understanding"* of God's character. However, the story of Job in the Old Testament is biblical evidence that humanity can know a great deal about God yet not *really* know or *understand* Him or His ways. Short of a miracle, no one can see God, audibly hear him, or sit down with Him to dine. He is Spirit; therefore believing that He exists, that He is our "Father" and that our human nature is frail comes entirely through our faith in the Word and the evidence in all creation. Therefore, our *understanding* of God must come from our faith in what the Bible says about Him.

GOD THE CREATOR

Even though exactly how the earth was created is still the subject of much debate, Genesis relates that as Creator, God simply spoke creation into being. However, in the creation process, He used order so that one thing created was sustained by another thing created. In other words, what good was water unless it was helpful to something? Though He did tell us He created the universe and everything in it, He didn't specifically tell us how long a day was. 1 Peter 3:8 says a day is like a thousand years to the Lord, and a thousand years like a day. We do know that the Bible calendar, also called the Lunar Calendar, was based on the moon. And we know that in 46 BC, Julius Caesar introduced the Julian calendar, and in 1582, Pope Gregory XIII introduced the Gregorian calendar, which we use today. Though none of the calendars accurately gage time, Christians tend to think of the creation days as the same twenty-four hour span of time we are familiar with today.

Genesis tells us that the earth had no form or content when God formed it during the second and third days of creation. We also know that God's Spirit was actively involved in creation because the

Word says that the image of the Spirit of God hovered over the earth's surface. On the third, fourth, and fifth days of creation, God filled the earth with living beings and on the sixth day, he created human beings—one male and one female—and instructed them to reproduce their own kind and obey Him. From Romans 1:19 we know that God revealed His power and His divine nature in everything He created therefore man has no excuse for not believing that He exists..

GOD THE SUSTAINER

As sustainer, God, through His creation made every provision for people to live on planet earth. Streams in the garden, which He planted for Adam and Eve, provided sustainable drinking water. Mist and light from the skies helped food to grow providing all necessary nutrients for humans and animals to survive. Even though against its will all creation has been subjected to God's curse because of the fall, (Romans 8:20) and drought and floods have brought devastation to all living things, God still allows rain and sunshine to sustain the land so that creation can survive and the cycle of life can continue until He sends Jesus to collect His bride, the "true" church.

When we look to God in faith and believe that He is the one true God, and when we repent of our sins and walk in obedience to His moral code, He is faithful to sustain us through every heartache, tragedy, and misfortune; even though at times it may seem that He has forgotten us in our situation. Regardless of the intensity of the pain we experience, we awaken one day and realize that being alive seems somewhat easier when our heart is seeking Him in all things. We are to acknowledge God in all our ways (Proverbs 3:6). From there, He directs our path and our communication with Him sustains us through our future trials and tribulations. God desires to sustain us and He desires that we let Him. When we take things into our own hands and try to make them happen without Christ's help, we position ourselves for heartache.

GOD THE JUDGE

As the "just" judge, God brings balance to everything that is unbalanced regardless of the reason it got that way. We never know when or how He will bring balance but He promises that He will—He never waivers to the right or to the left. His Word says He judges everything about us based on what He finds in our heart and those judgments are based on His principles, which were established to protect His creation from the evil that He alone was aware of before the fall. When we neglect those principles we do ourselves a great disservice.

The Scriptures do not tell us that prior to the fall, Adam and Eve were aware of the evil that eventually befell them; in fact there is every indication that they were not aware of evil except in the words God used to describe the tree in His warning; "you may eat of every tree except the tree of the 'knowledge' of good and evil." They had to eat the fruit before they could "know" evil. They knew only that God wanted them to trust Him and to believe what He said. I like the footnote in my Bible that says *"Adam and Eve failed to heed God's warning because they did not understand the reasons for His commands and chose to act in another way; a way that appeared better to them than God's way."*

Even today when we are faced with a decision, we may or may not ponder it; maybe we act without considering the consequences. Maybe the decision we made without God's approval hurt someone else, putting their life out of balance in some way—emotionally, physically, or financially. God, our just and fair judge who looks at the heart expects us to repent and when we refuse He will hold court and decide the just and fair punishment for the transgression.

In 2 Chronicles, chapter 33, we find an amazing story of God's judgment against a king, and the King's repentance. Manasseh became king at the age of twelve, and God permitted him to reign fifty-five years. For many of those years Manasseh ruled wickedly in Jerusalem. He followed the detestable practices of the pagan nations, building their altars in the Temple of the Lord. He sacrificed his own sons in the fire in the valley of Ben-Hinnom and practiced sorcery, divination, and witchcraft. He consulted with mediums and psychics and set up a carved idol in God's temple leading the people of Judah and Jerusalem to do exceeding evil. He was so rebellious and self-serving he ignored all God's warnings. Among corrupt kings, Manasseh would rank near the top. He danced with the devil to such a degree, the Lord sent Commanders to take him prisoner. They bound him in chains, put a ring in his nose, and took him to Babylon.

Manasseh was deeply distressed, and in his suffering he cried out to God in the manner of King David and genuinely repented from his heart. Manasseh knew who God was but he chose to do evil anyway. The Bible says that God was deeply moved by Manasseh's prayers and listened to his request. God relented and allowed Manasseh to go back to Jerusalem to his kingdom, then Manasseh finally realized that the Lord alone was God; there was no other—not even in all the mediums, psychics, and witchcraft. Can you imagine praying so powerfully that your prayer *deeply* moves God?

Manasseh committed horrible sins; imagine burning your children in a fire. But when he repented, God forgave and redeemed him. He went on to become a great leader. I have heard many people say that God could never forgive them for the horrible things that they had done but no one is outside the reach of God's forgiveness when they *truly* repent. Though God was patient with Manasseh, He judged and punished Manasseh for his sin. As humans, it is difficult for us to *understand* God's longsuffering while He waits on someone to return to Him because during the time of His patience for one person, many others may suffer terribly or even die. However, this characteristic shows us how great His love is for all humanity and is an example of just how far He will go to attack evil and punish evildoers.

GOD THE ONLY GOD

Deuteronomy documents what God told the children of Israel about who He was.

"Now search all of history, from the time God created people on the earth until now, and search from one end of the heavens to the other. Has any nation ever heard the voice of God speaking from fire—as you did—and survived? Has any other God dared to take a nation for himself out of another nation by means of trials, miraculous signs, wonders, war, a strong hand, a powerful arm, and terrifying acts? Yet that is what the Lord your God did for you in Egypt, right before your eyes. He showed you these things so you would know that the Lord is God and there is no other. He let you hear His voice from heaven so He could instruct you. He let you see His great fire here on earth so He could speak to you from it. Because He loved your ancestors, He chose to bless their descendants, and He personally brought you out of Egypt with a great display of power. He drove out nations far greater than you, so He could bring you in and give you their land as your special possession, as it is today. So remember this and keep it firmly in mind: The Lord is God both in Heaven and on earth, and there is no other. If you obey all the decrees and commands I am giving you today, all will be well with you and your children. I am giving you these instructions so you will enjoy a long life in the land the Lord your God is giving you for all time" (Deuteronomy 4:32-40 NLT).

God was not shy about the greatness of His power, and He was quick to remind the Israelite children of all He had done for them. And, He reminded them of what they had to do to continue receiving His blessing—if they would obey, He would provide.

In Deuteronomy 6:4-9, God is clear about how we are to worship Him. He says for us to listen up and love Him with all our heart, soul, and strength, and we are to fully commit ourselves to His commands. In everything we do, we are to continually teach His ways to our children. No, this isn't just for the Jews! Remember that if you are a Christian, you are a Gentile Jew, adopted and grafted into the tree where the dead Jewish branches were cut off. As Judeo Christians we also are required to follow these commands.

1 Corinthians 8:4-6 confirms again who God is, teaching us that an idol is not a real God, and that the God of Heaven and earth is the only true God. It cautions that some people really do worship many gods and lords of the earth, and in heaven, but they are "so-called gods" and not the real true Holy God. It tells us that true Christians know there is only one true God, the Father who created everything, and we live for Him. There is only one Lord—Jesus Christ—through whom God made everything and through whom we have been given life. No Jesus? No eternal life!

Compare your daily life to the commands God laid out in Deuteronomy. Does it resemble the instructions in the Scriptures or is it dreadful—worried about the day's chores, or those things that will be neglected or lost if your mental and verbal focus is on the Lord? Is your travel time spent talking about or to the Lord, or is it spent talking or texting on the cell phone? Are you listening to praise and worship music that will fill your heart with the ways of Jesus and settle your spirit, bringing you peace? Or are you listening to or singing along with songs that may be taking your mind someplace it shouldn't go? And yes, most secular songs do that!

What is bedtime like in your home? Is there prayer and conversation with the children about who God is and what He wants from them, and their need for Jesus—'if they will do this, He will do that?' Do your children see evidence of His commands on you personally, or do they see an assortment of diamonds, gold, and silver? No, these aren't bad things in and of themselves but if they become your love and your idol they violate God's will for your character. Do you show open worship for God or do you worry about what others will say if they see you express your commitment to Him? Today, few Christians make a show of all the different ways they say they are sold out to Jesus, but He requires us to carry Him in our heart and attitude, on our face, and in our actions so that others will see that He is the God we worship. I struggle with obeying these requirements all the time, and I believe that many other Christians do as well. Regardless, He has commanded us to live differently from how the world lives.

God admonishes us to be like Him. In the Old Testament He gives us several descriptions of His character. These help us *understand* what He wants us to be like. Through them we are able to define His attributes so that we can emulate them.

Chapter 7 of Deuteronomy tells us how much God hates false religions. He commanded the children of Israel to completely destroy seven nations that were more powerful and more numerous than they were. He commanded the Israelites not to intermarry or make treaties with them, and to not be merciful. God cautioned them that if they disobeyed Him regarding the people of these pagan nations they would lead away the Israelite's children to worship other Gods instead of the Holy and one true God. He told them that if this happened, His anger would burn against them and He would quickly destroy them.

Can you look at your nation today and compare it to what God said about the nations he would destroy because of their heart attitude and neglect of Him? How does it compare to those nations? Can you look at the abuse, the sexual sin, the divorce, and the moral decay of our people today and compare it to those nations God spoke about then?

Chapter 12 of Deuteronomy is another caution to the Israelites not to worship God in the same way the pagan people worshiped their gods. He gave them specific instructions about where and how to worship Him—the right place, the correct honor for Him, and what to bring. He told them to feast in the presence of the Lord and to rejoice because of all He had blessed them with.

Chapter 25 of Deuteronomy tells how God showed the pagan Amalekites no mercy. They had attacked and struck down the Israelites when they were tired and weary from a long journey after fleeing Egypt. The Amalekites did not fear God so they cudgeled His people that were straggling behind in their flight to freedom. God told the Israelites that when they got rested from their exodus out of Egypt to go and destroy the Amalekites—to erase their memory from under heaven and to never forget it! Do you think God doesn't hate sin and those who reject Him and hurt His Children? He does! Remember the story of the Christian Armenian's march to Aleppo and into the Assyrian Desert written about in part 1, chapter 3? The Christians—primarily pregnant women—that were lagging behind were struck down and cudgeled to death because they were too tired and weary to keep going. That horror against the Armenians parallels what the Amalekites did to the children of Israel when they were fleeing Egypt. God's command to destroy the Amalekites was powerful but it shows exactly how much he hates it when people worship something other than Him. He will not fail to destroy everything that opposes Him although he doesn't like to. Through Ezekiel the Sovereign Lord says, *"Do you think I like to see wicked people die? Of course not! I want them to turn from their wicked ways and live!" (Ezekiel 18:23 NLT)*

God is creator, infinite, all knowing, unequaled, without limit, and most wise. He is gracious, merciful, forgiving, long-suffering, perfect, and holy. He hates false religion, a lying tongue and all sin. He is light, love, and he loves His elect. God is a Shepherd who abounds in goodness and will not be mocked. He is the one who heals and who kills. According to His plan He will reveal Himself to every person at the time of His choosing.

GOD'S POWER

God is all-powerful, and He uses those He chooses for His purposes. He hardened Pharaoh's heart and sent horrific plagues to hurt the people of Egypt in order to free the Israelite children. Moses didn't perform those miracles; he was simply a vessel for God who told the Israelites that He had done these miracles to show them His power.

God allowed Satan to destroy all Job possessed, including his children, and then He restored to Job everything He had allowed to be taken from him. Afterwards, Job confessed that he abhorred (hated) himself and would repent in ashes and dust because he did not fully *understand* God's power, which God uses as He sees the need.

God said it was "His great pleasure" to crush His own Son in order to save mankind from hell. He allowed a demon spirit to enter Judas Iscariot, a disciple chosen by Jesus, so that Judas could betray Jesus, thus making possible His way to the cross for the redemption of mankind. After the betrayal God allowed the demon spirit to leave Judas. When Judas realized what he had done under the power of the demon spirit, he felt intense regret. The Bible says that he repented and returned the thirty pieces of silver he was paid for the betrayal. Then he went away from everyone and hanged himself. God is all-powerful and can use anyone as He pleases but no doubt He gives everyone an opportunity to repent!

When Jesus was delivered to Pilate for judgment, Pilate cautioned Him that he had the power both to crucify Jesus and to release Him. But Jesus reminded Pilate that he would have no authority over Him if it hadn't been given to him from above. How often we forget that all power remains in God's hands; that we can do nothing outside (without) Him!

Assyria was a great evil empire and terrible enemy of the Israelite nation. Because of Assyria's heartless cruelty Israel feared them more than any other empire. Nineveh, the capital of Assyria was home to 120,000 residents living in spiritual darkness. God told Jonah to go there and preach, warning the people of His plan to destroy them if they didn't repent. But Jonah hated those people and believed they did not deserve God's redemption. Dedicated to his personal views, which were contrary to God's, Jonah ran from God and boarded a ship headed for Tarshish.

Then the all-powerful God brought a storm of such magnitude it threatened the ship's safety as well as the lives of everyone aboard. When the removal of all the cargo failed to calm the struggling ship, they questioned Jonah about his purpose for being aboard. When he confessed he was running from the Lord, the ship's crew threw him overboard where a large fish swallowed him. For three days and nights, God let Jonah wallow in the belly of the fish until he repented of his disobedience. Then God caused the fish to regurgitate Jonah onto dry land. Having learned a huge lesson in obedience Jonah decided to do as God instructed. He went into the city of Nineveh and preached on the streets, warning that God would destroy the entire city in forty days if the people didn't repent. The people listened, and then repented, and God changed His mind about destroying them.

Every part of the city and its inhabitants deserved destruction. The people had tested God and pushed their filthiness in His face until He could stand it no more. The all-powerful God orchestrated everything He needed to redeem this dark and evil people. God is merciful and gives us every opportunity to turn from our wickedness. He isn't just a punishing God; He is also a God of love and redemption. These Bible stories of long ago serve to reassure us today that if we will repent of our sin and do what He says—be obedient—this awesome God of the Bible will be faithful to do what He says He will do—redeem and restore us. Are you listening to the warnings of our time as the people of Nineveh listened to Jonah in his time?

Is God *the* God of your life or do you have gods of greed, and selfishness, (having your own way—unable to flex)? Selfishness may include simple things like demanding a particular bed, or chair, pew at church, or place at the table, a particular cup or glass from which to drink, being possessive about the remote control. Or it may be slightly more serious such as a rebellious attitude of entitlement—a self-appointed right to un-forgiveness. Are you a source of contention for those in your family or loop of friends and acquaintances? Are the things you rebel against fully unimportant, yet you must always have your way? Is the god you worship the god of indecent behavior—pornography and lust of all kinds? Is your god a can or bottle of alcohol, which you think you can't live without or believe you can put down anytime and never pick up again? Are you addicted to drugs whether they come from the street or the pharmacy? Test yourself. Maybe you are a Christian who has a position of power that you use to violate God's commands and hurt His children. Maybe you have achieved some type of celebrity status and think of yourself as "important stuff." Maybe in your heart there is hate that causes you to think about killing someone. If you see yourself in bondage to any of these gods of the flesh it is time to have a little talk with Jesus. Fess up, and tell God that you want to become more like He who sacrificed Himself for you. No human can do or be anything unless He gives the power.

GOD THE REDEEMER THROUGH JESUS' BLOOD

I believe that more than anything else I learned in church growing up as a child and young teen was how much God through Jesus Christ was my redeemer. There is an old hymn I learned in those days, which I still love today. The lyrics tell me that Jesus is a blessed redeemer, that He is mine, and that my redemption is a foretaste (or preview) of glory divine. To redeem something is to liberate or set it free so it can be made new again. Each time we fall into sin and then go to Jesus guilty and repentant, truly sorry for our sins, He intercedes to God the Father on our behalf; then He liberates us—sets us free from our guilt—and reconnects us to our Father, God. We must allow Him to do that, otherwise we will never find joy, or peace of mind before we die. He does this for us now because He died more than two thousand years ago so that through Him we could be reconciled to God the Father when we ask to be. What a redeemer we have in Jesus! God became human in the Person of Jesus Christ so we must always remember to pray to the Father "in the name of Jesus" because He is the only one who can redeem us—set us free from guilt and shame.

JESUS CHRIST: SAVIOR, LAMB OF GOD

"In the beginning the Word (Jesus) *already existed. The Word was with God, and the Word was God. He* (Jesus) *existed in the beginning with God. God created everything through Him,* (Jesus) *and nothing was created except through Him. The Word gave life to everything that was created, and His life brought light* (He is the light of the world) *to everyone. The light* (Jesus) *shines in the darkness, and the darkness* (evil-the devil or Satan) *can never extinguish it" (John 1:1-5 NLT).* Parenthesis added. Since Jesus was crucified, no man can be saved except that he believes in Jesus.

When John the baptizer, saw Jesus coming toward him he said, *"Look, the Lamb of God who takes away the sin of the world . . . " "I did not recognize him as the Messiah . . . " "I saw the Holy Spirit descending like a dove from heaven and resting upon Him* (Jesus) *. . . " "I saw this happen to Jesus, so I testify that He is the Chosen One of God" (John 1:29,32,34 NLT).* Parenthesis added

Jesus said, *"I am the bread of life . . ." (John 6:35 NLT);* " *. . . I am the gate for the sheep." (John 10:7 NLT);* "*I am the good shepherd . . ." (John 10:11 NLT);* "*You call me Teacher and Lord, and you are right because that's what I am . . . " (John 13: 13 NLT).*

JESUS: THE GOOD SHEPHERD

John 3:16 is probably the most recognized and memorized verse in the Bible. Numerous people who have never darkened the door of a Christian worship center have heard about how God sent His Son to be a blood sacrifice for all humanity. In addition to being heralded as the Son of God, according to John the Apostle, Jesus taught that He was also the Good Shepherd. In John chapter 10, Jesus said that all who came before Him were thieves and robbers, and that the 'true' sheep (the true children of God) did not listen to the robbers. He said that, as a Good Shepherd He would sacrifice His life for the sheep. He confessed that He knew His own sheep, and that they also knew Him just as He knew His Father and His Father knew Him. Parenthesis added.

Isaiah recorded that the Lord would come with great power and an arm that would rule for Him, and that He would feed His flock like a Shepherd, gather the lambs with His arm, and carry them in His bosom.

Hebrews 13:20 records that the Lord Jesus is the great Shepherd of the sheep. Peter called Jesus the "Chief" Shepherd saying that when He appears, His children will receive an incorruptible crown of glory! Isn't it awesome knowing what we can expect and look forward to when we dwell with and worship Jesus in heaven?

JESUS: BREAD OF LIFE; A LIGHT TO MANKIND; CHRIST SUPREME

In John 6:27, Jesus teaches the disciples that He is the Bread of Life. Born without sin, He is the perfect example for us in character. Colossians chapter 1 tells us that through Jesus Christ, we can share in the inheritance that belongs to God's people who live in the Light. Through Him we are rescued from the kingdom of darkness (the evil one) and we are transferred into the kingdom of God's Son who purchased our freedom with His death, and forgave our sins.

The New Testament parallel to Isaiah chapter 53 says, *"Christ is the visible image of the invisible God. He existed before anything was created and is supreme over all creation, for through Him, God created everything in the heavenly realms and on earth. He made the things we can see and the things we can't see—such as thrones, kingdoms, rulers, and authorities in the unseen world. Everything was created through Him and for Him. He existed before anything else, and He holds all creation together. Christ is also the head of the church, which is His body. He is the beginning, supreme over all who rise from the dead. So, He is first in everything. For God in all His fullness was pleased to live in Christ, and through Him God reconciled everything to himself. He made peace with everything in heaven and on earth by means of Christ's blood on the cross"* (Colossians 1:15-20 NLT).

From the book of Revelation we know that Christ has received all authority to judge the earth. He is called Jesus Christ, the faithful witness, the firstborn from the dead, and the ruler over the kings of the earth. He is the First and the Last, He who lives, the Son of God, Holy and True, the Amen, and the Faithful and True witness. He is the Beginning of the Creation of God, the Lion of the Tribe of Judah, the Root of David, and the Lamb of God. The Bible calls Him The Word of God, King of Kings and Lord of Lords, Alpha and Omega, the Bright and Morning Star, and the Lord Jesus Christ. This makes him supreme! With so much honor, power and authority given Him, why would any Christian not clamor to faithfully walk the path of His statutes? Possibly it is because we don't really know or *understand* Him or His ways; but the Word tells us to get *understanding*!

JESUS: THE SERVANT

Through Isaiah, God told us exactly what was to come for the suffering Servant who would suffer for the sins of all people. Chapter 53 is an agonizing description of *how* Jesus would suffer.

"Who has believed our message? To whom has the Lord revealed his powerful arm? My servant (Jesus) grew up in the Lord's presence like a tender green shoot, like a root in dry ground. There was nothing beautiful or majestic about His appearance, nothing to attract us to Him. He was despised and

rejected—a man of sorrows, acquainted with deepest grief. We turned our backs on Him and looked the other way. He was despised and we did not care. Yet it was our weakness He carried; it was our sorrows that weighed Him down. And we thought His troubles were a punishment from God, a punishment for His own sins. But He was pierced for our rebellion, crushed for our sins. (Not His own) *He was beaten so we could be whole. He was whipped so we could be healed. All of us, like sheep, have strayed away. We have left God's paths to follow our own. Yet the Lord laid on Him the sins of us all. He was oppressed and treated harshly, yet He never said a word. He was led like a lamb to the slaughter. And as a sheep is silent before the shearers, He did not open his mouth. Unjustly condemned, He was led away. No one cared that He died without descendants, that His life was cut short in midstream. But He was struck down for the rebellion of my people. He had done no wrong and had never deceived anyone. But He was buried like a criminal; He was put in a rich man's grave. But it was the Lord's good plan to crush Him and cause Him grief. Yet when His life is made an offering for sin, He will have many descendants. He will enjoy a long life, and the Lord's good plan will prosper in His hands. When He sees all that is accomplished by His anguish, He will be satisfied. And because of His experience, my righteous servant will make it possible for many to be counted righteous, for He will bear all their sins. I will give Him the honors of a victorious soldier, because He exposed Himself to death. He was counted among the rebels. He bore the sins of many and interceded for rebels"* (Isaiah 53 NLT). Parenthesis added

God promised that much would be accomplished because of the anguish that Jesus suffered. These Scriptures reassure us that His suffering would not be for naught. They confirm that many will be counted righteous or saved because He was a Righteous Servant who gave His life to rescue those who were condemned. All they had to do was believe in and serve Him. The Lord also promised that Jesus would be "satisfied" or pleased that He suffered when He saw all that it did for humanity—all those who would be saved because they believed on Him and repented of their sin. So how great was Jesus' suffering on the cross? Rick Renner is the founder and pastor of The Moscow Good News Church in Russia. He has authored more than ten books and his daily television broadcast can be seen across Russia. In his book titled *Paid in Full*, Pastor Renner gives the excruciating details of Jesus' crucifixion.

Renner says that to crucify means to punish a criminal in a way that brings them intense pain and public humiliation. It was indisputably the cruelest and most barbaric form of punishment in the ancient world. In Jesus' time, Roman troops occupied Jerusalem and because of it, there were frequent insurrections between the people and the soldiers. To deter attempts to overthrow the government the Romans used crucifixion to send a strong message to those who might be thinking of revolting.

When a person was crucified, they were laid on a wooden crossbeam. The arms were outstretched and five-inch iron nails were pounded through the wrists into the crossbeam. Then the crossbeam with the victim attached was hoisted up and then dropped into a notch on top of a post that was already placed in an upright position. When the crossbeam with the body attached was dropped into the groove, the victim suffered excruciating pain as the sudden jerking motion wrenched wrists and hands. Then the weight of the victim's body caused his arms to be pulled out of their arm sockets.

After the wrists were nailed down and the victim was in the upright position on the cross, the legs were then positioned so that the feet were pointed downward with the soles pressed against the post. Once in position, a long nail was driven in through the top of the feet and between the bones, and then into the beam post. Positioning the nails between the bones prevented tearing through the skin and meat when the victim arched upward, gasping for breath. Though arching the body was to prevent asphyxiation, the pain on the feet was unbearable so the victim would release the arch quickly but repeat it often trying to breathe. With each arch and release of the body, the shoulders dislocate, popping out of joint, followed by the elbows and wrists. These dislocations caused the arms to extend up to nine inches longer than usual and resulted in terrible cramps in the victim's arm muscles, making it impossible for him to push himself upward in order to breathe. Now asphyxiation begins. Due to extreme loss of blood and hyperventilation the victim would dehydrate quickly. After several hours, the victim's heart begins to fail, the lungs collapse and excess fluids fill the lining of the heart and lungs adding to the slow process of asphyxiation. Motivated by their rage and hatred, Roman soldiers amused themselves by nailing their prisoners in different postures.

    This description of crucifixion is what Jesus experienced when He was nailed to the cross. Added to His torture was the agony caused by the constant grating of His recently scourged back against the upright post every time he pushed up to breathe. Jewish law required that the person being crucified would be stripped naked for all to see. And according to Roman custom, the soldiers who carried out the crucifixion had a right to the victim's clothing. Standing near the foot of the cross, and as Jesus hung there naked; asphyxiating to death, His lungs filling with fluid so that He couldn't breathe, the soldiers parted His garments, casting lots to see who got what.

    Jesus' totally naked body was flaunted in humiliation; His flesh was ripped to shreds; His body bruised and bleeding; His crucifixion was disgusting, repulsive, nauseating, humiliating, debasing, shameful, and the most painful method of death. And for what reason did He suffer in such a way? Jesus died for our sins, in fulfillment of God's plan for salvation for every person that would receive it. Those who killed Jesus were simply carrying out the Lord's divine plan (1 Corinthians 2:8). It was His mission to die for all humanity. Daniel 7:14 says that "He (Jesus) was given authority, honor, and sovereignty over all the nations of the world, so that people of every race and nation and language would obey Him. His rule is eternal—it will never end. His kingdom will never be destroyed." (NLT)

THE HOLY SPIRIT; THE SOURCE OF OUR COMFORT

"I am telling you these things now while I am still with you. But when the Father sends the Advocate as my representative—that is the Holy Spirit— He will teach you everything and will remind you of everything I have told you (John 14:25, 26 NLT).

God is Holy and He is spirit. When Moses questioned God's ability to feed 600,000 wandering Israelites, during the exodus out of Egypt, the Scripture says the Lord asked Moses if he believed that His arm had lost its power. Then the Lord came down in a cloud and spoke to Moses. Afterwards, He gave to seventy elders the same Spirit He gave to Moses. When the Spirit rested upon them they prophesied. God's Spirit also rested on two men who had stayed behind in the camp. That's power!

God is spirit, and through a dove He gave his spirit to His son Jesus, and then after Jesus' death and resurrection the Holy Spirit came to live in all who believed in Him as the Messiah. As our encourager and comforter the Holy Spirit helps us *understand* the Word of God, inspires us to worship God, and will cause us to desire salvation. He helps us attain peace, and gives us power to live a Christian life, and brings us God's mercy. Romans 8:9 assures us that our sinful nature cannot control us if the Holy Spirit lives within. Are you controlled by your sinful nature? If so, the Holy Spirit is missing from your heart. Ask Him to come and dwell in your heart.

1 Corinthians 6:17 comforts us with the knowledge that a person who is joined to the Lord is one spirit with Him. In other words, we cannot be joined to Christ without the Holy Spirit. The Spirit is the power of our new life in Christ and works in us to help us become like Christ. The Holy Spirit is so important in our life that the Scripture says, *"Every sin or blasphemy can be forgiven—except blasphemy against the Holy Spirit, which will never be forgiven. Anyone who speaks against the son of man, can be forgiven, but anyone who speaks against the*

Holy Spirit will never be forgiven, either in this world or in the world to come" (Matthew 12:31, 32 NLT).

NLT Life Application Study Bible Footnote: *"The unpardonable sin is the deliberate refusal to acknowledge God's power in Christ. It indicates a deliberate and irreversible hardness of heart. Sometimes believers worry that they have accidentally committed this unforgivable sin. But only those who have turned their backs on God and rejected all faith have any need to worry. Jesus said they couldn't be forgiven—not because their sin is worse than others but because they will never ask for forgiveness. Rejecting the prompting of the Holy Spirit removes us from the only force that can lead us to repentance, and restoration with God."*

2 Corinthians 1 tells us that God offers comfort to all—that He is the source of our comfort. That source is the power of the Holy Spirit that dwells within us. He comforts us in all things so that we can comfort others.

If we desire deep Christianity we must seek further wisdom and renewed *understanding* about God, Jesus, and the Holy Spirit. We must read the Word of God, and then pray to the Father in the name of Jesus, and through faith listen to the conviction of the Holy Spirit. What we receive from that obedience will be confirmed in the Word.

CHAPTER EIGHT STUDY QUESTIONS

1. What does Deuteronomy 32:39-41 mean to you?

2. Do you believe the Genesis account of creation? If not, why?

3. What does it mean to acknowledge God in all your ways?

4. Read the story of Manasseh in 2 Chronicles 33. Why was God so angry with Manasseh?

5. Why was God so touched by Manasseh's prayer?

6. What does it mean to be redeemed by the blood of Jesus?

7. In Deuteronomy 4:32-40, what did God remind the Israelite children that hey had to do to continue receiving His blessing?

8. How do you feel about the ways God showed His power as outlined on pages 327-329? Why do you think a Holy God would go to such lengths to show His power? ("He wanted to rescue His children" is not the intended answer to this question, so search for a deeper meaning to His actions.)

9. Study Isaiah 53. If you have gained a better understanding of how Jesus suffered to save mankind, do you see Him or imagine Him differently now?

10. From what you learned about the Holy Spirit on pages 337-338 how do you think your new knowledge of Him will change your life?

DANCING WITH THE DEVIL

NINE

WHAT IT MEANS TO BE A CHRISTIAN
- A SUMMARY -

The man who says I know Him but does not do what He says is a liar and the love of God is not in his heart (John 2:15-17 NLT).

The Bible gives Christians many personal responsibilities: love toward others, hating what is wrong, holding tightly to what is good, and taking delight in honoring each other. Christians are to avoid laziness, and work hard and serve the Lord enthusiastically. We are called to rejoice in confident hope, be patient in trouble, continue to pray about something, be ready to help others, and eager to practice hospitality. We are to bless those who persecute us, be happy with those who are happy instead of being jealous about their happiness, weep with those who weep, and live in harmony with each other. Yes, all these instructions are in the Bible (Romans 12) and they are charged to us as a personal responsibility to live sacrificially for God. But research shows that Christians have a difficult time putting them into practice.

In a survey titled *"Barna Lists the 12 Most Significant Religious Findings"* researcher George Barna reveals that Americans are comfortable with religious faith, and most adults and teens see themselves as people of faith, having definite opinions about religion.

Barna also says they possess well-honed beliefs, and invest substantial amounts of time, money and energy in religious activities, and that faith and spirituality remain hot issues in people's lives.

These are good things, but Barna reports that even though mass media keeps prolific stories involving religion foremost in people's minds *"people do not have an accurate view of themselves when it comes to spirituality. American Christians are not as devoted to their faith as they like to believe. They have positive feelings about the importance of faith, but their faith is rarely the focal point of their life, or a critical factor in their decision-making. The fact that few people take the time to evaluate their spiritual journey, or to develop benchmarks or indicators of their spiritual health, facilitates a distorted view of the prominence and purity of faith in their life."*

Barna's report divulged that if people's faith is objectively measured against a biblical standard of how faith is to be practiced, Americans are spiritually lukewarm. He says, *"Very limited effort is devoted to spiritual growth. Most Americans experience 'accidental spiritual growth' since there is generally no plan or process other than showing up at a church and absorbing a few ideas here and there. Even then, few people have a defined understanding of what they are hoping to become, as followers of Christ."*

In his book, *My Utmost for His Highest*, Oswald Chambers says, *"the reason some of us are such poor specimens of Christianity is because we have no Almighty Christ. We have Christian attributes and experiences, but there is no abandonment to Jesus Christ."* In other words, we don't "sell-out" to the things and ways of Jesus. Unyielding, we refuse to pay the price.

In our busy and often troublesome life, many of us have forgotten what it means to be a "sold-out" Christian. Let's review what it means to change our mind, commit to sacrificially living for Christ, and *understand* the importance of "repentance," a word used often in this chapter.

Instead of letting the Holy Spirit rule, teach and direct us through our study of the Word, and bring us contentment with Jesus, many of us look for ways to fill a certain emptiness with something that will make us feel good and keep us happy. The devil is overjoyed to assist us in our search for these things that don't include Christ. Mostly we think a spouse or lover will meet our need. Pets, children, or grandchildren, or maybe something new and different, such as a vehicle, house, furniture, clothes, or jewels. Some seek travel, or celebrity or business status. Others of us quest for a huge bank account, or changing residences or spouses often. But, until emptiness is filled with the spirit of the Lord, and He is allowed to live in that void and become number one in our life, we will never be satisfied nor dedicated to Jesus.

Dedicated Christians commit to a devoted belief in The Trinity—Father, Son and Holy Spirit—and a place called "heaven." We commit to make a choice to change our mind about worldviews and treasures, and accept Jesus as the one who is able and willing to save us and fill the void in our heart. We can do that only when we believe that Jesus is the way, the truth, and life and that through Him we can be reconciled to God the Father. When we have faith and trust in Jesus Christ, we will repent with heartfelt repentance when we fail. The Greek word for repent is Metanoia—meaning to change your mind – Meta (change) noia (mind).

Dedicated Christians believe that Jesus now sits at the right hand of the Father, forever interceding on behalf of His children. Why is it necessary for Jesus to intercede to the Father for us continually? Because we have an enemy who wants to steal us away from Jesus, he convinces us to sin and then we make a choice that the Lord doesn't approve. But when we repent to the Savior, He intercedes to God for us. If we don't repent, but continue to sin we are choosing to dance with the devil. Jesus can't intercede on our behalf because He will not over-ride our free will to dance.

Please don't make that mistake! Jesus loves you and He paid the ultimate price for your soul and wants you to be secure in Him. Can you think of anyone you love enough to shed your blood for? Most of us think more about preserving our life than giving it up for someone else; however, Jesus gave His life for everyone. But just because He gave His life for all people doesn't mean that all people automatically get to heaven when they die. No! Getting to heaven means we purposefully build a soul saving relationship with Jesus by taking the action as outlined above. When God sent Jesus in a body like the body we sinners have, He declared an end to sin's control over us by giving His Son to be sacrificed unto death for our sins. He did this so that the just requirement of the law would be fully satisfied for us who no longer choose to follow our sinful nature but instead follow the Spirit. Those who let the sinful nature control their minds and actions do not have the Spirit of Christ living in them and do not belong to Him at all. If we live by the dictates of our sinful nature, we will die physically and spiritually. However we are called to become like Christ and Christ was called to be the firstborn among many brothers and sisters—His dedicated followers (See Romans 8).

All people, including Christians often function under characteristics that violate God's Word. But we must eventually identify them, and give them up. (Note: Many of these characteristics are outlined in chapter 11.) Christians dedicated to Christ must make a commitment to read the Scriptures daily because from them we get an *understanding* of what God requires for us to maintain a Christian life and a relationship with Him that He approves.

The difference in a relationship with God and having religion is that a true relationship shows in a Christian's behavior, attitude, appearance, compassion, service, and words. Religion is perfunctory—something that is done often or repeated without thought. Also, "religion" can be simply going to church every Sunday and then pleasing our carnal senses in between—forgetting about Christ. In contrast, Christianity is something we live daily by keeping our thoughts on Jesus and His character. The Bible teaches that those still under the control of their sinful nature can never please God (Romans 8:8 NLT). If we don't please God, then how can we enter heaven?

Christians aren't free to live life influenced by any negative background, environment, or prior experiences. Instead, we must use Scripture to help us put the past behind, become born again spiritually, and overcome the negative influences in our life. We must let the Holy Spirit rule in our heart through the renewing of our mind. *"Except a man be born again, he cannot see the kingdom of God" (John 3:3 KJV)*. The only way to be born again is to turn around—to change our mind about sin, and do away with it. That requires making the choice to let Jesus be the priority in our life.

As Christians we don't have the freedom to say anything we choose. The Scriptures teach us that the words we speak have the power to heal or to kill and we are held accountable for them. Further, we are not permitted to hurt others with our actions. The Scriptures teach that even children are known by their conduct, whether it is pure and right. To say, "this is just the way I am. Take me, or leave me," is not Christianity. The Word tells us that we have power within us to make change in our lives. We can't accept Jesus as our Lord and Savior, and then go about life as we did before we accepted Him. We can't let Him become a religious symbol hanging around our neck, never worshipping Him. Some of the most adamant Christ objectors flaunt the largest crosses and Christian tattoos on their bodies.

The walls in many Christian homes are decorated with crosses, and at each turn Scriptures are displayed. Yet the occupants are living in open sin that violates God's commands. They curse others living in the home, and use the "F" word frequently. Wearing a cross around your neck or on your clothing, or displaying them on the walls of your home does not mean that you have a saving relationship with Christ. A genuine relationship with Him comes when you worship Him because of who He is—God's Son—and what He has done for you—died on the cross to give you a chance for eternal life. Christians celebrate the birth of Christ at Christmas and His resurrection at Easter. Celebrating His birth without believing He is the Messiah or without serving Him with all your heart is hypocrisy and treason against God. Equally, to deny His resurrection by keeping Him on the cross instead of ascended to the Father is to deny the indwelling power of the Holy Spirit and reject much of the New Testament, particularly the Scriptures that tell us the Holy Spirit is our comforter. Why do we need a comforter? 2 Timothy 3:12 tells us that "all" that live Godly in Christ Jesus will suffer persecution, and when we do, we have a comforter in the person of the Holy Spirit. We must know how to let Him take control of our life and comfort us with His peace but if we keep him on the cross, He can't send the Holy Spirit to dwell with and comfort us; we won't have the power we need to overcome.

We must remember that we have an enemy that doesn't want us to do things that build a relationship with Christ. Because he is wicked and jealous of Jesus he works night and day to discredit us before God. If the devil can get Christians to turn their hearts away from the Lord and their family and friends, and serve themselves through their actions and their attitudes then Satan is pleased. True worshipers of Jesus do not want to do such things and these are the ones that will be raptured as the Bible teaches in Thessalonians; they will be raptured because they were counted worthy to escape all the things to come and will be able to stand before the Son of Man (Luke 21:36). Those found too unworthy to be raptured will suffer the great tribulation, when they will be forced by the anti-Christ to either serve Satan or Christ. Those who choose Christ during the tribulation will be required to die for Him just as He died for them more than 2000 years ago. Today, Christians in the Middle East are being forced to choose between Islam and Christianity. For them, choosing Christianity means death by be-heading.

The Bible is full of Scriptures that caution Christians to avoid "falling away." To fall away puts us in disobedience to God and on the broad path to hell if we don't repent.

A CALL TO GROW IN THE WORD AND NOT 'FALL AWAY'

You have been believers so long now that you ought to be teaching others. Instead, you need someone to teach you again the basic things about God's word. You are like babies who need milk and cannot eat solid food. For someone who lives on milk is still an infant and doesn't know how to do what is right. Solid food is for those who are mature, <u>who through training have the skill to recognize the difference between right and wrong</u> (Hebrews 5:12-14 NLT).

Think about it! The Apostle Paul taught Christians that those who remain an infant in Christ—living on milk, never advancing in the Word—don't know how to do what's right! What does that really mean when compared to a stable relationship with Christ? I believe the answer lies in the second part: Hebrews 6:1-6.

So, let us stop going over the basic teachings about Christ again and again. Let us go on instead and become mature in our understanding. Surely we don't need to start again with the fundamental importance of repenting from evil deeds and placing our faith in God. You don't need further instructions about Baptisms, the laying on of hands, and the resurrection of the dead, and eternal judgment. And so, God willing, we will move forward to further <u>understanding</u>. For it is impossible to bring back to repentance those who were once enlightened— those who have experienced the good things of heaven and shared in the Holy Spirit, who have tasted the goodness of the word of God and the power of the age to come—and who then turn away from God. It is impossible to bring such people back to repentance; by rejecting the Son of God, they themselves are nailing him to the cross once again and holding him up to public shame (Hebrews 6:1-6 NLT).

Remaining an infant in Christ means we are walking on shaky ground; our faith is not strong enough to withstand attacks by the enemy. We are unable to give an answer about the reason we believe, because we have not studied the Scriptures, as we should. Once this happens we easily "fall away" from doing the right thing. These

Scriptures also tell us to grow in Christ by learning and *understanding* their meaning so we can assist others growing in the Lord, helping them avoid falling away. If we are to mentor or disciple another person, including our children, we have an urgent call to move forward in our own faith. It is only then that we become qualified to disciple others. These Scriptures in Hebrews are difficult teachings but they stress the importance of learning and *understanding* the Word, something the Bible teaches repeatedly. Further, these Scriptures stress the importance of obeying the Lord, and repenting when we mess up.

"Dear friends, if we deliberately continue sinning after we have received knowledge of the truth, there is no longer any sacrifice that will cover these sins. There is only the terrible expectation of God's judgment and the raging fire that will consume his enemies. For anyone who refused to obey the Law of Moses was put to death without mercy on the testimony of two or three witnesses. <u>Just think how much worse the punishment will be for those who have trampled on the Son of God, and have treated the blood of the covenant, which made us holy, as if it were common and unholy, and have insulted and disdained the Holy Spirit who brings God's mercy to us</u> 26-29. 37, 38 - For in just a little while, the Coming One will come and not delay and my righteous ones will live by faith. <u>But I will take no pleasure in anyone who turns away</u>" (Hebrews 10:26-29, 37, 38 NLT).

Here again, we read more "hard teaching." We, who attend church, yet willfully violate the Scriptures after learning that the violation is sin against the Lord will have a far greater punishment than those who refused to obey the Law of Moses, because willfully violating the Scriptures is desecrating or blaspheming the blood of Jesus. There is no sacrifice greater than that of the Son of God that we can claim in order to be saved. It is a matter of the life and death of our soul to turn from sin and remain in Christ, for He says, *"remain in me and I will remain in you."* The Scriptures teach that people that have barely escaped a lifestyle of deception, in other words, just barely gotten free of the clutches of the great deceiver—Satan—by accepting Jesus, can be lured back into sin and when that happens they become a slave to sin. When we sin against the Lord, we hurt our own soul and all who hate the Lord, love death—physical and spiritual (Proverbs 8:35, 36).

"And when people escape from the wickedness of the world by knowing our Lord and Savior Jesus Christ and then get tangled up and enslaved by sin again, they are worse off than before (they were saved). *It would be better if they had never known the way to righteousness than to know it and then reject the command they were given to live a holy life. They prove the truth of this proverb: "A dog returns to its vomit." And another* (proverb) *says, "A washed pig returns to the mud" (2 Peter 2:20-22 NLT).* Parenthesis added.

In the Old Testament book of Ezekiel and in the New Testament book of Romans God let His people know that He wanted them to turn from sin and obey Him so they could live and not die.

'Do you think that I like to see wicked people die? Says the Sovereign Lord. Of course not! I want them to turn from their wicked ways and live. However, if righteous people turn from their righteous behavior and start doing sinful things and act like other sinners, should they be allowed to live? No, of course not! All their righteous acts will be forgotten, and they will die for their sins. (Die a spiritual death) *Yet you say, 'The Lord isn't doing what is right* (being fair)*!' Listen to me O people of Israel. Am I the one not doing what's right, or is it you? When righteous people turn from their righteous behavior and start doing sinful things, they will die for it. Yes, they will die because of their sinful deeds. And if wicked people turn from their wickedness, obey the law, and do what is just and right, they will save their lives. They will live because they thought it over and decided to turn from their sins. Such people will not die. And yet the people of Israel keep saying, 'The Lord isn't doing what's right!' O people of Israel, it is you who are not doing what's right, not I. Therefore, I will judge*

each of you, O people of Israel, according to your actions, says the Sovereign Lord. Repent and turn from your sins. Don't let them destroy you! Put all your rebellion behind you, and <u>find yourselves a new heart and a new spirit.</u> For why should you die O people of Israel? I don't want you to die, says the Sovereign Lord. Turn back and live!" (Ezekiel 18:23-32 NLT.) Parenthesis added (New Testament parallel on pages 355, 356, Romans 11:18-24) To "turn back" means to go back to where you have already been. To turn back you must have left something or someplace otherwise you cannot "turn back" to it.

CHRISTIANS JUDGING OTHERS

In Ephesians chapter 5 the Apostle Paul wrote to the "dear children of God" warning them about behavior that could separate them from the Lord.

"Imitate God in everything you do, because you are His dear children. Live a life filled with love, following the example of Christ. He loved us and offered himself as a sacrifice for us, a pleasing aroma to God. Let there be no sexual immorality, impurity, or greed among you. Such sins have no place among God's people. Obscene stories, foolish talk, and coarse jokes—these are not for you. Instead, let there be thankfulness to God. You can be sure that no immoral, impure, or greedy person will inherit the Kingdom of Christ and of God. For a greedy person is an idolater, worshipping the things of this world. <u>Don't be fooled by those who try to excuse these sins, for the anger of God will fall on all who disobey Him.</u> Don't participate in the things these people do. For once, you were full of darkness, (evil) *but now you have light from the Lord. So live as people of the light! For this light within you produces only what is good and right and true. Carefully determine what pleases the Lord. Take no part in the worthless deeds of evil and darkness; instead, expose them. It is shameful even to talk about the things that ungodly people do in secret. But their evil intentions will be exposed when the light shines on them, for the light makes everything visible. This is why it is said, Awake, O sleeper, rise up from the dead, and Christ will give you light. So be careful how you live. Don't live like fools, but like those who are wise.*

DANCING WITH THE DEVIL

Make the most of every opportunity in these evil days. Don't act thoughtlessly, but understand what the Lord wants you to do. Don't be drunk with wine, because that will ruin your life. Instead, be filled with the Holy Spirit, singing psalms and hymns and spiritual songs among yourselves, and making music to the Lord in your hearts. And give thanks for everything to God the Father in the name of our Lord Jesus Christ (Ephesians 5:1-20 NLT). Parenthesis added

One doesn't hear songs from Psalms, or hymns in many of today's churches, so most young people don't know that these inspirational worship songs exist. Instead, they are hearing and watching "entertainers," not genuine worship. Though these Scriptures are very clear about how Christians are to live and worship on earth, across America and around the world countless numbers of people who say they are Christian live as they please, giving no thought to these instructions in Ephesians, and in reality, other warning Scriptures throughout the Bible. But this is the time to judge so that we won't become a victim of evil.

As a Christian, try to judge your personal behavior to determine if it pleases the Lord as outlined in Ephesians 5:1-20. Will you be able to ascend with Jesus when the time of the rapture comes? Once you judge your life and the routine things you do and say, will you find that your heart is pure before the Lord or that you have been dancing with the devil? After judging yourself, and putting your findings into perspective, compare the admonitions in these few passages of Scripture to the behavior of your loved ones, your friends, and even what you see on the news about so-called Christians. Scripture teaches that it is easy to see who God's children are by the fruit they bear (Matthew 7:18-20). We can tell if it is good or evil—bringing harm, hurt, pain, or misfortune to others, or insulting to Christ. Behavior that disagrees with the Word is evil behavior.

To assess the behavior of others does not mean that you are violating the Scripture, which says not to judge others lest you yourself be judged (Matthew 7:1). Imagine the injustice to your child if you refuse to judge his or her behavior because the Bible says not to judge others. As parents you are to judge your children's behavior to help them follow Christ. A child of God cannot judge what is in another person's heart, but we can look at behavior and if we really know the Word of God as we should know it, we are qualified to make a determination about whether that behavior would be pleasing to God and we can evaluate whether that person is in danger of being separated from God. Ephesians says we are to expose them. How often do we see anyone exposing the sin of a brother or sister to help snatch that person from the fire? Instead, we are more apt to make excuses for them, tolerating their behavior. Many church pastors won't call for a "salvation" conference with members they know to be living in sin. Pastors and laypersons alike must remember that the Lord is coming back for a purified church.

Do you know someone who has accepted Jesus as their savior at some point in their life and then turned away from Him completely? Have you heard someone say they are Christian but are just not serving Christ right now? Well, let me encourage you to pray for them continually because the Bible says that Christ does not know them and if Christ doesn't know them, and they die in their condition, their soul won't live eternally with Him. Unless they repent with unprecedented fervor they will be forever separated from Him. Some Christians will say that we are not to judge if another person is a Christian, but the Bible says we are to judge. As a mature Christian we are to *understand* sin well enough that we can see it in the brother or sister who is playing with "fire."

Paul warned the Christians at Corinth:

"I wrote to you in my letter not to associate with immoral people; I did not at all mean with the immoral people of this world, or with the covetous and swindlers, or with idolaters; for then you would have to go out of the world. But actually, I wrote to you not to associate with any <u>so-called brother</u>, if he should be

an immoral person, or covetous, or an idolater, or a reviler, or a drunkard, or a swindler—not even to eat with such a one; For what have I to do with judging outsiders? Do you not judge those who are within the church? But those who are outside, God judges. Remove the wicked man from among yourselves" (1 Corinthians 5:9-13 NAS).

Take count of the people you are acquainted with who call themselves Christians and go to church; maybe they go to your church. How many of these people let it be known that they live in open sin—an immoral life that violates Scripture? Do you visit or dine with these so-called Christians? The Scriptures in 1 Corinthians 5 teach that true Christians—those obedient to the Word are not to associate with those so-called Christians living in sin while claiming they are saved. In fact, we should remove the wicked "so-called" brother—a Christian, or someone who calls himself a brother—from among us so that other saints aren't influenced by their sin—particularly, young, tender saints just coming to the Lord. We must live an example of Christianity so they will know right from wrong.

However, just eight chapters forward in Corinthians 13 the Bible teaches us what love is: patient and kind, not irritable, and several other characteristics of God, including love that never gives up. As Christians we are to remove the wicked person but never give up on them. We are to mentor and disciple them, trying to help restore them to Christ while preventing their sin from influencing the lives of the innocent ones. Not every Christian can mentor such a person because they themselves are still on milk and lack biblical *understanding*. We Christians are to build our faith until it is Holy, and pray in the power of the Holy Spirit, keeping ourselves preserved for eternal life with Jesus. When we do this we will *understand* when a brother or sister in Christ has deviated from the truth.

Jude, brother of Jesus says we are to *"be merciful to those* (Christians) *who doubt; snatch others* (brothers or sisters) *from the fire and save them; to others* (Christians) *show mercy, mixed with fear—hating even the clothing stained by corrupted flesh" (Jude 1:22 NLT).* Parenthesis added. The fear referenced here is a caution to the righteous—those who have been faithful to Jesus—to be careful so they don't get caught-up in a brother or sister's sin, even avoiding their clothing because it is so stained with wickedness. That person is dancing with the devil. Remember that the Word says that even the elect can be deceived if it were possible. When we associate with friends and loved ones who claim to love Jesus and yet they violate the Scriptures, our love for them can taint our own hearts and minds about what is or is not acceptable behavior in the Lord's eyes. Our love for them helps us tolerate those things the Lord objects to. Instead of helping them come out of *their* sin, we are more apt to change *our* mind about sin.

A question for Christians to ponder is this: How will we know to help these people, as the Scripture instructs, if we can't recognize that they are in sin? Research shows that most people who call themselves Christians today don't know what the Bible calls sin. If we refuse to judge their behavior how can we help them? How will we live with the guilt of having done nothing to help them if we leave them to eternal separation from God because we don't want to be guilty of judging them or offending them? We are to judge the behavior of those brothers and sisters inside the church, and help snatch them from the fire. But we are to do it with huge doses of love. Unfortunately, in today's world few people will agree to a one-on-one discussion about their behavior that violates Scripture and many will not listen to such a message from the pulpit. In a church I attended for about 10 years, several couples there were living in open sin. When the pastor began a series of sermons on lifestyle sin most of those couples left the church, for they did not want to hear such messages.

The Gentiles were a heathen (pagan) people whom God spoke about through Hosea saying they were not His people and He did not love them. That statement from God is difficult for Christians to accept. But, those heathen people seemed hopelessly confused by darkened minds and hardened hearts, and much like most of the world today (68% of humanity) they had disregarded God and His statutes and He was angry. Without shame they practiced all impurity and lustful pleasure.

The Jews hated the Gentiles and called them uncircumcised heathens and outsiders. They were not allowed citizenship in Israel because their behavior was so wicked. They lived in a world without hope of salvation until God sent the Apostle Paul to bring them into the knowledge of Jesus Christ, offering them eternal life through Him if they would believe, trust, and follow Him, and not fall away. To help them, Paul had to tell them what they were doing that violated God's statutes.

In offering them salvation, God was hoping to make His people (the Jews) jealous, then maybe they would run to Him for salvation, which some did. But the Jews who refused to accept Jesus were broken away from the tree to make room for the new believers, the Gentiles. However, the Apostle Paul warned the Gentiles who were grafted into the tree after branches of disobedient Jews were broken off to make room for them, not to brag about being grafted in to replace the discarded branches. Speaking to the gentiles Paul said:

"You are just a branch, not the root." "Well," you may say, "those branches were broken off to make room for me." "Yes, but remember—those branches (the Jews) *were broken off because they didn't believe in Christ, and you are there because you do believe. So don't think highly of yourself, but fear what could happen; for if God did not spare the original branches* (the Jews) *He won't spare you either. Notice how God is both kind and severe. <u>He is severe toward those who disobeyed, but kind to you IF</u>* (notice the big if!) *<u>you continue to trust in His kindness. But IF</u>* (notice the big IF again!) *<u>you stop trusting, you also will be cut off.</u> And if the people of Israel* (the Jews) *turn from their unbelief, they will be grafted in again, for God has the power to graft them back into the tree. You,* (Gentiles) *by nature, were a branch cut from a wild*

olive tree—(A generation of people not of the lineage of Isaac). *So, if God was willing to do something contrary to nature by grafting you into his cultivated tree, He will be far more eager to graft the original branches* (the Jews) *back into the tree where they belong (Romans 11:18-24 NLT).* Parenthesis added (See OT parallel: Ezekiel 18:23-32 pages 349, 350)

These Scriptures parallel Ezekiel 18:23-32 completely. If we were not born Jewish, and didn't come from the lineage of Isaac, but have accepted Jesus as savior, then we are Gentile, having been grafted in to the Jewish tree, saved by God's mercy, grace, and love for His chosen people, the Jews. Since we did not come from Isaac's descendants, how much more grateful we should be that He showed us this mercy. Therefore, having been given such mercy, shouldn't we Gentile Christians be clamoring to serve Him with all our heart, soul, and mind? We should be fully aware of the enemy that wants to destroy us by taking us back to our pagan roots.

Can you evaluate your Christian life and determine if you are teetering on the verge of being discarded from the tree, as the disobedient and unbelieving Jews were who had no faith in Jesus? I don't think there is any question that we can lose our right standing with God based on neglecting our spiritual growth, lack of *understanding* of the Scriptures and of sin, and our willful disobedience of His commands. To walk in the deep faith that the Lord requires of us means being willing to make a special effort to please the Lord in all our ways.

WALKING IN FAITH

Without faith, we have no Christian life. It is faith that determines every aspect of our walk with the Lord. But so do our deeds. In the example of Abraham when he obeyed God regarding his son Isaac, James (brother of Jesus) wrote a lesson to us all; *"You see then that a man is justified by works, and not by faith only" (James 2:24 NKJV).* (I also recommend an in depth study of 1 Corinthians 3. It is another hard teaching that is difficult to understand in relation to other Scriptures referenced here. Each person must reach their own satisfaction regarding the Scriptures on this passage.)

"For the time has come for judgment to begin at the house of God; and if it begins with us first, what will be the end of those who do not obey the gospel of God? Now, if the righteous one is scarcely saved, where will the ungodly and the sinner appear?" (1 Peter 5:17-18 NKJ) Faith that doesn't bring about change in ungodly actions, or conviction that makes us ashamed of our sin and persuades us to "turn around," is not a saving faith. James 2:19 says *"You say you have faith, for you believe in one God. Good for you! Even the demons believe this, and they tremble in terror."* Behaving as God commanded—living as representatives of the character of Jesus and passionately loving God—shows our willing respect for God's graciousness toward us in that He would send a Savior to redeem us if we would accept and obey Him.

Don't be confused about working your way to heaven. The Lord doesn't want us to believe that we can get to heaven by performing great and impressive acts. Giving loads of money to organizations is a good thing and certainly God is pleased with such actions. But if we make grandiose gestures while living in sin thinking that God will overlook our sin because of our gesture, then we are trying to "work" our way to heaven. Further, what we give others on behalf of charity should be given secretly for when we give to boost our own ego so that we look good in other's eyes people will worship us, and neglect worshiping the Jesus of the cross and what He did for us. Humans tend to admire and chase after people who function in abundance. Possibly they think this extravagance will pour out onto them. Working all day at the church doesn't guarantee us a mansion in heaven if other spiritual requirements don't line up with Scripture. Flying around the world to help countries in disaster won't automatically justify any hard-hearted attitudes or disobedience we may have of God's commands.

DANCING WITH THE DEVIL

The only thing that justifies us before God is our willingness to ask Jesus to live in our heart, to cleanse our heart and mind of all sin, to lead us on a day-by-day basis, and to forgive us when we transgress. We are not ashamed to proclaim our faith in Jesus Christ even when we know we will be persecuted for that proclamation. This is a genuine relationship with the Lord. Jesus Himself said that if we love Him we will willingly obey Him and if we say we love Him but don't do what He says then we are liars. Doing what He says includes those actions visible to others, and those thoughts of the heart, which *aren't* visible to others. Doing great things to get to heaven is not the same thing as doing your part in obedience to the Scriptures. God requires both faith and working to do good to avoid evil in order to have eternal life with Him.

The criminal on the cross who asked Jesus to remember him when He came into His Kingdom made poor life choices but then at the last minute he turned to Jesus for salvation. Suddenly he had great faith that Jesus was the Savior and his story demonstrates that even a genuine "last minute" heart conversion makes us right with God. However, the person who chooses to live for the devil thinking he will repent on his deathbed may want to reconsider because it may already be too late if he has repeatedly rejected God's call. Scripture says that at some point God abandons them to their foolish thinking (Rom. 1:28 NLT). The reality is that Jesus could very well say, *"I never knew you. Get away from me, you who break God's laws"* (Matthew 7:23 NLT). The Lord looks at the attitude of the heart. Friendship with the world is enmity with God. It can be seen easily in our outward behavior or it can be hidden deep within our heart. We must also be careful not to pretend we love the Lord by saying so with our mouth while our hearts are far away meditating on ungodly things such as un-forgiveness, anger or even hatred, and lust.

At some point, each of us will give a personal account to God. It is in our best interest to work at transforming our hearts to the heart of God before we meet Him at the judgment. We are to be patient of other Christians yet intolerant of their sin. In the letters to the seven churches Jesus showed John what he had against each one, which I cover in detail in chapter 10. God requires us to look closely at our faith, our church and our denomination and test its beliefs and teachings against the Scriptures. We are to know Biblical truth and not man's view about it. When we seek God He gives discernment in our spirit. Please don't go to church and listen to someone else tell you what the Bible says and then neglect your own Bible study and prayer. The person in the pulpit could be diluting the true gospel. Be careful about listening to TV evangelists. They may be false teachers. How will you know? By studying to learn the Word of God and asking Him to give you wisdom and *understanding* about how to discern the spirits as to whether they are of God or the devil. Be careful how you translate those things you read. Including this book, you must compare all things to Scripture and seek God for an answer. Just as no human can be perfect, no human can fully and accurately translate Scripture for humans are not fully disciplined, nor are they all-knowing (Omniscient).

As Christians we are required to work at living in a way that the fruit of our actions is without accusation; when compared to Scripture, people would struggle to find fault with our behavior. Critics will come against us all the time, especially when we speak up for the Lord, but as Proverbs teaches, the godly are to be as bold as lions. John, the disciple Jesus loved, penned this Scripture of Jesus' teaching: *"If you love me, obey my commandments" (John 14:15 NLT).* The writer of Philippians wrote: *"For God is working in you, giving you the desire and the power to do what pleases Him" (Philippians 2:13 NLT).* The Bible is not difficult to *understand*; the difficult part is making a choice to do what it says regardless of what our friends and family members or the secular world may think of us. Our willingness to build our faith in Jesus Christ must override everything else in our life. Without that kind of faith, we cannot live a resourceful life in Christ.

THE RESPONSIBILITIES OF GRACE

When we accept Jesus Christ as our Lord and Savior, we live under the grace of God in that He was gracious toward us to send his Son to take on our sins and reconcile us to His Father. Christians, who accept Jesus as their Savior, are obligated to the responsibilities of God's grace. They must live as representatives of the character of God—a life of righteousness that honors His grace. The only way to live a righteous life is to "learn" and then "make a choice," otherwise we indulge what pastor, and martyr Dietrich Bonhoeffer called "cheap grace." When something is cheap usually it has very little quality or value.

German author, Theologian, and Christian Martyr Dietrich Bonhoeffer, defined "cheap grace" as *"the grace we bestow on ourselves. Cheap grace is the preaching of forgiveness without requiring repentance, baptism without church discipline, communion without confession . . . Cheap grace is grace without discipleship, grace without the cross, grace without Jesus Christ, living and incarnate."* Grace without these attributes is worthless grace. Jesus does all the work and we can live according to our desires. When I hear Christians use the word "grace" excessively in conversation or from the pulpit, and their only discussion about the Lord is how much He loves His children, I listen up quickly. This can easily cause believers to transfer the biblically mandated responsibilities of their actions to Jesus, enabling them to act like the devil.

In some cases listeners may be sitting under the influence of a *New Age* teaching—an attempt by historical New Agers to shift the truth of the Word of God, taking traditional Christian religion and making it a mystical religion that makes humans "gods" and alters the divinity and sovereignty of the one true God. We must listen and *understand*; otherwise we will miss the most important command for salvation the Lord has for us, which is "follow Me!" We must decide what the Bible says about how we are to do that because we never want to hear the words, "I never knew you!"

FOLLOWING JESUS

When we make the decision to follow Jesus, change begins in our heart. But the mind is still tied to the old ways. There will be a struggle to conform to the ways of God because old hurts, habits, and behaviors are still with us. To allow the "things of the Lord" to heal and renew our mind we must mentally *understand* that our mind must be changed. (Romans 12:1-2) When the mind is healed we forgive others and our self, then the rest of the body can be healed.

Jude told Christians they were to: 1) Encourage each other; 2) Pray in the power of the Holy Spirit; 3) Wait for Jesus to take them home; 4) <u>Show mercy to those losing their faith;</u> 5) Rescue from the flames of judgment Christians living in sin; 6) Be merciful to nonbelievers, hating their sin but being careful to not let it contaminate their lives.

Therefore, put on every piece of God's armor so you will be able to resist the enemy in the time of evil. Then after the battle you will still be standing firm. Stand your ground, putting on the belt of truth and the body armor of God's righteousness. For shoes, put on the peace that comes from the Good News so that you will be fully prepared. In addition to all of these, hold up the shield of faith to stop the fiery arrows of the devil. Put on salvation as your helmet, and take the sword of the Spirit, which is the Word of God (Ephesians 6:13-17 NLT).

Christians must beware of extravagantly desiring spiritual success by seeking great things for self, jeopardizing their position with the Lord. Christians must be willing to give up their own convictions and traditional beliefs in order to break through any barriers that might be keeping them from the knowledge, the wisdom and the fullness of God. We must surrender to Jesus everything in our lives, for with each passing day the fullness of what we are to become has not yet been revealed to us.

The evidence of our true love for Christ is the spontaneity of the love we allow to flow naturally from His nature that is within us.

Then the proof that our relationship is right with God is that we do our best whether we feel inspired or not. God inspires all good things and He should be the inspiration for our causes and our issues because we are devoted to Him through our communication with Him in prayer and the written Word.

GET OFF THE MILK AND ON THE MEAT

The "true" children of God make every effort to get off of milk and feed entirely on meat. Once this is accomplished they will know when they are hearing a diluted version of the Scriptures. The true children do not practice sin or deliberately keep sin in their lives. God's children are educated about the difference in good and evil and realize that the entire world is under the influence of Satan, the evil one. The true children of God realize that He judges sin. In Romans chapters 1 and 2, Paul cautioned Christians that God gets angry about the sin committed by wicked people who suppress the truth about Him. He said the truth was obvious to them and they could clearly see His eternal power and divine nature. They knew Him but wouldn't worship Him or even give Him thanks. Because of this He abandoned them to do whatever shameful things their heart desired. Those people were deeply involved in all kinds of wicked sins and refused to *understand* how God felt about their sin. They broke promises, were heartless, and had no mercy. Paul warned that those people knew that God's justice for this kind of behavior required that they must die but they continued their behavior anyway. And the Word says that something worse than them doing it themselves was that they encouraged others to behave in like manner. In Romans chapter 2, Paul spoke the following to those Christians:

"Because you are stubborn and refuse to turn from your sin, you are storing up terrible punishment for yourself. For a day is coming when God's righteous judgment will be revealed. <u>He will judge everyone according to what they have done. He will give eternal life to those who keep on doing good, seeking after</u>

the glory and honor and immortality that God offers. But He will pour out His anger and wrath on those who live for themselves, who refuse to obey the truth and instead live lives of wickedness. There will be trouble and calamity for everyone who keeps on doing what is evil—for the Jew first and then for the Gentile. But there will be glory and honor and peace from God for all who do good—for the Jew first and also for the Gentile. For God does not show favoritism. When the Gentiles sin, they will be destroyed, even though they never had God's written law (The Ten Commandments). *And the Jews, who do have God's law, will be judged by that law when they fail to obey it. For merely listening to the law doesn't make us right with God. It is obeying the law* (The Ten Commandments) *that makes us right in His sight (Roman 2:5-13 NIV)*

In Romans chapter 3, the Word tells us that all people are under the power of sin—that no one is righteous. Yet, through the death of Jesus on the cross, He gave us undeserved righteousness, freeing us from the penalty of our sin when we confess and repent. He declares sinners to be right in His sight when they believe in Jesus. But we cannot boast about this freedom and forget God's law for it is only when we have faith that we truly fulfill the law. Romans chapter 7 teaches that it is the law that helps us *understand* right from wrong. When the law showed us things that were wrong in God's eyes, sin took advantage of those commands and deceived people. Paul told how this happened to him and it happens to people today. I am convinced that when we get off the milk and feast on the meat, which includes all of God's Word, sin will *not* take advantage of (or rule) us, even though we will occasionally sin.

REVOLUTIONARIES FOR JESUS

The Barna Group research shown at the beginning of this chapter attributes much of today's lack of faith among Christians to the numerous distractions common in most people's lives. Barna listed three general patterns that he says will define the future of American Faith: diversity, which includes new forms of spiritual leadership, different expressions of faith, and greater variety in when and where people meet together to be communities of faith; media, which includes new technologies that will significantly reshape how people experience and express their faith, and the ways in which they form communities of faith; and then, bifurcation, (which is divergence) or a widening gap between the intensely committed and those who are casually involved in faith matters. I believe this is where we are today as a Christian nation. We are already seeing a widening gap between the people who truly understand what being a good Christian is all about and those who are toying with Christianity—they can't let go of certain aspects of the worldly life, and live much of their life as the non-believer lives.

Barna says that "dedicated" Christians are breaking away from the organized church and are holding tight to being fully committed to Biblical Christianity. He calls them "Revolutionaries" and defines them as having a clear sense of the meaning and purpose of their life; they describe their relationship with and faith in God as their top priority; they consider themselves "Christian" and read the Bible and pray regularly; their faith being very important in their life, their main objective is to love God with all their heart, mind, strength and soul; they describe God as the "all-knowing, all-powerful being who created the universe and still rules it today;" they have made a personal commitment to Jesus Christ that is important in their life; they believe that when they die they will go to heaven only because they have confessed their sins and accepted Jesus as their savior and say that their faith in Christ has "greatly transformed" their life. Based on these characteristics, can you see yourself as a "true" child of God—a Revolutionary? I can and I am quite happy about it.

God has set a race before us, which we are to run with endurance, keeping our eyes on Jesus.

"Therefore, since we are surrounded by such a huge crowd of witnesses to the life of faith, let us strip off every weight that slows us down, especially the sin

that so easily trips us up. And let us run with endurance the race God has set before us. We do this by keeping our eyes on Jesus, the champion who initiates and perfects our faith. Because of the joy awaiting Him, He endured the cross, disregarding its shame. Now He is seated in the place of honor beside God's throne. Think of all the hostility He endured from sinful people; then you won't become weary and give up" (Hebrews 12:1-3 NLT).

The weight that slows us down can be many things. However, it is usually something that Satan has convinced us we can't live without—or can't live with. We become weary and want to give up but the Lord wants us to get off the milk, get on the meat of the Word, stay strong, and turn to Him in our faith. If for any reason you have abandoned your first Love, the Lord, He wants you to get back in the race. He loves you and He desperately wants to say to you one day, "well done, my son; well done, my daughter." If you want to hear the words "well done" instead of "but I have this complaint against you" when you see Him face to face, then do all you can to get back in the race.

And so, dear brothers and sisters, I plead with you to give your bodies to God because of all He has done for you. Let them be a living and holy sacrifice— the kind He will find acceptable. This is truly the way to worship Him. Don't copy the behavior and customs of this world, but let God transform you into a new person by changing the way you think. Then you will learn to know God's will for you, which is good and pleasing and perfect (Romans 12:1, 2 NLT).

When we Christians are able to run a winning race, as Paul outlined in Hebrews chapter 12 and truly live for and worship Christ, as Romans 12 teaches, then we have become true Revolutionaries for Christ.

CHAPTER NINE STUDY QUESTIONS

1. Review Romans 12 and evaluate whether your life represents the responsibilities God laid out for Christians.

2. What is your opinion of George Barna's research, which shows Christians to be spiritually lukewarm? Based on his findings would you consider yourself to be a lukewarm Christian?

3. Can you think of anyone you love enough to be willing to die for him or her?

4. Do you see yourself as a dedicated Christian? List some characteristics you think you possess that confirm you are? List those characteristics, which you think confirm you aren't.

5. What does it mean to remain an infant in Christ?

6. What does it mean to put on the battle armor of Christ?

7. God gives us free will and does not force us to follow Him. What must you do to avoid falling away from Christ?

8. Are you confused about the biblical meaning of "judging others? When are you to judge others and when are you not to judge others?

9. Why were the Gentiles not allowed citizenship in Israel?

10. Why did God offer salvation to the wicked Gentiles?

TEN

"BUT I HAVE THIS COMPLAINT AGAINST YOU"

"But I have this complaint against you. You don't love me, or each other as you did at first! Look how far you have fallen! Turn back to me and do the works you did at first" (Revelation 2:4, 5 NLT).

God called the Israelites wicked and stubborn. The Bible records how they were willfully and persistently rebellious. From the time of their wilderness wonderings recorded in the Book of Genesis to the letters to the Seven Churches spoken of in the book of Revelation, God has put forth every effort to reconcile His people to Himself and to offer salvation to all humanity. But, all peoples have rebelled against Him, characterizing Him as an unjust or unbelievable God. Even after Jesus was crucified the world still rejected Him and even today there is a great delusion—a seduction purposed to blind the eyes of the saints and destroy their dedication and love for Him.

In their book, *The Seduction of Christianity*, T.A. McMahon and the late Dave Hunt say that this incredible worldwide delusion is gathering momentum. They caution that *"every person on earth during these last days prior to Christ's return must face it and choose God's truth or Satan's lie. So compelling will be the seduction that Jesus warned that "even the elect" would be deceived "if it were possible."* They say *"such language ought to put every Christian on his guard."*

DANCING WITH THE DEVIL

Hunt and McMahon wrote this warning in 1985, more than thirty years before I began writing, *Dancing With The Devil*. They caution that *"we should not become fatalistic, but work even more diligently to rescue as many* (souls) *as we possibly can before it is too late."* They say that *"the Bible repeatedly makes it clear that the issue is "truth" and that Paul warns that all those who 'did not receive the love of the truth so as to be saved' would be given from God himself 'a deluding influence so that they might believe the lie.'"* (See 2 Thessalonians 2:10, 11) Parenthesis added

About 2700 years ago Isaiah so lucidly described what the people were like then, that one could easily think he was speaking about the people of today.

"Listen! The Lord's arm is not too weak to save you, nor is His ear too deaf to hear you call. It's your sins that have cut you off from God. Because of your sins He has turned you away and He will not listen anymore. Your hands are the hands of murderers, and your fingers are filthy with sin. Your lips are full of lies, and your mouth spews corruption. No one cares about being fair and honest. The people's lawsuits are based on lies. They conceive evil deeds and then give birth to sin. They hatch deadly snakes and weave spider's webs. Whoever falls into their webs will die, and there's danger even in getting near them. Their webs can't be made into clothing and nothing they do is productive. All their activity is filled with sin, and violence is their trademark. Their feet run to do evil, and they rush to commit murder. They think only about sinning. Misery and destruction always follow them. They don't know where to find peace or what it means to be just and good. They have mapped out crooked roads, and no one who follows them knows a moment's peace. So, there is no justice among us, and we know nothing about right living. We look for light but find only darkness. We look for bright skies but walk in gloom. We grope like the blind along a wall, feeling our way like people without eyes. Even at brightest noontime, we stumble as though it were dark. Among the living, we are like the dead. We growl like hungry bears; we moan like mournful doves. We look for justice, but it never comes. We look for rescue but it is far away from us. For our sins are piled up before God and testify against us. Yes, we know what sinners we are. We know

we have rebelled and have denied the Lord. We have turned our backs on our God. We know how unfair and oppressive we have been, carefully planning our deceitful lies. Our courts oppose the righteous, and justice is nowhere to be found. Truth stumbles in the streets, and honesty has been outlawed. Yes, truth is gone, and anyone who renounces evil is attacked. The Lord looked and was displeased to find there was no justice. He was amazed to see that no one intervened to help the oppressed. So He himself stepped in to save them with His strong arm, and His justice sustained Him. He put on righteousness as his body armor, and placed the helmet of salvation on His head. He clothed himself with a robe of vengeance and wrapped himself in a cloak of divine passion. He will repay His enemies for their evil deeds. His fury will fall on His foes. He will pay them back even to the ends of the earth. In the west, people will respect the name of the Lord; in the east they will glorify Him. For He will come like a raging flood tide driven by the breath of the Lord. The Redeemer will come to Jerusalem to buy back those in Israel who have turned from their sins, says the Lord" (Isaiah 59 NLT).

Fast forward from Isaiah to Revelation at the end of our Book of Instruction, the Holy Bible. By now, Jesus has come from Heaven, shed His blood for all humanity and gone back. Yet in their stubbornness people still refuse to listen, remaining on the path to God's wrath. However, being merciful toward His children once again, Jesus called John the Beloved up to heaven and showed him the great and mighty things to come. He gave John powerful words of warning for the churches and the Christians that were attending church on a regular basis. Reading these warnings today, I am filled with anxiety about the punishment that awaits those who have compromised their devotion to Jesus by getting caught-up in non-Christian sensualities and have not repented. It seems as though a drug fogs their mind and renders them unable to reason.

THE MESSAGES TO THE SEVEN CHURCHES

Throughout the Scriptures God continually warned the people about what He had against them—not just what he had against the pagans and heathens, but also His children. Revelation, the testament of "things to come," was dictated by Jesus and written by the disciple John whom the Bible refers to, as "the one Jesus loved." John walked with Jesus during His time on earth. He witnessed Jesus' crucifixion and just before Jesus died, He gave John the responsibility of taking care of His mother, Mary (John 19:26-27).

When John was exiled to the Isle of Patmos for preaching the gospel, he believed his work for Jesus was finished—that he would soon die. But it was on this Island that the Jesus he loved and who loved him revealed Himself miraculously to John in a vision and told him to write down what He said. Jesus wanted Christians to understand two things: where they stood in relationship with Him, (see chapter 5) and what they could expect in the end time.

The Lord, dressed in clothing representative of His High Priesthood, and standing among the lampstands (the Churches) said to John, *"I am the living one; I was dead, and behold I am alive forever and ever! And I hold the keys of death and Hades. Write, therefore, what you have seen, what is now and what will take place later. The mystery of the seven stars that you saw in my right hand and of the seven golden lampstands is this: The seven stars are the angels of the seven churches, and the seven lampstands are the seven churches" (Revelation 1:18-20 NLT).* Then beginning with the Church in Ephesus Jesus began to tell John what He wanted the seven churches to know. If we believe that these messages don't apply to us today then we are living a lie that holds powerful consequences for us.

TO THE CHURCH IN EPHESUS

"I know all the things you do. I have seen your hard work and your patient endurance. I know that you don't tolerate evil people. You have examined the claims of those who say they are apostles but are not. You have discovered they are liars. You have patiently suffered for me without quitting. <u>*But I have this complaint against you.*</u> *You don't love me, or each other as you did at first! Look how far you have fallen! Turn back to me and do the works you did at first. If*

you don't repent, I will come and remove your lampstand from its place among the churches. But this is in your favor: you hate the evil deeds of the Nicolaitans just as I do. Anyone with ears to hear must listen to the Spirit and <u>understand</u> what He is saying to the churches. To everyone who is victorious (overcomes), *I will give fruit* (the right to eat) *from the tree of life, which is in the paradise of God"* *(Revelation 2:1-7 NLT).* Parenthesis added

For a long time in history the Church in Ephesus had refused to tolerate sin among its members. They had done many good things in the name of the Lord and had revered Him highly. They compared the teaching to God's Word and discarded what they found to be untrue. (Note: Unlike the Christians at Ephesus, many Christians today don't do this, so false teachers are misleading them. But as we see here in Revelation, Jesus fully expects us to compare the teaching to the Scriptures) The Church in Ephesus hated the practices of the Nicolaitans who were believers that had compromised their faith so that they could justify their sin and "fit in" with what the unbelieving people around them thought was acceptable behavior.

The Christians at the church in Ephesus had fallen so far from loving the Lord as He wanted them to that He found it necessary to caution them strongly to "turn back," which means to make a complete turn around and go the opposite direction or the cost would be high. Basically, He would wipe out the effectiveness of their church. Notice how the Lord stressed the importance of loving Him, and your church family. One of the areas of obedience that I have stressed with intense fervor in this book is God's admonition for us to *get understanding,* which the Lord emphasized in each of the letters to the seven churches. *Understanding* who God is teaches us how to forgive.

TO THE CHURCH IN SMYRNA

The Lord's admonition to the church in Smyrna about the coming persecution of His children was powerful and direct.

DANCING WITH THE DEVIL

"I know about your suffering and your poverty—but you are rich! I know the blasphemy of those opposing you. They say they are Jews, but they are not because their synagogue belongs to Satan. Don't be afraid of what you are about to suffer. The devil will throw some of you in prison to test you. You will suffer for ten days but if you will remain faithful even when facing death, I will give you the crown of life. Anyone with ears to hear must listen to the Spirit and <u>understand</u> what He is saying to the churches. Whoever is victorious will not be harmed by the second death" (Revelation 2:9-11 NLT).

The City of Smyrna was situated on the Aegean Sea about 25 miles north of Ephesus. The Jewish population in Smyrna opposed Christianity, and the non-Jewish citizens favored Rome and supported emperor worship, which is what the Japanese people did for hundreds of years until the surrender of Hirohito during WWII. The church at Smyrna was a church in poverty, and it suffered persecution at the hands of the 'devil-led' opposing forces that surrounded them. Jesus was telling them that some would die for their faith but to stay faithful and strong in the time of suffering.

Do you realize that in standing strong for your faith you may be faced with death as your choice? Around the world today there are Christians and ministries suffering for the cause of Christ and the cross, and in America the government is already persecuting the church. Unless we speak up, our right to religious freedom will be removed entirely. If we give it away freely we will be forbidden to even speak of Christianity and if we do speak of Christianity we will die because of it. However, Jesus says to not turn from Him during this time. He will not necessarily exempt us or remove us from persecution but when we are persecuted unto death, and have stood faithful He will take us to heaven to be with Him for eternal life. Today no one wants to discuss being persecuted for Christ. Instead, blindly we prefer to believe that we have a government who cares for its people enough to protect and preserve their Christian freedoms. I assure you; we don't! Further, many Christians today believe that

God will not permit Americans (especially Christians) to be persecuted or killed although they realize that many Christians before us were persecuted and killed. And today as I write, many Christians around the world are being persecuted or killed.

TO THE CHURCH IN PERGAMUM

The message to the church in Pergamum was given with a warning about the power of God's two-edged sword, which represents His ultimate authority and judgment.

Jesus said, "I know that you live in the city where Satan has his throne, yet you have remained loyal to me. You refused to deny me even when Antipas, my faithful witness, was martyred among you there in Satan's city. <u>But, I have a few complaints against you.</u> You tolerate some among you whose teaching is like that of Balaam, who showed Balak how to trip up the people of Israel. He taught them to sin by eating food offered to idols and by committing sexual sin. In a similar way, you have some Nicolaitans among you who follow the same teaching. Repent of your sin, or I will come to you suddenly and fight against them (those teaching the false religion) *with the sword of my mouth. Anyone with ears to hear must listen to the Spirit and <u>understand</u> what he is saying to the churches. To everyone who is victorious I will give some of the manna that has been hidden away in heaven. And I will give to each one a white stone, and on the stone will be engraved a new name that no one understands except the one who receives it"* (Revelation 2:12-17 NLT). Parenthesis added

Most of us know it is difficult to stand firm against the pressures and temptations of the anti-Christ society that surrounds us, but it would be especially difficult when to do so might cost us our life. Sinful people had infiltrated the church in Pergamum and the Christians there were challenged every day to compromise, or leave their faith, or die for it. Antipas was the first leader of the Christian church to be slain. He was roasted to death slowly inside the statue of a bull at the Throne of Satan. Though he faced death, Antipas refused to compromise his faith.

The Throne of Satan, or The Great Altar of Zeus, existed in Pergamum at the time John wrote the letters to the churches. About 2000 years after Revelation 2:13 was written, German archeologists removed the massive Altar of Zeus from the ruins of Pergamum, an ancient Greek City, and took it to Berlin, Germany where it was restored as the centerpiece of the Pergamum Museum there. Germany's Kaiser Wilhelm II, whom you read about in chapter 3, A World Obsessed with Evil, celebrated the Altar's erection in Berlin in 1902. In chapter 3 you also read about Wilhelm's hatred for the Jewish people. Considering his hatred for the Jews and his admiration for the Altar of Zeus, possibly he worshipped Satan during the celebration when the throne was being erected in Berlin. In so doing he invited Satan and the demons into his territory. The evidence lies in the atrocities in Germany during WWI and WWII.

In 1933, Adolph Hitler was elected Chancellor of Germany and then became dictator in 1934. At that time he ordered the construction of the Tribune at Zeppelin Field where he held his Nazi rallies. Architect Albert Speer used the Pergamum Altar as the model for the Zeppelintribune. The Fuhrer's pulpit was the center of the tribune, which was built from 1934 to 1939. After WWII the Soviets disassembled the Altar and took it to Leningrad, Russia in 1948 as part of their spoils of war. (Note: 1948 was the same year that Israel became an independent state.) Ten years after its erection in Russia, the Soviets returned the Altar to Germany where it is now memorialized at the Pergamum Museum in Berlin. As you read the next paragraph keep in mind that this Throne of Satan was the place of persecution and death of many Christians that were offered to Zeus as a sacrifice.

On July 24, 2008, American Presidential candidate Barak Hussein Obama gave a speech in Berlin titled *"The World that Stands as One."* Obama gave his speech at the Tiergarten, a 495-acre park in the middle of Berlin. He stood in front of The Berlin Victory Column—a 226-foot monument—a Nazi symbol topped by a golden winged figure representing Borussia, the female personification of Prussia, and Victoria, the cult goddess of military victory. Just a short distance from The Berlin Victory Column where Obama made his speech, sat the Great Altar of Zeus—the Throne of Satan. Before leaving Berlin, Obama visited the Great Altar of Zeus and upon his return to the United States, he immediately commissioned the construction of a Greek-columned stage from which he made his acceptance speech in Denver, Colorado for his party's nomination. The New York Post ran an enlightening Convention Special supplement on August 28, 2008 with the telling headline: "'O' MY GOD: DEMS ERECT OBAMA TEMPLE." Campaign managers tried to explain away the design as being a conglomeration representing the portico of the White House with the US Capital building. But experts agreed that it was a replica of the Great Altar of Pergamum—or Throne of Satan. President Obama was elected to two terms as president of the United States. Take some time to do some research and see how many of our Christian freedoms were removed during his tenure and ask why a president of a Christian nation would desire to do such a thing and why the nation would allow it? (Refer to chapter 4, p 177)

Some in the church at Pergamum were tolerating those who taught or practiced what Christ opposed. Are you sitting in church, wanting God to accept you yet you tolerate pornography, sexual sin, cheating, gossiping, and lying, and other things God hates? Have you compromised your integrity? Do you bring speakers into your church that compromise the Word of God, or who say things that lead believers away from God's truth? Are you paying attention to what is happening around you and in your government?

TO THE CHURCH IN THYATIRA

The message Jesus sent to the church at Thyatira had such a strong warning, He promised that all the churches would have no doubt that He was Lord when He would finally come against them because of the evil they tolerated. He assured them that He knew what they were doing (permitting the teaching of sexual sin) and He promised that they would know that He was the one who searched the thoughts and the intentions of every person and would punish accordingly.

He said, "I have seen your love, your faith, your service, and your patient endurance. And, I can see your constant improvement in all these things. <u>But I have this complaint against you.</u> You are permitting that woman—that woman who calls herself a prophet—to lead my servants astray. She teaches them to commit sexual sin and to eat food offered to idols. I gave her time to repent, but she does not want to turn away from her immorality. Therefore I will throw her on a bed of suffering, and those who commit adultery with her will suffer greatly unless they repent and turn away from her evil deeds. I will strike her children dead. Then all the churches will know that I am the one who searches out the thoughts and intentions of every person. And I will give to each of you whatever you deserve. But, I also have a message for the rest of you in Thyatira who have not followed this false teaching ('deeper truths,' as they call them—depths of Satan, actually). I will ask nothing more of you except that you hold tightly to what you have until I come. To all who are victorious, who obey me to the very end; to them I will give authority over all the nations. They will rule the nations with an iron rod and smash them like clay pots. They will have the same authority I received from my Father, and I will also give them the morning star! Anyone with ears to hear must listen to the Spirit and <u>understand</u> what He is saying to the churches" (Revelation 2:19-29 NLT).

The Old Testament Jezebel was a pagan queen of Israel and was considered the most evil woman that ever lived. Her name is synonymous with people who completely reject God. She held great power and controlled her husband Ahab, and 850 assorted pagan priests. Her quest was to get what she wanted and her ultimate plan was to wipe out the worship of God in Israel. Her most outstanding success was contributing to the downfall of the northern kingdom of Israel.

Called by some as "a messenger of Satan" Jezebel was so powerful under the demonic influence in her life that she systematically eliminated those people who represented God in Israel and she tried to have Elijah, the prophet of God, killed. The Bible says that no other person so completely sold himself to what was evil in the Lord's sight as Ahab did under the influence of his wife, Jezebel. When God got angry enough at the evil they had done, He promised to destroy all of their male descendants and the entire family. He pledged that dogs would eat Jezebel's body, and that dogs and vultures together would eat members of her family. The story of Jezebel and Ahab can be found in 1 Kings 21:1-29.

American born Madalyn Murray O'Hair was not a legal ruler over priests—pagan or otherwise—but her quest was to wipe out the worship of God in America and remove any reference to Him in public schools or institutions. In the Murray v. Curlett lawsuit, the Supreme Court's landmark ruling ended official Bible-reading in American public schools in 1963—just one year after the Supreme Court ruled to prohibit officially sponsored prayer in schools. Though many give her the title "atheist" O'Hair's son, William J. Murray Jr., who eventually became a Christian, referred to his mother not as an atheist, but as evil—a Satan worshipper who hated God. In 1995, O'Hair, her son, Jon Garth Murray, and her granddaughter Robin were murdered and mutilated by the criminals she had hired to help her destroy Christianity in America. The only law she respected was "Do what thou wilt"—a phrase coined by Aleister Crowley, an occultist atheist who called himself "the Great Beast 666." The British Press referred to him as "the wickedest man in the world."

O'Hair, her son, and granddaughter were found buried on a ranch in Central Texas. Their bodies had been sawn into dozens of pieces and their remains revealed extensive mutilation. Christians who had objected so strongly to her quest to destroy their worship of their Christ were not the ones who took her life; it was the evil criminals she had hired to help her do her dirty work against God and Christianity. It is interesting that both of these women, the biblical Jezebel and America's O'Hair, who tried with all their power to destroy God, his children, and take people to hell with them, both died horrible deaths.

The woman in the church at Thyatira was not the Jezebel written about in 1 Kings. Yet her Jezebel spirit was so wicked in her efforts to seduce Christians away from their belief and service to Jesus that He compared her to the Old Testament Jezebel. Jesus had John write down His words as a warning to us today. Though she called herself a Christian prophet, in reality she was "a messenger of Satan" in the manner of the OT Jezebel. She taught that sexual immorality, which was directly opposed to the commandments of the Lord, was acceptable among church members. And she encouraged them to eat food offered to idols. Jesus called her teachings false, and promised to destroy her and her children, and to give each of her followers the punishment they deserved. It's too bad that our Supreme Court wasn't able to see O'Hair as "a messenger of Satan." Had they studied the Word, maybe they would have judged differently, and changed the course of our nation as well.

Because of its destructiveness to humans, Jesus declared sexual immorality a serious offense. It overrides God's plan for our life, fracturing our ability to be obedient to Him. It caters to our personal selfish plans and desires, showing complete disregard for the Lord's commands. It subjects us to disease and changes our life and personality in ways we can't count or foresee. It destroys families, churches, communities and nations. It extinguishes the integrity we need to build and maintain good relationships and it affects the spirituality of our children, grandchildren, and other family members, putting them in danger of being unclean before the Lord. Why do we let this great sin take charge of our lives? Because Christians don't study the Word enough to *understand* how seriously God defines this behavior as evil.

TO THE CHURCH IN SARDIS

"I know all the things you do, and that you have a reputation for being alive—but you are dead. Wake up! Strengthen what little remains, for even what is left is almost dead. I find that your actions do not meet the requirements of my God. Go back to what you heard and believed at first; hold to it firmly. Repent and turn to me again. If you don't wake up, I will come to you suddenly as unexpected as a thief. Yet there are some in the church who have not soiled their clothes with evil. They will walk with me in white, for they are worthy. All who are victorious will be clothed in white. I will never erase their names from the Book of Life, but I will announce before my Father and His angels that they are mine. Anyone with ears to hear must listen to the Spirit and <u>understand</u> what He is saying to the churches" (Revelation 3:1-6 NLT).

When Jesus looked at the church in Sardis He saw a dead church. The people had a reputation for being alive but Jesus knew differently. Some of the church members were involved in evil. Those members not involved in evil were ineffective because they tolerated evil in their members. Those participating in evil had slipped so far from Scripture that they no longer met God's requirements. I believe this means His requirements for salvation. Those found to be worthy of salvation were doing nothing to help those members lost in sin. Though some members were lost and some were saved, Jesus called the entire church a dead church because they were productive at nothing Spiritual. Today, many churches resemble Jesus' description of the church in Sardis. In His letter to them, once again, Jesus wanted another church to recognize that in His eyes they had serious problems.

If you recognize that your church is dead and you are a true servant of God—not soiling your clothing with evil doing—you are in a position to help turn around your church. Attempt to awaken the dead believers by urging them to return to the joy and service of their beginning with Jesus. Encourage them to deepen their *understanding* through an in-depth Bible study. Use the Bible to help them *understand* the importance of growing in knowledge and wisdom about the ways of God. Reassure them that self-satisfaction and remaining inside a perceived safety cocoon will lead to spiritual death but if they will rejuvenate a compassionate love and service toward others, and unify the body, God will place them in a responsible role of teaching, leading, and serving, which will help bring others back to the Lord.

TO THE CHURCH OF PHILADELPHIA

Most of the citizens of Philadelphia had been forced to forsake the city for suburban areas due to their worry over the aftershocks of an earthquake in A.D. 17. Surely the condition of the city and their ongoing battle to keep barbarians at bay weakened them, but Jesus praised their faithfulness to the gospel and promised to protect them giving them a place of honor in the Temple of God.

Though He had no complaints against them, Jesus told John to write a letter of praise, approval, encouragement, and promise to His beloved church in Philadelphia.

"I know all the things you do and I have opened a door for you that no one can close. You have little strength, yet you obeyed my word and did not deny me. Look, I will force those who belong to Satan's synagogue—those liars who say they are Jews but are not—to come and bow down at your feet. They will acknowledge that you are the ones that I love. <u>Because you have obeyed my command to persevere, I will protect you from the great time of testing that will come upon the whole world to test those who belong to this world.</u> I am coming soon. Hold on to what you have so that no one will take away your crown. <u>All who are victorious will become pillars in the Temple of my God, and they will never have to leave it.</u> And I will write on them the name of my God, and they will be citizens in the city of my God—the New Jerusalem that comes down from

heaven from my God. And I will also write on them my new name. Anyone with ears to hear must listen to the Spirit and <u>understand</u> what He is saying to the churches" (Revelation 3:7-13 NLT).

I have underlined parts of the above Scriptures to show that for me they confirm that the Lord promises to remove his faithful and obedient children before the tribulation—the great time of testing. The Lord is faithful to secure our eternal life with Him when we are faithful to obey His commands and persevere through the painful times in our life. Jesus suffered much to become the sacrifice for our sins—the mediator and bridge between God and us so that we could be redeemed. When we weaken under the trials of life and succumb to the tactics of the enemy, we lessen what Jesus did for us on the cross. But when we stay faithful and strong, He is able to work in us that which we can't work in ourselves. Our victory over sin and our trustworthiness enables the Lord to work miracles and blessings in our lives on earth and is commendable before God in heaven. Does your church look like the church in Philadelphia? If not, what can you do to make it so?

TO THE CHURCH IN LAODICEA

Famous for its successful manufacturing and white-collar business industry, Laodicea was the wealthiest of the seven cities. But despite its many attributes the water supply had problems. By the time the water was piped to its destination it was neither hot nor cold but was simply lukewarm. Jesus compared the condition of the Christians to the piped-in lukewarm water because they had become complacent and indifferent. In His message to the Laodicea church, Jesus instructed John to say this:

"I know all the things you do, that you are neither hot nor cold. I wish that you were one or the other! But since you are like lukewarm water, neither hot nor cold, I will spit you out of my mouth! You say, 'I am rich. I have everything I

want. I don't need a thing.' And you don't realize that you are wretched and miserable and poor and blind and naked. So I advise you to buy gold from me—gold that has been purified by fire. Then you will be rich. Also, buy white garments from me so you will not be shamed by your nakedness and ointment for your eyes so you will be able to see. I correct and discipline everyone I love. So be diligent and turn from your indifference. Look, I stand at the door and knock. If you hear my voice and open the door, I will come in and we will share a meal together as friends. Those who are victorious will sit with me on my throne, just as I was victorious and sat with my Father on His throne. Anyone with ears to hear must listen to the Spirit and <u>understand</u> what He is saying to the churches" (Revelation 3:14-22 NLT).

In many ways, the church at Laodicea was much like countless churches of western civilization today. Because the city of Laodicea was economically sound, those that attended the church were well to do. Though our nation's present economic condition leaves much to be desired there is still a great deal of wealth flowing and a sizable portion gets rolled into the church. That is what happened to the church in Laodicea. The Christians completely forgot what it meant to sell-out their hearts to Jesus and sacrifice something of themselves for Him and for others. Their minds had become numb to what Christ had done for them, and they focused on their self-sufficiency due to their wealth. Their material possessions had become more special to them than an eternal life with Christ but He wanted them to *understand* that their possessions and achievements were worthless when compared to an everlasting future. Therefore His admonishment was a threat that if they didn't get active in relationship with Him—if they didn't open their eyes; if they didn't recognize how wretched and miserable and poor and blind they were—He would spit them out of His mouth . . . in other words, turn His back on them.

Notice that in all the letters to the churches except two, the Lord addressed what was wrong with their belief *and* their actions. He cautioned them to listen to His Holy Spirit, which lives in the heart of everyone who accepts Him as Savior. He also wanted them to do something that He had encouraged them to do from the beginning to the end of His Word, and that was to *understand*.

One of Jesus' gravest warnings was a caution about how badly the enemy wanted to deceive God's children. Satan used humans to teach God's children a new way of thinking about Christ and His sacrifice, and the real meaning of grace. But the Lord cautioned them that this new way of thinking was wrong and they should return to their first love. In other words, the people were implementing a "shift" away from the original gospel—an attempt to convince a true believer that God winks, and looks the other way when His children play with what the Bible calls sin. The Lord didn't approve of this shift when He cautioned the churches back then and He doesn't approve of it today.

PARADIGM SHIFT – TOLERANCE – RELATIVISM STRONGHOLDS OF THE SEEKER FRIENDLY CHURCH

A present day expression for the "shift" that Jesus warned about in Revelation and which is causing Christian's of today to compromise their beliefs is "paradigm shift." This deceptive teaching, which is designed to *tickle the ears of the listener*, and *dilute the Word of God*, is a complete reversal of the gospel from what we have always believed it to be, and it seduces the seeker friendly ear, which belongs to those people looking for Scriptures they can twist to help them justify their sin. After learning of the phrase "paradigm shift" I spent hours in research looking for Biblical support from credible theologians and pastors on the topic of Christians in a battle against accountability to the Scriptures. In the process I was compelled to dissect and *understand* how the phrase "paradigm shift" related to the church. I learned that basically it is biblical truth, taught perfectly upside down—grace and unmerited favor from a loving and unconditional God with no admonitions against sin or repentance of sin. Under the "paradigm shift" teaching, one can rest assured of their place in heaven regardless of their earthly lifestyle. Dietrich Bonhoeffer called it "cheap grace." (See chapter 9 page 360).

The theories behind tolerance and relativism have become deeply embedded in our society and culture, as well as religious denominations. Much like "paradigm shift" they dilute the true gospel of the Bible for the purpose of deceiving God's children. Christians usually become "tolerant" of the sins of the culture when they get tired of fighting the spiritual battle that is raging between the things of the world and the things of God.

Tolerance can be defined as "the ability and willingness to tolerate something; in particular it is the existence of opinions or behaviors that do not necessarily conform to the standards of God's predefined moral code. Tolerance is, among other things, permissiveness; a disposition that allows freedom of choice and behavior; a disposition that accepts and is patient with the beliefs, opinions or practices of anti-God thinkers. In this one definition alone, it is easy to see how tolerance is contrary to God's directive for personal discipline, and His admonitions to "follow Him." Tolerance can also be 'accepting the existence of something unacceptable to God while still disapproving of it.' Probably this is where most Christians stand regarding tolerance. This was Jesus' complaint about the church in Sardis.

Tolerance is a broad-minded acceptance of differing views about something, whether or not it is beneficial to all people even if it permits harm. A tolerant person is often double minded in that they tolerate when tolerating benefits them in some way. However they are intolerant when being tolerant does not conform to the view they hold, making them uncomfortable. Endorsing tolerance requires one to respect, accept, and appreciate the "rich diversity of our world's cultures, our forms of expression, and ways of being human." Tolerance means being in harmony with "difference" even when it compromises or opposes the Word of God.

DANCING WITH THE DEVIL

I love this analogical definition: "Tolerance is the ability of a host plant to develop and reproduce fairly efficiently while sustaining disease." This definition of tolerance is absolutely correct in relation to our culture and the present day Christian perspective on biblical sin. When one seems strong in their appropriateness toward the commands of the Lord—that is, attending church, reading the word, moral behavior, etc.—yet tolerates, permits, and defends an inappropriate or ungodly behavior in others, preferring to say nothing, they are someone who is able to function in a fairly normal existence, even looking good on the outside, but are diseased in mind and heart.

Relativism holds that all standards, regardless of their origin, are susceptible to change according to the wishes of the one desiring change; that all things or behaviors are justified or permitted. In other words, tolerance and relativism do not conform to any moral code or standard. Instead, they accept all things regardless of their origin or the consequences.

"Oh, the joys of those who do not follow the advice of the wicked, or stand around with sinners, or join in with mockers. But they delight in the law of the Lord, meditating on it day and night (Psalms 1:1, 2 NLT).

Christians must be careful not to fall into the "tolerant church" movement because it does not honor God's statutes of "absolutes." Instead it encourages a willingness to tolerate something, in particular the existence of opinions or behaviors that oppose God even though the tolerant person may not necessarily agree with those opinions and behaviors.

The average Christian that loves the Lord, the church, and the Holy Scriptures goes about life as a loving and caring child of God. They focus on the beatitudes, the definition of love as defined in 1 Corinthians 13, and live a life that glorifies the Lord and keeps them out of hell. Few Christians are aware of the terms 'emerging' or 'seeker-friendly' or 'apostate' church and those that have heard these terms don't really *understand* what they mean. Therefore, people struggle to sift through the apostasy and get to the gospel truth. Some simply give up and ignore it, but this proves to be a huge mistake.

T.A. McMahon wrote the best explanation of "seeker friendly" I have found. McMahon calls the seeker-friendly or seeker-sensitive church "a *'movement' designed to evangelize through the use of the latest marketing techniques."* He says, *"Mega churches across the nation have fallen in step with the leading 'seeker-friendly' churches. In an effort to draw in crowds of un-churched people* (a modern day politically correct term for the lost) *mega churches seem to spare no expense to attract the masses. They design and build properties complete with opulent sanctuary scheme and décor meant to entertain and please the senses through the use of large screens, and state-of-the-art sound and lighting systems for multimedia, drama, and musical presentations. Building 'commons' areas sport libraries that could rival libraries built for large communities, and food courts that easily compete with those in a shopping mall complete with Starbucks and McDonald's franchises. Many churches have bowling alleys, NBA regulation basketball courts and bleachers, exercise gyms, spas, locker rooms, and auditoriums designed for concerts and dramatic productions."* Parenthesis added

McMahon says that *"while these churches are 'pack'n em' in,"* he questions if this latest trend of reaching-the-lost-through-whatever-turns-them-on (catering to the senses of the flesh instead of the heart) mindset can be accurately evaluated as successful in terms of spiritual salvation. He says, *"The stated goal of the seeker-friendly church is reaching the lost,"* and agrees that the goal is biblical and praiseworthy. But he suggests, *"These marketing tactics compromise the gospel and inhibit maturing in the faith. They are hearing a diluted version of the gospel designed to bring in the unbelievers instead of a nourishing meal featuring the 'meat' of the Word with emphasis on sound doctrine and discipleship."* Parentheses added

Author Ray Yungen has researched and studied religious movements for over twenty-five years. In his book, *A Time of Departing*, he refers to the New Age as the great apostasy or falling away spoken of in II Thessalonians. Yungen says that the term New Age was coined from the early writings of Alice Ann LaTrobe-

DANCING WITH THE DEVIL

Bateman Bailey, who was primarily responsible for the Western esoteric movement—a by-product of the occulted Theosophical Society. Born into privilege in upper class Manchester, England society in 1880, she became very religious and married a man who eventually became an Episcopal minister. After moving to the United States her minister husband became physically abusive so she took her three children and moved to Pacific Grove, California where she became acquainted with theosophy—which is any of a number of philosophies maintaining that knowledge of God may be achieved through spiritual ecstasy, direct intuition, or special individual relations.

Alice claimed that in 1919 a voice urged her to write books for the public. In 1920, she married occultist Foster Bailey, and between 1919 and 1949 she wrote 19 books for her "voice" by means of telepathic communication. Basically she was listening to a demon spirit. Yungen relates that Bailey's *prophecies* foretold what she termed *"the regeneration of the churches,"* which states: *"The Christian church in its many branches can serve as a St. John the Baptist, as a voice crying in the wilderness, and as a nucleus through which world illumination may be accomplished."* In other words, Yungen says *"instead of opposing Christianity, the occult would capture and blend itself with Christianity and then use it as its primary vehicle for spreading and instilling New Age consciousness. The various churches would have their outer trappings of Christianity while still using much of the same lingo. If asked certain questions about traditional Christian doctrine, the same answers would be given. But it would all be on the outside; on the inside a contemplative spiritualty would be drawing in those open to it."*

Christians: please pay attention to what Yungen is saying here—the New Age does not oppose Christianity but would capture Christianity and blend in with it. To know the difference, one must know the Word *and* the New Age belief and agenda! This requires a study of the New Age movement in order to successfully separate it from Christianity.

DANCING WITH THE DEVIL

The website for the Center for Contemplative Spirituality gives this definition of contemplative spirituality: *"We come from a variety of secular and religious backgrounds and we each seek to enrich our journey through spiritual practice and study of the world's great spiritual traditions. We desire to draw closer to the loving Spirit which pervades all creation and which inspires our compassion for all beings."* There is absolutely nothing biblical about such goals. Studying the world's "spiritual traditions" for the purpose of drawing closer to the loving Spirit is an exercise in futility because any spiritual tradition other than that which exalts Christ is falsehood. The only way to draw closer to God is through the path He has ordained—Jesus Christ and the Word.

Yungen speaks of a "new ecumenism," which is promoted by contemplative writers like Thomas Merton who spoke to both Hindus and Buddhists at a conference in India; *"We are already one, but we imagine we are not. What we have to recover is our original unity."* Contemplative writer Vivekananda wrote: *"The Christian is not to become a Hindu or a Buddhist, nor a Hindu or Buddhist become a Christian. But each must assimilate the spirit of others."* Tilden Edwards wrote: *"The new ecumenism involved here is not between Christian and Christian, but between Christians and the grace of other intuitively deep religious traditions."* Yungen relates that in a regional Catholic syndicated newspaper article a Catholic retreat master offered the notion that *"today Catholics have an obligation to seek God in other traditions."* This means remaining in your original religion of choice but being aligned with Eastern mysticism.

Biblical Christianity is not to align with any religion that worships any gods or unifies with any beliefs that are contrary to the Holy Bible, or that compete with the Trinity. As we can see from the letters to the seven churches, the Lord isn't going to tolerate a "paradigm shift" from His Word to any other religion that waters down the truth in order to deceive His children. Christians that are truly desiring 'ears to hear' listen to what the spirit of the Lord is speaking to their heart. Then they run willingly back to their first love, the Lord of the Bible, which is the true gospel, Jesus Christ, and

DANCING WITH THE DEVIL

Him crucified. If after evaluating your heart you discover that you have listened to a "paradigm shift" and endorsed tolerance of beliefs that don't honor God, please give up your dance with the devil, and let the Lord dance you into heaven on the straight and narrow path. Though you will give up some pleasurable things of the world you will never be sorry for choosing to dance with Jesus.

CHAPTER TEN STUDY QUESTIONS

1. Why do you think God called the Israelites wicked and stubborn?
2. Study Isaiah 59. Make a list comparing how you think Christians of today are like the people in Isaiah 59.
3. What was the main complaint Jesus had against the church in Ephesus, Pergamum, Thyatira, Sardis, and Laodicea?
4. What is a spiritual paradigm shift?
5. According to German Pastor Dietrich Bonhoeffer, what is the meaning of cheap grace?
6. After reading about tolerance and relativism will you be able to recognize such teachings in your church? List some of the characteristics you think you will be able to recognize when you hear them spoken.
7. Define the following: seeker friendly; apostate; emerging; ecumenism; esoteric; occult; cult; regeneration; telepathic; theosophy; and contemplative prayer.
8. Define the New Age belief and agenda. You will need to do some serious research.
9. Who was Thomas Merton? Who are Tilden Edwards and Brian McLaren?
10. What do you think it means for the Catholic religion to suggest that their members are "OBLIGATED' to seek God in other traditions? Do you agree?

ELEVEN

❧⋅❦

"TURN TO ME NOW WHILE THERE IS TIME; GIVE ME YOUR HEARTS"

That is why the Lord says, "Turn to me now while there is time. Give me your hearts. Come with fasting, weeping, and mourning. Don't tear your clothing in your grief, but tear your hearts instead." Return to the Lord your God, for He is merciful and compassionate, slow to get angry and filled with unfailing love. He is eager to relent and not punish (Joel 2:12-13 NLT).

Guard your heart above all else, for it determines the course of your life (Proverbs 4:23 NLT).

I pray that your heart will be flooded with light so that you can <u>understand</u> the confident hope He has given to those He called—His holy people who are His rich and glorious inheritance (Ephesians 1:18 NLT).

Come close to God, and God will come close to you. Wash your hands you sinners; purify your hearts, for your loyalty is divided between God and the world (James 4:8 NLT).

IT'S ALL ABOUT THE HEART

My aggressive search through the Bible for Scriptures about "the heart" showed me how little I knew about how important our heart is to the Lord. I could recall having heard a few teachings on "the heart," but it wasn't until I committed to such intense research that I was able to really *understand* exactly what the Lord meant when He said *"turn to me now while there is time; give me your hearts."*

All of Jesus' teachings came through the heart of His compassionate Father. They were meant to give people time to turn their hearts back to Him and worship Him entirely before they died or before Jesus returned for His "pure" church. When I realized there was a small part of my heart that had not been completely released to Jesus, and that He was trying to win me completely, I made the decision to change my heart to conform to the way Christ wanted me to live. That meant spending much time in the Scriptures so that I could learn. I discovered how important it was for me not to have Jesus unhappy with me for any reason.

The above Scriptures tell us that certain heart conditions can separate us from God, causing us to miss heaven, for it is the heart that tells the Lord all about us: *"I, the Lord, search the heart, I test the mind, even to give every man according to his ways, according to the fruit of his doing" (Jeremiah 17:10 NKJV).* And, *"those who are still under the control of their sinful nature can never please God" (Romans 8:8 NLT).* Scripture confirms that God will judge us based on what is in our heart, our mind, and our ways or actions, and according to the results of what we have done, whether they were good or bad—whether our actions conveyed a deliberate hurt upon another or whether they were unintentional actions.

Our heart and mind must function in sync as God designed them. Otherwise our character is out of balance, because inside our heart is where God placed every aspect of goodness—our ability to love, be compassionate, form a conscience, function with integrity, and lend mercy. This is why He searches our heart to see what is there. To be spiritually lost is to refuse to evaluate the condition of our own heart, and make a decision to change what needs changing so we can conform to God's character.

Regardless of what we say with our mouth, such as "I am a Christian" God will give to us based upon what He finds going on inside our heart. If He searches our heart and finds that we have put Him above all people and things and that our life is ruled based on integrity as well as our relationship with Him—that we "live" an attitude of agape love, compassion, humbleness, goodness, and mercy—He will write our name in the Lamb's Book of Life. He will never remove our name if we continue down this narrow path, desiring eternity with Him for He says, "Remain in me and I will remain in you." However, if our heart confirms to Him that we are un-repentant, and hard-heartedly "committed" to any of the following heart conditions, He will bar the gates of heaven and we can't enter no matter how much we plead saying, "but Lord, I cast out demons in your name . . ." for He will say, *"I never knew you. Get away from me, you who break God's laws." (Matthew 7:23 NLT)*

Christians tend to think of sin as lust, lying, murder, hate, un-forgiveness, rape, violence, and the like—which they are! But rarely do we think of heart attitudes as sin. However, the Word says differently. The Lord rejects and turns away a heart that doesn't love Him more than it loves the desire to hold on to sinful attitudes and behaviors that He hates. He will say, "You don't really know me" (See 1 John 2: 3, 4). The Lord will not accept or co-exist with the following heart conditions—all of which are mentioned in the Scriptures. If readers will truly digest each word and its synonyms, comparing them to their own heart attitude and behaviors—their thoughts, etc., I believe they will find a way to make positive life changes.

Unbelief is *skepticism, agnosticism, and atheism.*
Lying is to be *deceptive, dishonest, twofaced, insincere, and double-dealing.*
Adultery is *infidelity, disloyalty, betrayal, treachery, and faithlessness.*
Sexual immorality is *abuse of sexual ethics; violating God's design for sex.*
Wickedness includes *evil, sin, impiety, malice, and being bad in general.*
Maliciousness is to be *vicious, spiteful, hurtful, mean, hateful, and offensive.*
Envy is *jealousy, covetousness, greed, bitterness, resentfulness, and begrudgery.*

DANCING WITH THE DEVIL

Strife is *trouble, conflict, discord, fighting, dissention, friction, and rivalry.*
Deceit is *dishonesty, treachery, deception, trickery, duplicity, guile, and fraud.*
Violence is *ferocity, aggression, vehemence, viciousness, passion, and intensity.*
Evil-mindedness is *a mind that thinks of evil continually.*
Untrustworthy is to be *unreliable, dishonest, disloyal, deceitful, treacherous, and devious.*
Unloving means being *unable to love or show love.*
Unforgiving is to be *merciless, remorseless, vindictive, ruthless, callous, and unmoved.*
Unmerciful is to be *cruel, severe, harsh, unkind, and unforgiving.*
Inventor of evil things is to be a *creator of that which causes harm.*
Covetousness is to be *greedy, materialistic, envious, jealous, and longing.*
Backbiting is being *vicious, spiteful, backstabber, or speaks unkind remarks.*
Contentiousness is to be *controversial, combative, quarrelsome, or belligerent.*
Fornicating is *having sex outside of marriage.*
Unclean is to be *impure, contaminated, tainted, sinful, immoral, or unworthy.*
Jealousy is *envy, suspiciousness, watchfulness and demanding loyalty.*
Lewdness is *coarseness, vulgarity, profanity, vileness, obscenity, offensiveness, and immorality.*
Idolatry is the *worship, adoration, admiration, idolization, fanaticism, devotion, and obsession of something except God.*
Sorcery includes *witchcraft, wizardry, magic, enchantment, witchery, and necromancy.*
Selfish ambition is to *fulfill one's own desires, even to the harm of others and ourselves.*
Passion seeking is *pursuing one's own desires, cravings, and hunger, thus neglecting the Lord.*
Evil desire means *desiring to do things that cause harm or destruction.*
Thievery includes *burglary, shoplifting, robbery, larceny, stealing, and pilfering.*
Bitterness is *resentment, unpleasantness, sullenness, anger, animosity, hostility, cynicism, indignation, and sourness.*
Wrath includes *anger, rage, fury, and madness. God's wrath will punish evildoers.*

DANCING WITH THE DEVIL

Anger includes *annoyance, irritation, fury, rage, antagonism, resentment, and wrath.*

Clamor is a *demand, outcry, uproar, commotion, or racket.*

Evil speaking means *saying words in a way that causes harm or intends to cause harm.*

Lover of self means *loving ourselves in ways that are harmful to us and to others.*

Lover of money is to *seek money over purity and honor, or the Lord, or another person.*

Boasting is being *cocky, arrogant, self-important, conceited, and bragging*

Pride is *arrogance, conceit, smugness, egotism, vanity, and immodesty.*

Blasphemy is *profanity, sacrilege, wickedness, irreverence, violation, and desecration.*

Disobedient to parents means to be *defiant and rebellious against them*

Unthankful is *the act of not appreciating.*

Unholy is to be *ungodly, godless, irreligious, impious, blasphemous, sacrilegious, profane, irreverent, wicked, evil, immoral, corrupt, depraved, and sinful.*

Slanderous is to be *defamatory, disparaging, libelous, false, misrepresentative, scandalous, malicious, abusive, insulting, and informal mudslinging.*

Without self-control is being *unable to conquer emotions, thoughts, and actions.*

Brutal means to be *savage, cruel, vicious, ferocious, brutish, barbaric, barbarous, wicked, murderous, bloodthirsty, cold-blooded, callous, heartless, ruthless, merciless, sadistic heinous, monstrous, abominable, or atrocious.*

Traitor is one who is a *betrayer, backstabber, double-crosser, renegade, turncoat, defector, deserter, collaborator, informer, mole, snitch, or double agent.*

Headstrong means to be *willful, strong-willed, stubborn, obstinate, unyielding, contrary, perverse, wayward, and unruly.*

Haughty is to be *proud, arrogant, vain, conceited, snobbish, superior, self-important, pompous, supercilious, condescending, patronizing, scornful, contemptuous, disdainful, full of oneself, stuck-up, snooty, hoity-toity, uppity, big-headed, high and mighty.*

DANCING WITH THE DEVIL

Lover of pleasure rather than God means *enjoying sensualities that God disapproves of and neglecting our love for Him.*

Cowardly is to be *faint-hearted, lily-livered, spineless, chicken-hearted, craven, timid, fearful, weak-kneed, gutless, yellow-bellied, and wimpy.*

Abominable is to be *loathsome, detestable, hateful, odious, obnoxious, despicable, contemptible, damnable, diabolical, disgusting, revolting, repellent, repulsive, offensive, repugnant, abhorrent, reprehensible, atrocious, horrifying, foul, vile, wretched, base, horrible, awful, dreadful, appalling, nauseating, horrid, nasty, disagreeable, unpleasant, distasteful, terrible, shocking, god-awful, beastly, cursed, and accursed.*

Drunkenness includes *intoxication, inebriation, insobriety, tipsiness, impairment, intemperance, overindulgence, debauchery, heavy drinking, alcoholism, and dipsomania.*

Murderer is a *killer, assassin, serial killer, butcher, slaughterer, hit man, or gunman.*

Extortion is *blackmail, shakedown, or exaction.*

Revelers are *partygoers, merrymakers, and carousers.*

Revilers are *those who criticize in an abusive or angrily insulting manner.*

Whisperer/gossipers are *those who tell others information that isn't confirmed as truth, or those who whisper a confidence about another.*

When a person's heart is unchanged after accepting Jesus it can harbor any one of the above listed sin attitudes. If the person makes no effort to dig them out and get rid of them the heart will never be converted and that condition of the heart holds dire consequences for that person. Further, in life they will experience nothing but heartache and death because they are comfortable with sin, and not interested in the true Word of God. A person harboring any of these iniquities can become detached from worship, disinterested in fellowship with the saints, un-teachable, uninterested in prayer, and scornful toward God. The person with an unconverted heart can be self-righteous, unable to see their own faults, immoral with no guilt, not hungry for spirituality, is a seeker of personal pleasure, and is lustful.

We can bury these anti-Christian characteristics inside our heart and allow them to become a hindrance to our salvation. This is why the Lord cautioned us to guard our heart above all else, for it determines the course of our life—earthly and eternal.

The Lord says, *"Come now, let us reason together"* (Isaiah 1:18 NKJV). When God designed our brain He gave us the ability to reason through what the heart was saying by balancing our emotional capacity—the senses—between the heart and the brain, so that we would be able to reach a logical analysis about how to live a life pleasing to Him. He will test our mind and then determine if we renewed it to cooperate with our heart, which should love Christ. We must compare our heart and mind to those things on the list—those things that force us to face the truth about ourselves. We should focus on each word to see if we can see ourselves in any of them. When we study Scripture with a humble and repentant heart, we gain wisdom from the words, and the Holy Spirit, which lives inside of us helps us apply those words to our everyday life. If we determine that we have even one of these characteristics in our heart, under no circumstances should we justify its presence there.

THE UNHEALED HEART

The unhealed heart has low self-esteem, judges other Christians with a critical spirit, does not trust, is hypersensitive, and unforgiving. It holds grudges, is bitter, gossips, feels unworthy, promotes self and is angry and unreasonable. It cannot see its on faults. When our heart is unhealed we are unable to come together and reason because our mind is not able to accurately determine the love characteristic of God, which we are told to emulate. We reject God's ways because we blame Him for the hurt we feel and we function entirely from our own emotions. We cling to entitlement—"I have a right to feel the way I do." But we soon discover that we have guarded our heart against God and not against our enemy who loves that we keep protecting our unhealed heart. Most of us with unhealed hearts defend our heart attitude against every argument that will help us heal. Further, when we live with someone who has rejected God, and their heart is unsaved or unhealed, our relationship with them becomes dismal, because their thoughts and ways settle on us. Eventually the relationship will die due to an inability to work through the issues because there is no willingness to reason with others using a heart and mind sold out to the Lord's principles.

Our stubborn rebellion enables us to refuse to let our heart be a storehouse for the Lord's Word. Because I care about other's souls, I challenge people to search out and endorse those things of the Lord that help us convert to His ways so that our heart can be healed. Christians with an unhealed heart cling to rebellion, which is usually revealed in contentiousness, causing or likely to cause offense or controversy. The rebellious Christian often carries anxieties that usually manifested in childhood, or a severe hurt or abuse in adulthood. It has occupied their heart for so long they are comfortable with its presence there and can't recognize it as sin—a detriment to building godly relationships. Although he or she may claim to be a Christian who attends church, reads the Bible, and prays regularly they are still unable to deal with painful issues. They are unable to reason, based on a biblical *understanding* of the difference in good and evil. Therefore, the spirit of rebellion is invited by the host to stay and build a contentious grievance in unfavorable situations that arise. Living with the spirit of rebellion enables us to live a lie whether it is a spoken lie or a life of pretense, which is often the case in a rebellious person.

My mom would never allow us children to lie. If she found that we had, we were appropriately punished. Mom *understood* that Satan is the Father of lies and we are most like him when we lie. She also *understood* that liars have no integrity and if we children were to have any kind of a life of honor, we had to *understand* how serious an offense lying was. When our words are lies, our heart becomes a lying heart in every part of our life. But if we seek God's ways in truth we allow our heart to be converted—turned away from sin, and healed. Then we become willing to seek God with our heart, soul and mind, helping us dispense peace toward others instead of living in rebellion, which is a playmate to stubbornness and like the sin of witchcraft. If we fail to fix the issues in our own hearts, how can we help our children fix the issues in their hearts, which will hinder all of their earthly relationships and their relationship with the Lord?

THE HEALED AND CONVERTED HEART

The healed and converted heart is much more comfortable than the unhealed or unconverted heart. It is filled with compassion, willing to find resolve, forgiving, kind, and it loves unconditionally. It is humble in spirit, conscionable, helpful, sacrificial in giving, and committed to praying for others. It is patient, sensitive toward others, considerate, and respectful. Life is so much more fun when we carry a healed heart around with us. Under a healed heart, others will look at us and see Jesus, which is rewarding to the onlooker and to us.

My heart has experienced a great deal of hurt and dealing with that hurt has been an on-going, everyday effort. But before I could deal with my hurt, my heart had to see the person that hurt me as God sees them—with love! I had to be able to return to the Scriptures and obey them. Any wound, whether physical or emotional takes time to heal, but if we are patient, willing, and obedient to God's Word, we will eventually find that our heart begins to feel better and better until one day we discover that we are healed.

In this chapter, I have included a few Scriptures that tell all about the heart. They admonish and comfort us as well as help us search our own heart to see what is there. But, there are many other Scriptures about the heart that are worth reviewing, which I have not included here so I encourage readers not to neglect those.

HEART SCRIPTURES

"The Lord observed the extent of human wickedness on the earth, and He saw that everything they thought or imagined was consistently and totally evil. It broke His *heart*. And the Lord said, *'I will wipe the human race I have created from the face of the earth'*" *(Genesis 6:5-6 NLT)*. The Lord is clearly tenderhearted toward His creation. But He also shows how important it is to destroy evil. God showed how horrible man could become.

"He (King Rehoboam) did evil because he had not set his *heart* on seeking the Lord" *(2 Chronicles 12:14 NIV)*.

"Oh, that their *hearts* would be inclined to fear me and keep all my commands always, so that it might go well with them and their children forever" *(Deuteronomy 5:29 NIV)!* The attitude of the *heart* is connected to our success (the wellspring) in life.

"Love the Lord your God with all your *heart* and with all your soul and with all your strength. These commandments that I give you today are to be on your *hearts*" *(Deuteronomy 6:5-6 NIV)*.

"Therefore, change your *hearts* and stop being stubborn" *(Deuteronomy 10:16 NLT)*. To be stubborn means to be determined, obstinate, and pig-headed. We've all known someone like this, and have probably been stubborn at one time or another in our own life. But God says stubbornness is a bad heart attitude and should be discarded.

"Those who hear the warnings of this curse should not congratulate themselves, thinking, 'I am safe, even though I am following the desires of my own stubborn *heart*.' This would lead to utter ruin! The Lord will never pardon such people" *(Deuteronomy 29:19-20 NLT)*. Stubbornness and eternal security in Christ do not coexist.

"Now your (Saul's) kingdom must end, for the Lord has sought out a man (David) after His own *heart*. The Lord has already appointed him to be the leader of His people because you (Saul) have not kept the Lord's command" *(1 Samuel 13:14 NLT)*.

"The Lord doesn't see things the way you see them. People judge by outward appearance, but the Lord looks at the *heart*" *(1 Samuel 16:7 NLT)*.

"Give me an *understanding heart* so that I (Solomon) can govern your people well and know the difference between right and wrong. For who by himself is able to govern this great people of yours" *(1 Kings 3:9 NLT)*. This Scripture cautions that leaders throughout the world should know the importance of governing with an *understanding heart*. But, what is it these leaders are to *understand?* The difference in good and evil!

"Never before had there been a King like Josiah, who turned to the Lord with all his *heart*, and soul, and strength, obeying all the laws of Moses. And there has never been a king like him since" *(2 Kings 23:25 NLT)*.

The greatest asset a nation can have is a leader with a heart dedicated to God and who leads the people with godly principles. Nothing I have learned in my lifetime has been as important and helpful toward my *understanding* of life as what I have learned through my study of the Scriptures and the history of the world regarding the behavior of mankind. Our educational system has erred unforgivably in the matter of our country by neglecting to stress to all students the importance of *understanding* what the leaders of the world's nations have done to set in motion the destruction of humanity, particularly godly nations. (See Chapter 3) If new generations never learn the history of the world and the evil therein, they will never *understand* how to deal with it, or how to determine the difference in good and evil.

"If I had cherished sin in my *heart*, the Lord would not have listened" *(Psalms 66:18 NIV)*. King David was confessing that he knew God would not hear his prayers if he continued to love sin.

"I have hidden your word in my *heart* that I might not sin against you" *(Psalms 119:11 NIV)*. When we hide His Word in our heart He becomes real to us, then we are able to fall in love with

Him. When we fall in love with Him we are ashamed about the things we do that hurt the Lord just like when we are ashamed about the things we do that hurt those people close to us in heart. When we fall in love with Jesus, our walk with Him becomes "more willing" and forgiveness gets easier. In forgiveness, we lose our anger and then we can experience healing.

"Search me, God, and know my *heart*; test me and know my anxious thoughts" *(Psalms 139:23 NIV)*. Being willing to let the Lord search our heart, to test our attitude and thoughts, provides no faster way for Him to speak to us because when we invite Him to sift us He desires to purify our hearts!

"Do not let my *heart* be drawn to what is evil so that I take part in wicked deeds along with those who are evildoers; do not let me eat their delicacies" *(Psalms 141:4 NIV)*. I can remember many times in my life when I allowed my heart to be drawn into the wicked deeds of evildoers. Words like wicked and evildoers may sound very strong coming from a Christian, but to God, sin is wickedness and those who do sinful things, are evildoers. When we put words into perspective according to how the Lord defines them and then evaluate our life on that basis He gives us revelation that causes us to change our direction.

"My sons, do not forget my teaching, but keep my commands in your *heart . . .*" *(Proverbs 3:1 NIV)*. Do you know that we can keep His commands in our heart but ignore them? We can live a lie, forgetting that our heart knows all about Him. I know, because I did that, so guard your heart for it holds the rules to a life that is pleasing to God.

"Trust in the Lord with all your *heart* and lean not on your own *understanding*" *(Proverbs 3:5 NIV)*. How many times a day do you say, "But I don't *understand?*" If you are like me you probably say it often. We are not all knowing like the Lord. We only know what directly affects us and what we retain from the things we are taught. There are many things we do not *understand* and there are many things we think we *understand* but God tells us not to lean on our own understanding because we don't really *understand* in the way He wants us to *understand*. We tend to *understand* from a worldly perspective and not from the spiritual perspective, which is His way. It is very important that we *understand* what He is saying to us.

"Then He taught me, and He said to me, '"Take hold of my words with all your *heart*; keep my commands, and you will live"' *(Proverbs 4:4 NIV)*. Our spiritual life or death is directly connected to our willingness to dedicate our heart to knowing God's Word.

"He will turn the *hearts* of the parents to the *hearts* of the children, and the *hearts* of the children to the *hearts* of the parents; or else I will come and strike the land with total destruction" *(Malachi 4:6 NIV)*. The Lord cares deeply about parent/child relationships and He is grieved in His heart when parents and children deliberately hurt each other and when they disrespect each other; and He is so serious about us doing it right that if we don't, He will order His wrath against our land.

"Blessed are the pure in *heart*, for they will see God" *(Matthew 5:8 NIV)*. Do you want to see God? How pure is your heart?

"But I tell you that anyone who looks at a woman lustfully has already committed adultery with her in his *heart* *(Matthew 5:28 NIV)*. When the Lord listed the un-repented sins that would keep us out of heaven, physical adultery was on the list. However, sins of the heart will also keep us out of heaven. Therefore, the un-repented heart-sin of adultery will keep us out of heaven just as physical adultery will. Yet, heart adultery and physical adultery are the most accepted sins among Christians today and looked upon as all right with God. I encourage every Christian to re-evaluate your position on adultery before it is too late.

"For the people's *heart* has become calloused; they hardly hear with their ears, and they have closed their eyes. Otherwise they might see with their eyes, hear with their ears, *understand* with their *hearts* and turn, and I would heal them" *(Matthew 13:15 NIV)*.

MEDICAL DOCTORS AND THE HEART

Medical doctors call the heart a vital organ and are relentless in trying to teach us how to care for it so that we can live a long and healthy life on earth. Though most believers want to go to heaven, few want to die. However, the Scriptures tell us that the Lord's greatest concern for our heart is that it be spiritually healthy so that we can have eternal life after we abandon this earthly body. Imagine what the world would be like if doctors and pastors encouraged protecting the heart from both perspectives.

Many people have had out-of-body experiences. Their heart stopped for a while and their soul left their body. After a few minutes of death they were resuscitated. Medical personnel has witnessed and documented many cases, and Dr. Maurice Rawlings was one such doctor. He was an atheist who begrudgingly and under pressure from associates prayed for a dying man who claimed to be in hell each time his heart stopped while being resuscitated. Dr. Rawlings' rebellious prayer changed both his life and the life of the dying man. His experience is spellbinding and his book, *To Hell and Back* is recommended reading.

HELL—A PLACE TO AVOID

What better place to talk about hell than in this chapter about the heart, since it is the heart that determines which path we take—the path to hell or the path to heaven.

In the year 2000, Bruce Bickel and Stan Jantz co-wrote an article titled *Whatever Happened to Hell*, which appeared in that year's March issue of HOMELIFE, a Christian family magazine. Bickel and Jantz gave what I believe is a perfectly clear *understanding* of hell and how humanity has ignored it in favor of the comfort and beauty of heaven.

Their article explains how hell has always been a detested subject and how surveys of public opinion consistently show that more people believe in heaven than believe in hell. They claim that folks would much rather spend eternity in a Jesus-built mansion than a lake of fire. Consequently, the biblically illiterate public prefers to classify hell as a myth or fairy tale, too bizarre to believe. Bruce and Stan also support that some so-called religious experts align with the popularity of denying the existence of hell; after all, a God of love couldn't send people to hell.

In agreement with Bruce and Stan, I have heard numerous sermons just within the past few years that tell of 'God's love for all mankind' but with no mention of hell, sin, or accountability. If we allow ourselves to see God as love only, ignoring His justice, then maybe we won't feel the discomfort of guilt and conviction for our sin.

Also, Bruce and Stan report in their article that *"many people deny the literal existence of hell—these are usually people who do not read the Bible."*

The Bible describes hell as a place of torment, and since God is holiness, without sin, He cannot and does not reside there. Therefore, hell keeps us eternally separated from Him. In the book of Matthew hell is described as a place of darkness, a fiery furnace where there will be weeping and gnashing of teeth, eternal fire and eternal punishment.

Until they have faith in Jesus, God's judgment falls on all sinners; therefore unrepentant sinners will occupy hell. According to the New Testament, the objects (people) of God's wrath range from the pious hypocrites (Matthew 23:33) and those failing to help the poor (Matthew 25:31-46 and Luke 16:19-31) to the vile and the murderers (Revelation 21:8). Hell exists for the requital and retribution of evil deeds. It is the place for God's final judgment. Through Hell, God finally rectifies wrongs through his avenging wrath. The damned will be paid back for the harm they have done. The Gospel of Romans, chapter 2 refers to Hell as a place of God's wrath. Wrath is an emotion or feeling in the Godhead and thus, God's personal action (See Romans 1:18-32).

DANCING WITH THE DEVIL

The Gospel of 2 Thessalonians 1 refers to Hell as everlasting destruction. Wicked people are imprisoned there so that they cannot harm God's people. In Hell, the damned receive their due for "things done while in the body." (2 Colossians 5:10; 2 Peter 2:13; Jude 15; Revelation 14:11). The Gospel of Revelation calls it the abyss, a place of torment—a fiery lake of burning sulfur.

Scripture suggests that there are degrees of punishment in hell. In Mark 12:35, 40 Jesus taught that we are to watch out for teachers of religious law. *"They parade around in flowing robes and receive respectful greetings as they walk in the marketplaces. They love the seats of honor in synagogues and the head table at banquets. Yet they shamelessly cheat widows out of their property and then pretend to be pious by making long prayers in public. Because of this, they will be more severely punished."*

Jesus taught, *"Whoever rejects the Son will not see life, for God's wrath remains on him"* (John 3:36). As long as God's wrath abides on them, the damned must exist. Jesus' picture of hell as the place where *"the worm does not die, and the fire is not quenched,"* (Mark 9:48) indicates that this manifestation of God's wrath is unending. Other passages in the New Testament reiterate Jesus' dreadful warning by describing hell as *"everlasting torment."*

I agree with Bruce and Stan that hell is serious punishment, and I want to avoid it at all costs. However, I came really close to accepting a doctrine that because I was basically a good person, and loved and prayed to the Lord, and still went to church, and still did good things for others, I was well on the pathway to heaven even though I was willfully sinning. But one day through a process of events, God brought me to my knees, opened my eyes, and showed me where I was headed.

Throughout this book, I have referenced many Scriptures about Satan, hell, the Lord Jesus, God, and Heaven. I have included biblical information about how God will look at our hearts, and I have offered many Scriptures about the soul that will go to heaven to live eternally with God, and the soul that will go to hell to live eternally with Satan and his band of angels. Bruce and Stan laid out their own research about who will populate hell, which they liken to being more populated than Disneyland on Memorial Day.

They say, *"Satan will be the celebrity inmate. He will be in misery for eternity, and since misery loves company, the beast and the false prophet will join him. 'And the devil, who deceived them, was thrown into the lake of burning sulfur, where the beast and the false prophet had been thrown. They will be tormented day and night for ever and ever.'"* (From Rev. 20:10) *"All the rest of the fallen angels will be there too. 'For . . . 'God did not spare angels when they sinned, but sent them to hell, putting them into gloomy dungeons to be held for judgment.'"* (2 Peter 2:4). *"All those who rejected Christ's free gift of salvation will be tortured occupants of hell. 'If anyone's name was not found written in the book of life, he was thrown into the lake of fire.'"* (Rev. 20:15)

As Bruce and Stan mentioned in their article, many occupants of hell will be surprised to find themselves there since they were expecting heaven as their home due to their "religious" life on earth. They will spend eternity in torment because Jesus said He never knew them. (Matthew 7:23 NLT) Their sanctimonious behavior was worthless in God's eyes. Remember the story of the rich man and a sick poor man named Lazarus? When the rich man arrived in hell he couldn't believe he was there.

Where do you want to spend eternity? Humble your heart and let the Holy Scriptures teach you about God, heaven and hell; open your heart to allow the Holy Spirit to speak truth to your mind; don't listen to false teachers or those who distort or neglect some of the truth. Instead, test and evaluate what you hear from the pulpit against what the Bible says. Ask the Lord to show you truth and help you live according to His will instead of your own. Preserve your soul for heaven where you will spend a joyful eternity with the Lord for He says, "Turn to me now, while there is time; give me your *hearts.*

DANCING WITH THE DEVIL

CHAPTER ELEVEN STUDY QUESTIONS

1. What do you think God meant when He said, "Turn to me now while there is time; Give me your hearts?"

2. What does it mean to have your heart flooded with light?

3. Review the heart conditions listed on pages 393-396. Choose 5 to 10 that you can identify as a problem in your own heart. What steps can you take to correct these negative traits that can separate you from God if you don't repent?

4. List 5 characteristics of an unhealed heart. Can you recognize any of these in your own heart?

5. Name 10 characteristics of a healed heart. Can you recognize any of these in your own heart?

6. What is the greatest asset a nation's leader can possess? Why?

7. How does one hide God's Word in their heart so they won't sin against Him?

8. What is a calloused heart?

9. What does it mean to have an out-of-body experience?

10. How does the Bible describe hell?

TWELVE

~~~

IN MY FATHER'S HOUSE

In my Father's house there are many mansions; if it were not so, I would have told you. I go to prepare a place for you (John 14:2 KJV).

No eye has seen, no ear has heard, and no mind has imagined what God has prepared for those who love Him (1 Corinthians 2:9 NLT).

When I received the inspiration for this chapter, daylight savings time had been in effect for several days and each day the sun dropped behind The Teton Range of the Northern Rockies at about 7:00 in the evening. As it did, a blue haze settled across the mountains. It was so beautiful I could not stay motivated to sit at my desk and write, but instead was compelled to take a ride.

The date was March 15, 2012, and I was on a tight schedule to leave Wyoming within three weeks for an April 3rd interview with Mrs. Kitty Werthmann, an Austrian born World War II survivor. An urgent need to finish the manuscript haunted me continually and for hours each day I labored at my laptop. My research had been intense and I was mentally exhausted, so when I looked out the window and saw the beauty before me I knew I had to get outside and mingle in God's landscape.

DANCING WITH THE DEVIL

Compiling a manuscript of such intense content caused me to feel melancholy, and on that particular evening I was somewhat pensive. I climbed into my Jeep and drove toward the airport where the park began, and pulled into a roadside overlook. Not wanting to leave the beautiful music on the radio I lowered the car window before I stepped out onto the ground. Light rain fell as I leaned against the fender and watched the clouds move in from the west and cover the highest peaks of the Range.

I was expecting a friend to fly in from Denver that night and was a little anxious for her safety. Landing a jetliner safely on the ground through the narrow passageway at the foothills of the Teton Range takes a skilled pilot. Concern for all air travelers is foremost in the minds of most residents there. However, the view from inside the plane is breathtaking and the experience exhilarating. There is never a time that I don't enjoy breaking through the clouds at the Jackson Hole Airport and seeing that majestic range stretching out its beauty to greet me. Not knowing when my friend was to arrive I said a little prayer for her safety before allowing my mind to move on to search for the spiritual reason I so urgently needed to take this specific drive.

As I stood there in the misty rain observing the beauty around me and pondering this book, I thought about the condition of our nation. I thought about my dance with the devil just a few years earlier, and how I believed I was saved because I had served Jesus for years and after all, I was a good person—maybe in the same way the rich man who neglected Lazarus thought he was a good person. Recognizing my own transgression I could now see how other Christians who believed in Jesus thought they too, were saved but were involved in sin that forced God to turn His back to them.

These thoughts caused me to weep particularly for others, and on this night I wept for myself as well, because leaving those beautiful mountains even for a brief time has always been sad for me. At each departure, I wondered if or when I would be able to return. At that moment it seemed like I had just arrived but it had been six years earlier and every year flowed through my mind that evening like the Snake River meandered through the valley floor about a half-mile from me.

In vivid color I recalled all my beautiful experiences while I lived in the mountains, and I also thought of the sad ones. Earlier that day my daughter had phoned to tell me how happy she was to be moving into a new home on the military base where she and her husband were stationed. But along with her joy I detected sadness in her voice as she questioned me about when I was coming home. Clearly she needed some "mommy" time.

Through a swirling mist I watched the lights throughout the valley flicker on and brighten the night. As the snow machines maneuvered the melting snow atop the ski slopes, I recalled my first trip through the area in 1996 with a good friend. For two weeks, we had toured the Northwest and had seen amazing sights but for me nothing compared to this majestic place with its sprawling ranches, amazing starlit nights and the most beautiful rivers I had ever seen. Instantly I had fallen in love. Everything around me had pierced my soul. As I stood there remembering the past, I thought about how the research for this book had changed my life. I thought about what was—the evil our world had seen. And, I thought about what was to come—the horrors spoken of in the Bible and the life and death, and the sorrow of it all. After reminiscing through the happiness and the sadness of my time in the mountains, I spoke a fond farewell to all that surrounded me and headed back to the cabin to write.

Before I took my little ride that evening I had no clue as to what should be said in this last chapter. I drove along the highway and thought of heaven and how wonderful the Word says it is. I believe the Holy Spirit was guiding me to use this chapter to tell of what the Bible says about heaven's glory, and the awesomeness of what God has prepared for those who love and worship Him. Everything we worship on earth, as we should worship Him, is miniscule compared to the beauty that is awaiting us with Him in heaven. Clearly, the awesome beauty that lay before me did not compare to that which many people have forgotten about His Word, which is *"No eye has seen and no ear has heard, no mind has imagined what God has prepared for those who love Him" (1 Corinthians 2:9 LT).* I believe this Scripture could also refer to the awesomeness of Jesus and not just heaven.

The Lord promises to write the names of the truly repentant—those who believe in Him with a born again heart—in the Lambs Book of Life. As I prayed over this chapter, it suddenly occurred to me that despite my past faults and failures I was one who had always returned to Jesus in repentance and I was an encourager of the brethren. Now I was to remind others that the love God gives will never hurt, and in heaven the redeemed will have the peace that so many say they pray for here on earth but never attain. People that go to heaven will no longer be sad because there will be no more pain of any kind, and they will have no reason to fear anything. A daughter of any age will no longer need to shudder with fear in the dark hours of night when she hears her bedroom door open ever so gently because she knows the pain that is coming to her in the quiet footsteps approaching her bed. God will be her father and she will have no reason to fear Him and she will no longer remember those painful times on earth.

Defenseless children—those that were murdered in the womb, those forced to live in a closet or a box, those starved or chained outdoors, those sent away into the night as unwanted, those tortured and brutalized by wicked men and women in war as well as peace, those taken into slavery of any kind—will have the best their heavenly father offers. Though these children were last on earth, having been given no right to life, they will be first with their Father in heaven. For every person that was beaten or abandoned, for those that were stalked, harassed, or molested there will be peaceful love and rest in their heavenly father's arms. Those who lost out on a quality life on earth because they weren't able to forgive themselves or others even though the Lord forgave them will never again experience the pain of worthlessness. Defenseless women that were beaten, and degraded by husbands and boyfriends will find their first sense of peace, acceptance, and wellbeing in the presence of the Holy Father.

The Holy Spirit reminded me of the many mansions in the Father's house and that there is one prepared for every name written down. He spoke to my heart to remind His children that He gets the last dance. For them it will be the best dance they have ever danced and they will no longer remember their dances with the devil.

Yes, heaven is real and beautiful in every way. Isaiah spoke of it; the Apostle Paul reminded the Corinthians of it; as time passed and the Holy Spirit revealed, scribes wrote about it. John saw the Holy City—the New Jerusalem, coming down from God out of heaven and the one sitting on the throne was like brilliant gemstones encircled by the glow of emeralds.

"Then one of the seven angels who held the seven bowls containing the seven last plagues came and said to me, 'Come with me! I will show you the bride, the wife of the Lamb.' So he took me in the spirit to a great, high mountain, and he showed me the holy city, Jerusalem, descending out of heaven from God. It shone with the glory of God and sparkled like a precious stone—like jasper as clear as crystal. The city wall was broad and high with twelve gates guarded by twelve angels. And the names of the twelve tribes of Israel were written on the gates. There were three gates on each side—east, north, south, and west. The walls of the city had twelve foundation stones, and on them were written the names of the twelve apostles of the Lamb. The angel who talked to me held in his hand a gold measuring stick to measure the city, its gates, and its wall. When he measured it, he found it was a square, as wide as it was long. In fact, its length and width and height were each 1400 miles" (Revelation 21:9-16 NLT).

Over the years I've made numerous trips from Austin, Texas

to Jackson Hole, Wyoming. My route indicated a distance of 1440 miles. As I traveled I would amuse myself by trying to imagine a city made with streets of gold, and 12 foundations of precious gemstones the distance from Austin to Jackson, and Las Vegas to Kansas City, which averages about 1400 miles square. Then I would look at the sky and try to imagine 1400 miles high. That's not possible! The average height a commercial jetliner flies is 35000 feet. A mile is 5280 feet. The math for 1400 miles high is 73,920,00 feet.

The Word tells us that the walls of heaven measure 216 feet thick and are made of jasper; the city's main street is made of pure gold, as clear as glass; foundations are made of stones inlaid with twelve precious stones: jasper, sapphire, agate, emerald, onyx, carnelian, chrysolite, beryl, topaz, chrysoprase, jacinth, and amethyst (Revelation 21:18-20 NLT).

John saw that the, *"twelve gates were made of pearls—each gate from a single pearl! There was "no temple in the city—for the Lord God almighty and the Lamb are its temple. And the city has no need for sun or moon, for the glory of God illuminates the city, and the Lamb is the light. The nations will walk in its light, and the kings of the world will enter the city in all their glory. Its gates will never be closed at the end of the day because there is no night there. And all the nations will bring their glory and honor into the city. Nothing evil will be allowed to enter, nor anyone who practices shameful idolatry and dishonesty—but only those whose names are written in the Lamb's Book of Life"* (Revelation 21:21-27 NLT).

Then the angel showed John a river with the water of life, clear as crystal, flowing from the throne of God and of the Lamb. It flowed down the center of the main street. On each side of the river grew a tree of life bearing twelve crops of fruit with a fresh crop each month. The leaves were used for medicine to heal the nations (Revelation 22:1, 2 NLT). (Please read Ezekiel 47:12 for more about this scripture)

> *"No longer will there be a curse upon anything. For the throne of God and of the Lamb will be there, and His servants will worship Him. And they will see His face, and His name will be written on their foreheads. And there will be no night there—no need for lamps or sun for the Lord God will shine on them. And they will reign forever and ever"* (Revelation 22:3-5 NLT). *Then the angel said to me, "Everything you have seen is trustworthy and true. The Lord God who inspires His prophets, He has sent His angels to tell His servants what will happen soon. Look, I am coming soon! Blessed are those who obey the Words of prophecy written in this book"* (Revelation 22:6, 7 NLT).

Heaven! A place so beautiful, no one can imagine it. We who are His children are waiting for the new heaven and a new earth in which righteousness dwells. (2 Peter 3:13) We are citizens of heaven, where the Lord Jesus Christ lives. And we are eagerly waiting His return as our Savior. He will take our weak mortal bodies and change them into glorious bodies like His own, using the same power with which He will bring everything under His control. (Philippians 3:20, 21) What God has promised His children if they overcome worldly obstacles and sensual pleasures is a tremendous gift for the sacrifice they make on earth. You don't really want to let Satan steal all this from you, do you? Nor do you want to let him keep you from the most awesome loving Father you could ever imagine—a life that is unbelievably peaceful and happy. In heaven, we will no longer sin; we will not be subject to the laws of physics; we will eat and touch; we will never be sick again; we will recognize one another; we will have relationships free of doubt, jealousy, and gossip. We will live in the New Jerusalem and we will be with Christ.

DANCING WITH THE DEVIL

CONCLUSION

My prayer for *Dancing with the Devil* has been and still is that it would be anointed to speak to those Christians in bondage to anything that the Bible teaches is sin that separates them from God. Also, that it would be a ministry of emotional healing, which often brings physical healing. But, I didn't realize the degree to which "Christians" are blinded to biblical truth.

For example, I was somewhat surprised to learn the different views among Christians on fornication, adultery, and homosexuality—something the Lord clearly calls sin. Nor did I realize the different views on the Genesis account of creation. Attacks by the enemy, which were designed to discredit me were overwhelming and may never be resolved. Conversational misunderstandings with people I considered dear friends left me reeling in shock and still remain unresolved. The cost of personal sacrifice has been painful as it will be for every Christian who decides to remove all stops in order to give reverence to God and keep His commandments. According to Ecclesiastes 12:13, giving reverence to God is the duty or purpose of all mankind.

Nowhere within the struggles of the past ten years of seeking the Lord for His will and direction about how to write did He ever once tell me that this would be easy or that I would be writing things that would tickle people's ears, making them feel good about being Christian. In fact, every time I approached the computer to write about peace, tranquility, harmony, or other aspects of living a prosperous and trial-free Christian life I encountered unbelievable interference and obstacles.

Occasionally I found myself in situations that tested my ability to genuinely follow Christ, and in times of weakness and discord I would question whether He *really* loved me. Further, there were times when, as if I could demand anything from God, I would cry out to Him for an answer as to why He didn't just release me from this terrible burden. But the conviction to publish *Dancing with the Devil* never left me. Instead, it became fire in my bones!

    Obediently I submitted to God, and the process has taken six years from start to finish—an education far beyond anything I could have attained on my own merit without the Holy Spirit who swayed me to an uncompromising commitment not to write in a way that would affirm transgressions. He did not convict me to speak only of His love for mankind but instead He convicted me to speak of His justice and His wrath. Much has already been written about His love and how He beckons us to come unto Him and He will accept us just as we are. And, yes, He does accept us just where we are but He also tells us to get cleaned up, to renew our minds, to love Him with all our hearts, obey His commands, and mature into Christians who can get off the milk and feed on solid meat and walk in forgiveness. Few people are willing to hear this kind of teaching in today's world of personal fulfillment and self-imposed entitlement.

    As a child of God, don't doubt for a moment that He loves you. In fact, He loves you so much that He sent His son to earth and let Him die a horrible death on a wooden cross so that you and I could be redeemed. Don't doubt for a moment that the Bible is full of Scriptures that tell of His amazing grace and because He is gracious, you and I are saved by our faith in His son. Don't doubt that God is patient and merciful, slow to anger, desiring that all be saved to eternal life with Him rather than condemned forever to the place of agony. Don't question who God is but instead recognize Him by what the Bible calls Him: El Shaddai (Lord God Almighty), El Elyon (The Most High God), Adonai (Lord, Master), Yahweh (Lord, Jehovah), Jehovah Rapha, (The Lord That Heals). He is all this and much more. Don't doubt that all the good and positive things the Bible says about God are true, because they are. However, please don't doubt for a moment that God is righteous, and just. He hates sin, disobedience, rebellion, perversion and lies. And He will condemn and destroy those who don't repent of and turn away from these sins.

DANCING WITH THE DEVIL

Dancing with the Devil was written to help the reader *understand* that evil is real, that it does exist and it always comes to us through people. *Dancing with the Devil* was written to help others see how easily we can fall into temptation, flirt with sin, and sometimes linger there until our joy of salvation through Christ leaves us. The Lord says His people perish for lack of knowledge; therefore my quest is to reach the heart and mind of every Christian—the very young, the teenager, the young adult, the middle aged, and the very mature—and try to persuade them to get accurately educated about the Word of God before it is too late.

When is too late? Spend one week focusing on the world news. If you really *understand* the Word of God, you will be able to compare world news reports with what the Bible says will happen in the latter days. You will recognize that we are living in evil times; that the anti-Christ's are at work 24/7 trying to stop people from becoming the bride of Christ. Equally, in avalanche style, new laws are being implemented that force Christians to violate the Scriptures and adhere to the anti-Christian view known as the persecution of the church.

Dancing With The Devil was written to appeal to Christians to recognize and personalize the fact that God looks at the condition of the heart, the thoughts of the mind, deeds and misdeeds, and then to search truthfully their inner heart for any sin that displeases Him. My further appeal is for each person to search their outward behavior—including appearance, language, and attitude—to see if it too, displeases God, and if it does, then turn from it, and seek Him with all their heart, soul, and mind. Once done, their next step is to renew their mind with the things of the Lord, then guard their heart so that they will be able to choose the right path because it is very narrow and difficult to find!

Where pride is an issue, I challenge you to submit to the Lord with a humble heart asking Him for forgiveness and then He will show you how to get rid of the pride and commit fully to Him.

Those who do this will not only grow in relationship with Him they will build beautiful relationships with family and friends. He will heal each person's mind and emotions. I encourage each and every Christian to a quest for wisdom and *understanding* because without *understanding*, wisdom is handicapped.

And finally, now that you have finished reading *Dancing With The Devil*, I encourage you to set this book aside for a couple of weeks and spend some time in prayer, asking the Lord to open the eyes of your heart and allow you to see what's inside; then go and read this book again, keeping your Bible close by. I encourage you to pray for *understanding* before beginning each chapter.

May the Lord Bless you and Protect You; May the Lord Smile on You and be Gracious to You; May the Lord Show you His Favor and Give You His Peace! Numbers 6:24-25 NLT

CHAPTER TWELVE STUDY QUESTIONS

1. What did Jesus mean when He said, "I go to prepare a place for you?"

2. What does repentance mean to you?

3. How many gates are in the Holy City, Jerusalem? How many angels guard those gates as foretold in Revelation 21:9-16?

4. What are the twelve gates made of?

5. According to Revelation 21:9-16, how many miles square is heaven?

6. Whose names are written on the gates of heaven?

7. How many foundations does the New Jerusalem have?

8. According to Revelation 21:2-7, who will occupy heaven?

9. What is heaven's main street composed of?

10. Why do you think God bestows such extravagance on His children in heaven?

ABOUT THE AUTHOR

Whether or not Kathleen was walking closely with Jesus, throughout her life she always felt she belonged to Him—that He was her Savior and God was her Father. But it would be a distinct moment when Kathleen would know that the Lord was telling her she needed to make some changes. She came to a truthful understanding of what being a Christian really meant and then took immediate steps to walk a walk that would assure her that she was heaven bound. Soon the Lord showed her how she could help others who were walking where she had walked. Through six years of intense Bible study and research, and regenerating herself to Christ-like behavior, *Dancing With The Devil* became a reality.

Kathleen is a social graces instructor, a substitute teacher, and speaker. She loves the Lord and His children and is hugely concerned about the lifestyle many of them choose to live. She believes that all who profess salvation through Jesus Christ should learn the Scriptures and make the greatest possible effort to live Christianity to the fullest degree.

Kathleen is a passionate patriot and supporter of the U.S. Constitution and the American Flag, and she abhors the horror of human trafficking. She hopes to see a greater effort in rescuing victims and to eventually provide a domicile where they will have an opportunity to return to a normal way of life, find some joy and happiness, and eventually get to know Jesus and the heavenly Father.

Kathleen can be reached through her website www.kathleendryden.com. kathleen@kathleendryden.com

DANCING WITH THE DEVIL

END NOTES

INTRODUCTION
p. 7 – Pew Research Center World Distribution of Christian Population 2010; www.pewresearch.org

p. 9 – John Hagee, Cornerstone Church, San Antonio, TX; Paraphrase of *"Ten Characteristics of the Antichrist"* 01/08/2015

CHAPTER ONE
p. 15 – The Barna Group – *"Most American Christians Do Not Believe that Satan or the Holy Spirit Exist"* April 10, 2009 www.barna.org (Permission Granted)

p. 16 – William J. Bennett, *"Why We Fight; Moral Clarity and the War on Terrorism,"* 2002, pp. 7, 8; Doubleday, a Division of Random House, Inc., 1540 Broadway, New York, New York 10036 (Fair Use)

p. 21 – *New Living Translation Life Application Study Bible*, Tyndale House Publishers, Inc., Wheaton, Illinois, 1996, 2004 – Footnote for Job 28:28; 1 Samuel 5:24-31

pp. 22, 23 – Evil Defined, Merriam-Webster 1913 Online Dictionary and WordNet Dictionary

p. 29 – NLT Footnote *"David was in no mood to listen when he set out for Nabal's property."*

p. 36 – Edmund Burke, Irish Statesman, Author, and Philosopher (1729-1797) – Notable Quotes *"All that is necessary for the triumph of evil is that good men do nothing."*

CHAPTER TWO
p. 46 – The Barna Group, *American Lifestyles Mix Compassion and Self-Oriented Behavior*, February 5, 2007, www.barna.org (Used by Permission)

p. 50 – David Wilkerson, *The Vision* (out of print; revised as THE VISION AND BEYOND in 2003.) Permission granted by World Challenge Inc, P.O. Box 260 Lindale, Texas, 75771; www.worldchallenge.org.

p. 52 – David and Deborah Dombrowski, Lighthouse Trails Publishing, P.O. Box 908, Eureka, Montana 59917; www.lighthousetrailsresearch.com, 406-889-3610

p. 52 – David Hunt, (1926-2013) with T.A. McMahon, *The Seduction of Christianity*, Harvest House Publishers 1985 (Fair Use Permission Granted)

p. 53 – Andrea R. Jain, Asst Professor Religious Studies, Indiana University-Purdue University Indianapolis; Author, *Selling Yoga: From Counterculture to Pop Culture* – Quote from article, *History of Yoga*, 24 Indian News, August 8, 2015; *"yoga is undoubtedly a Hindu movement for spiritual meditation;"* "*dilutes its Hindu identity.*"

p. 53 – United Nations – www.un.org/en/events/yogaday International Day of Yoga

p. 54 – Milestones of Swami Satchidananda – www.swamisatchidananda.org -
   1972: Dean Ornish Meets and Begins Studying with Swami Satchidananda
p. 54 – Charles Colson, *The Struggle for Men's Hearts and Minds*, 1986
p. 54 – Charles Colson, Life of – Wikipedia

CHAPTER THREE

p. 63 – WWII in History as translated from the German into English by Ingrid Rimland - Horror at NeuStettin; www.thebirdman.org report of the events at Camp Vilmsee of the RAD on February 16, 17, 18, 1945
p. 65 – Dietrich Bonhoeffer, (1906-1945) – Quote from Website: www.bonhoeffer.org.
p. 65 – Edmund Burke, (1729-1797) – Irish Orator, Philosopher and Politician – Notable Quotes
p. 66 – John Stuart Mill, (1806-1873) – Writer/Publisher – Notable Quotes
p. 70 – Philip G. Dwyer, *The Evil Men Do! It Still Makes Me Shudder*, Memoirs of Massacres and Atrocities during the Revolutionary and Napoleonic Wars 2009 (Fair Use permission granted)
p. 71 – Napoleon Bonaparte Biography – Wikipedia
p. 71 – 1812 French Invasion of Russia, www.history.com
p. 73 – History of Pogroms – *Bolshevism: The Road to Revolution* by Alan Woods. Part Two: The First Russian Revolution
pp. 73-75 – Study of Riots, Pogroms and Genocide by Paul R. Brass for the Sawyer Seminar on "Processes of Mass Killings," Center for Advanced Study in the Behavioral Sciences, Stanford University, December 6 and 7, 2002
pp. 73-75 – Nikolay Alexandrovich Romanov, Nicholas II of Russia (1868-1918), Wikipedia – Family Background
p. 74 – Bolshevism: The Road to Revolution by Alan Woods, Part 2 – The First Russian Revolution Sections 4 and 5 ("Nicholas the Bloody")
p. 74 – Russification – Black Hundred Gangs, www.historylearningsite.co.uk
p. 76 – Assassination at Sarajevo, (Franz Ferdinand) CN Trueman, History Learning Site, www.historylearningsite.co.uk
p. 76 – Rodolphe Archibald Reiss, (1875-1929) Professor of Criminology, University of Lausanne, Switzerland; Report Upon the Atrocities Committed by the Austro-Hungarian Army during the First Invasion of Serbia; Published by Simpkin, Marshall, Hamilton, Kent & Co., Ltd., London 1916
p. 79 – Wilhelm II, German Emperor, Life in Exile, Wikipedia
pp. 77-79 – 1917 Lenin Returns to Russia - www.history.com/this-day-in-history/lenin-returns-to-russia-from-exile
pp. 77-79 – Vladimir Lenin; Wikipedia
p. 79 – The Financial Panic of 1907, Running from History; History and Archeology, Article Smithsonian Magazine by Abigail Tucker, October 10, 2008
p. 79 – History – European Battles 1907-1915
p. 80 – Religion in Georgia (the country) – Wikipedia

DANCING WITH THE DEVIL

p. 80 – Ottoman Empire (1301–1922)
www.bbc.co.uk/religion/islam/history/ottoman/empire

pp. 80-83 – Charles F. Horne, Records of the Great War, Vol. III, ed., National Alumni 1923, Memoirs and Diaries – The Armenian Massacres

p. 83 – Democracy in America, American Politics – Criminal Justice and Mass Incarceration – The Moral Failures of America's Prison-industrial complex, 07.20.2015 18:48 by w.w./Chattanooga

p. 83 – Michael S. Schmidt, *U.S. to Release 6,000 Inmates From Prisons by October 6, 2015*, The New York Times

p. 84 – The Massacre of the Armenians 1915 – Eyewitness to History, www.eyewitnesstohistory.com (2008)

p. 84 – Walter Kalaidjian, *The Edge of Modernism by American Poetry and the Traumatic Past* © 2006, The Johns Hopkins University Press

p. 86 – WWI 1915 German Submarine Sinks Lusitania: www.history.com/this-day-in-history

pp. 84-86 – U.S. Entry into WWI, 1917, Office of the Historian, U.S. Department of State

p. 89 – The Aims of the Big 3; History Public Domain (Before 1923)

p. 90 – The League of Nations, 1920 Office of the Historian, U.S. Department of State

p. 91 – The Versailles Treaty; History, www.militaryhistory.com

p. 92 – Washington Naval Conference (1921-1922), Office of the Historian, U.S. Department of State

pp. 92, 93 – Washington Naval Treaty: Disarmament, www.militaryhistory.com

p. 94 – Statement of Principles of International Policy; U.S. Department of State, Publication 1983 Peace and War: United States Foreign Policy 1931-1941 (Washington D.C., U.S. Government Printing Office 1943)

p. 94 – Second Sino-Japanese War – Wikipedia; WWII Sites in China, Nanking Massacre, Mass Murder in 1937, War Rape in World War II

p. 94 – History – The Rape of Nanking; Diary and Documents of Reverend James M. McCallum

pp. 95, 96 – History – The Rape of Nanking; From the Diaries of John Rabee, German Businessman, and Member of the Nazi Party

p. 96 – History – The Rape of Nanking; From the Letters of Robert O Wilson, Surgeon, American-administered University Hospital – Safety Zone, Nanking

p. 97 – Death of Japanese Emperor Hirohito – *Hirohito, Mastermind of Japanese Involvement in WWII*; Hope of Israel Ministries

p. 99 – Frank Capra, *"Why We Fight"* Series of 7 Films (1942), U.S. Government, Office of War Information, Bureau of Motion Pictures 1940-1943

pp. 99, 100 – Definitions – Britannica Encyclopedia – Nazism (National Socialism)

p. 100 – History: Hirohito's Rule of Government

pp. 101, 102 – History: Joseph Stalin "Man of Steel"

pp. 102, 103 – Germany/Soviet Union Relations Before 1941 – Wikipedia

DANCING WITH THE DEVIL

p. 103 – William L Shirer, *The Rise and Fall of the Third Reich, A History of Nazi Germany*; p. 796; A **Touchstone Book** published by Simon & Schuster, Inc. (1959, 1960, 1987, 1988, 1990)

p. 103 –Adolph Hitler, *Mein Kampf*, German Chancellor, Füher, and Dictator 1925 Published in England

p. 104 – Operation Barbarosa, www.militaryhistory.com; www.historylearningsite.co.uk

pp. 104, 105 – History: German and Russian Invasion of Poland, 1939

pp. 105, 106 – History: The Plan to Take America by Surprise; Japanese Attack on Pearl Harbor

pp. 108, 109 – History: Targeted for Disposal – Dietrich Bonhoeffer

p. 109 – History: Tortured for Christ – Richard Wurmbrand, (1909-2001) Lutheran Min., Voice of the Martyrs Ministries

pp. 110, 111 – History WWII: Unleashed Rape – The Russian Red Army's march across Germany

pp. 110, 111 – History: America's Stain - 11,000 Rapes during WWII

p. 111 – Anthony Beevor, *The Fall of Berlin, 1945*, Penguin Books, Kindle Edition, P342-343 - Quote

p. 111 – Antony Beevor, *The Second World War*, Back Bay Books, Rep. ed. 0507-201

pp. 112-117 – Kitty Werthmann, Austrian born WWII Survivor – Personal Interview 04-03-2012

p. 118 –Aleksandr Solzhenitsyn, *The Gulag Archipelago;* The Harvill Press, 01.30.2003; *52 Methods of Russian Torture*, Kindle ed.; Amazon Digital Services LLC. 11.26.2010

pp. 118, 119 – Laura Hillenbrand, *Unbroken*, Random House 1st ed., 2010

p. 119 – Geneva Conventions; www.militaryhistory.com

pp. 120, 121 – Blaise Pascal (1623-1662) French Mathematician, Physicist, Inventor, Writer, and Christian Philosopher (Notable Quotes)

pp. 121, 122 – Jay Sekulow, *Rise of ISIS, A Threat We Can't Ignore*, Howard Books, An Imprint of Simon & Schuster, Inc. 2014

p. 122 – 2014 Global Report on Trafficking in Persons published by the United Nations Office on Drugs and Crime

pp. 122, 123 – The Vienna Forum to Fight Human Trafficking 13-15 February 2008, Austria Center Background Paper – Introduction Page 2

pp. 124, 125 – Women and Revolution No 41 Summer/Autumn 1992

pp. 124, 125 – United Nations Children's Fund Statistics

p. 127 – Obama's speech to the Washington Fellowship for Young African Leaders Educational Summit in Washington DC, July 28-30, 2014)

p. 128 – The Vienna Forum to Fight Human Trafficking 13-15 February 2008, Austria Center Vienna, and Background Paper – Introduction Page 1

p. 128 – Article: The World Health Organization

p. 129 – Article – Executive Summary: Geneva Centre for the Democratic Control of Armed Forces – Women in an insecure World, Violence Against Women, Facts, Figures, and Analysis, in Slaughtering Eve

pp. 129, 130 – World News Article: Rape in India – 2013

p. 130 – Article: 1999 Report on Domestic Violence in Russia

p. 130 – 2012 Report by the Thompson Reuters Foundation on G20 Nations (Re: Russia)
p. 131 – BBC News, US and Canada, December 15, 2011, National Intimate Partner and Sexual Violence Survey
p. 131 – Centers for Disease Control and Prevention
p. 131 – Steubenville Ohio High School Rape Case, 08.11.2012
pp. 131, 132 – Jon Krakauer, *Missoula*, Rape and the Justice System in a College Town, Anchor, Rep. ed. 01.12.2016
p. 132 – News Report – Infant Rape in America – San Antonio, Texas and Northern Michigan
p. 133 – 2010 Survey by U.S. Centers for Disease Control & Prevention

CHAPTER FOUR

pp. 139, 140 – Robert C. Winthrop, (1809-1894) Quote from his speech titled *The Bible* presented to the Annual Meeting of the Massachusetts Bible Society in Boston, MA as documented in *Addresses and Speeches on Various Occasions 1835-1851* (Page 172) by Robert C. Winthrop, Little, Brown and Company Boston: 1852 Public Domain
pp. 141-144 – American History: Patrick Henry's Speech "Give Me Liberty or Give me Death" 1775 Public Domain
p. 144 – John Stuart Mill (1806-1873), Political Philosopher and Economist – Notable Quotes
p. 146 – Supreme Court Ruling on Ten Commandments in School, (1980) and Ruling on Same Sex Marriage (June 1015)
p. 147 – Franklin Graham, Christian Evangelist and Missionary, CEO Billy Graham Evangelistic Association and Samaritan's Purse – Quote from his 2012 speech found at www.billygraham.org
p. 149 – DNC Vote on whether to use God's name in their Political Slogans 2012
pp. 149-152 – The Barna Group *A New Generation of Adults Bends Moral and Sexual Rules to Their Liking*" (2006), www.barna.org (Used by Permission)
pp. 152, 153 – The Millennia Invasion, November 12, 2001 (Newsweek); May 2013 issue of Time Magazine
p. 154 – 1968 Movie Green Beret's (Quote)
p. 155 – US Constitution and Bill of Rights
pp. 155-157 – Jonathon Edwards; Sermon: *"Sinners in the Hands of an Angry God,"* July 8, 1741
p. 158 – U.S Government Selective Service Mandate to Register
p. 158 – Estimate of Illegals in America
pp. 159, 160 – Paul Harvey; Speech: *"If I were The Devil,"* April 3, 1965 American Broadcaster, (1918-2009)
pp. 160, 161 – William J. Bennett, *"Why We Fight"* Doubleday 2001. Bennett is an American Conservative Pundit, Politician, and Political Theorist
p. 163 – American Fam. Assoc. Article - 04.23.2014 titled "7 common careers Christians may no longer hold in America."
p. 164 – Supreme Court Ruling on Same Sex Marriage (June 2015)

pp. 164, 165 National Health Interview Survey "Assessing American's Health and Behavior"
pp. 168, 169 – Judicial Watch Inc. and Mexico's Intelligence Sources
pp. 170-172 – Paul McGuire, *The Day the Dollar Died; Are You Ready;* – M House Publishers, Los Angeles, CA. (Used by Permission)
p. 172 – John Hagee, Pastor Cornerstone Church, San Antonio, Texas (Quote); www.jhm.org
p. 177 – www.alliancedefendingfreedom.org, www.wallbuilders.com
p. 177 – www.wallbuilders.com; documents on government instigated anti-god activities against the U.S. Constitution
p. 177 – Ann Corcoran, www.refugeeresettlementwatch.com
p. 177 – Dinesh D'Souza, *"The Roots of Obama's Rage;"* "2016 – Obama's America;" Doc Film, "America" 2014
p. 177 – Barak Obama, *The Audacity of Hope;" "Dreams of my Father,"*
p. 177 – Ibid. Hitler
p. 179 – History – WWII – German Naval U-Boats off America's East coast

CHAPTER FIVE

p. 197 – Roger Miller, *"Husbands and Wives"* written and recorded by Roger Miller, 1966, Album - Words and Music
pp. 201, 202 – *Cast Away*, (2000) Award Winning Movie Directed by Robert Zemeckis, Distributed by 20th Century Fox
pp. 203, 204 – Ed Wardle, Documentary Film Producer; *Alone In the Wild* (2009)
pp. 220-222

    Criminal Justice and Behavior, Vol. 14, p. 403-26[1]
    National Principals Association Report on the State of High School[2]
    U.S. Dept. of Justice, Special Report Sept., 1988[3]
    Fulton County Georgia jail populations & Texas Dept. of Corrections, 1992[4]
    U.S. D.H.H.S., Bureau of the Census[5][SEP]
    Center for Disease Control[6]
    U.S. Department of Health and Human Services, National Center for Health Statistics, Survey on Child Health, Washington, DC, 1993[7]
    Deane Scott Berman *"Risk Factors Leading to Adolescent Substance Abuse,"* Adolescence 30 (1995)[8]
    P.L. Adams, J.R. Milner, and N.A. Schrepf, *"Fatherless Children"*, New York, Wiley Press, 1984[9]
    Nicholas Zill, Donna Morrison; Mary Jo Coiro, *"Long Term Effects of Parental Divorce on Parent-Child Relationships, Adjustment and Achievement in Young Adulthood,"* Journal of Family Psychology 7 (1993)[10]
    David M. Fergusson, John Horwood and Michael T. Lynsky, *"Parental Separation, Adolescent Psychopathology, and Problem Behaviors,"* Journal of the American Academy of Child and Adolescent Psychiatry 33 (1994)[11]

Denise B. Kandel, Emily Rosenbaum, Kevin Chen, *"Impact of Maternal Drug Use and Life Experiences on Preadolescent Children Born to Teenage Mothers,"* Journal of Marriage and the Family 56 (1994)[12]

Alfred A. Messer, *"Boys Father Hunger: The Missing Father Syndrome,"* Medical Aspects of Human Sexuality, January 1989[13]

U.S. Department of Health and Human Services, National Center for Health Statistics, National Health Interview Survey, Hyattsville, MD, 1988[14]

E.M. Hetherington and B. Martin, "*Family Interaction*" in H.C. Quay and J.S. Werry (eds.), Psychopathological Disorders of Childhood. (New York: John Wiley & Sons, 1979)[15]

J.B. Elshtain, *"Family Matters..."* Christian Century, July 1993[16]

Ronald E. Johnson, C.Ph.D and author of *Teaching Eagles to Soar*, Tate Publishing, 2009 (Fair Use Quote)

pp. 222, 223 - The Bureau of Census Survey of Income and Program Participation collected in 2009 and published in the report *Living Arrangements of Children: 2009*

p. 224 – David Blankenhorn, "Fatherless America" Random House (1995) (Fair Use Quote)

p. 227 – Ronald M. Enroth, *Churches That Abuse*, Zondervan, July, 1993

p. 228 - Trends in U.S. Corrections—State and Federal Prison Population 1925-2011–Fewer than 200,000 U.S. Citizens imprisoned in 1925. Bureau of Justice Statistics Series

p. 229 - U.S. Department of Justice, Office of Justice Programs, Bureau of Justice Statistics, Prisoners in 2010 Revised 2/9/12

p. 229 – The Barna Group, *The Spirituality of Moms Outpaces that of Dads* dated May 7, 2007, www.barna.org (Used by Permission)

pp. 231, 232 – Ralph Waite, Actor, Producer, Television Series *"The Waltons"* 1974-1981;" Presbyterian Minister

CHAPTER SIX

p. 262 – Former U.S. President William Jefferson Clinton – Quote regarding the Clinton/Lewinsky Scandal

p. 262 – Matt Nolen, *"Why Do We Think"* from CD "Song of My Life" 1995 – Producers Paul W. Wright III, et al.

p. 262 – World Health Organization – Statistics on Abortion

p. 263 – The Kermit Barron Gosnell Case, February 18, 2010 – FBI and State Police Investigation

pp. 265-267 – Conception and Fetal Development

p. 267 – USabortionclock.org – Statistics on Abortion in American 022413

p. 267 – Alan Guttmacher Institute – Abortions in America, www.guttmacher.org

p. 268 – www.physiciansforlife.org/content/view/1164/26/ 01.02.2012 (Women murdered because they were pregnant)

p. 274 – Footnote: NLT Life Application Study Bible, Proverbs 17:27 Contradictory Speech

CHAPTER SEVEN

p. 288 – Ibid. Bonhoeffer

pp. 308, 309 – E. L. James, *Fifty Shades of Grey*, Vintage Books, 04.03.2012

p. 309 – Grace Randolph, YouTube Book review of *Fifty Shades of Grey* by E.L. James

p. 309 – Quote by Sophie Morgan of the Observer, August 2012 Book Review (Ibid - *Fifty Shades of Grey*)

pp. 310-312 – Steve Gallagher, *At the Altar of Sexual Idolatry*, 1986 N.P. (Used by Permission)

CHAPTER EIGHT

pp. 334-336 – Rick Renner, *Paid in Full*, Harrison House Publishers, 08.06.2013 (Fair Use) Renner is an Author and the Pastor of Moscow Good News Church in Russia

p. 338 – Ibid. NLT Footnote

CHAPTER NINE

pp. 341, 342 – Barna Group, *Barna Lists the 12 Most Significant Religious Findings* 12.20.2006 www.barna.org; Used by Permission

p. 342 – Oswald Chambers, (1874-1917) *My Utmost for His Highest*, Barbour Pub. Tyndale Momentum Rep. ed. 10.01.2012, Quote by Oswald Chambers

p. 360 – Dietrich Bonhoeffer (1906-1945) – Quote from website; www.bonhoeffer.com

pp. 363, 364 – George Barna, *Revolution*, Tyndale Momentum, 10.01.2012 –The Barna Group, www.barna.org (Fair Use)

CHAPTER TEN

pp. 367, 368 – Ibid. *The Seduction of Christianity*, Harvest House Publishers 1985 – (Used by Permission)

pp. 374, 375 – The Great Altar of Zeus – Obama's Speech in Germany, July 24, 2008

pp. 376, 377 – Madalyn Murray O'Hair – Wikipedia

p. 386 – Ibid. T.A. McMahon, Quote on Definition of Seeker Friendly Church –
(Used by Permission)
pp. 386, 387 – Ray Yungen, *A Time of Departing* – (Used by Permission)
p. 388 – Contemplative Prayer defined –
www.centerforcontempletativespirituality.com

CHAPTER ELEVEN
p. 404 – *Maurice Rawlings*, (1922-2010) T*o Hell and Back*, Thomas Nelson Publishers, 1993
pp. 404-407 – Bruce Bickel and Stan Jantz, *"Whatever Happened to Hell"* - Homelife Family Magazine (2000) (Used by Permission)

DANCING WITH THE DEVIL
RECOMMENDED READING

The Holy Bible
W.S. McBirnie, (1923-1995) *Anti-Christ*, Acclaimed Books 1978
David Wilkerson, (1931-2011), *The Vision*, Spire Books, 1979 Revised as THE VISION AND BEYOND, 2003 (World Challenge Ministries), Evangelist, Author; Founder: Times Square Church NYC
David Hunt, (1926-2013) with T.A. McMahon, *The Seduction of Christianity*, Harvest House Publishers 1985 – Hunt founded The Berean Call, A Ministry of Biblical Discernment. He was concerned about our western culture being invaded by Eastern psychological and selfish philosophies, ecumenism, and Islamic politics and religion. Since the Attack on the World Trade Center in NYC, Hunt's video, *Israel, Islam, and Armageddon* has become a tool to educate the church.
Roger Oakland, *Faith Undone*, Lighthouse Trails Publishing, www.lighthousetrails.com 2007 – Oakland is an Author, Lecturer, Missionary, and Evangelist – www.rogeroakland.co,
Ray Yungen, *A Time of Departing 2nd Ed 2006* Lighthouse Trails Publishing, www.lighthousetrails.com – Yungen is an Author, Speaker, and Research Analyst
John Hagee, *The Three Heavens,* Worthy Publishing, May 12, 2015 – Senior Pastor, Cornerstone Church, San Antonio, TX
Paul McGuire, *The Day the Dollar Died; Are You Ready; Mass Awakening; A Prophecy of the Future of America 2016-2017* – M House Publishers, Los Angeles, CA – McGuire is an Internationally recognized Prophecy Expert, Speaker, and Author; Founder of Paul McGuire Ministries, Paradise Mountain Church, Newhall, CA – www.paulmcguire.us
William J. Bennett, *Why We Fight*, Doubleday, April 2002 – Bennett is an Author, Former U.S. Sec. of Education, and Political Theorist
Steven Gallagher, *At the Altar of Sexual Idolatry*, 1986 – Gallagher is the President of Pure Life Ministries, Dry Ridge, KY; He is an Author, Columnist, Pastor and Bible Counselor
George Barna, *Revolution*, Tyndale Momentum, October 1, 2012 –The Barna Group Research, www.barna.org
Oswald Chambers, (1874-1917) *My Utmost for His Highest*; Barbour Publishing Inc., www.barbourbooks.com – Chambers was a Scottish Baptist and Holiness Movement Evangelist and Teacher
Antony Beevor, *The Fall of Berlin, 1945;* Deckle Edge, April 29, 2003; *The Second World War*, W&N 2012 – Beevor is a British Military Author and Historian, winner of numerous awards including the Pritzker Literature Award for Lifetime Achievement in Military Writing; Acclaimed by Booksellers as the bestselling historian of the BookScan era, with more than seven million copies sold

DANCING WITH THE DEVIL

Laura Hillenbrand, *Unbroken*, Random House, 1st Ed 2010; Unbroken is the story of Olympic Runner and Gold Medal Winner, and WWII POW and American hero Louis Zamperino; how he prevailed in resilience and survival while held as a POW under the Japanese and then how he came to redemption

Aleksandr Solzhenitsyn, (1918-2008) *52 Methods of Russian Torture*, The Kindle Edition, Amazon Digital Services, LLC, 11.26.2010; *The Gulag Archipelago*, The Harvill Press, 01.30.2003 – Solzhenitsyn was a Russian Novelist, Historian, and Outspoken critic on the Soviet Union, totalitarianism, and forced labor camps where he spent 11 years in exile for speaking out against Joseph Stalin

Eric Metaxas, *Bonhoeffer; Pastor, Martyr, Prophet, Spy*, Thomas Nelson, Rpt. Ed. August 2011; Other recommendations on Bonhoeffer include *The Writings of Dietrich Bonhoeffer; Bonhoeffer: The Cost of Freedom* – www.bonhoeffer.org published by Focus on the Family, 1997

Maurice Rawlings, (1922-2010) *To Hell and Back*, Thomas Nelson Publishers, 1993 – Rawlings was an American Cardiologist, Author and Researcher of Near Death Experiences

Mary Neal, *To Heaven and Back*, - WaterBrook Press, May 29, 2012 – Neal is an Author and Orthopedic Spine Surgeon in Jackson Hole, WY

John Ramirez, *Out of the Devil's Cauldron: A Journey from Darkness to Light*, Heaven and Earth Media May 15, 2012 *Unmasking the Devil: Unmasking the Patterns and Cycles of the Underworld*, Destiny Image, October 20, 2015 – Ramirez is a former high ranking priest in the Satanic Cult; Presently: He is a born-again Christian, Evangelist, Author, and Speaker – John Ramirez Ministries, www.johnramirez.com

Jay Sekulow, *Rise of ISIS*, Howard Books, an Imprint of Simon & Schuster, Inc., 2014 – Sekulow is Chief Counsel for the American Center for Law and Justice

Adolf Hitler, (1889-1945) German Politician, Chancellor, Füher and Dictator – Hitler's book *Mein Kamph*, will educate every person about how the truly evil and demonic mind thinks.

DANCING WITH THE DEVIL

www.ingramcontent.com/pod-product-compliance
Lightning Source LLC
Chambersburg PA
CBHW030441090526
44586CB00044B/450